CAHIERS DE DROIT FISCAL INTERNATIONAL

GENERAL REPORTS, EU REPORT
AND SUMMARY & CONCLUSIONS OF ALL BRANCH REPORTS

by the International Fiscal Association

2022

CAHIERS DE DROIT FISCAL INTERNATIONAL

**Studies on International Fiscal Law
by the International Fiscal Association**

Volumes 106A and 106B

**106A: Group approach and separate entity approach
in domestic and international tax law**

General report
Johanna Hey (Germany)
Arne Schnitger (Germany)

EU report
Niall Casey
Jasna Voje

Summary and conclusions of all branch reports

**106B: Big data and tax – domestic and
international taxation of data driven business**

General report
Gary D. Sprague (USA)

Summary and conclusions of all branch reports

List of Cahiers published since 1939

This book was printed on FSC certified paper

© 2022 International Fiscal Association (IFA)
World Trade Center
P.O. Box 30215
3001 DE Rotterdam
Netherlands

Once a year the Cahiers de Droit Fiscal International are published and distributed free to all the members of the Association. These Cahiers contain a wealth of domestic and international material in dealing with the main subjects to be discussed at the following IFA Congress. They comprise IFA branch reports together with a general report on each of the two subjects selected.

The printed publication of the Cahiers consists of the general reports of both Subject 1 and Subject 2, together with an EU report, an OECD report (on both subjects if applicable) and the summary and conclusions of all branch reports. The digital publication consists of the general reports, the EU and OECD reports (if applicable), as well as all branch reports including the biographies, abstracts and directives.

IFA members can access the online versions of the Cahiers via the secured part of the IFA website. The digital publication contains easy access to all reports making it more available for its audience. All reports can be downloaded for off-line consultation.

The new Cahiers are made available annually in June.

INTERNATIONAL FISCAL ASSOCIATION

The International Fiscal Association (IFA) is a leading independent and neutral non-governmental, international non-profit organisation devoted to the study of international tax law. It comprises taxpayers, their advisers, government officials and academics and is a unique forum for discussing international tax questions.

The objects of the Association are the study and advancement of international and comparative law in regard to public finance, specifically international and comparative fiscal law and the financial and economic aspects of taxation. These objects are achieved by scientific research, the holding of national and international congresses, publications by means of its *Cahiers de Droit Fiscal International* treating two major subjects annually, cooperation with other organisations whose objects are mainly or partly fiscal, especially the International Bureau of Fiscal Documentation, the EU and the OECD and all other appropriate methods.

IFA is headquartered in the Netherlands and has approximately 13,000 members worldwide, deriving from 114 countries, with 71 branches.

The inauguration of IFA took place in the Peace Palace of The Hague, the Netherlands, on 12 February 1938.

The IFA's headquarters address is:

IFA General Secretariat
World Trade Center
P.O. Box 30215
3001 DE Rotterdam
Netherlands
Tel.: 31-104052990
E-mail: a.gensecr@ifa.nl
Internet: www.ifa.nl

— Detailed information about IFA is available on the website
— A list of Cahiers is available in the back of this book

Subject 2
Big data and tax – domestic and international taxation
of data driven business

The views expressed are those of the reporters and not necessarily those of the respective IFA branches or the International Fiscal Association.

General report Subject 1

Group approach and separate entity approach in domestic and international tax law

Johanna Hey (Germany)
Arne Schnitger (Germany)

Group approach and separate entity approach in domestic and international tax law

Table of contents

Johanna Hey (Germany)[1]
Arne Schnitger (Germany)[2]

Summary and conclusions

Until nowadays the separate entity principle is not only the starting point, but still also the leading principle of corporate taxation, domestically as well as internationally.

Due to the separate entity principle corporate profits can be taxed independently of the shareholders and before distribution. At the same time, corporate profits are separated from the personal income tax allowing tax deferral. In many countries, there is a significant gap between the low corporate income tax and the higher progressive personal income tax. For that reason, corporatio ns are used also domestically to shelter income from the higher personal income tax. Change of control and loss forfeiture rules in many countries break the separate entity principle in order to prevent loss trafficking.

The separate entity principle is incapable of reflecting the economic situation of groups. Group tax regimes overcome the separate entity approach in one way or the other, but normally incomplete. Even though group tax regimes are widespread and their number has increased in recent decades a real unitary taxation of the group is a rare exception. More common is the mere attribution of separately determined profits and losses among group members. Given the importance of the separate entity principle for the international allocation of tax revenues, the application of group tax regimes to cross-border groups has also made little progress. European law prevents EU Member States from excluding corporates resident within other member states of the Union from the access to the tax group but does not require the offsetting of foreign losses unless they are final. Furthermore, not the group but only the single group member is entitled to DTT relief.

Since the profit allocation in cross-border cases is based on the separate entity approach, the Authorized OECD Approach (AOA) applies a transaction based allocation of profits also between headquarters and branches, even though they are not legally independent.

While on the one hand the separate entity is needed to demarcate the tax jurisdictions from each other, it is at the same time perceived as a tax planning instrument. The separate entity approach is the starting point of any base erosion and profit shifting. Therefore, an increasing number of measures is deviating from the separate entity principle, particularly in cross border situations in order to counter the sheltering of profits in low-taxed subsidiaries or the erosion of the tax base by payments into low-taxed subsidiaries. There is quite a large array of anti-BEPS measures neglecting the separate entity, such as interest and royalty barriers or hybrid mismatch rules. The wide-spread CFC regimes negate the deferral of taxation by the separate entity principle but do not lead to a group taxation. The effective tax burden is determined for the single subsidiary and then immediately

[1] Professor for Tax Law and Director of the Institute for Tax Law at the University of Cologne, Germany.
[2] Partner and Head of the National Tax Office at PricewaterhouseCoopers in Berlin, Germany.

The reporters are grateful for extensive research support from Frederik Schildgen (Institute of Tax Law, University of Cologne) and Kerstin Holst (PWC).

attributed or deemed as distributed. The cross-border attribution is limited to profits, losses are recognized only in the single subsidiary. These anti-avoidance rules sometimes require majority capital ownership or control, regularly they apply if the threshold of 25% of voting rights, capital ownership or profit participation is reached or exceeded. Thus, they clearly are not meant to reflect the economic unit of a consolidated group, but rather insinuate a certain influence needed to establish tax planning structures. Not only are the requirements not limited to cases of control, but also the legal consequences do not lead to group taxation. Rather, the separate entity approach is breached on a selective basis.

Even though some authors claim that only formulary apportionment could overcome the problems of the broken international tax system, the 2015 BEPS recommendations of G20/OECD followed a transactional approach based on the separate entity principle. The profit split method can be seen as a tendency towards a formulary allocation of profits following the group approach, but it still is not the standard method. Also BEPS 2.0 with the two pillars still clings to the separate entity. Even though different to the BEPS recommendations of 2015, the pillars were not primarily born as anti-avoidance measures. Pillar One as well as Pillar Two aim to overcome only the most prominent excesses of the separate entity principle. The subjective scope is based on the idea of control that enables tax planning opportunities. It is no longer merely rule-based but follows the notion of economic substance by defining the group as for financial reporting. Both pillars apply only to cross-border groups of a certain size (20 Billion/750 Mio. EUR). The size of the group revenue is meant to mirror economies of scale for tax planning. Furthermore, the high complexity of the new rules makes their restriction to large MNEs inevitable. Nevertheless, even for this limited number of multinational groups neither Pillar One nor Pillar Two result in group taxation but in a mixture of elements of the separate entity and a group approach. The formulary apportionment method of Amount A of Pillar One applies only to a limited portion of the group profit and adds to the persisting transfer pricing system. For purposes of the global minimum tax of Pillar Two (GloBE) the effective tax rate is not determined on a group-wide basis (worldwide blending), but in between on a jurisdictional basis. Although the EU intends to implement GloBE across Europe, it has not yet taken this as an opportunity to resume the initiative to introduce a European wide group taxation under the CCCTB.

Overall, the present mix of elements of the separate entity approach and of a group approach may limit opportunities to exploit the separate entity principle for aggressive tax planning. Given the limited scope of application on the one side and the complexity on the other side, the pillars do not have the potential to drive the international corporate tax system more into the direction of a group approach. They neither make any of the more specific anti-BEPS rules obsolete.

1. Introduction

1.1. Relevance of the subject

Historically, the separate entity principle has been the mainstay of the corporate income tax. The taxation of the corporation independently of its shareholders is to this day the global standard for corporate taxation. Today, however, companies above a certain size are regularly organized in groups that form a single economic unit but legally consist of a large number of separate entities. This holds true not only for MNEs, but also for many SMEs.

Therefore, many countries foresee rules that deviate from the separate entity principle. Special group taxation regimes, for instance, provide for the prevention of double taxation of subsidiary profits but also for intra-group offsetting of profits and losses. These special group tax schemes are usually limited to domestic tax groups.

In international taxation, the separate entity principle not only has the function of separating the corporate level from the shareholder level, but also of international profit allocation. Entities situated in one territory are outside of the tax jurisdiction of other territories. Thus, for over 100 years, separate entity accounting and the arm's length principle have been the cornerstones of the international approach to intercompany payments for tax purposes. Transfer pricing rules aim both to establish a tax base similar to the one of a stand-alone taxpayer and to prevent the shifting of profits between different separate taxpayers. The scope of this legal concept has even been expanded and is now also applied to permanent establishments despite them being a legally integrated part of the business. The rules on the attribution of profits to permanent establishments are directed towards the separate allocation of taxable profits. Under the Authorized OECD Approach (AOA) the permanent establishment is treated as a functionally separate entity, aligning the allocation of profits between the head office and its permanent establishments with the determination of transfer prices between associated entities.

Additionally, there is an ongoing trend to introduce special provisions which apply depending on the shareholding structure of the corporation and distinguish between stand-alone corporations and corporations that are part of a group or are controlled corporations. These provisions depart from the principle that corporations are taxed independently from their shareholders. The tax consequences arising from such special provisions are quite varying. On the one hand, some of these measures intend to reflect the economic unit of the group in order to facilitate organizational flexibility within the group. On the other hand, control or belonging to a group is observed as being the starting point for the shifting of profits and is, therefore, at the same time often the reason for the application of special anti-avoidance measures. Other special rules such as hybrid mismatch rules link the tax treatment in one jurisdiction to the tax consequences in another jurisdiction and/or another taxpayer in order to prevent qualification conflicts.

These more recent provisions reflect that the separate entity approach in the context of multinational group taxation is seen internationally as the main trigger for base erosion and profit shifting (BEPS). This has led to special anti-avoidance rules based on control. Beyond these individual measures, however, there are also more fundamental considerations of an economically appropriate taxation of multinational groups. It has been argued against the arm's length standard from time to time that it contradicts the nature of integrated companies. This puts concepts of unitary taxation like the proposal of the EU Common Consolidated Corporate Tax Base (CCCTB)[3] on the map again. It also is the starting point for a group-based allocation of taxing rights discussed by the OECD/G 20 under Pillar One[4] of the work on the challenges of the digitalized economy. Unlike national group tax rules, however, this debate is not about fully overcoming the disadvantages of the separate entity

---

[3]   Proposal for a directive on a Common Consolidated Corporate Tax Base (CCCTB) of 25 October 2016, COM(2016) 683 final. See also EU report, part 2.3.
[4]   OECD, Tax Challenges Arising from Digitalisation – Report on Pillar One Blueprint: Inclusive Framework on BEPS, 2020.

principle but about changing the international allocation of taxation rights and limiting the fiscal downside of the separate entity principle, i.e. international tax planning opportunities.

1.2. Terminology: What is meant by separate entity and group approach?

The term "separate entity approach" describes the treatment of a legal entity as an independent tax subject. In principle, the same rules apply to transactions between the company and its shareholders as to transactions with third parties.

The term "group approach" stands for all deviations from the separate entity approach and means that tax consequences for the taxed entity depend on other taxable entities; it is not meant in any formal way (i.e. it also covers special provisions for controlling shareholders and not only situations where there is actually a group under commercial law or for accounting purposes). While group taxation rules in the narrower sense are concerned with avoiding tax disadvantages of a multi-entity company organization, special rules, applying under the condition of control or significant participation, are intended to exclude the tax planning opportunities which the separate entity principle entails.

Anti-avoidance provisions based on control or a special degree of affinity between two entities can result in double taxation in conflict with the idea of a unitary business and the group approach. However, such anti-avoidance-rules are also not necessarily compatible with the separate entity approach if, for example, as a legal consequence general principles of income determination such as the deductibility of expenses are suspended.

1.3. Aims of the general report

Many aspects of the topic, like group taxation (2004),[5] CFC regimes (2013),[6] the future of transfer pricing (2017)[7] or interest deductibility (2019),[8] have been discussed in detail before at IFA congresses. However, only an overall view of the group- and control-related provisions aimed at here allows an assessment as to whether and to what extent the tax systems internationally are moving away from the separate entity principle.

One aim of the subject is to understand the function of the group (or related party) criteria in the domestic as well as in the international context and to examine whether:
- Special rules for groups reflect the economic reality of a unitary business;
- Rules reflect group membership and/or control as an indicator of tax planning opportunities and the absence of conflicting interests;
- The application of certain rules only to groups can reflect considerations of feasibility and enforceability because information is available only to group members or can be made available but cannot be derived from third parties;
- The size of groups is used as an approximative indicator for tax planning capacities achieved through economies of scale. However, such special tax regimes for (international) groups, especially if conditioned by certain revenue thresholds, at

---

5   IFA, Group taxation, Cahiers Vol. 89b (2004).
6   IFA, The taxation of foreign passive income for groups of companies, Cahiers Vol. 98a (2013).
7   IFA, The Future of Transfer Pricing, Cahiers Vol. 102b (2004).
8   IFA, Interest deductibility: the implementation of BEPS Action 4, Cahiers Vol. 104 (2019).

the same time deviate from the ideal of tax neutrality and create different classes of taxpayers.

Many of the special rules for related parties are characterized by considerable complexity. Even within the European Union, where the Anti-Tax Avoidance Directive (ATAD)[9] ensures a minimum standard, different regulatory techniques are used. This applies all the more when states individually deviate from the separate entity principle on the basis of the OECD BEPS recommendations. On the one hand, this raises the question of what consequences arise when different concepts of group or control clash. On the other hand, the legal comparison can help to identify best practices In terms of compliance costs and avoid extra tax burden. Finally, the branch reports show trends that allow a classification of the ongoing OECD discussion (Pillars One and Two) on a fundamental reorganization of the international tax system for multinational groups.

2. Separate entity approach and tax liability

2.1. The rationale of the corporate income tax and the separate entity principle

The separate entity principle is an inherent element of the corporate income tax, allowing the taxation of corporate profits independently of the shareholders and before distribution. With the separation of assets in corporations under company law during the 19th century, the need to tax profits before distribution or sale of shares arose historically. On the one hand, taxing corporate profits when they arise is a dictate of competitive neutrality in comparison to sole proprietors and fiscally transparent partnership where profits are immediately attributed and taxed. At the same time, corporations are a "convenient mechanism for the collection of tax".[10] The corporate income tax ensures that tax authorities have timely access to corporate profits, avoiding in the budgetary interest long term tax deferral. On the other hand, a direct allocation of undistributed profits to the shareholders is not only hindered by practical difficulties, which is particularly true in the case of big multi-layer corporate groups, but also because until distribution the shareholders lack legal authority over the (retained) corporate profit. Consequently, the separate entity principle appears to be enshrined as a principle in international taxation that is indispensable.

Moreover, in times of international tax competition, separating the taxation of legal entities from the taxation of the individuals behind the entity allows the application of different tax rates, sheltering the personal income tax rate from the downward pressure on mobile capital income. Nowadays, in most countries the corporate income tax is (significantly) lower than the top bracket of the personal income tax.

In principle, tax law respects the legal entity as a separate tax subject, regardless of further requirements. However, in order to prevent the misuse of shell entities for tax purposes, the draft EU-"Unshell-Directive"[11] now makes the recognition of corporations,

---

[9] Council Directive (EU) 2016/1164 of 12 July 2016 laying down rules against tax avoidance practices that directly affect the functioning of the internal market.

[10] D. Rosenbloom, Tax Notes International, 15 December 2003, 989 (992).

[11] Proposal for a Council Directive laying down rules to prevent the misuse of shell entities for tax purposes and amending Directive 2011/16/EU, COM(2021) 565 final, see also below 6.1.1.

which are located in EU Member States, for purposes of treaty eligibility and shielding of income dependent on substance requirements.

The rationale of the taxation at the corporate level depends on the respective corporate income tax system. Classical systems of (unmitigated) economic double taxation at the level of the corporation and the shareholder assume that the corporation has its own ability to pay taxes. Sometimes, the definitive burden of corporate income tax is also justified by the advantages of incorporation and limitation of liability.[12] Against this, in (full) shareholder relief systems, the corporate income tax has the character of a temporary preliminary burden. However, this classification only concerns the relationship between corporate income tax and personal income tax. Within the corporate income tax, the separate entity principle cannot justify multiple taxation in principle, even within the framework of classical systems.[13] Within the corporate income tax corporate profits are meant to be taxed once, but only once (principle of single taxation)[14]. As splitting an enterprise into several legally independent entities does not establish any additional ability to pay (tax capacity) the profits of each entity should consequently be only taxed once. This poses the question of the allocation of the tax burden to the entities within a shareholding structure. The separate entity principle can be used to determine at which level the profit is taxed. Following this principle, the tax subject is the individual corporation. Consequently, if group tax regimes do not apply, the profit is always first taxed at the level of the entity in which the profit is recognized. In shareholding structures, economic double taxation on distributed profits is avoided by taking into account prior taxation at the level of the shareholder (see 3.3).

2.2. Scope of the corporate income tax and determination of the legal entity as taxable unit of the corporate income tax

Separate entity taxation requires a separation of assets. Regularly corporate law is used as a basis to determine when a separate taxpayer can be assumed. However, internationally different concepts apply as to when a separate entity exists for tax purposes. The decisive factor is the legal separation from the individual. In principle, the legal personality of the entity is used as a starting point. Sole proprietorships are generally neither in corporate law nor in tax law considered separate entities. As a rule, they also do not benefit from an option to be subject to corporate tax.

In many jurisdictions, the tax status of partnerships as separate (opaque) entities or as transparent entities does not depend on the respective civil law status and their legal personality but is an autonomous decision of the corporate tax legislator. Even though commercial partnerships are commonly considered to have legal personality many countries treat them fiscally transparent (e.g. Austria, Denmark, Finland, Germany, Luxembourg, New Zealand,[15] Norway, South Africa, Sweden). To the contrary, Hong Kong taxes partnerships as separate entities even though they are not considered to have legal personality under

---

[12] E.g. Canada, Germany, India.
[13] E.g. Switzerland with a strong separate entity approach, nevertheless, grants a participation exemption of dividends in case of a participation > 10%.
[14] R.S. Avi-Yonah, International Taxation of Electronic Commerce, Tax Law Review 1997, 507 (517-520); R.S. Avi-Yonah, Global Taxation, 2016, 12.
[15] In New Zealand, only a limited partnership has a legal personality, however all partnerships are fiscally transparent.

common law. Some states differentiate according to liability and tax limited partnerships as separate entities, see Australia, France (only the limited partners), Italy, Poland and Turkey.

Some countries provide for check-the box schemes[16] for (closely held) entities, both in favour of transparent taxation[17] and opaque taxation.[18] Particularly well-known is the "Check-the-Box" regime of the US. Its broad scope of application widely allows to eliminate the shielding effect of the legal entity and to establish a kind of group taxation by the option for transparent taxation. Such options can be used to offset losses and profits of different corporations, to simplify intercompany transactions and to avoid the application of the CFC Subpart F regime[19] (by disregarding intercompany transactions for tax purposes) and to combine (or separate) the tax attributes of various entities.

Furthermore, REIT systems can also deviate from the separate entity taxation and achieve one-level taxation by exempting the legal entity from corporate income tax at the REIT level and taxing distributions at the shareholder level.

2.3. Classification of foreign entities

The linking of the status as a corporate tax subject with civil and corporate law necessarily requires a special qualification insofar companies are incorporated abroad. Neither the corporate law status nor the tax law classification of the jurisdiction of establishment is binding for the source state. The classification of entities established under foreign law requires a case-by-case resemblance test in most jurisdictions.[20] For simplification purposes some countries provide for lists of qualified foreign entities.[21] Italy deems all foreign entities to be opaque; in Mauritius non-resident partnerships are subject to corporate income tax, while resident partnerships are not.

The uncoordinated juxtaposition of separate entity taxation and transparent taxation results in hybrid entities as addressed in BEPS Action 2 as qualification of one entity by different states might differ. The OECD hybrid mismatch rules reconcile only the tax consequences, and, therefore, avoid addressing the characterization of the hybrid entity itself.[22] In contrast, since 2008 Danish tax law provides under its anti-hybrid rule, that entities, which would be normally transparent under Danish tax law, are subject to corporate income tax if they are in their residence jurisdiction treated as separate entities for tax purposes. A similar rule applies in Poland.

---

[16]   In both directions: United States.
[17]   In this direction only: Italy under special circumstances (consortium relief), New Zealand for closely held resident companies. Chile stipulates this as a small business privilege.
[18]   In this direction Turkey. See also Germany (since 2022) for business partnerships, for cross-border cases restricted to partnerships liable to corporate income tax in the state in which their management is located.
[19]   For the US Subpart F rules see US report, 2.3, 2.6, 2.10.
[20]   See in detail German branch report part two 2.1; see also Australia, Canada, France, Finland, Luxembourg.
[21]   E.g. Dutch branch report, 2.1. fn 51.
[22]   OECD, Neutralising the Effects of Hybrid Mismatch Arrangements, Action 2 – 2015 Final Report, 2015, para. 295.

2.4. Size related provisions and rules against splitting up corporations

The separate entity principle poses problems with regard to size-related provisions, because it allows taxpayers to undergo thresholds by splitting up a corporation into various entities. Such thresholds can be found for various reasons.

Firstly, profit- and/or turnover-related thresholds were used for granting tax reliefs or subsidies as small (and closely held) corporations in some countries enjoyed privileges like a lower corporate income tax rate or an option for transparent taxation.[23] In addition, provisions giving relief to smaller entities below defined thresholds can be also seen as an attempt to give procedural relief for smaller companies from administrative burden.

Secondly, as a fairly new trend, thresholds are used to define when special anti-avoidance measures apply depending on the size of the legal entity/group. The thresholds of these new provisions depend either on profits or revenues to focus on (big) MNEs as there may the presumption, as an outcome of economies of scale, that tax-planning is only cost-effective for larger groups. In the Netherlands, in the context of MNE headquarters emigration a draft bill is discussed that would apply e.g. a deemed profit distribution in case of cross-border relocations only for companies with deemed profits of more than EUR 50 million (stand-alone basis). In addition, some countries apply their CFC legislation only if certain thresholds are exceeded depending either or on the amount of CFC income and a relative share of passive income to exclude small controlled foreign entities (e.g. below 5% in Australia or below a third in Austria). Article 7 paragraph 4 ATAD allows such de minimis exclusions for the income inclusion in case of a non-genuine arrangement (accounting profits of no more than EUR 750 000, and non-trading income of no more than EUR 75 000) as well.

Thirdly, most countries apply country by country reporting according to OECD BEPS Action 13 recommendations and the Multilateral Competent Authority Agreement on the Exchange of Country-by-Country Reports (CbC MCAA). However, the application is (again) limited to groups with an annual consolidated turnover of at least EUR 750 million.

Furthermore, taxes developed in the BEPS era also focus on MNEs as countries implementing digital service taxes or similar instruments restrict them usually to big groups as also foreseen in the EU proposal for a digital service tax.[24]

Such provisions which apply depending on the size of the entity bear the risk of being circumvented by splitting-up entities. In order to avoid that taxpayers undergo such thresholds on the one hand Denmark and Spain test such thresholds only on group level. On the other hand, Germany, the Republic of Korea, Poland and Switzerland address such planning by the application of its GAAR provision. Another legislative strategy is the introduction of SAARs to prevent members of above-threshold-sized economic groups from receiving these benefits. Such rules can be found in Argentina, Belgium, Chile, France and Japan.

---

[23]   Australia, Belgium, Chile, Hungary, Japan, Republic of Korea, Poland, Spain.
[24]   Proposal for a Council directive of 21 March 2018 on the common system of a digital services tax on revenues resulting from the provision of certain digital services, COM/2018/0148 final – 2018/073 (CNS).

3. Determination of the tax base under the separate entity approach

3.1. No tax consolidation but determination on a stand-alone basis

The separate entity approach leads to an income determination on a stand-alone basis. As a consequence, dividend distributions are non-deductible whilst interest payments (provided no thin capitalization/interest barrier rules apply) in general reduce the entity's taxable profit, no matter whether they are paid to affiliates or third parties.

Financial reporting standards require companies to prepare consolidated group accounts as well as stand-alone financial statements. In many countries financial accounting also forms the starting point for tax accounting, usually with numerous modifications for tax purposes. Other countries base income taxation on an autonomous tax accounting (e.g. Australia). However, also in countries with tax accounting linked to financial accounting, tax accounting is always, also for purposes of group taxation, based on the stand-alone financial statements. Therefore, one can conclude that financial group accounting is mostly irrelevant for tax purposes and serves no basis to introduce group taxation.

3.2. Change of control and loss forfeitures rules

Due to the separate entity approach losses can be carried forward in the same entity in line with the general system of loss utilization rules. However, it is impossible to offset losses against the income of the shareholders (i.e. the separate entity approach excludes the transfer of losses to another entity). Therefore, losses can usually not be transferred via corporate reorganization to another entity (some tax laws explicitly foresee a forfeiture of losses in case of a reorganisation)[25]. Instead, losses forfeit under those rules if the former entity ceases to exist which hinders reorganization within corporate groups.

Change of control rules aiming to prevent loss trafficking go into the opposite direction. Even while the legal entity remains unchanged such rules foresee that losses cease to exist if the shareholders change (i.e. as otherwise a separate shell might be used to trade losses or interest carry forwards to use them for other business activities). In order to limit such loss trafficking many countries[26] adopted change of control provisions which foresee a look through to the shareholder level to identify whether losses of an entity can still be used. Change of control rules are, therefore, a serious departure from the separate entity principle implying that the economic identity of the entity changes with the personal identity of the shareholders. However, they are neither a sign of a legislator following a group approach nor do they lead to transparent taxation as they do not result in an attribution of losses to the shareholder level but solely trigger their expiry. In principle, this can only be justified on the basis of preventing abuse. Therefore, most states allow proof that the economic identity of an entity which shareholders change, remains unchanged, as e.g. the business

---

[25]   France, Germany and Poland (no change of control rule applies in the acquisition of shares); usually the Republic of Korea, Uruguay (in split-up cases, subject to dispute).

[26]   No rule at all is reported for Chinese Taipei, Turkey and Hong Kong.

continuity test in Australia.[27] Other countries foresee a business purpose escape test,[28] which underlines that those rules are meant to be anti-abuse provisions. A notable exemption is Japan that solely focuses on the change of control.

Significant differences exist with regard to the question of when a change of control is to be assumed. Often it takes a change of more than 50% of the voting power (Australia, Chile, Canada,[29] Denmark, Finland, Germany, Italy, Mexico, New Zealand, Portugal, Singapore [>49%]). However sometimes a change of control of more than 75% (Austria) is required but in some cases the threshold is much lower (Czech Republic: at least 25%; the Netherlands 30%). While some countries apply change of control rules only on a one-tier basis (Austria, UK), others follow a multi-tier approach (Chile, Finland, Germany).

Some countries (like Belgium, Canada, Chile, Denmark, Finland, Germany, Hungary, UK) do not apply such provisions for an intra-group change of control. In Belgium, this exemption applies to transfers between companies that are consolidated for financial reporting purposes. In contrast, the German rules require a 100% participation in all companies involved. The Danish rule includes a transparency (look-through) rule: if at least 25% of the share capital in the company in question is owned by another company, the change of control test applies to the shareholders of the parent company. Full consolidation regimes (see 4.1.2.) effect the broadest exemption within a group.

The treatment of losses differs in the context of group reorganisations and cannot be concluded from the group exemptions. Some countries provide exemptions to the denial of losses,[30] some explicitly deny losses in the case of a reorganisation.[31] Either way, exemption or denial does not necessarily fit the (non-)existence of group exemptions. Change of control rules are also common after a tax-neutral transfer of assets between group members (South Africa).

Overall, one can conclude that change of control rules break with the separate entity principle by looking through to the shareholder level to identify whether the economic

---

[27] See also Austria (change in control & changes in the business purpose and the organizational structure of that company; Czech Republic (company's activities are 80% the same as in the period when the tax loss arose); Italy (no dormant company); Netherlands (>50% assets are operational and the combined activities of the entity have not decreased to less than 30% compared with the activities in the oldest year in which these losses originated); New Zealand (no major change in the nature of the business activities).

[28] Belgium (legitimate financial or economic reasons: change of control is not merely inspired by tax reasons), Finland (if business reasons can be substantiated), Norway (a transaction would normally not be mainly motivated by tax unless the acquirer is able to utilize the tax position), Singapore (not for the purpose of deriving any tax benefit or obtaining any tax advantage (no tax-motivation, e.g. company rescue)), Luxembourg and Switzerland (no explicit rule, but denial of losses if transfer of shares only due to tax reasons); Restriction of losses dependent on asset value: Colombia (in merger situations), Italy (in merger situations), Sweden (losses admitted to the extent of 200% of the purchase price), Ukraine (in merger situations).

[29] Alternatively, the change of control rule applies if 75 % of the fair market value of the equity is acquired.

[30] Argentina (in order to transfer accumulated losses and outstanding tax exemptions from the predecessor entity to the successor entity, their holders have to prove that they have held at least 80% of ownership interest in the capital for two years before the reorganization date), Colombia (up to the net asset value), Czech Republic (spinoff/merger: retention of transferred activities test), Denmark (look through enables survival of losses), Finland (merger carve out if acquiring company or its shareholders or both together have held more than 50 % of the shares of the merging or dividing company as from the beginning of the lossmaking year), Italy (positive vitality test: allowed up to net equity value or if positive ruling (business reasons)), Japan, Norway (usually no denial of losses within a tax group).

[31] Germany, France, Poland (no change of control rule applies in the acquisition of shares); usually Republic of Korea, Uruguay (in split-up cases, subject to dispute).

activity changes. This deviation from the separate entity principle is not reflected in the legal consequences since losses are not attributed to the shareholder but instead, the carry-forward of the losses of the single entity is denied.

3.3. Prevention of economic and international double taxation

The separate taxation of corporations raises concerns of economic double taxation with respect to dividend distributions and capital gains received by their shareholders. Most countries provide, therefore, shareholder relief with dividends being either often fully tax-exempt at the level of the receiving corporation (DRD)[32] or an indirect tax credit being granted.[33] However, no country resolutely follows a classic shareholder taxation system anymore. When applying a DRD, usually 95%[34] or 100%[35] of dividends are effectively tax exempt; rarely other fractions are exempted.[36] Both, DRD and the granting of a tax credit require regularly but not always[37] a qualifying participation of 5%[38] or 10%.[39] Higher thresholds in order to apply this relief can rarely be found.[40]

---

[32] Argentina (domestic subsidiaries), Australia (foreign subsidiaries), Belgium, Canada, Chile (domestic subsidiaries), Czech Republic, Denmark, Finland, France, Germany, Hong Kong, Hungary, Italy, Japan, Republic of Korea, Luxembourg, Mauritius, Mexico (domestic subsidiaries), Netherlands, New Zealand (foreign subsidiaries), Norway, Peru (domestic subsidiaries), Poland, Portugal, Singapore, South Africa, Spain, Sweden, Switzerland, Turkey, Ukraine, UK, Uruguay.

[33] Argentina (foreign subsidiaries), Australia (domestic subsidiaries), Chile (foreign subsidiaries), Colombia (foreign subsidiaries), Republic of Korea (foreign subsidiaries), Mauritius (foreign subsidiaries, sometimes combined with partial exemption), Mexico (foreign subsidiaries), New Zealand (domestic subsidiaries), Peru (foreign subsidiaries), Portugal (foreign subsidiaries, but only if participation exemption does not apply, e.g. tax rate threshold not met), Spain (foreign subsidiaries, exemption method can be applied optionally).

[34] Denmark, France, Germany, Italy, Japan (foreign subsidiaries), Spain.

[35] Argentina, Australia, Austria, Belgium, Canada, Chile, Chinese Taipei, Czech Republic, Finland, Hungary, Japan (domestic), Republic of Korea (100% participation), Luxembourg, Mauritius (domestic), Mexico (domestic), Netherlands, New Zealand, Norway (> 90% participation), Peru (domestic), Poland, Portugal, Singapore, South Africa, Sweden, Switzerland, Ukraine, UK, Uruguay.

[36] France (exemption of 99% of dividends between members of a tax group), Japan (exemption of 50% of the dividends received for participation between 5% and 1/3 [domestic subsidiary], exemption of 20% for participation < 5% [domestic subsidiary]), Republic of Korea (exemption of 50% of the dividends for a participation above 50%, below 100% [domestic subsidiary]), Norway (exemption of 97% for participation < 90%).

[37] There is no such qualified shareholding requirement in: Argentina (domestic cases), Austria (EU & EEA and comprehensive agreement on mutual assistance), Canada (domestic subsidiaries), Chinese Taipei, Hungary, Italy, Mauritius (exemption), Mexico (exemption), New Zealand, Norway (for 97% exemption), Peru (domestic subsidiaries), Singapore, South Africa, Ukraine, Uruguay.

[38] France, Mauritius (Imputation), Netherlands, Spain.

[39] Australia (exemption), Austria (non-EU/EEA/comprehensive agreement on mutual assistance cases), Canada (foreign subsidiaries: taxpayer must hold 1% participation in any share class & taxpayer and related taxpayers must hold at least 10% of shares of any class), Czech Republic, Denmark, Germany, Luxembourg, Mexico (imputation), Peru (foreign subsidiaries), Poland, Portugal, South Africa (foreign subsidiary), Sweden, Switzerland, UK.

[40] Argentina (for foreign subsidiaries, > 25 % direct participation or > 15 % for indirect participations), Japan (> 1/3 participation for 100% exemption of domestic dividends, > 25% participation for exemption of foreign dividends), Republic of Korea (100% [> 50%] participation for 100% [50%] exemption of domestic dividends, foreign subsidiaries: 25% participation for indirect tax credit for foreign dividends), Poland (Switzerland cases: > 25% participation, non-EU/non-Switzerland but treaty-partner cases: > 75% participation).

In many jurisdictions the exemption of dividends is restricted if
- the payment has been deductible at the level of the paying corporation (due to a different qualification (hybrid mismatch), following article 4 paragraph 1 let. a) of the EU Parent Subsidiary Directive[41] and also fulfilling requirements set up under Action Item 2 of the BEPS project)[42] as e.g. under Austrian, German and Spanish tax law.
- if the profit of the distributing subsidiary has been taxed significantly lower than at the parent level in order to prevent the use of foreign entities in low-tax jurisdictions similar to the aim of CFC tax regimes (see 4.2).

Countries that exempt dividends from corporate taxation also regularly exempt the profits from the alienation of such shares. Losses from the depreciation and disposal of such shares are, accordingly, in most cases also not tax deductible. However, Austria (domestic cases and option for cross-border cases), Canada (capital gains 50 % subject to tax), Chile and Japan do not tax-exempt capital gains from shares despite the corporate tax exemption of dividends. Furthermore, Japan recently introduced anti-abuse rules to prevent an abusive receipt of tax-exempt dividends prior to a fully taxable alienation of shares.

The exemption of capital gains and losses can lead to a non-utilization of losses due to the separate entity taxation principle if no tax group is available or was concluded (see 4.1). However, on the one hand some countries (like Switzerland) foresee the possibility to deduct losses from the impairment of shares which allows for a use of losses – de facto introducing elements of a group approach – despite the fact that dividend income and capital gains are still tax exempt. Germany, on the other hand, also disallows losses from the impairment or disposal of loans to foreign or domestic related entities to prevent an abuse transfer of losses.

Nowadays, most jurisdictions apply the different methods to prevent economic double taxations also in cross-border cases. Most of the countries, especially the EU member states, apply the DRD with regard to dividends received from foreign subsidiaries. However, sometimes countries impose additional or different shareholding requirements.[43] Hong Kong does, in contrast, not tax dividends from abroad in general irrespective of the shareholding due to a strictly territorial based tax regime. Only a few countries switch to an indirect tax credit system for dividends from foreign subsidiaries.[44] Australia, and New Zealand, antithetically, credit taxes indirectly for domestic dividends and exempt foreign ones. Chinese Taipei in contrast only allows a direct tax credit for dividends from foreign subsidiaries. Such an approach is also followed by Finland for dividends from subsidiaries in non-EU/Double Tax Treaty(DTT)-partner states. Both countries thus apply a classical shareholder taxation in such cases.

---

[41] Council Directive 2011/96/EU of 30 November 2011 on the common system of taxation applicable in the case of parent companies and subsidiaries of different member states.
[42] OECD, Neutralising the Effects of Hybrid Mismatch Arrangements, Action 2 – 2015 Final Report, 2015, para. 103.
[43] E.g. Canada, Japan, Poland.
[44] Argentina, Chile, Republic of Korea, Mauritius (a partial exemption can also be applicable to certain cross-border cases), Mexico, Peru, Spain (exemption method can be applied optionally).

3.4. Transfer pricing for transactions between related parties

The requirement to foresee principles on how transfer prices for transactions between related companies are set, is again based on the fact that tax systems followed the separate entity approach for some time and that the taxable income for the individual entities is determined on its profits. In order to prevent that transfer prices are used to shift profits between different states, the arm's length standard has been a key cornerstone of international taxation for years to overcome the lack of conflicting interests between affiliated companies, through legal requirements. It is, therefore, not surprising that on the one hand some countries foresee transfer pricing rules that apply only in cross-border situations (e.g. Belgium) which can potentially lead to an infringement under European law.[45] On the other hand, some states apply transfer pricing rules also in domestic situations (such as e.g. Finland, Uruguay and partially Germany) as this also allows to distinguish between the taxation at the level of the company and its shareholders, leading to a more stringent separate entity approach when determining the profits in general.

Looking at the different ways accepted by the OECD to determine a transfer price in line with the arm's length standard, the methods tend either towards the separate entity or the group approach. On the one hand one can see that the Comparable Uncontrolled Price Method, Resale Price Method as well as the Cost Plus Method deem the legally independent entities to be also economically independent. Consequently, the income needs to be determined based on a standalone basis considering the functions and risks of (only) those entities. The same holds true for the Transactional Profit Split Method which compares profit margins of single entities with comparable transactions. In its first report, the OECD introduced such transfer pricing methods following the separate entity approach.[46] Not surprisingly it is, therefore, still the first choice in almost all countries to determine transfer prices (such as in Argentina, Australia, Austria, Canada, Chile, Chinese Taipei, Denmark, Finland, France, Hong Kong, Italy, Japan, Republic of Korea, Luxembourg, Mexico, Netherlands, New Zealand, Norway, Peru, Poland, South Africa, Spain, Switzerland, Turkey, the UK and Ukraine).

On the other hand, there are profit methods such as the Comparable Profit Method or the Global Formulary Apportionment which aim at dividing the profit of the overall group between the group companies. The Profit Split Method as an approach following the group approach was, however, developed at a later point in time. In more detail it was described by the OECD in the Transfer Pricing Report 1995/96/97, even though it was back then still qualified as a last resort option,[47] and finally accepted as an equivalent method with the Transfer Pricing Report 2010.[48] Its areas of application were finally set by the Transfer Pricing Guidelines in 2017 for 1) cases, where parties to a transaction make unique and valuable contributions, 2) highly integrated operations and 3) transactions involving the shared assumption of economically significant risks by all parties.[49] These conditions confirm the conclusion that the Profit Split Method conceptually follows the group approach. Some countries like Australia, the Republic of Korea (for intangibles) and

45   ECJ, 21 January 2010, Case C-311/08, SGI, ECLI:EU:C:2010:26.
46   OECD, Transfer Prices and Multinational Enterprises, 1979.
47   OECD, Transfer Prices and Multinational Enterprises and Tax Administrations 1995/96/97, paras. 2.49 and 3.1.
48   OECD, Transfer Prices and Multinational Enterprises and Tax Administrations 2010, para. 2.2. In regard to the work of the European Joint Transfer Pricing Forum on the profit split method, see EU report, part 2, section 5.
49   OECD, Public Discussion Draft BEPS Actions 10: Revised Guidance on Profit Splits, 2017.

the UK apply the Profit Split Method more widely; in some countries it is still only applied where appropriate (People's Republic of China, Denmark) and in some countries it is still not a common method at all (Colombia, Finland, Hong Kong, Japan, Luxembourg, New Zealand, Peru, South Africa). In Argentina, the use of this method must be reported to the local tax authorities.

Furthermore, in its Action items 8-10 of the BEPS reports the OECD adjusted the existing transfer pricing methods with a holistic approach to tax intangibles in order to align transfer prices with value creation.[50] In this context, in particular highly capitalized group entities that did not have the economic capacity to control their financial risks were targeted by the new interpretation of the OECD. The fact that intangibles are not only allocated based on the legal ownership but on the DEMPE function concept indicates that elements of a group taxation approach were transferred into the classical transfer pricing methods. From now on the functional involvement of group companies has to be considered as well when determining the allocation of risks and functions. Seven years after the final BEPS reports were issued more and more countries adopted this new interpretation as well (such as Australia, Austria, Republic of Korea, Italy, Luxembourg, Netherlands, New Zealand, Peru, the UK, Ukraine and Uruguay). However, there are still a considerable number of countries who have not implemented those rules (such as Canada, Chile, Colombia, France, Mexico, South Africa).

Finally, in its Transfer Pricing Guidelines 2017 the OECD also deals with the treatment of group synergies for transfer pricing purposes. Under these principles one needs to distinguish whether group synergies can be classified as "incidental benefits" (i.e. the mere fact that a group exists triggers the assumption of guarantee) or as "deliberate concerted group actions" (i.e. other group entities grant an actual guarantee).[51] Only the latter needs to be separately remunerated. This indicates that the setting of transfer prices still leans more towards the separate entity approach. The fact that a company belongs to a group is, in contrast, decisive if the higher creditworthiness is based on an implicit guarantee. In such a case no separate guarantee agreement is required to compensate for the higher creditworthiness applying a more consolidated group taxation approach.

3.5. Transactions between the head office and its branch

The allocation of profits between the head office and its foreign branch was for a long time based on the direct and indirect method. When applying the indirect method, a consolidated view is applied as company profits have to be divided between the head office and its permanent establishment on the basis of an apportionment key such as sales, number of employees or total wages and salaries. This approach very much follows from the fact that head office and branch have no separate legal personality and allocating profits on a group approach was, therefore, rather logical.

The direct method already incorporates to a certain extent the idea of an independent status of the branch as it provides for the principle that the branch profits are determined separately. Nevertheless, the scope of the notion of independence under the direct method is limited. Thus, no intra-company service relationships (such as goods deliveries and

---

50   OECD, Aligning Transfer Pricing Outcomes with Value Creation, Actions 8-10 – 2015 Final Reports, 2015.
51   OECD, Public Discussion Draft BEPS Actions 10: Revised Guidance on Profit Splits, 2017, paras.1.157–1.173.

service transactions) between the head office and the branch can be assumed under the direct method. Consequently, the notion of independence under the direct method is only decisive to allocate profits between the head office and the branch which occur as a result of a legal transaction of the taxpayer with other persons ("external transactions").

However, this changed with the introduction of the AOA in 2001, when the OECD published discussion drafts on the taxation of permanent establishments based on the working hypothesis of taxation according to the so-called Functional Separate Entity Approach (FSEA). The FSEA foresees that branches are to be treated as fictitiously independent for the purposes of the attribution of profits. The introduction of this fiction is a noteworthy turning point. In contrast and ironically to the opposite, the League of Nations drafts of a model treaty from 1927 treated subsidiaries as permanent establishments of their parent companies. After the final reports were issued in 2008, the FSEA was reflected in the revised version of the OECD commentary as well as the revised OECD-MTC 2010 providing for a revised wording of article 7 (2) OECD-MA. Some countries such as Austria, Chinese Taipei, Colombia, Denmark, Japan, Switzerland and Ukraine introduced the AOA as a general principle to determine branch profits. The Republic of Korea for example has included the AOA only in a few DTT but not in their domestic tax law while some countries like Canada, Peru, Singapore and South Africa have not enacted such principles. Belgium, Finland, France, and Hungary have not officially implemented the AOA but follow it as it is foreseen under OECD principles.

The introduction of the FSEA pursues a number of different objectives, such as to harmonize the determination of profits (the accrual of profits was treated differently before in different states),[52] achieve certainty,[53] avoid double taxation[54] and to achieve convergence of OECD principles on the determination of transfer prices and the apportionment of profits.[55] In essence, its introduction can be seen as an attempt to achieve uniformity in the taxation of permanent establishments and subsidiary corporations. However, already under the view of the OECD not all transactions between the head office and its branch are possible such as guarantee fees to transfer credit risks as both have the same creditworthiness as the enterprise.[56] Correspondingly under Austrian tax law no loan, renting or license agreements are possible and also other countries such as New Zealand restrict the possibility to assume dealings as well.

Furthermore, there are still a number of differences between those two forms of establishment such as that almost all countries do recognize branches as not being entitled to apply the DTT. Only some countries based in the EU such as Belgium and Portugal grant branches treaty entitlement in order to prevent a discrimination under EU law despite

[52]   OECD, Report on the attribution of profits to permanent establishments, 2010, Part I para. 2: "Practical experience has shown, however, that there was considerable variation in the interpretation of these general principles and of other provisions of earlier versions of Article 7".

[53]   OECD, Report on the attribution of profits to permanent establishments, 2010, Part I para. 3: „The Committee acknowledged the need to provide more certainty to taxpayers".

[54]   OECD, Report on the attribution of profits to permanent establishments, 2010, Part I para. 3: "This lack of a common interpretation created problems of double taxation and non-taxation".

[55]   OECD, Report on the attribution of profits to permanent establishments, 2010, Part I para. 55, Part II para. 4, Part III para. 25: „In this context, it should be noted that the aim of the Authorised OECD Approach is not to achieve equality of outcome between branch and subsidiary in terms of profits but rather to apply the same transfer pricing principles that apply to associated enterprises when attributing profits to a PE".

[56]   OECD, Report on the attribution of profits to permanent establishments, 2010, Part I, para. 103.

existing EU jurisprudence.[57] Also losses of a foreign PE are deductible in Austria (recapture mechanism) and as well as other countries such as Canada, Chinese Taipei, Finland, Japan, Mexico, New Zealand, Peru, Turkey which apply the credit method in order to avoid double taxation, tax-deductible.

Some countries such as Canada, Korea or the US[58] have taken a step further to treat subsidiaries and permanent establishments the same by e.g. introducing a branch profit tax. However, most other countries have no similar branch profit tax but only other rules for source taxation might trigger withholding taxes such as in e.g. Argentina. This limitation of the fiction to apply to the PE corresponds also with the OECD view that no withholding taxes can be levied on so-called dealings.[59]

However, despite those limitations one can summarize that the taxation of branches developed much more into the direction of applying the separate entity approach and treating the branch as an own taxpayer beside the fact that it is legally part of the same enterprise.

4. Special regimes of the allocation of income for (tax) groups

4.1. Group tax regimes

4.1.1. Rationale and history of group tax regimes

The core rationale of any group tax regime is the reflection of the economic unit and the ability-to-pay of the group which does not depend on the number of legally independent subunits. While economic double taxation of distributions between related entities is avoided in many jurisdictions also outside tax groups, the main purpose of all group tax regimes is the immediate offsetting of losses. The immediate offsetting of intra-group profits and losses is even more relevant if the use of losses is restricted.

The development of group tax regimes is diverse. In Germany, the case law on substance over form developed such a regime already in the 1920s and 1930s as a response to the introduction of the separate taxation of entities by the corporate income tax.[60] In the early 20th century Danish administrative practice also allowed for tax consolidation. Early legislative adopters of group tax regimes were Denmark (1960), the UK (1967), Germany (1968)[61], Norway (1979), Luxembourg (1981) and France (1980s). Other countries enacted group tax regimes later on[62] as a reaction to the vastly increased number of enterprises

---

[57] Also ECJ, 21 September 1999, Case C-307/97, Saint-Gobain, ECR 1999, 438.

[58] US: Sect. 884 IRC.

[59] OECD, Report on the attribution of profits to permanent establishments, 2010, Part I, paras 11, 203; Part IV, para. 167.

[60] Even earlier, in 1896 the Prussian High Administrative Court assumed such a view in the context of the Prussian local business tax.

[61] The group tax regime was adopted only in 1968 after the Federal Fiscal Court held the previous case law incompatible with the separate entity principle.

[62] According to A. Michelsen, general report, IFA, Tax treatment of Corporate Losses, Cahiers, Vol. 83a (1998), only 15 out of 34 countries allowed intra group loss relief; Y. Masui, general report Group Taxation, Vol. 89b (2004), reported group tax regimes in 20 out of 30 jurisdictions. 2021: 22 out of 37 jurisdictions.

organized in groups. Since the IFA report of 2004 a number of countries have introduced group tax regimes such as the Republic of Korea (2010), Belgium and Hungary (both 2019). Mexico has abolished its group tax regime.

However, still quite a few jurisdictions do not provide for group tax regimes, namely Argentina, Canada, Chile, Colombia, Czech Republic, Hong Kong, India, Mauritius, Peru, South Africa, Switzerland, Turkey, Ukraine, and Uruguay. Mexico recently repealed the group tax regime and now only offers a temporary system to offset losses (i.e. saved taxes are recaptured every three years). Some of these countries grant group-related relief in case of corporate re-organization like a transfer of losses (Argentina, Switzerland) and/or tax-neutral transfer of assets (Argentina, South Africa). However, the immediate offset of profits and losses is not foreseen under those regimes. Canada tolerates an array of planning instruments to allow for "manual consolidation". In contrast, one reason for the introduction of the Italian group taxation system was also to address the "manual" consolidation practices of taxpayers.

It is interesting why some countries do not provide any group taxation measures. The main reason is certainly the negative effect on the tax revenue. However, there are also systematic reservations by countries with a strong separate entity approach which find it more difficult to regard groups as economic units (i.e. from this perspective a group relief system is regarded more of a preferential regime than the adequate tax system to reflect the ability-to-pay of groups). Furthermore, in South Africa legislative initiatives to introduce a group taxation failed, because such a system was seen as some form of tax avoidance. Quite differently, some countries like New Zealand considered the group contribution system to be an anti-avoidance measure in order to prevent an abuse of a progressive corporate tax rate structure. The early Prussian case law on group taxation in Germany was also considered to counter abusive structures. Today, both the group contribution in New Zealand and the "Organschaft" in Germany are considered taxpayer-friendly regimes. Australia still considers its elective tax consolidation system also an anti-avoidance measure.

4.1.2. Concepts

Group taxation systems vary widely with regard to their conceptual design. One central difference is whether the group can for each case deliberately choose the group member that makes loss compensating payments to or "receives" losses from a loss-making group entity (group contributions or group relief) or whether group treatment is achieved by aggregation or even consolidation of the income at the top level of the group, based solely on a particular financial link between the group members (e.g. Austria, Denmark, Italy, Spain, US).

Another central difference is the degree of consolidation: Does the regime merely effect an aggregation of the income of the group members or is there a full-fledged consolidation as known from financial reporting?

In general, four different approaches can be distinguished.

1. Full consolidation[63] regimes	Australia, Netherlands, New Zealand, United States
2. Profit and loss attribution and elimination of inter-company results	France, Spain
3 Profit and loss attribution	Austria, Denmark, Germany,[64] Hungary,[65] Italy, Japan, Republic of Korea (partial elimination of inter-company results), Luxembourg, Poland, Portugal
4. a) Group Contribution (profit transfer to loss-making entities, payments are required) and b) Group Relief (loss transfer to profit-making companies)	a) Belgium (payment to the extent of tax saving), Finland, New Zealand Norway, Sweden b) Singapore, UK (partial elimination of inter-company results)

Approaches 1-3 result in the determination of an aggregate (approaches 2 and 3) or consolidated (approach 1) income of the group. Approach 4 neither effects an aggregate treatment nor an all-or-nothing loss offset within the group. In this order, the approaches reflect the economic unit of the group with approach 1 being the most adequate reflection while approach 4 still adheres to the separate entity principle.

New Zealand seems to be the only country that provides two conceptually different systems that can be understood as group tax regimes. Italy and Denmark explicitly foresee two systems, a worldwide and a merely domestic one.

In most group tax regimes, also those based on full consolidation, the single group members remain subjects when determining the income. Only in a second step income and losses of the single entities are contributed, aggregated or consolidated. A genuine group taxation based on consolidated accounts with full elimination of the subsidiaries as separate entities, is, therefore, a rare exception. Such full consolidation group tax regimes, which effectively treat the group as one single taxpayer[66] can be found in Australia, the Netherlands and New Zealand and bear their own problems: In the Dutch group tax regime (fiscale eenheid) the profits of the fiscal unity are determined as if the group of entities is one single taxpayer and, thus, all transactions (transfers of assets, reorganizations) are considered "internal" transactions. However, due to anti-avoidance considerations, it is necessary to attribute loss and interest carry-forwards to separate group entities, if they stem from before entering the group. Furthermore, the full consolidation concept of the fiscal eenheid is under pressure from CJEU case law (see 4.1.4).

---

[63]   For purposes of this report, the term full consolidation is used for systems that apply a full-fledged consolidation as known from financial reporting.

[64]   The German group tax system also requires profit transfer and loss compensation payments and has, insofar, similarities to group contribution regimes.

[65]   In Hungary, the loss compensation is either limited by law or by the taxpayers discretion; group members with positive income pay their share of the final tax showing an element of a group contribution regime.

[66]   Spain and Hungary also treat the group as one taxpayer. The group tax regimes however stop short of a full consolidation. The situation in Poland underlines the importance of certainty about the status of the taxpayer.

4.1.3. Requirements to form a tax group

In most states[67] the requirements to form a tax group are mostly based on bright-line tests in regard to participation thresholds. Thus the rules are more typecast than those for consolidation under commercial/accounting law. The participation requirements underlying such rules are often stricter than the participation requirements to define control in financial reporting (e.g. IFRS 10 does not solely focus on control based on voting rights or shareholding thresholds but also considers the overall circumstances of the individual case including contractual relationships outside the corporate relationship. In this case control may also be given if the participation is below 50%). Only Denmark applies the same definition of control for tax and accounting purposes.

The participation thresholds vary by country. In general, group taxation requires a participation of at least 75%[68] or 80%,[69] more often 90%,[70] 95% or even the whole ownership[71] of shares.[72] The relatively low participation requirement of 66% for the tax grouping regime in New Zealand can be explained by its history as an anti-avoidance instrument. In Austria, Italy and Germany a taxable group can be established already with a participation of more than 50% of the voting rights. However, the establishment of the German Organschaft requires the conclusion of a profit and loss transfer agreement, under which profits of the subsidiaries are transferred and losses are compensated. Furthermore, minority shareholders need to be entitled to compensation payments for their minority shareholding. For that reason, in practice also in Germany group taxation usually takes place only in cases where the parent has complete or almost complete control.

Furthermore, group tax regimes are in general optional. Only Denmark deviates from this principle with compulsory group taxation rules for domestic groups introduced in 2005.

4.1.4. Determination of the group profit, treatment of intra-group transactions

The principle that the income is determined taxable on a stand-alone basis (see under 3.1.) remains unchanged even if group tax regimes apply (i.e. the income of the individual group members is still determined on a stand-alone basis and consolidated financial statements have no relevance when determining the group's tax base). Even in countries applying the full consolidation system like Australia, the Netherlands and New Zealand, the consolidated income statement is generally not determined based on the consolidated statement for financial accounting but on special tax accounting rules. However, in New Zealand it is possible for some groups to use the consolidated financial results as practical starting point.

In any group tax regime, even in those systems where the tax personality of the individual group member ceases to exist and is transferred to the group, the group members

---

[67]   The Danish control concept depends on the financial reporting concept of control.
[68]   Hungary, Poland, Portugal; Singapore, Spain (reduced to 70% for listed companies), UK.
[69]   United States.
[70]   Belgium, Chinese Taipei, Finland, Norway, Sweden (reasoned with company law squeeze-out threshold)
[71]   95%: France, Luxembourg, Netherlands; 100%: Australia, New Zealand (consolidation regime), Japan, Republic of Korea.
[72]   Due to EU law such shareholding can in a EU context also be indirectly held. ECJ, 27 November 2008, Case C-418/07, Papillon, ECR 2008, I-659.

remain the tax subjects when determining the taxable income in the first step. Therefore, intra-group transactions such as the transfer of assets are in general not disregarded in this first step.

Since most jurisdictions stop short of the elimination of such inter-company results, intra-group transactions are still recognized for tax purposes. Consequently, such intragroup transactions must still meet the arm's length standard. However, transfer pricing rules lose their importance within a group in Hungary and Portugal even though the group members must still calculate their taxable income as separate entities.

In full consolidation regimes intra-group transactions are usually disregarded. This also applies to restructurings and transfer of assets. They, however, may still be monitored for anti-avoidance purposes (i.e. to prevent the formation of a group solely to execute tax-neutral restructurings as in the Netherlands). Due to EU law reasons (see 4.1.7.1) the Dutch system, actually a full consolidation system, offers another striking exception. Interest deduction limitations and dividend withholding rules, which were originally intended to be solely applied outside of the tax groups, especially in relation to foreign related companies, are currently also applied within domestic tax groups.

The tax neutral transfer of assets between group members is often not the immediate outcome of the group tax regime but of other special tax provisions foreseen to allow for a tax-free transfer of assets or tax free reorganizations. On the "no gain no loss basis" the UK allows within the same chargeable gains group, for example, not only a tax-neutral transfer of capital assets but also an offset of capital losses against capital gains. Furthermore, countries allow under their reorganization acts a tax neutral transfer of single assets between members of a group even though no group taxation or group relief system is available (e.g. Argentina, South Africa, see also 4.1.1.)

As a rule, the possibility to offset results of group members is limited to the time of the existence of the group. Therefore, pre-group losses can usually not be offset with group profits. Exceptions to this can be found in Australia, New Zealand and Poland where pre-group losses can be offset with group profits while some jurisdictions allow losses of a group company to be settled with profits of the respective entity before tax consolidation (e.g. Austria, Denmark, Hungary, Italy, Luxembourg, the Netherlands, Portugal). However, Germany does not allow any offsetting, so losses "get locked in" until the membership of an entity in the group ends. In Denmark losses carried forward can only be offset by another group company to the extent that both entities were subject to group taxation when the (offset) loss occurred.

Summarizing the above one can conclude that with regard to the consequences triggered by a tax group no full consolidation is implemented in the different group tax regimes that can be observed in practice today. In contrast, all systems foresee to a certain degree different elements of a separate entity approach.

4.1.5. Group tax regimes and tax avoidance

Group tax regimes trigger several questions regarding the application of anti-avoidance rules. Inherent to all group tax systems is that they offer the possibility to offset profits and losses. Therefore, the mere fact that the tax burden of an entity is reduced by this effect of a tax group cannot be seen per se as constituting tax avoidance.

However, the fact that tax groups offer the possibility to allocate income to other group entities (especially in group contribution systems) and taxpayers can have the choice which companies to include in the tax group triggers the concern of legislators that this might be seen as an invitation to tax optimization. As a consequence some countries foresee all-in-all-out models such as Denmark for the cross-border consolidation (while the domestic system is compulsory in any case) and Italy (for the cross-border consolidation) as well as Australia (this does not hold if the parent is a foreign company; in this case cherry-picking is allowed), Chinese Taipei, Japan, Portugal, Spain and the UK. The Portuguese group tax regime foresees that the controlling company of the tax group cannot be controlled by any other resident company, effecting an implicit all-in-all-out model. Furthermore, minimum periods during which the group must be sustained (e.g. three years in Austria, Poland, five years in Luxembourg, ten years in Denmark for the cross-border consolidation system) can be observed.

In addition, group tax regimes trigger the risk of double dipping as already observed in the context of the Action item 2 of the BEPS project (see under 6.3). Thus, countries like Denmark, Germany, Luxembourg and New Zealand foresee dual consolidated loss rules (DCL) under which losses cannot be offset against income in other group entities to the extent that the loss can also be offset in another jurisdiction.

Furthermore, group taxation regimes can have an effect on the application of anti-avoidance rules. Transaction-related anti-avoidance rules like interest or royalty barrier rules might not apply with regard to intra-group transactions in a full consolidation system. However, also less far-reaching group tax regimes which do not eliminate transactions but only aggregate the separately determined income of each group entity can impact the application of anti-avoidance rules within a group. This can be studied in Denmark, Germany and Hungary where such rules only apply at the level of the controlling entity of the tax group.

The non-application of SAARs in tax groups can be explained by their purposes. As interest and royalty barrier rules aim at preventing the shifting of profits between related companies, it makes no sense to apply them for transactions within a tax group which can only be domestically established. Special rules for the application of SAARs on a tax group can be integrated in the provisions of the group tax regimes. Often, however, such group escapes are part of the special anti-avoidance rules. The requirements for such group escapes do not always match the requirements that allow to form a tax group. The German change of control rule for example contains a group escape, requiring complete control while the majority of voting rights suffices to form a tax group.

4.1.6. Group tax liability

In most group tax systems, group members do not cease to be tax subjects, but remain at least obliged to determine income and, in some cases, to file tax returns (Austria, Denmark, Germany, Luxembourg). In other systems, the obligation to file tax returns as well as to pay tax for the group is transferred to the ultimate parent company (Australia, Chinese Taipei, Denmark, Hungary, Italy, Republic of Korea, New Zealand, Poland). However, in order to reduce the risk of default by the fiscal authorities, the other group members are often held liable for the group's tax liabilities or the shares of it attributable to them (Australia, Denmark, Germany, Italy, Republic of Korea, the Netherlands, New Zealand, Poland, Portugal). In the United States groups have a choice of four methods to allocate the tax liability of the group to the group entities.

In the case of group contribution systems that have no impact on the personal tax liability, all group members continue to pay their own taxes.

4.1.7. Cross-border tax groups

4.1.7.1. Groups under European Law

It will be shown that European countries tend to have group taxation systems that appear more open to foreign group entities. This can only be understood against the background of European law.

One essential objective of European law is the establishment of a single market, where national boundaries do not impede trade and movement. Consequently, if domestic situations are treated more favourably than cross-border situations a measure can be found discriminatory. In manifold decisions the CJEU decided, that foreign entities may not be (entirely) excluded from tax group membership. Already in the first decision of the CJEU on direct taxation, the famous case avoir fiscal of 1986,[73] it was stated that a foreign entity with a domestic PE may not be discriminated against a domestic entity. Also, the denial to offset foreign losses with domestic profits is regarded discriminatory. Due to reasons to safeguard a balanced allocation of taxing rights it, however, has been found in Marks & Spencer[74] and X Holding[75] that the exclusion of current foreign losses (as opposed to final losses which can no longer be used to offset foreign profits) from the domestic group taxation is justified. Otherwise, groups could freely decide in which member state they offset such losses. As found in Groupe Steria[76] such reasons of justification do not hold for other benefits – aside of a loss offset – that arise from the application of group tax regimes. Many European countries, for example, effectively tax exempt dividends from non-group members to 95 % (or any ratio below 100 %, see 3.3) while a group tax regime may allow a full exemption. In cross-borders cases, such treatment would be an unjustified discrimination of foreign entities which would fulfil the requirements for group membership if they were domestic. Member states may comply in two different ways. They either may grant such advantages also in cross-border cases or deny such advantages even within the group (as recently happened e.g. in France and Spain for the DRD or in the Netherlands for other advantages [see 4.1.4).

4.1.7.2. Inherent restriction of group tax regimes to domestic groups (profits and losses)

In regard to the ability-to-pay of the economic unit, domestic and cross-border groups with non-resident entities do not differ. Nevertheless, hardly any jurisdiction allows cross-border group taxation with the chance to include foreign losses into the domestic tax group (see 4.1.7.2). The main reason is the effect of the separate entity principle in international tax law, which prevents the taxation of the profits of non-resident subsidiaries before distribution. This also excludes cross-border loss consolidation.

A cross-border group taxation regime would require a symmetric inclusion of foreign losses and profits. Furthermore, a full cross-border consolidation would need a consent of countries about the allocation of taxing rights which is politically hardly conceivable. As Yoshihiro Masui wrote almost two decades ago in 2004 in the IFA General Report on group taxation:

---

[73]   ECJ, 28 January 1986, Case 270/83, Avoir Fiscal, ECR 1986, 273.
[74]   ECJ, 26 February 2006, Case C-253/03, Marks & Spencer, ECLI:EU:C:2006:129.
[75]   ECJ, 25 February 2010, Case C-237/08, X Holding, ECLI:EU:C:2010:89.
[76]   ECJ, 2 September 2015, Case C-386/14, Group Steria, ECLI:EU:C:2015:524.

"the Achilles heel of any worldwide consolidation system is how to agree on a common formula to divide the amount of revenue between the jurisdictions concerned".[77]

4.1.7.3. Non-resident (foreign) entities

Historically, most group tax regimes were restricted to resident entities. However, today in many countries non-resident entities with their domestic permanent establishments can also be part of the group, which is also required under European law.[78] However, in general the prerequisite is that the application of the group rules, namely loss offsetting, is matched by taxable profits in the same jurisdiction, whereby the different group tax concepts require different techniques.

Any of the countries that apply a full consolidation take a different approach on how to extend their tax group to foreign entities:

In Australia, only domestic companies may participate in the group. A foreign parent may, however, act as non-consolidated head of the group. In New Zealand, non-resident companies can offset profits and losses occurred in New Zealand with group members. In the Netherlands, following a rather wide European approach of non-discrimination, a PE can be a controlling and controlled member of the group.

Furthermore, many European countries, which apply a group attribution system, allow domestic permanent establishments of non-resident entities as a controlling member of a tax group which includes the domestic entities owned by the PE into a tax group (e.g. in Austria, Denmark, France, Germany, Italy, Luxembourg, Portugal).

With regard to the controlled members of a group, a domestic PE of a foreign entity can become a controlled group member of a domestic group in Austria, Denmark (compulsory), France, Hungary, Luxembourg, and Portugal. To the contrary, in Germany, for example, at least the place of effective management and, therefore, tax residency has to be in Germany in order to be included in the tax group (and therefore allowing that resident entities founded in the EU or EEA can participate in a tax-group).

Further, predominantly European states do not even require a tax residence of a controlling entity or PE in their territory such as in Belgium, Finland (if non-discriminatory clauses are applicable), Italy (also in the domestic system), Luxembourg, the Netherlands, Norway, Portugal, Spain and the UK, allowing for a horizontal integration of sister companies in a tax group. To the contrary such residence is required in Austria, Germany, Poland, Singapore and Sweden.

Group contribution schemes are generally restricted in such a way that only payments to resident companies are deductible (as e.g. in Norway)[79]. However, no domestic tax residency of the ultimate parent is required, thus, group contribution between sister companies of a foreign parent are permissible. In Nordic countries (Finland, Norway, Sweden) payments from and to[80] non-resident companies may also be included, provided that the recipient

---

[77]   Y. Masui, General Report Group Taxation, Vol. 89 b (2004), p. 57.

[78]   ECJ, 12 June 2014, Case C-39-41/13, SCA Group Holding, ECR 2014, I-1759; EJC, 14 May 2020, Cases C-749/18 and C-40/13, B and others, ECR 2020, I-370.

[79]   Currently due a Supreme Court Ruling: With the exception of payments covering final losses of a EEA-resident company.

[80]   If only a tax-treaty non-discriminatory clause applies, Norwegian companies may not deduct payments to such PEs.

is liable to tax with it (which is generally the case if the foreign company has a permanent establishment in the country of the paying company). A further premise is the residence in an EU/EEA state or a treaty-jurisdiction, with which a non-discriminatory clause has been agreed on. Even while the CJEU has concluded already some time ago that based on the freedom of establishment it is not necessary to allow a deduction for a profit transfer if the recipient is tax resident abroad,[81] the Finnish system has recently been challenged by the EU Commission in regard to payments covering a final loss of an EU/EEA affiliate. Subsequently, new legislation covering the deduction of final losses has been introduced in Finland. According to the new law, a parent entity located in Finland could deduct the final losses of its subsidiary located in another EEA (European Economic Area) country by applying a specific group deduction.

In only very few jurisdictions (Austria, Denmark, Italy) foreign subsidiaries can be group members even without a domestic permanent establishment, but then only under very restrictive conditions. Austria, for example, allows only first tier foreign subsidiaries to be part of the group, and only under the condition that the foreign subsidiary is not financially integrated with a foreign group member.

If non-resident subsidiaries without a domestic permanent establishment can become part of a tax group, the attribution of profits differs. In Austria, profits are not attributed immediately but only after distribution (i.e. the separate entity principle shelters foreign profits from taxation also if the taxpayer opted for the group taxation). However, in Italy and Denmark profits are attributed immediately.

4.1.7.4. Foreign losses

Only a few – not surprisingly European[82] – countries such as Austria, Denmark and Italy provide for the option to include foreign losses in a group tax regime (often as a legislative measure of tax competition). Not surprisingly, such rules trigger the concern that foreign losses are abusively imported which is why Austria and Denmark apply special provisions in order to prevent abuse and double deduction of foreign losses. Thus, also under those regimes foreign losses are not equally treated in comparison to domestic losses as e.g. under Austrian tax law the losses have to be calculated by applying Austrian law as well as the foreign tax law of the non-resident subsidiary and only the lower amount is deductible only up to 75% of the group profit. Furthermore, both countries safeguard their tax basis by recapture mechanisms, adding back the formerly deducted losses as soon as foreign profits arise. The same mechanism applies if a foreign entity leaves the tax group or if the tax group is terminated (i.e. the tax value of the remaining foreign tax losses will be recaptured in both countries).

---

[81]   ECJ, 18 July 2007, Case C-231/05, Oy AA, ECR 2006, I-474.
[82]   Considering that the decision of the ECJ in Marks & Spencer with regard to the requirement to import foreign losses has still not been waived. ECJ, 26 February 2006, Case C-253/03, Marks & Spencer, ECLI:EU:C:2006:129.

4.1.7.5. Groups in the DTT law

DTTs rely on the separate entity principle when determining tax residence in order to allocate taxing rights. This explains why neither the OECD Model Convention, nor individual double tax treaties contain special rules on how treaties are applied with regard to tax groups. In general, the consequences depend on the underlying concept of the different group taxation regimes.[83]

Only such group tax regimes in which the group itself becomes the tax subject, trigger the question of tax treaty entitlement of the group. Here one has to distinguish between the entitlement of the single group member and the question of an (additional) entitlement of the group as whole. As long as the group members are subject of the income determination they do not lose their tax treaty entitlement, if one understands tax subject correctly not necessarily as "liable to tax". However, in New Zealand only the tax group is entitled to the DTT. The Polish example shows, furthermore, that without clear rules in this regard considerable legal uncertainty remains.[84] In principle, the same problem might arise in Australia where a full consolidation is applied and group members are deemed to be part of the head company (i.e. group members would not be "liable to tax"). However, as the Australian treaties usually do not adopt the model convention wording "liable to tax" but refer to the actual domestic qualification of tax residency, DTT entitlement is a rather remote problem for Australian group member entities.

If a group contribution system, which leaves the tax personality of the single group members unaffected, applies, every single group member stays entitled under the DTT. The same holds true for profit attribution regimes where DTT benefits are granted to the individual group members.

4.1.8. Groups and local/regional business taxes

Similar problems as in cross-border-groups arise if countries apply business taxes at sub-federal levels (regional or local) and entities reside in different regions. Such regional or local taxes are levied in Canada, France, Germany, Hungary, Italy, Japan, Republic of Korea, Portugal, Spain, Switzerland and the US. It is striking that neither Switzerland nor Canada, both states in which the sub-federal level plays a major role, provide for any possibility to offset gains and losses in a group taxation system (i.e. in Canada the absence of special regional allocation rules is considered to be the primary reason why no group taxation is foreseen).

However, if tax groups are foreseen and local taxes exist, the approaches of the different group taxation regimes to deal with the regional allocation of the tax base differ:

Germany, Japan and the US grant the possibility of group taxation also for state or local tax purposes and allocate profits based on formulary apportionment. This apportionment is not only applicable to tax groups but to all corporations with interstate or intercommunity activities. As a consequence the application of the arm's length principle is not decisive in a cross-regional context.

---

[83]   See on this fundamentally S. P. Link, Konsolidierte Besteuerung im Abkommensrecht, München 2009.
[84]   B. Kuźniacki, Tax Notes International, October 14, 2013, 143.

In Spain, the Basque country and the Navarra region levy their own taxes. As a consequence companies can only enter a tax group for those taxes if all the activity of the companies entering the tax group are carried on in the region.

In France group taxation affects the determination of the local value added tax. Where an entity fulfils the holding conditions to be a member of a tax group, the relevant turnover that determines its effective rate of taxation corresponds to the aggregate turnover of the same (potential) group.

The Hungarian group tax regime, introduced in 2019, does not apply for Hungarian local business tax purposes. Therefore, the tax base must be assessed for each entity on a stand-alone basis and transactions between related parties need to meet arm's length conditions. The Italian local value added tax and the Portuguese local tax are similarly solely levied on a stand-alone basis.

4.2. CFC regimes

Foreign resident companies that are affiliated can be used in order to shift income from high to low tax countries via the establishment of centralized functions such as financing and licensing of intangibles (i.e. those functions can be more easily established in affiliated companies resident mostly in low-tax jurisdictions). Therefore, the starting point for the application of Controlled Foreign Company (CFC) rules is the separate entity principle as foreign companies are used as a "blocker" between a source of income and its shareholders. Such CFC rules are commonly introduced by states in order to allow that certain types of income earned by foreign subsidiaries can be taxed in the state of the shareholder. At first glance CFC rules seem, therefore, to resemble group taxation regimes as they pierce the legal body of a company and also allocate income of foreign CFC entities to its shareholders (i.e. group taxation regimes and CFC rules both foresee that income will be allocated from one entity to another group entity). However, looking at the details of those CFC regimes one can see that they also contain elements following more a group approach:

The principles of how income has to be allocated to resident shareholders can be distinguished between 1) income allocation rules (such as applied e.g. by Belgium, Chile, Finland and Turkey) and 2) deemed profit distribution rules (such as in e.g. France and Republic of Korea). The difference of those concepts can on the one hand make a difference regarding different aspects such as timing of allocation of income.[85] On the other hand, the different legal consequences speak either towards the separate entity approach or the group approach. CFC regimes that deem a profit distribution rather follow the separate legal entity approach, as the body of a foreign company is respected and only the point in time, when a distribution occurs, is shifted. Alternatively, rather a group approach can be assumed if foreign income is directly allocated to the shareholder under local CFC rules.

In order to allow CFC rules to apply they generally require some form of control of resident shareholders over the foreign entity (i.e. mostly a 50% holding in the capital or voting rights). Some countries consider all shares held by associated companies for the purpose of the 50% shareholding test as foreseen under article 7 paragraph 1 let. a) of the

---

[85]   Example see M. Lang, Bulletin for Fiscal Documentation 2003, 51 (55-56); A. Rust, Die Hinzurechnungsbesteuerung, 2007, 66-104; partly disagreeing with Rust: B. Kuźniacki, Intertax 2015, 758 (769-772).

ATAD Directive[86] applying a group view (such as in Austria, Czech Republic, Denmark, Italy, Luxembourg, Mauritius). However, other countries such as Canada (limited to five resident shareholders), the Republic of Korea and Norway take a broader view and see a control also given if independent resident shareholders hold more than 50% of the shares in a foreign company (despite the fact that those independent shareholders are neither unanimously exercising their voting or any other shareholder rights nor forming some other group with a special common interest).

When determining CFC income, countries such as Finland and France in general follow a separate entity approach which means that the income and low taxation test is done for the different foreign standalone entity. Certain countries such as Germany, however, allow that the allocation of income foreseen under foreign group taxation principles has to be respected as well when determining whether foreign income is taxed at a sufficient level. This leads to a situation that a foreign entity is not expected to be low taxed only because another foreign entity is paying the tax for the income due to an allocation of a foreign group taxation system. Even more far-reaching are the consequences of the check-the-box election under US tax law which can be used within the US Subpart F rules to disregard passive transactions which would normally be subject to CFC taxation.

Most importantly, most countries do not allow for an allocation of foreign low-taxed losses to the shareholders resident in its jurisdiction. This as well as the fact that many jurisdictions foresee thresholds from which percentage or amount of passive income an income inclusion is triggered, clearly speaks in favour of that CFC rules more serve the purpose to disallow tax planning opportunities arising from the separate entity principle than establishing a taxation following the group approach. Some countries allow the deduction of foreign low-taxed losses against foreign low-taxed income. However, usually such an offset is only allowed within the CFCs, following again a stricter separate entity approach (i.e. in such a case losses of a CFC can be carried forward in order to reduce future CFC income). However, some countries such as Peru and Poland allow no such carry forward at all.

Furthermore, most countries only include so-called "passive" or "tainted" income in the CFC tax base and only selected countries such as Denmark and Sweden include all income. However, in the Swedish case the area of application is narrowed down by a white list exemption or a focus on CFC rules for states mentioned on a blacklist. This and the fact that CFC rules of almost all countries require some kind of low-taxation of the income speaks in favour of that CFC rules should only balance negative effects stemming from the application of the separate entity approach and abusive shifting of income.

5. Groups and associated corporations in the tax procedure

Tax procedure rules commonly follow the separate entity approach in group tax regimes if the individual group members' income is the starting point for the group's aggregate or consolidated income. Those jurisdictions audit, therefore, corporations independently, even though they may be members of a tax group. Only a few exceptions exist, e.g. Japan, where only the group is audited. In the Republic of Korea, the audit of a dominant group member

---

[86] See also EU report, part 2, section 6.

also includes the audit of other members. In Italy, the overall taxes of the domestic group are audited if an error has been detected during the audit of one member of the tax group.

However, a few jurisdictions consider tax groups to be the single taxpayer (Australia, Hungary New Zealand and the Netherlands). In these jurisdictions groups consequently are audited as one taxpayer.

Among those jurisdictions that do not consider tax groups to be one single taxpayer, formal rules of a joint audit for group members can sometimes be found. In Germany, groups and controlled corporations are audited jointly under administrative guidelines if external sales exceed an amount of EUR 25 million. Large corporate groups are also audited jointly in Canada in order to reduce compliance costs. Furthermore, entities are regularly audited simultaneously (e.g. Belgium, Czech Republic, Denmark, Finland, France, Norway) due to practical considerations, even if no special tax procedure rules for tax groups or even group taxation regimes exist.

One of the reasons that group companies are audited independently can be the fact to preserve local jurisdiction applicable for the different entities. Furthermore, tax secrecy provisions can also preclude the involvement of representatives of other group members in some countries.

Many countries also foresee in their procedural provisions the requirement to report significant holdings in other entities,[87] membership in a group and/or transactions with related entities (see e.g. Australia, Chile, France, Norway). In addition, rules on the disclosure of beneficial ownership have to be observed and members of multinational groups are regularly obliged to prepare special transfer pricing documentation, sometimes limited to size-related thresholds. All of those obligations are based on the presumption that tax planning opportunities among related parties exist and greater scrutiny to audit intercompany transactions is therefore necessary.

6. Provisions on base-erosion and profit shifting

6.1. Intra-group withholding taxes or non-deductibility of outbound payments due to royalty capping rules

Base erosion is seen as one of the most common problems in international tax law nowadays which is why the term made it to the title of the BEPS project, one of the most important initiatives of the OECD during the last decade. The possibility of taxpayers to erode the tax base is based on the taxation according to the separate entity principles and the fact that interest payments, lease payments as well as payments for the provision of services are per-se deductible, even if the recipient is part of the same corporate group but outside the scope of domestic tax law.

Base erosion can be combatted by introducing or applying rules that strengthen source taxation. Such rules can be explicitly or implicitly tailored to group scenarios (base erosion payment rules). Other rules also apply on outside-group cases but effectively reduce base erosion (withholding tax rules). Another differentiator is if such rules are designed to

---

[87] E.g. Finland: need to report holdings of at least 10% in other corporations.

consider the tax burden of the payee. Such consideration would support single taxation within a group.

6.1.1. Measures not requiring group membership

One classical way to prevent base erosion is the levying of withholding taxes on outbound payments which is generally not restricted to intra-group payments. However, in a European context such withholding taxes mostly can not be used as an instrument to prevent base erosion, as the levying of withholding taxes on interest and royalty payments made between associated companies of different EU member states is not possible under the interest and royalty directive.[88]

Furthermore, also DTT often prevent the levying of such withholding taxes. Therefore, this instrument has become a bit "out of fashion" and only selected countries such as e.g. Colombia, Mexico, New Zealand and Peru broadly apply withholding taxes to safeguard domestic tax revenues.

In reversal of the described restrictions of EU and DTT law to the levying of withholding taxes, the proposed EU-"Unshell-Directive",[89] however, denies tax residency certificates to shell companies that lack substance and are resident in an EU Member State.. Further, EU Member States shall disregard any agreements that provide the elimination of double taxation concluded with the member state of residence of the shell entity. Payments to the shell entity that constitute "relevant income" (in particular interest payments, royalties, dividends, income from financial leasing, income from immovable property and certain movable property, income from outsourced services) are thus subject to withholding taxes, if there is no tax treaty or agreement between the countries of the payor and of the shareholder. EU member states would consequently look through the shell company when applying measures to eliminate double taxation. If the shell company, for example, receives a payment, and the shareholder of the shell company is not resident in the EU, the Member State of the payor would levy its withholding tax according to its domestic tax law, ignoring the shell entity. However, any agreement or tax treaty entered into between the Member State of the payor and the country of the shareholder may still apply. If both the payor and shareholder are EU resident, EU directives may apply as well. Additionally, an EU resident shareholder would include the payment in his taxable income as if it had directly accrued to him – without prejudice to any treaty it has concluded with the country of the payor. In this regard, the (separate) entity principle is not fully neglected, because only certain items of income (the "relevant income") are directly attributed. The shareholder as well may be able to claim relief for any tax paid at source, based on EU directives or tax treaties or other agreement. Any tax paid by the shell can be credited. The treatment as a shell entity is safeguarded by intensive reporting obligations, an extended exchange of information as well as penalties ensuring the compliance with the directive' obligations. Concerning some aspects – the attribution of income (i.e. not allowing the deferral of income in interposed entities) and the definition of relevant income – there is some similarity with the concept of CFC regimes. Different to conventional CFC regimes, however, the Shell Directive is

---

88   Council Directive 2003/49/EC of 3 June 2003 on a common system of taxation applicable to interest and royalty payments made between associated companies of different Member States.

89   COM(2021) 565 final of 22 December 2021, see also EU report part 2, section 12.

supposed to apply without a minimum participation threshold nor is it linked to a minimum tax rate.

Similarly to the levying of withholding tax, but stricter, Argentina restricts the deductions of royalties and certain fees to foreign beneficiaries regardless of the affiliation. Such limitations are not applicable in DTT cases.

Furthermore, such withholding taxes can, in a group context, also arise due to the application of an interest barrier or debt-to-equity rule such as in Canada and Switzerland. However, in those instances the respective provisions aim at limiting the deduction of payments and the levying of withholding taxes is a rather mechanical consequence from the fact that those rules often trigger a constructive dividend which triggers withholding taxes.

6.1.2. Deduction restrictions explicitly tailored to intra-group payments

Tax base erosion can also be prevented by limiting in general the deductibility of outbound payments to affiliates. They can apply to any payments characterized as base erosion payment. Such rules can apply irrespective of the nature of the underlying intercompany transactions and have, therefore, the intention to safeguard the domestic tax base to the widest extend possible. In this context the US Base Erosion and Anti-Abuse Tax (BEAT[90]) needs to be mentioned as one of the most well-known provisions limiting the deductibility of outbound payments. BEAT covers, irrespective of the foreign tax burden, all outbound payments to related parties (leaving aside the depreciation of assets) and is, therefore, a strong legislative measure to ringfence the own tax jurisdiction. Poland recently introduced a similar rule.

Rules restricting the deductibility of interest payments are classical base erosion measures of states to protect their tax base. This is based on the fact that financing structures are an important instrument of international tax planning to make use of different tax rates and the flexibility to either finance via debt or equity. Provisions that limit the deduction of related-party interest payments can be found in Canada, Belgium and the Republic of Korea. Provisions specifically aiming at reducing the deductibility of interest payments on debt-push-down are nowadays more and more rare and can only be found e.g. in South Africa.

Some countries such as Chile, Chinese Taipei, Colombia, and Switzerland foresee a debt-to-equity ratio to determine the deductible payments of interest on related-party debt. Denmark applies such a debt-to-equity ratio in addition to an interest barrier rule. Regarding the legal consequences, those debt-to-equity rules follow a strict separate entity approach as they do not consider if the overall group may be highly leveraged.

In some jurisdictions provisions can be found that limit the deduction of intra-group royalties (as e.g. in Chile, Germany and Ukraine). Furthermore, the German and Chilean royalty barrier rules are also worth mentioning as they intend to limit the deductibility of royalty payments if payments are taxed below a certain rate. These provisions, therefore, already include elements of a taxation based on a group approach (i.e. as the taxation of another related entity is decisive for their application). However, the German rules are subject to heavy discussions with regard to their permissibility based on European law or article 24 of the OECD-MTC which is why some countries such as Germany already included a treaty override in order to apply those rules.

---

[90]   See US report, 2.10.

In summary, regarding the legal consequences of the regulation of outbound payments, such provisions generally still follow the separate entity approach very strictly and often do not contain elements following the taxation on a group basis. Regarding the requirements, such rules however recognize that group membership facilitates base erosion.

6.1.3. Deduction restrictions implicitly tailored to intra-group interest payments

Often rules on the limitation of interest deductions apply to payments towards related and third parties as under the laws of Australia and European countries following the ATAD Directive such as e.g. France, Germany and the Netherlands. Sometimes they only apply in cross-border situations (such as in the case of e.g. Australia and the Republic of Korea), and sometimes – especially in EU countries due to the EU law principles – they apply with regard to domestic situations as well (such as in Austria, Finland, France and Germany). Only some countries such as Hong Kong, Singapore and Uruguay have no specific provisions with regard to interest payments.

In the context of Action 4 of the BEPS Action Plan best practices for the design of rules to avoid the reduction of profits through the deduction of interest expenses can be found. Those are implicitly tailored to intra-group debt. The OECD recommends legislative measures that shall ensure that external interest payments remain deductible. This is being achieved by restricting the deductibility of the net interest expense in each entity according to 10-30% of the EBITDA.[91] This shall also ensure that an entity's interest deductions and thus the allocation of a group' debts are directly linked to its economic activity and revenue-generating activities.[92] Under article 4 paragraph 1 subparagraph 1 ATAD[93] a limitation of 30% of the EBITDA applies. Furthermore, an interest carryforward and a carryforward of unused interest deduction potential can be foreseen. Therefore, it is not a surprise that European countries such as Belgium, Czech Republic, Denmark, France, Germany, Hungary, Italy, Luxembourg, the Netherlands (20%-EBITDA threshold as of 2022), Portugal as well as in Japan, Mexico, and from 2021 onwards Peru, introduced such rules.

With the limitation of deductibility of interest payments applying the 30%-EBITDA threshold, the interest barrier rules on the one hand follow more strictly the separate entity approach as the existence of the corporate body is not questioned. On the other hand, interest barrier rules have elements following a group approach as well as they aim to influence the group to allocate interest within the group according to the EBITDA. Such an aim ignores the fact that the generation of tax advantages is only one aspect of intra-group debt financing (besides business considerations such as the management of currency risks and capital preservation considerations). Consequently, this approach does not necessarily lead to the intended pro rata allocation.

In order to allow a deduction of interest payments if a proportional allocation of debt within the group is given, the OECD as well as article. 4 paragraph 5 let. B) ATAD foresee a

---

[91] OECD, Limiting Base Erosion Involving Interest Deductions and Other Financial Payments, Action 4 – 2016 Update, 2016, para. 99.
[92] OECD, Limiting Base Erosion Involving Interest Deductions and Other Financial Payments, Action 4 – 2016 Update, 2016, para. 23.
[93] See also EU report, part 2 section 7. Suggestions for an interest barrier regulation can also be found in art. 13 of the Proposal for a directive on a Common Consolidated Corporate Tax Base (CCCTB) of 25 October 2016, COM(2016) 683 final.

group ratio rule which allows an entity to deduct net interest expense up to its group's net interest/EBITDA ratio. Alternatively, article 4 paragraph 5 let. A) ATAD allows to fully deduct interest costs comparing the taxpayer's equity over its total assets to the equivalent ratio of the group. E.g. Germany and Norway introduced such escape rules. However, no such escape for an equity test within the group is provided for under e.g. Belgium and Spanish interest barrier rules.

Germany and the UK follow the principles foreseen under article 4 paragraph 1 subparagraph 1 let. a) ATAD and apply the interest barrier rule only on the income of the group[94] (see already 4.1.5).

It can be expected that rules on base erosion will also play an important role in preventing the stripping of earnings in the future as long as no dramatic shift to a more comprehensive group taxation will occur.

6.2. Hybrid mismatch-rules

Hybrid structures are characterized by the fact that the qualification of entities for tax purposes is assessed independently (following the separate entity approach) and differently by the countries involved (see under 2.3.). Qualification conflicts arising out of this were used in order to achieve a lower overall tax burden. Neutralizing such inconsistencies was one of the main goals of the OECD and led within the BEPS project to an own action item[95] and at the EU level to the Anti-Tax Avoidance Directive I (ATAD I) and the Anti-Tax Avoidance Directive II (ATAD II) requiring member states to combat hybrid structures. Furthermore, qualification conflicts can also be achieved through the use of permanent establishments and differences in the allocation of income which is why the OECD has published a separate report in this regard as well (the so-called Branch Mismatch Report).[96] Especially, the deemed branch payment rules are of interest insofar as they make use of qualification conflicts that arise due to the fact that states do not apply the AOA and the fiction of the branch being a fiction legal entity in the same way (i.e. also such a fiction triggers qualification conflicts and the requirement to introduce further anti-abuse rules).

Not surprisingly anti-hybrid rules have been established over the last years in a number of (especially Europeans) countries such as in Australia, Austria, Belgium, Czech Republic, Denmark, France, Germany, Hungary, and Italy. However, still various countries such as Canada, Chinese Taipei and Hong Kong have not introduced such rules. Mostly anti-hybrid rules apply to any kind of income. However, Korean anti-hybrid rules apply only to interest payments.

On the one hand hybrid-mismatch rules start from the separate entity approach as the negative tax consequences are caused by the standalone taxation of the involved entities. On the other hand, group taxation rules can also be the reason for hybrid structures because the corresponding income occurs at another group entity which is only considered and

---

[94]   The German rules operate on the existence of a tax group, the UK rules operate on the existence of a consolidated group, as defined for IFRS purposes.

[95]   OECD, Neutralising the Effects of Hybrid Mismatch Arrangements – 2014 Deliverable, 2014; Neutralising the Effects of Hybrid Mismatch Arrangements, Action 2 – 2015 Final Report, 2015.

[96]   OECD, Neutralising the Effects of Branch Mismatch Arrangements, Action 2: Inclusive Framework on BEPS, 2017.

offset in one of the countries (see also under 4.1.5).[97] However, the fact that the hybrid mismatch rules require the testing of tax consequences in another tax jurisdiction and also at the level of another taxpayer indicates, that those rules also follow a group view in order to prevent untaxed income.

When solving such qualification conflicts an agreement needs to be found which state limits its taxing rights and which state is entitled to tax. It is probably the biggest achievement that Action Item 2 led to a consensus in a relatively short time frame which state is entitled to tax if the different qualification conflicts arise, which has not been achieved in the discussions around a more global formular taxation.

The scope of the hybrid mismatch rules is on the one hand limited to arrangements between related parties and intra-group arrangements (i.e. to group situations where there is a certain proximity between tax treatment by the persons involved in the arrangement). This can be explained by the fact that a conflict of qualification is not always intended in which case the hybrid mismatch rules should not apply. However, if a qualification conflict arises within a group leading to Deduction/No Inclusion (D/NI) or Double Deduction (DD) result an abuse is always assumed (i.e. there is no possibility of giving counter-evidence that the qualification conflict was triggered "accidentally").

On the other hand, the hybrid mismatch rules apply also to so-called "structured arrangements". Such structured arrangements are given if the value of the tax incongruence has been included in the terms of an arrangement or the facts and circumstances of the arrangement indicate that a qualification conflict was intended. In other words the hybrid mismatch rules apply also to unrelated parties insofar that it can be assumed that the independent parties were acting with a common goal to achieve a qualification conflict and the tax benefits were to be shared.

Summarizing above, anti-hybrid-rules worship the separate entity approach and try to prevent negative consequences arising from qualification conflicts in the form of double non-taxation. However, the application of anti-hybrid rules introduces a new level of complexity in international taxation which can be illustrated by the almost 500-page length of the OECD Action Item 2 report, which accounts for almost one third of the total volume of all BEPS reports. The reason for this is that hybrid mismatch rules make the tax treatment in one jurisdiction dependent on the taxation in other jurisdictions or at other taxpayers. Not surprisingly, complexity arises from this linking of tax rules as the possible tax scenarios from the combination of different tax regimes are manifold. Therefore, it is a good example that maintaining the separate entity approach and introducing a group view in parallel increase complexity and administrative burden.

6.3. Country-by-Country Reporting

A central component of the OECD's anti-BEPS strategy is transparency. This is where Action Item 13 with the Country-by-Country Reporting (CbCR) comes in.

Having a CbCR reporting done on a per entity basis would have been pointless as its main purpose (similar to financial reporting) is to give an overview of the overall taxes paid by an MNE in the different jurisdictions. Therefore, the CbCR is in contrast to material tax provisions based on a group approach and foresees the reporting of consolidated numbers

---

97   OECD, Neutralising the Effects of Hybrid Mismatch Arrangements – 2014 Deliverable, 2014, para. 73.

such as income, the overall taxes paid, and certain indicators of the economic activity and allocates them to the tax jurisdictions in which the MNE group operates.[98]

CbCR has been introduced in all countries represented by the branch reports for MNEs with an annual revenue of over EUR 750 million (or the equivalent in the national currency) per year. The thresholds rely on the consolidated financial accounts in order to identify corporations' obligation to file a country by country reporting.

7. Special taxes for (international) groups (DPT, DST etc.)

"Anti-BEPS taxes" like diverted profits taxes or digital service taxes have in common that they shall apply only to large companies or groups. Although the actual taxpayer remains the separate entity, the group revenue is determining the tax base (i.e. the group's financial accounts is insofar decisive).

The diverted profits tax of Australia, implemented in 2017, applies only to "significant global entities" ("SGE"), which are either a parent company with annual global income of A$1 billion or more, or a member of a consolidated group for accounting purposes where the global parent entity has an annual global income of A$1 billion or more.

The UK diverted profits tax (DPT), which was introduced in 2014 as the first kind of such taxes, does not contain a size-related threshold. Even though designed to apply on big multinational groups, it still focuses on the separate entity – i.e., it is assessed whether a particular entity avoided a UK PE or incurred an intragroup expense or diverted intragroup income. However, the requirements for the variant that focuses on the intra-group payments obviously reflect group membership.

Digital service taxes (DST) focus on big multinational groups as well. The original EU-proposal for a digital service tax[99] contains two thresholds to limit its scope which needs to be surpassed in order for an entity to be subject to the tax:

1. the total amount of worldwide revenues reported by the entity for the latest complete financial year for which a financial statement is available exceeds EUR 750 million, and
2. the total amount of taxable revenues obtained by the entity within the EU during that financial year exceeds EUR 50 million.

The testing of the two thresholds is based on the total consolidated group revenues.

Some European member states (Austria, France, Italy, Spain) as well as the UK implemented digital service taxes,[100] which are largely based on the EU proposal in particular with regard to the (group) threshold (e.g. as of 2020 Austria applies a digital advertising tax on business entities with a global annual revenue of at least EUR 750 million). However, the second threshold determining the local revenue is often significantly lower (Austria: EUR 25 million; Italy EUR 5.5 million; Spain EUR 3 million). Other countries discuss the introduction of similar instruments (see Belgium, New Zealand).

---

[98]   OECD, Transfer Pricing Documentation and Country-by-Country Reporting, Action 13 – 2015 Final Report, para 16.
[99]   Proposal for a directive on the common system of a digital services tax on revenues resulting from the provision of certain digital services of 21 March 2018, COM(2018) 148 final. The work on this proposal has been put on hold and will be abandoned with the introduction of rules on Pillar One (see below 9.2).
[100]   Those unilateral taxes will be removed with the introduction of rules on Pillar One.

These taxes do not lead to any kind of group taxation and lack a coordinated approach in the country where the remuneration for the digital service is paid and the country of the recipient. Instead they generalize that additional taxes for digital services have to be levied given that companies in that industry tend to divert income taxes due to the non-physical nature of their business. Therefore, these new taxes bear the risk of double taxation also as they are not covered by existing DTT. However, the EU proposal aims at preventing double taxation within a group as payments to other entities belonging to the same group are to be excluded. Spain follows this element of the EU proposal and excludes digital service activities if a 100% direct or indirect ownership is given.

As transitional measures, these special national anti-BEPS- taxes on the profits of the digital economy are supposed to be removed after Pillar One has been implemented.[101]

8. Intermediate conclusion

Despite the fact that manifold special rules for groups and controlled companies exist, the separate entity principle still dominates the world of income tax today. This does not only trigger on the one hand challenges for taxpayers which generate profits and losses in different jurisdictions due to the fact that no cross-border consolidation is available. It also requires companies to deal with the determination of various rules such as e.g. transfer prices (and discussions in audits about them) in order to allocate profits between the different jurisdictions according to the subjective arm's length principle.

The separate entity principle is on the other hand also the basis for the worries of legislators that companies engage in tax planning and the shifting of profits. As a consequence, legislators react with different legislative measures such as interest and royalty barrier rules or hybrid mismatch rules, just to name to few, which try to counter the potential negative consequences arising from the separate entity principle. These anti-avoidance rules are directed against the exploitation of the separate entity principle and apply regularly if the threshold of 25% of voting rights, capital ownership or profit participation is exceeded as also stipulated under article 2 paragraph 4 ATAD. Other provisions, such as CFC regimes, regularly foresee an income inclusion for subsidiaries controlled by a participation of at least 50%, as regulated in article 7 paragraph 1 ATAD. However, since the ATAD only contains a minimum standard, it tolerates notable exceptions like Portugal, Finland, and Sweden that apply the income inclusion already in cases of a participation of more than 25%. Such low thresholds are problematic as the assumption of an influence on the decisions of the affiliates which justifies the application of anti-abuse provisions, seems to be not necessarily accurate. There are, however, also group escapes which mitigate the application and consequences of such anti-avoidance rules like foreseen in article 4 paragraph 5 ATAD for the application of the interest barrier and introduce some elements of a group taxation.

Furthermore, group tax regimes do not change the observation about the importance of the separate entity principle fundamentally. Even though they are widespread, they are limited both in scope and in their consequences when being applied. Additionally, they exclude the possibility for a group taxation in cross-border situations. This limitation

---

[101]   See https://home.treasury.gov/news/press-releases/jy0419.

is striking as for financial reporting purposes it is acknowledged that in group situations parent companies can shift capital, liquidity and profits due to the control over its subsidiaries through intra-group transactions. Consequently, parent entities are required to provide consolidated financial statements in which the group is treated as one single entity even though financial accounting is linked (as tax law is as well) to the legally independent company.

Tax law, despite following the same intention to avoid deliberate allocation among group entities, does not follow a comparable path (so far) and legislators refrain from enacting tax provisions allowing a full consolidation to reflect the economic unity of a group. Instead, the group approach, which also considers tax consequences of other taxpayers in other jurisdictions, is only introduced where necessary to prevent negative consequences from the application of the separate entity principle. In summary, the current status can, therefore, be described as some kind of hybrid situation where legislators stick to the separate entity principle but engage in group-oriented tax provisions where necessary to fix undesired tax consequences.

9. Perspectives

9.1. International group taxation as the panacea of all BEPS issues?

The aim of the G20/OECD BEPS initiative in 2012 was to restrict aggressive tax planning pursued by MNEs which was particularly based on the shielding effect resulting from the separate entity principle. The results are the 2015 OECD recommendations that among others restrict the separate entity principle in various ways described above (see under 4.2. and 6.3.).

Furthermore, a system of worldwide group taxation with a formulary apportionment of profits was seen as the ultimate solution of all problems addressed in the BEPS project and, therefore, as the future of a new international tax system.[102] This concept is also embedded in the dragging EU Commission proposal for a Common Consolidated Corporate tax base (CCCTB).[103] Even while this idea sounds promising, one can be sceptical with regard to the outlook of a successful implementation. Because what has not been agreed upon for quite some time in the EU is unlikely to be passed in a worldwide consensus.

As a consequence the OECD's Inclusive Framework decided to continue its pathway with proposals in the area of taxation of digital business models by suggesting so-called Pillar One and Pillar Two rules with the objective of reaching a consensus-based solution.

Even while the political outcome of these trends is still unclear, both proposals allow a view on the discussion of the future in international taxation. In particular the question arises, whether Pillar One and Two as an extension of BEPS 2.0 will include more group-

---

[102] R.S. Avi-Yonah et al. Allocating Business Profits for Tax Purposes: A Proposal to Adopt a Formulary Profit Split, Florida Tax Review 2009, p. 497; R.S. Avi-Yonah, A Proposal for Unitary Taxation and Formulary Apportionment to Tax Multinational Enterprises in P. Dietsch and T. Rixen (eds.), Global Tax Governance, 2016 , p. 289; M. F. de Wilde, Intertax 2011, p. 62 (82), mediating Maarten F. De Wilde, Sharing the Pie, 2017, pp. 378-430, https://papers.ssrn.com/sol3/papers.cfm?abstract_id=2564181.

[103] Proposal for a directive on a Common Consolidated Corporate Tax Base (CCCTB) of 25 October 2016, COM(2016) 683 final; see EU report part 2, section 3.

like international taxation principles or whether those proposals remain trapped in the separate entity principle.

9.2. Pillar One

In order to move away from the traditional arm's length principle as the heart of the separate entity principle, a greater share of (residual) profits should be allocated to market/user jurisdictions with the creation of standalone nexus rules that do not make reference to the physical presence by the following building blocks of Pillar One:
1) Amount A: sets a new taxing right for market jurisdictions with 25% of a multinational enterprise's (MNE's) residual profit being reallocated.
2) Amount B: is meant to foresee a fixed return for certain baseline marketing and distribution activities taking place physically in a market jurisdiction (with the outcomes consistent with the arm's length principle) even while the work on Amount B has been postponed and is meant to be concluded in 2022.
3) Processes to improve tax certainty through effective dispute prevention and resolution mechanisms.

Amount A will only apply to specific big multinational groups that exceed a sales threshold of EUR 20 billion and a before tax return on sales of 10%. The formerly foreseen activity test according to which it needs to be determined whether the business activity is so called "automated digital services" (ADS) and/or "consumer facing businesses" (CFB), has been abandoned during the process when the Statements on the Two-Pillar Solution were agreed upon.[104]

Under Amount A, 25% of the MNE's residual profits will be allocated to the market jurisdictions in which the in-scope MNE has a nexus. The residual profits are defined as group profits that exceed a threshold of 10% of group revenue and will be allocated to the nexus jurisdictions on a revenue-based allocation key. The revenue numbers required for determining the nexus and the allocation key will be sourced to the market jurisdictions where goods or services are used or consumed. The details of the Pillar One rules with regard to Nexus and Revenue Sourcing have been laid out in the Public consultation document of 1 February 2022.[105]

In the course of the nexus test, which was further refined in the Public consultation document, market states are identified in which the MNE is economically participating (beyond mere sales to customers located there from a remote location). This test is generally carried out on the basis of revenue thresholds foreseeing that the nexus test is met if the group revenue of an in-scope MNE exceeds EUR 1 million (for jurisdictions with a GDP equal to or greater than EUR 40 billion) or EUR 250,000 (for jurisdictions with a GDP of less than EUR 40 billion) in a jurisdiction.

The formulary apportionment mechanism of Amount A provides for common rules for the determination of the apportionment based on a range of possible indicators, or, in cases where a 'back-stop' is needed, based on an allocation key that is expected to provide a

---

[104] OECD, Statements on a Two-Pillar Solution to Address the Tax Challenges Arising From the Digitalisation of the Economy, July and October 2021.
[105] OECD, Pillar One – Amount A: Draft Model Rules for Nexus and Revenue Sourcing, 2022.

reasonable approximation of the market jurisdiction (i.e. the 'back-stop' allocation keys are provided to ensure that no revenue goes unsourced particularly with regard to third-party distribution arrangements, components, certain services, and intangible property). The revenue sourcing rules provide for a schedule setting out the detailed rules for applying the revenue sourcing principle for different types of revenue. As a starting point the revenue must be sourced on a transaction-by-transaction basis according to the category of revenue earned from the transaction (i.e. for each revenue generating item it must be determined where the revenue item should be sourced). The draft Model Rules differentiate eight different sourcing rules for different types of revenue categories. If transactions comprise of different elements that fall under more than one revenue category, they must be qualified according to their predominant character.

While Amount A tries to develop new allocation rules which determine profits and revenues on a group basis, Amount B takes a different direction. As the work for Amount B will continue through 2022, at the time of writing the Blueprint still foresees Amount B. Amount B is applicable if an entity acquires products from a related party for resale to third parties and performs associated "defined baseline marketing and distribution activities" in the local market.[106] In order to avoid disputes a list of positive and negative criteria will be developed in order to define which activities are covered by Amount B.[107]

If Amount B is applicable, a "fixed return" for "baseline marketing and distribution activities" is expected to be applied. The intention of Amount B is, therefore, to simplify the administration of transfer pricing rules.

Even while a lot of factors such as the final definition of "baseline marketing and distribution activities" as well as the applicable fixed fee remuneration still need to be defined, Amount B clearly follows the classical standalone approach. In fact it is expected that Amount B will be in line with the results determined under the transactional net margin method.

This assumption is also supported by the fact that Amount B is intended to operate under a "rebuttal presumption". This means that the distribution entity will need to apply Amount B, unless the taxpayer can provide sufficient evidence that another transfer pricing method is more appropriate (which conceptually also indicates towards the concept of a taxation on a standalone basis).

From the overall setup it can be concluded that Pillar One includes elements of a group taxation when testing and determining Amount A. It is expected that uncertainties will arise under this new allocation of taxing rights based on a group approach which is why the members of the Inclusive Framework discuss the introduction of dispute prevention and resolution mechanisms.

Amount B, in contrast, follows a more classical transfer pricing and separate accounting approach. To what extent Pillar One will function in the direction of a group approach in order to allocate profits internationally depends in particular on the amount of profits assigned to Amount A in comparison to Amount B. This question is a political one and has therefore deliberately been left open in the Blueprint.[108]

[106]   OECD, Tax Challenges Arising from Digitalisation – Report on Pillar One Blueprint: Inclusive Framework on BEPS, 2020 paras. 658 et seq.

[107]   OECD, Tax Challenges Arising from Digitalisation – Report on Pillar One Blueprint: Inclusive Framework on BEPS, 2020, paras. 667 et seq.

[108]   OECD, Tax Challenges Arising from Digitalisation – Report on Pillar One Blueprint: Inclusive Framework on BEPS, 2020, para. 513.

9.3. Pillar Two – GloBE

The proposal of the Global Anti-Base Erosion (GloBE) rules (i.e. Pillar Two) was issued on 20 December 2021,[109] almost at the same time as the corresponding proposal for a European Directive[110] and follows a very different approach. Instead of developing new parameters to reallocate taxing rights between the different states with an emphasis to consider the need of market states to tax, GloBE discusses several mechanisms which are intended to establish a global framework of a minimum taxation in order to limit excessive tax competition by a race to the bottom in general.

(1) The country of residence is expected to pass an Income Inclusion Rule (IIR) in relation to all so-called Constituent Entities (i.e. consisting of subsidiaries and permanent establishments) which foresees a top-up tax for foreign low-taxed entities to ensure a minimum-taxation.

(2) The source state is expected to apply an Undertaxed Payments Rule which provides for either a [partial] denial of the deduction of cross-border intra-group payments) or a (reversed) IIR applying a top-up tax with regard to all Constituent Entities as a backstop to the IIR described under (1).

(3) A subject-to-tax rule which entitles source countries to protect their tax base by denying treaty benefits for deductible intra-group payments made to jurisdictions with low or no taxation is still expected to be issued in the course of the year 2022.

The shared logic of all of these measures is their supplementary character (i.e. they only kick in if the tax burden is considered to be too low). As a consequence, the GloBE rules still stick to the separate entity principle as a starting point. This can be taken from the fact that the Model rules still require that the income of the Constituent Entities is determined under the accounting principles applied in order to prepare the Consolidated Financial Accounts before any consolidation adjustments eliminating intra-group transactions on a stand-alone basis.[111] Furthermore, the GloBE rules acknowledge the requirement that transactions between Constituent Entities located in different jurisdictions need to comply with the arm's length principle.[112] Insofar, one has, on the one hand, the impression that the GloBE rules are systematically comparable to the anti-hybrid rules following the separate entity principle.

On the other hand, the GloBE rules foresee certain elements following a group approach. Firstly, the GloBE rules are only applicable if the consolidated revenue threshold of EUR 750 million for a group is exceeded. Secondly, the GloBE rules foresee the possibility that an Ultimate Parent Entity may elect to apply its consolidated accounting treatment to eliminate income, expense, gains and losses from transactions between Constituent Entities that are included in a tax consolidation group and are located in the same jurisdiction. Even without exercising this option, the GloBE rules foresee a strong element of a group

---

[109] OECD, Tax Challenges Arising from Digitalisation of the Economy–Global Anti-Base Erosion Model Rules (Pillar Two), 2021.

[110] Proposal for a Council Directive on ensuring a global minimum level of taxation for multinational groups in the Union, 22 December 2021.

[111] OECD, Tax Challenges Arising from Digitalisation of the Economy–Global Anti-Base Erosion Model Rules (Pillar Two), 2021, 3.1.2.

[112] OECD, Tax Challenges Arising from Digitalisation of the Economy–Global Anti-Base Erosion Model Rules (Pillar Two), 2021, 3.2.3.

approach by testing the low taxation of the Constituent Entities on a consolidated basis for each territory following the jurisdictional blending.[113] However, this suggested group approach also has limits given that GloBE rules do not foresee for a global blending as currently foreseen under US GILTI rules.[114]

Therefore, one can conclude that the GloBE rules under Pillar Two is a mixed bag foreseeing elements of separate entity and group taxation.[115] This can also be derived when examining the Undertaxed Payment Rule (UTPR).[116] This rule requires the source state to either limit the deduction of payments or to make an equivalent adjustment (which under article 13 of the Directive is specified that the top-up tax amount under the UTPR shall be equal to the sum of the top-up taxes calculated under the IIR). While the first option (limitation of deduction) is very much a sign of the separate entity approach, the second option (application of a reversed IIR) can be seen as deviating from this principle and rather following the principle of a group taxation (because this option pierces the veil of other group entities without an existing shareholder relationship).

10. Final conclusions

Pillar One and Two do not provide for a system following a full consolidated group taxation. Both sets of rules only contain elements following a group view but do not, different to the EU CCCTB proposal, mean to establish a consolidated international tax group. In contrast, Pillar One only increases the taxing right of market states. Pillar Two is, furthermore, not meant to achieve a consolidation and cross-border use of losses but rather to ensure that foreign profits are not taxed below a minimum tax rate still to be politically agreed upon.

Furthermore, even under the low minimum tax rate foreseen under Pillar Two there remains the possibility to make use of tax rate differences. Taxpayers will, therefore, remain to evaluate opportunities to optimize the tax rate under the separate entity principle and, consequently, countries will not abandon anti-avoidance rules even if tax measures following GloBE will be introduced. Therefore, GloBE seems to be rather another complementary tool to be added to the tax laws which continue to be strongly oriented towards the separate entity principle.

---

[113]   OECD, Tax Challenges Arising from Digitalisation of the Economy–Global Anti-Base Erosion Model Rules (Pillar Two), 2021, 5.2.3. and 5.2.4.
[114]   For the US GILTI rules see US report, 2.3, 2.6, 2.10.
[115]   Similar EU report, part 2, section 11: Pillar Two Directive as "hybrid approach between the Separate Entity and the Group Approach".
[116]   Which is called under the Proposed Directive in the meantime "Undertaxed Profit Rule". See amended Proposal for a Council Directive on ensuring a global minimum level of taxation for multinational groups in the Union, 7 March 2022.

EU report Subject 1

Group approach and separate entity approach in domestic and international tax law

Niall Casey
Jasna Voje

Niall Casey[1]
Jasna Voje[2]

Summary and conclusions

The separate entity and group approach come through in different shades in the EU legal framework. On several occasions, the case law of the Court of Justice (CJEU) confirmed where tax benefits of a group should be equally given to domestic and foreign companies. The CJEU also examined situations where control within a group was a relevant factor, although the tax consequences were applied at the entity level. In State Aid cases the Court ruled that the arm's length principle is enshrined in article 107(1) TFEU, hence focusing on the core principle of a separate entity approach. Similarly, the existing EU tax legislation also contains different approaches. The Parent Subsidiary Directive and Interest Royalties Directive revolve around the 'associated enterprises' – thus control within a group and provide benefits in such cases. The benefits are granted to the entity. The Anti-Tax Avoidance Directive as amended, is orientated strongly towards the separate entity approach. This separate entity orientation could be explained by the specific objective of the ATAD, which is to provide rules to prevent tax avoidance practices. Such practices are usually designed on the entity level in order to minimise the overall level of taxation of the group as a whole.

The (Proposal for a) Directive on ensuring a minimum effective tax rate for the global activities of large multinational groups takes a hybrid approach, by taking the group perspective (i.e. the financial accounts) as a starting point, but in its essence requires minimum taxation at an entity level (albeit with a jurisdictional blending). In addition, the soft law initiatives such as the Code of Conduct on Business Taxation examines whether or not EU Member States apply tax rules towards a (separate) entity established in its territory when it determines if a preferential business tax regime is harmful.

While the separate entity approach was, and continues to be, the guiding principle in international tax law generally, there have been a number of significant initiatives in EU policy making that trend more towards a group approach. The most illustrative example is the Common Consolidated Corporate Tax Base (CCCTB) proposal. First launched in 2011 as an optional system, it was relaunched in 2016. For the 2016 relaunch the proposal was split into (i) a common base proposal and (ii) a consolidation proposal and made obligatory for all in scope companies. After several years of discussion in the Council, to date no agreement has been reached. On 18 May 2021, the Commission Communication on business Taxation in the 21st century published by the Commission, announced that after five years of discussion

---

[1] Policy Officer at the European Commission, DG TAXUD, working on policy with respect to company taxation initiatives.
[2] Policy Officer at the European Commission, DG TAXUD, working on policy with respect to corporate taxation, exchange of information and administrative cooperation, withholding tax, transfer pricing and dispute resolution; DPhil candidate at University of Oxford, focus of the research on international and EU tax law.

The report represents the personal views of the authors, which do not purport to represent the view of the European Commission.

in Council the CCCTB proposal is to be withdrawn and replaced by a new proposal that is to be known as BEFIT: Business in Europe: Framework for Income Taxation. As stated in the communication, BEFIT will *provide for fairer and more efficient allocation of taxing rights between Member States*. Apart from the Communication, there is little in the public domain on the specific design on BEFIT and the internal policy development continues within the Commission Services. Therefore, it remains to be seen whether BEFIT will continue the trend set by the CCCTB towards a more group approach or whether it will maintain some features of the separate entity approach.

In sum, it can be said that the majority of EU tax law is geared towards the separate entity approach but the flagship proposed initiatives such as the CCCTB and its relaunch, and BEFIT show a trend towards the group approach.

Introduction

The domestic tax law of EU Member States is a matter of their exclusive competence. Still, in exercising their competencies, the Member States, must adhere to the EU law. Those limits set by EU law on the Member States' include, (i) the freedom of movement and the principle of non-discrimination and (ii) the prohibition of fiscal State aid. Despite Member States' exclusive competence in the field of taxation, the Treaty on the Functioning of the EU (TFEU) grants the Commission the right of a legislative initiative to propose secondary legislation (for adoption by the Council of the EU) aiming at the harmonization or the approximation of national tax laws.

Accordingly, the development of the EU tax law was two fold (i) positive harmonisation by means of policy, (ii) negative harmonisation by means of CJEU case law. The group approach more broadly exists since the first decades of the life of the European Communities. A Commission proposal on losses-offset by foreign subsidiaries and permanent establishments[3] was a step towards a cross-border group taxation regime but as it did not receive the necessary support from the Member States it was consequently withdrawn. The idea of the group taxation has nevertheless remained on the agenda of the Commission.

The amount of proposals and formally adopted directives with respect to substantive tax law[4] has exponentially increased in the last decade. Although the shift towards the group approach might have been successful only in the recent directives, such as the Anti-Tax Avoidance Directive, an idea of wholesome group taxation across border within the internal market and thus taxation of a group was already proposed in 2011 in Commission proposal on a Common Consolidated Corporate Tax Base.

With respect to EU secondary law, the CJEU also has the competence to provide interpretation of provisions in question. At the same time, the case law of the CJEU has also assessed national measures in the light of the fundamental freedoms and state aid.

---

[3]   CoM (90) 595 final, available at:
        https://eur-lex.europa.eu/legal-content/EN/TXT/PDF/?uri=CELEX:51990PC0595&from=EN.
[4]   The authors refer to 'substantive law' as meaning the tax rules that have an impact on the taxable base. In contract, 'procedural law' is one that refers to procedures such as dispute resolution, reporting obligations and exchange of information, and similar.

This report aims at presenting an overview of all these developments and shed light on whether the current tendency is leaning towards either separate entity or group approach. It will also attempt to provide more clarity in answering whether the two approaches can coexist. It is structured in a way that introduces EU law elements to relevant topics.

Part I: Separate entity approach and group approach in EU case law

1. Fundamental freedoms

1.1. General overview

The fundaments of the single market are based on four freedoms laid down in the Treaty on the Functioning of the EU (TFEU). These are (i) freedom of movement of goods, (ii) freedom of movement of persons, (iii) freedom of establishment and to provide services and (iv) freedom of movement of capital. The essential objective of Community law is the establishment of a single market, where nationals within the Community can trade and move without the impediment of national boundaries. In the widely globalised world, multinational companies operate cross-border, which inevitably often results in clashes between domestic tax regimes and the single market related to the group relief.

The freedom of establishment enshrined in article 49 TFEU shall include the right to take up and pursue activities as self-employed persons and to set up and manage undertakings. Restrictions on the freedom of establishment of nationals of a Member State in the territory of another Member State are prohibited. Such prohibition also applies to restrictions on the setting-up of agencies, branches or subsidiaries by nationals of any Member State established in the territory of any Member State.[5] The CJEU is not competent to examine a purely domestic situation and therefore only deals with cross-border situations where a fundamental freedom is applicable. If cross-border situations are treated less favourably compared to similar domestic situations, a measure can be found discriminatory due to unequal treatment of two comparable situations. It should then be further tested if such an unequal treatment is justified and proportional.

1.2. General legal principles developed by the CJEU

1.2.1. Free choice of legal form

CLT-UFA is a corporation with residency in Luxembourg that had a permanent establishment in Germany and was thus subject to corporate tax in Germany. The income was assessed at a tax rate of 42% applicable at that time to non-resident corporations. The case reached the CJEU, that considered a measure determining a higher tax rate applicable to permanent establishments as compared to a lower rate applicable to a German subsidiary in breach of

---

[5] Art. 49(1) TFEU.

freedom of establishment.[6] The CJEU emphasized that the freedom of establishment grants market participants the right to choose an appropriate legal form for their undertakings in other Member States. According to this, companies are permitted to open a branch in another Member State in order to pursue their activities under the same conditions as those which apply to subsidiaries. The CJEU considered that a permanent establishment and a subsidiary are objectively comparable and instructed the German Supreme Tax Court to apply the same overall tax rate to the income from the permanent establishment that had applied to a distributing subsidiary.

1.2.2. *Group taxation benefits such a loss relief applied equally*

Marks & Spencer, a multinational with its head office in the UK, had subsidiary companies resident in Belgium, Germany and France that were loss making. It sought to surrender these losses by way of group relief to shelter UK-taxable profits of the UK parent, but the UK's group relief provisions only allow for losses of a UK resident subsidiary (or UK permanent establishment of a non-UK resident subsidiary) to be surrendered to its UK parent and not losses incurred by a foreign subsidiary without a UK permanent establishment. They appealed against the refusal of group relief by arguing that the UK's restrictions on group relief to UK resident companies were not compatible with paragraph two of article 43 of the EC (now article 49 TFEU), in that by preventing the loss-surrender of a non-UK resident subsidiary, they constituted a barrier to the exercise of the freedom of establishment and made it less attractive to set up a subsidiary outside the UK. By following the opinion of the AG closely, the Court held that the UK's group relief rules hinder the exercise by the parent company of its freedom of establishment in contravention of articles 43 EC and 48 EC by deterring it from setting up subsidiaries in other member states. Albeit discriminatory, the measure was considered to be justified on the following grounds: balanced allocation of taxing rights, tax avoidance and the risk for using losses twice ("double dip"). Eventually, when the CJEU examined whether the UK law complied with proportionality, it found that only "terminal" losses would have to be considered by the UK. It remained somehow vague what type of losses would qualify as final/ terminal but following Marks & Spencer, it is clear that cross-border loss relief is not required by the Freedoms in the majority of cases.[7]

1.2.3. *Group taxation applied cross-border*

Group taxation regimes are usually discussed from the perspective of their main feature: loss compensation amongst group companies. The most important element of group taxation regimes is the fact that losses of one group entity can be relieved against the profits of another group company. Under the national laws of some Member States, group taxation regimes have additional consequences. The application of group taxation in a cross/border context however requires further considerations.

---

6   Case C-253/03, 23 February 2006.
7   Ibid para 35.

In case *X Holding*,[8] the CJEU, in contrary to the position submitted by the Commission,[9] rejected an obligation upon the Member State to include non-resident companies in the consolidated group. The Court considered that permanent establishments situated in another Member State and non-resident subsidiaries as not being in a comparable situation.[10] Consequently, the losses of these non-resident companies can legitimately be excluded (in contrast to those of a permanent establishment). The Court further clarified that any extension of a tax advantage granted to resident parent companies and their resident subsidiaries to be taxed as if they formed a single tax entity, would have the effect of allowing parent companies to choose freely the Member State in which losses of their non-resident subsidiaries are to be taken into account.[11]

However, when it comes to other cross-border payments, such as dividends, which are not inextricably linked to being within a consolidated tax group, we move in the territory of prohibition of discrimination. In more recent cases, the CJEU does not look at one tax provision (i.e. measure) in isolation, but instead examines a combination of tax provisions that could lead to an infringement on EU law where that combination had a more advantageous effect in domestic situations. A case where an infringement was indeed confirmed, concerned Groupe Steria, a French resident company that is the head of a French consolidation group.[12] Under French law, a French parent company that directly or indirectly, holds at least 95% of the shares in a French resident subsidiary, the companies can request for application of tax consolidation. This regime provides for 100 % participation exemption between companies that are part of the tax consolidation group. The participation exemption is otherwise limited to 95%. As the tax consolidation regime is limited to French resident companies, the benefit of the participation exemption is limited to domestic situations only. Groupe Steria received a dividend from a non-resident company for which it applied for the deduction of the 5% exemption. The CJEU confirmed the views of Groupe Steria that claimed that the differential treatment of French resident parent companies depending on the place of residence of their subsidiaries could make it less attractive for these French parent companies to establish a subsidiary abroad.[13] The fact that the tax advantage is only obtained if the resident subsidiary is part of a tax consolidation group does not lead to an objectively different position. Both in relation to resident and non-resident subsidiaries, the parent company bears the costs and expenses related to its shareholding in the subsidiary, and, moreover, the profits made by the subsidiary and from which the dividends distributed are derived are, in principle, liable to be subject to economic double taxation or to a series of charges to tax.[14]

As a subsequent matter, the CJEU provided clarity on the view taken in the *X Holding* case that it could be disallowed to include non-resident subsidiaries in a tax consolidation scheme.[15] The CJEU emphasized that the *X Holding* judgment cannot be interpreted in such a broad way that all different treatments of domestic and cross-border situations following

8   Case C-337/08, *X Holding BV v Staatssecretaris van Financiën*, 25 February 2010.
9   Ibid para 35.
10   Ibid para 38.
11   Ibid para 41.
12   CJEU 2 September 2015, C-386/14 (Groupe Steria), ECLI:EU:C:2015: 524.
13   Ibid para 20.
14   Ibid para 22.
15   Ibid para 25.

the application of the tax consolidation regime are compatible with EU law.[16] In *X Holding* case, the CJEU merely examined the residence condition as a condition of access to a tax integration scheme, and held that the condition was justified, taking into account the fact that such a scheme allows losses to be transferred within the tax-integrated group.[17] As regards tax advantages other than the transfer of losses within the tax-integrated group, a separate assessment must therefore be made as to whether a member state may reserve those advantages to companies belonging to a tax-integrated group and consequently exclude them in cross-border situations.[18] Because the difference in treatment concerns only incoming dividends, received by resident parent companies, i.e. concerning the fiscal sovereignty of one and the same member state, the allocation of taxing rights is not harmed by an extension of the full exemption to dividends from non-resident group companies.[19]

The decision in Groupe Steria makes it clear that national group regimes cannot treat cross-border situations that are in comparable situations unfavourably. The discrimination has to be remedied by either extending the benefits of a group approach to non-resident companies or eliminating the tax benefit granted to domestic companies.

2. State aid

2.1. *General overview*

While the fundamental freedoms only lead to one specific test, namely whether cross-border taxpayers or situations are treated less favourably than domestic taxpayers or situations, state aid control applies to purely internal situations as well. Article 107 of the TFEU ensures that aid granted by a Member State or through State resources does not distort competition and trade within the EU by favouring certain companies or the production of certain goods. State aid is defined as an advantage in any form whatsoever conferred on a selective basis to undertakings by national public authorities. Therefore, subsidies granted to individuals or general measures open to all enterprises are not covered by this prohibition and do not constitute State aid (examples include general taxation measures or employment legislation).

To be State aid, a measure needs to have these features:
- there has been an intervention by the State or through State resources which can take a variety of forms (e.g. grants, interest and tax reliefs, guarantees, government holdings of all or part of a company, or providing goods and services on preferential terms, etc.);
- the intervention gives the recipient an advantage on a selective basis, for example to specific companies or industry sectors, or to companies located in specific regions;
- competition has been or may be distorted;
- the intervention is likely to affect trade between Member States.

---

[16]   Ibid para 26.
[17]   Ibid para 27.
[18]   Ibid para 28.
[19]   Ibid para 29.

2.2. Fiscal state aid

At the end of the 1990s, the Commission increased its activity in the monitoring of national tax measures. While the Member States had endorsed the Code of Conduct in the area of business taxation, the Commission adopted its Notice on the Application of State Aid Rules to Measures Relating to Direct Business Taxation (the 'State-Aid Business Tax Notice').[20] The Commission launched several investigations against favourable tax measures adopted by Member States, many of them ending with a negative decision.

A detailed discussion on the investigations and court cases that follow is not necessary for the purposes of this report. What is relevant is that a measure that constitutes an advantage can be provided in various ways, including: (i) a reduction in the tax base (such as special deductions, special or accelerated depreciation arrangements, or the entering of reserves on the balance sheet); (ii) a total or partial reduction in the amount of tax, such as exemption or a tax credit; or (iii) deferment, cancellation, or even special rescheduling of tax debt,[21] provided it meets the other criteria of a state aid, especially selectivity.

In the Report on Implementing State-Aid Business Tax Notice, the Commission, quoting the General Court, emphasized that the State-Aid Business Tax Notice did not actually constitute a change in the State-aid approach in tax matters, but merely reflected a clarification, mostly based on the development of the Court's case law. It also stressed that the concept of aid is an objective one, to be applied on the basis of principles falling outside the scope of the Commission's discretion, and reaffirmed the constitutive criteria of the notion of aid.[22] With respect to the 'advantage', the Commission emphasized that State aid could also result from a selective application of methods of computation of the corporate tax base, such as the use of a particular transfer-pricing method (in cases quoted, the cost-plus method). While the Commission acknowledged that such methods are not, as such, caught under the prohibition of State aid, an advantage could still arise from its application if 'the economic reality of the transactions' is not properly considered (e.g., the exclusion of certain expenditures of the tax base or use of arbitrary levels of profit margins, etc.).[23] Even measures intended to avoid international double taxation, particularly, the switch from the credit to the exemption method for foreign income in certain circumstances can be subject to scrutiny under the State aid rules.[24]

2.3. State aid with respect to tax rulings

Since June 2013, the Commission has been investigating the tax ruling practices of Member States. A dedicated Task Force Tax Planning Practices was set up in summer 2013 to follow up on public allegations of favourable tax treatment of certain companies (in particular in the form of tax rulings) voiced in the media and in national parliaments. This Task Force was later transformed in a permanent unit of DG COMP. The Commission extended this

[20]   Commission Notice on the Application of the State Aid Rules to Measures Relating to Direct Business Taxation, OJ C 384/3 (1998).

[21]   Ibid para 9.

[22]   Report on the Implementation of the Commission Notice on the Application of State Aid Rules to Measures Relating to Direct Business Taxation, (C(2004)434) (2004), para. 3.

[23]   Ibid paras 10–13.

[24]   Ibid para 16.

information inquiry to all Member States in December 2014, including a list of tax rulings issued in recent years, on the basis of which individual tax rulings have been requested.

A State aid investigation into aid measures consists typically of a preliminary phase possibly leading to a first Commission decision to initiate a formal investigation. In this decision the Commission expresses doubts about the compatibility of an assumed State aid measure, such as a tax ruling. A decision to initiate a formal investigation is followed by a final decision, which can either conclude that the doubts expressed are not founded or which confirms the initial views of the Commission, resulting in a negative decision. An action can be taken against the final decision of the Commission by means of an appeal.

In judgments on the tax treatment of Fiat in Luxembourg,[25] Starbucks in the Netherlands,[26] and Apple in Ireland,[27] the General Court confirmed that, while Member States have exclusive competence in determining their laws concerning direct taxation, they must do so in respect of EU law, including State aid rules. Furthermore, the General Court also confirmed the Commission's approach to assess whether a measure is selective and whether transactions between group companies give rise to an advantage under EU State aid rules based on the so-called 'arm's length principle'. A confirmation that the arm's length principle can be used as a tool under article 107(1) TFEU to monitor the transfer pricing practices of the Member States gives the EU law an additional dimension and the Commission an important mechanism. In practical terms, the tax measure concerning the chargeable profits of a resident company (i.e. a subsidiary) or a non-resident company carrying on a trade in a Member State through a branch determines a certain level of profit attributable to that subsidiary or branch. Article 107(1) TFEU allows the Commission to check whether that level of profit corresponds to the level that would have been obtained through carrying on that trade under market conditions, in order to determine whether there is, as a result, any mitigation of the burdens normally included in the budget of the undertaking concerned, thus conferring on that undertaking an advantage for the purposes of that provision. Whether the CJEU will confirm the position taken by the General Court, is still to be seen.

3. CJEU interpretation of EU secondary law

3.1. Special anti-avoidance rules depending on 'group' or 'control'

The Court of Justice of the European Union, on 26 February 2019, delivered a judgement in the so-called "Danish Beneficial Ownership cases".[28] The key question for the court to consider here was whether dividend and interest payments were exempt from withholding tax, in circumstances where the payments were made from a Danish company to an EU resident company, if these payments were eventually passed on to an ultimate parent company that was resident in a third country (a non-EU country). These Danish companies were owned by a parent company which was resident in another EU Member State. These parent companies were in turn owned by companies resident in non-EU countries. Interest

[25]   Case T-755/15, 24 September 2019.
[26]   Case T-760/15 and T-636/16, 24 September 2019.
[27]   Cases T-778/16 and T-892/16, 15 July 2020.
[28]   N Luxembourg 1, X Denmark A/S, C Danmark I and Z Denmark ApS vs. the Danish Ministry of Taxation (Joined Cases C-115/16, C-118/16, C-119/16 and C-299/16.

payments were made by the Danish companies to their EU parent companies. These parent companies claimed an exemption from withholding tax under the EU Interest and Royalties Directive.[29]

The Danish tax authorities maintained that the withholding tax exemptions permitted by the IRD should not be granted, as the recipients of the payments were not the beneficial owners of the payments. The companies appealed the cases to the Danish High Court, which then referred a number of questions to the CJEU. The CJEU held that the term "beneficial owner" was not a formally identified recipient but instead the entity that benefits economically from the interest. The CJEU stated that the OECD Commentary on the OECD Model Tax Convention is pertinent for interpreting the term "beneficial owner".

The Danish High Court also asked that if the requirements to benefit from the IRD were met, would an EU Member State need to implement an anti-avoidance provision in its domestic law in order to deny the benefits of the Interest and Royalties Directive. According to the CJEU, the general EU anti abuse principle requires that an EU Member State denies a benefit if an arrangement constitutes abuse of rights, regardless of whether there is any specific anti avoidance legislation in domestic law. The Court then provided some guidance as to what constitutes an abuse of rights. Some indicators include, if the relevant funds are moved on short after they are received, this could suggest a flow through entity and therefore abuse. Another indicator could be if the recipient lacks substance or is part of a tax structure that normally would not come within the scope of the IRD. The case was then returned to the Danish high court to make a final decision based on this guidance from the CJEU.

While the final decision needs to be made by the Danish court, in practice the reference to the entity that benefits economically could allow the EU-resident parents to be found to be the beneficial owners, unless the payments were moved outside the EU in a short time. In that case, the EU-resident parents would only be look-through.

Part 2: Separate entity approach and group approach in EU policy

1. The Code of Conduct on Business Taxation Group

1.1. Background to the Code of Conduct on Business Taxation 1997

The Code of Conduct on Business Taxation 1997[30] is a soft law instrument agreed by the EU Member States, that aims to prevent harmful tax competition within the Union. The Code of Conduct Group was established by the Member States to monitor compliance with the Code of Conduct. The Code of Conduct applies to business tax incentives only and any preferential tax measure introduced by an EU Member State that meets the Gateway criteria is within its scope and can be examined by the Group. The two Gateway criteria are: (i) a measure must be capable of affecting in a significant way the location of business activity in the EU.

---

[29]   COUNCIL DIRECTIVE 2003/49/EC of 3 June 2003 on a common system of taxation applicable to interest and royalty payments made between associated companies of different Member States.

[30]   Resolution of the Council and the Representatives of the Governments of the Member States, meeting within the Council of 1 December 1997 on a code of conduct for business taxation: https://eur-lex.europa.eu/legal-content/en/TXT/?uri=CELEX%3A31998Y0106%2801%29.

Business activity in this context also includes all activities carried out within a group of companies; (ii) a measure must provide for a significantly lower effective rate of taxation than the levels which generally apply in the Member State in question. Once a tax measure meets both of these Gateway criteria, it is then subject to assessment by the Group against five assessment criteria. If a measure fails any one of these assessment criteria it can be found to be harmful by the Code Group and must be "rolled back". This means it must be amended or abolished by the Member State that introduced the tax measure.

Tax measures introduced by Member States include laws, regulations and administrative practices. When looking at whether the level of taxation is significantly lower, the Group will look at the statutory tax rate, the tax base, or any other relevant factor.

1.2. *The Code criteria*

When deciding if a tax measure is harmful, the Group assesses it against five assessment criteria. The first two assessment criteria look at whether a regime is ring-fenced – if advantages are only available to non-residents or in respect of transactions carried out with non-residents or if they are ring-fenced in such a way that they do not affect the national tax base. The third criterion examines if a tax measure has no economic substance requirements. The fourth criterion looks at whether *the rules for profit determination in respect of activities within a multinational group of companies depart from internationally accepted principles, notably the rules agreed upon within the OECD*. In this way, under criterion 4, the Code of Conduct group is examining if EU Member States apply the separate entity approach and transfer pricing rules when designing preferential business tax measures. Finally, under criterion 5 the Code looks at whether a tax measure lacks transparency.

The Code of Conduct group has agreed guidance to assist in its work and increase transparency. Of particular interest to this report is the Guidance on the interpretation of criterion four.[31] This guidance, like all the Code guidance, is based on past decisions of the Code of Conduct Group. The guidance does not replace the code principles and nor does it prejudge any decision of the Code Group. The Group continues to make its decisions on a "case by case basis". The guidance specifies that a measure should be subject to particular scrutiny by the Code Group under the fourth criterion if any one of five circumstances are met. Of particular relevance to this topic are circumstance one and circumstance three.

Circumstance one is whether a measure *deviates from the arm's length principle as applied in accordance with the most recent update of the OECD Transfer Pricing guidelines*. The guidance specifies two situations where this could be acceptable: (a) *this deviation is proportionate and justified with reference to the size of the SMEs as defined in the Commission Recommendation 2003/361/EC*, and (b) *the measure uses "safe harbour" rules for profit determination that are proportionate and justified with reference to the reduction of the administrative burden which the measure is expected to produce*.

Circumstance three is a situation where the tax measure *deviates from the principle that the profits to be attributed to a permanent establishment (PE) are the profits that the PE would have earned at arm's length, in particular in its dealings with other parts of the enterprise, if it were a separate and independent enterprise, regardless of the OECD approach chosen*. If any of the five circumstances are met, then a preferential tax regime will be subject to particular scrutiny

---

[31]   https://data.consilium.europa.eu/doc/document/ST-5814-2018-INIT/en/pdf

under criterion four by the Code Group, when carrying out its assessment. Nonetheless, an assessment must still always be made on a case by case basis.

2. Treatment of income from foreign subsidiaries and branches

The policy in this regard is dominantly based on preserving and improving the functioning of the Internal market by achieving neutrality of inter-group distributions of profit.

2.1. Dividend payments

On 22 December 2003, the Council adopted Directive 2003/123/EC[32] to broaden the scope and improve the operation of the Council Directive 90/435/EEC on the common system of taxation applicable in the case of parent companies and subsidiaries of different Member States, i.e. the Parent Subsidiary Directive (PSD). The 1990 Directive was designed to eliminate tax obstacles in the area of profit distributions between groups of companies in the EU by (i) abolishing withholding taxes on payments of dividends between associated companies of different Member States and (ii) preventing double taxation of parent companies on the profits of their subsidiaries. The amending Directive of 2003 contains three main elements (i) updating the list of companies that the Directive covers; (ii) relaxing the conditions for exempting dividends from withholding tax (reduction of the participation threshold); and (iii) eliminating double taxation for lower-tier subsidiaries. The scope of the PSD includes cross-border payments to permanent establishments situated in a Member State, even where the head office is located in the same Member State as the paying entity.

The amending Directive relaxed the conditions of this exemption to the parent company having to hold at least 10% of the shares in the subsidiary company for the exemption to apply. Two further amendments based on one Commission proposal[33] were adopted in 2014 and 2015, to accommodate (i) a specific anti-tax avoidance rule that makes the dividend taxable at destination if not taxed at source;[34] and (ii) a targeted anti-abuse rule (in the ATAD style but limited to the PSD).[35]

---

[32] Council Directive 2003/123/EC of 22 December 2003 amending Directive 90/435/EEC on the common *system of taxation applicable in the case of parent companies and subsidiaries of different Member States*, OJ L 345, 29 December 2011, p. 8–16.

[33] Proposal for a Council Directive amending Directive 2011/96/EU on the common system of taxation applicable in the case of parent companies and subsidiaries of different Member States, COM (2013/0814) final.

[34] Council Directive 2014/86/EU of 8 July 2014 amending Directive 2011/96/EU on the common system of taxation applicable in the case of parent companies and subsidiaries of different Member States, OJ L 219, 25 July 2014, p. 40–41.

[35] Council Directive (EU) 2015/121 of 27 January 2015 amending Directive 2011/96/EU on the common system of taxation applicable in the case of parent companies and subsidiaries of different Member States, OJ L 21, 28 January 2015, p. 1–3.

2.2. *Interest and royalties*

On 3 June 2003, the Council adopted Directive 2003/49/EC on a common system of taxation applicable to interest and royalty payments made between associated companies of different Member States.[36] The Interest and Royalties Directive is designed to eliminate withholding tax obstacles in the area of cross-border interest and royalty payments within a group of companies by abolishing withholding taxes on interest and/or royalty payments arising in a Member State. These interest and royalty payments shall be exempt from any taxes in the Member State where they are paid out of, provided that the beneficial owner of the payment is a company or permanent establishment in another Member State. On 11 November 2011, the Commission adopted a new proposal to recast the Directive with a view to expand its scope. The technical discussion at the Council stalled due to a divergence of views amongst Member States on whether the exemption from withholding tax should be made contingent upon the payments being "subject to tax" at the destination Member State. A consensus required was never reached, however the inability to agree on this by means of EU secondary law, was partially mitigated by the CJEU decision in the Danish cases (see Part I, section 3.1.).

3. Common Consolidated Corporate Tax Base

3.1. *Background*

In 2016, the European Commission re-launched the proposal for a Directive on a Common Consolidated Corporate Tax Base (CCCTB).[37] The CCCTB, first formally proposed in 2011, puts forward a group approach for the EU in a comprehensive cross-border group taxation system. The intention was for the re-launched CCCTB to be implemented through a two-step process beginning with the common base, and then followed by consolidation. To this end, the original 2011 directive was split into two separate proposals: the proposal for a Common Corporate Tax Base,[38] and the proposal for a Common Consolidated Corporate Tax Base. In addition, it was intended for the relaunched CCCTB to be mandatory for groups with worldwide combined revenues exceeding EUR 750 million.

The original CCCTB proposal was published in 2011. However, after a number of years of discussion in the Council without agreement, the proposal was withdrawn and replaced by the relaunched CCCTB. There are some important differences between the relaunched CCCTB and the original. Firstly, as noted above, the relaunched CCCTB is intended to be implemented in two steps, secondly the relaunched proposal will be mandatory for large groups, and thirdly the relaunched proposal will give strong incentives to R&D.

Differently from the proposal of 2011 which focussed on facilitating business, the relaunched CCCTB was proposed with a two-fold set of objectives: not only to improve the

---

[36]   Council Directive 2003/49/EC of 3 June 2003 on a common system of taxation applicable to interest and royalty payments made between associated companies of different Member States. OJ L 157, 26 June 2003, p. 49–54.

[37]   Proposal for a COUNCIL DIRECTIVE on a Common Consolidated Corporate Tax Base (CCCTB) COM(2016) 683 https://ec.europa.eu/taxation_customs/sites/taxation/files/com_2016_683_en.pdf

[38]   Proposal for a COUNCIL DIRECTIVE on a Common Corporate Tax Base COM(2016) 685: https://ec.europa.eu/taxation_customs/sites/taxation/files/com_2016_685_en.pdf

Single Market for businesses by supporting growth, jobs and investment in the EU, but also to combat tax avoidance.

3.2. Scope of the proposals

Article 2 of the common base (CCTB) proposal sets out the scope. The rules apply to any company that meets the following four conditions: (a) it takes one of the company forms listed in Annex I of the proposal, (b) it is subject to one of the corporate taxes listed in Annex II or to a similar tax subsequently introduced, (c) it belongs to a consolidated group for financial accounting purposes with a total consolidated group revenue that exceeded EUR 750 000 000 during the financial year preceding the relevant financial year and (d) it qualifies as a parent company or qualifying subsidiary as referred to in article 3 and/or has one or more permanent establishments in other Member States as referred to in article 5.

3.3. Consolidation - The Common Consolidated Corporate Tax Base

The second part of the proposal, the CCCTB Directive (the CCCTB) remains pending for examination in Council, until the Directive on a common base (CCTB) is agreed. The CCCTB proposal, among other elements, lays down the conditions for being in a group, outlines the form a group can take and regulates the transition in and out of the group. It sets out the rules for consolidation and the formula for apportionment of the group taxable base amongst EU Member States. The proposal also deals with business reorganisations with impact on the CCCTB group as well as with the treatment of losses and unrealised capital gains.

The eligibility for membership of the consolidated corporate tax group is determined based on a two-part test. The first part is control, the parent must have more than 50% of voting rights. The second part of the test is ownership: the parent must have more than 75 percent of equity or rights to profits (more than 75 percent of rights giving entitlement to profit). This test aims to ensure a high level of economic integration between members of the group. In order to ensure that these tests are effective, they must continue to be met throughout the year.

3.4. Formulary Apportionment

The mainstream CCCTB formula is set out in Chapter VIII of the proposal, article 29. The formula is made up of three equally weighted factors: labour, assets, and sales by destination. The aim of this formula is to achieve a balanced approach to the distribution of profits between EU Member States where both the origin and destination territories are given appropriate weight. The labour factor is divided between payroll and the number of employees, to take account of differences in wages across the EU (article 32). The assets factor consists of all fixed tangible assets. In order to avoid manipulation, intangibles and financial assets are excluded from the formula. Financial assets are only included in the sector-specific formula for financial institutions. When the outcome of the apportionment does not correctly represent the extent of business activity, there is a safeguard clause to provide an additional method of allocation (article 29).

Under the CCCTB proposal, when a company joins the group with losses, these pre-consolidation trading losses are kept ring-fenced from the group and can be set off only against the specific company's apportionment share of profits. When a loss-making company leaves the group, the company is not entitled to retain any losses incurred during the period of consolidation. These losses always stay at the level of the group.

3.5. Administration

One of the principal advantages to the CCCTB proposal is that once it is implemented, groups will be able to deal with a single tax administration in the EU (the principal tax authority). This will be based in the Member State where the parent company of the group (the principal taxpayer) is resident for tax purposes. Audits are begun and coordinated by the principal tax authority. The CCCTB is the initiative that most clearly represents the group approach to taxation in EU policymaking.

4. BEFIT

In May 2021, the Commission published the Communication on Business Taxation for the 21st Century. The Communication announced that the CCCTB proposal will be withdrawn and replaced by a new proposal: the Business in Europe: Framework for Income Taxation (BEFIT) proposal. This proposal is meant to move the EU towards a common set of rules for determining taxable income and provide for fairer and more efficient allocation of taxing rights between Member States. It should also be expected to improve the compliance burden for companies, which is of particular relevance given the volume of new legislation in this area.

The broad idea is that BEFIT will be a deeper, more structural reform to the EU's business tax framework that will be consistent with, and build on, the OECD Two Pillar Approach. BEFIT will aim to reduce compliance costs for business, reduce tax avoidance opportunities and also support jobs, growth and investment in the EU. Given that there is limited information on this proposal in the public domain, we cannot comment on it in any greater detail at this point. We must wait for further announcements from the European Commission for more details in order to assess if this proposal is likely to tend more towards either the group approach or the separate entity approach.

The Communication also set out a shorter term policy agenda for the Commission by announcing a number of additional proposals including legislation to address the debt equity bias (the DEBRA proposal) and a measure to deal with the abusive use of shell entities.

5. Transfer pricing rules

So far, the EU has not legislated in the field of transfer pricing. The separate entity approach and the arm's length standard thus remain the prevailing principles and the basis for the work done in this field.

In the last 15 years, the EU work in transfer pricing has mostly been done within the context of the European Joint Transfer Pricing Forum (EU JTPF). The mandate of the EU

JTPF entailed finding practical solutions to the application of the rules as developed at the OECD within the EU. The outputs of this group consisting of representatives from the Member States, business and NGOs are mostly consensus reports, used in many countries (also outside the EU) as soft law guidelines. The reports are regarded as complementary to, and supportive of, the OECD rules and guidelines.

Among other topics, the EU JTPF most recently focused on the practical application of the profit split method (PSM). The aim of the JTPF work was to take stock of how the PSM is applied within the EU and work towards a common approach to address the relevant challenges arising under the current OECD framework.

In March 2019, the EU JTPF agreed on a report on the application of the profit split method (PSM) within the EU,[39] following the OECD Revised Guidelines on the application of PSM.[40] The aim of the JTPF exercise was to take stock of how the PSM is applied within the EU and work towards a common approach to addressing the relevant challenges arising under the current OECD framework. The report addresses (i) when to use the PSM (i.e. in which circumstances it may be considered the most appropriate transfer pricing method) and (ii) how to split the profit based on the concepts described in the revised OECD Guidelines as well as by providing an inventory of recurrent splitting factors.

After the completion of the report on the PSM, the mandate of the EU JTPF expired and was not extended. As a result, work on the remaining BEPS Actions 8-10 and the OECD outputs did not continue. Still, the inclusion of a few new concepts features in Directive 2018/827 (DAC6).[41] While the Commission proposal[42] for the amending directive featured two transfer pricing related hallmarks, the Member States' ambition resulted in expanding and adapting Hallmark E by including (i) a reference to unilateral safe harbours, (ii) transfers of 'hard-to-value-intangibles' and (iii) intragroup cross-border transfer of functions and/or risks and/or assets with 50% decrease of projected EBIT.

6. CFC regimes and separate entity approach

In the EU, Council Directive (EU) 2016/1164 laying down rules against tax avoidance practices that directly affect the functioning of the internal market (the ATAD)[43] sets out rules on the Controlled Foreign Companies (CFC) in articles 7 and 8 of this Directive. The Directive is shaped as a minimum standard, which should be included in all EU Member States' corporate income tax laws.

---

[39] Available at:
https://ec.europa.eu/taxation_customs/sites/taxation/files/report_on_the_application_of_the_profit_split_method_within_the_eu_en.pdf

[40] Available at:
http://www.oecd.org/tax/beps/revised-guidance-on-the-application-of-the-transactional-profitsplit-method-beps-action-10.htm

[41] Council Directive (EU) 2018/822 of 25 May 2018 amending Directive 2011/16/EU as regards mandatory automatic exchange of information in the field of taxation in relation to reportable cross-border arrangements (OJ L 139, 5 June 2018, p. 1).

[42] https://ec.europa.eu/taxation_customs/sites/taxation/files/intermediaries-proposal-2017_en.pdf and annex:
https://ec.europa.eu/taxation_customs/sites/taxation/files/intermediaries-annex-proposal-2017_en.pdf

[43] Council Directive (EU) 2016/1164 of 12 July 2016 laying down rules against tax avoidance practices that directly affect the functioning of the internal market, OJ L 193, 19 July 2016, p. 1–14.

The directive builds upon the work performed at the OECD level in the framework of the BEPS project. The aim of the ATAD was to create a minimum level of protection against corporate tax avoidance throughout the EU, while ensuring a fairer and more stable environment for businesses. CFC rules are designed to prevent taxpayers with a controlling interest in a foreign subsidiary (CFC) from stripping the tax base of their country of residence by shifting income into the CFC.

The CFC rule attributes the income of a low taxed controlled subsidiary or a permanent establishment to its parent company or head office respectively. Two cumulative criteria— (i) control by a resident parent company and (ii) a low level of local country taxation—have to be fulfilled for a foreign entity to qualify as a CFC. The parent company or head office becomes taxable on the attributed income in the State where it is resident, if the actual tax paid by the CFC is less than 50% of the corporate tax that the CFC would have paid on the same profits in the Member State of the controlling parent entity.

EU Member States have the flexibility to either use a rule that targets specific categories of "tainted" income (Option A), or they can limit the rule to income that has been artificially diverted to the subsidiary exclusively from its controlling parent company (Option B) (article 7(2)(a) and (article 7(2)(b).

Option A provides that certain predefined categories of undistributed passive income of the CFC are attributed to the taxpayer. The income that is attributed is calculated based on the rules of the EU Member State where the taxpayer is resident and based on its participation in the CFC. In order to comply with the EU fundamental freedoms, article 7 provides for a substance carve-out. The aim of the carve-out is to limit the impact of these rules (within the EU and EEA) to situations where the CFC does not carry out a genuine economic activity. In practice, the CFC rule is limited to artificial situations within the EU. Member States may extend this carve out to third countries. Member States can exempt entities with low profits or profit margins where there is a lower risk of tax avoidance. Member states can also exempt some financial undertakings that are highly regulated at the EU level, provided that only one third or less of the predefined categories of income comes from transactions with the taxpayer or associated enterprises.

Option B provides that undistributed income of the CFC, which was transferred to it as a result of non-genuine arrangements put in place for the essential purpose of obtaining a tax advantage, is attributed to the taxpayer. In practice, this means that transactions which involve payments from the parent towards the controlled subsidiary are non-genuine to the extent that the payments are "inflated" and go beyond arm's length. For Option B Member States also have the possibility to exempt certain entities with low profits or profit margins that give rise to lower risks of tax avoidance.

Since the ATAD lays down a minimum standard of protection, Member States are free to define a CFC more broadly than article 7, provided that they remain in line with the fundamental freedoms. In addition, when transposing CFC rules Member States can use their white, grey, or black lists of third countries which can include the corporate tax level, or use white lists of Member States compiled on that basis.

7. Interest limitation rule

Article 4 of the ATAD contains the interest limitation rule. The policy rationale for this rule is to discourage companies from using artificial debt arrangements, which are designed to minimise tax liabilities. Since interest payments are generally tax deductible in the EU, as in most jurisdictions, some companies arrange their inter-company loans so that their debt is with one of the group's companies in a high-tax country where interest payments can be deducted. Meanwhile, the interest on the debt is paid to the group's "lender" company, which is situated in a low tax country where interest is taxed at a low rate. Tax planning strategies like this allow the group to reduce its overall tax burden. This means that the group has paid less tax by shifting its profits in loan arrangements between its companies.

The Directive proposes to limit the amount of financial costs (interest and other costs) that a company can deduct from its taxable income, based on a fixed ratio that refers to its earnings. This aims to make it less attractive for companies to artificially shift debt in order to minimise their taxes.

This rule works by limiting the deductibility of taxpayers' net borrowing costs to 30% of a taxpayer's taxable earnings before interest, tax, depreciation and amortisation (EBITDA). Of course, EU Member States can, in addition to this rule, provide targeted rules against intra-group debt financing, such as thin capitalisation rules insofar these are in conformity with EU law.

Member States that operate group taxation systems can consider the overall position of all group entities in the Member State, including in the event of operating group taxation based on the so-called 'separate entity' approach, e.g. group relief, profit contribution, etc. In addition, Member States may allow the transfer of profits or interest capacity between entities within a group.

The ATAD also provides for a derogation from article 4 according to which the Member States which have targeted rules for preventing BEPS risks as of 8 August 2016, and provided these rules are equally effective to the interest limitation rule set out in article 4, then such Member States may apply these targeted rules until the end of the first full fiscal year following the date of publication of the agreement between the OECD members on the official website on a minimum standard with regard to BEPS Action 4, but at the latest until 1 January 2024. The Commission Notice "Measures considered equally effective to Article 4 of the Anti-Tax Avoidance Directive" OJ 441 of 7 December 2018, p. 1 outlined the five Member States[44] that were found to have rules that the Commission Services consider to be "equally effective".

In line with the approach that Member States can adopt stricter measures if they wish, Member States can reduce the ceiling below 30%. In order to reduce the administrative and compliance burden of the rules, Member States are free to allow a safe harbour. This safe harbour may allow a deductibility of up to EUR 3 million of exceeding borrowing costs.

Given that base erosion and profit shifting through excessive interest payments normally happens between associated entities, article 4 allows Member States to provide for an exclusion of standalone entities. This is due to the limited risks of tax avoidance. Similarly, given that financing arrangements of long-term public infrastructure projects pose limited base erosion and profit shifting risks, Member States can accordingly exclude exceeding borrowing costs incurred on loans used to fund such projects. However, for this exclusion to apply, the project's operator, borrowing costs, assets and income are all required to be located in the European Union.

In order to ease the introduction of the ATAD's interest limitation rule, article 4 permits Member States to introduce a grandfathering clause for pre-existing loans. This is permitted provided that the terms are not subsequently modified. If there is a modification, then the

---

44   Greece, France, Slovakia, Slovenia, and Spain.

grandfathering rule no longer applies to any increase in the amount/duration of the loan but is instead limited to the original terms.

In situations where the taxpayer is a part of a consolidated group for financial accounting purposes, the group's level of debt at worldwide level may be considered in order to permit higher amounts of deductibility. There are two approaches outlined in article 4 to achieve this aim: the equity escape or the group escape.

The equity escape allows Member States to set down rules whereby the interest limitation rule does not apply if the taxpayer demonstrates that its equity over total assets ratio is broadly equal to or higher than the equivalent ratio of the group. The group escape allows taxpayers to deduct higher amounts of exceeding borrowing costs based on the indebtedness of the overall group at worldwide level vis-à-vis third parties. The Directive also allows an amount of unrelieved borrowing costs or interest capacity to be carried forward or back. The Member States can place a time limit on such carry forward or carry back in order to ensure a higher level of protection.

During the development of the ATAD and subsequent negotiations in Council, there was an understanding that highly regulated credit and financial institutions should be subject to limitations to the deductibility of interest in the same way as other companies. However, it was also understood that this sector presents special features, in particular extensive regulation, which require a customised approach. The discussions on how to design such a customised approach were not fully developed by the time that ATAD was adopted. Therefore, Member States are permitted to exclude from the scope of article 4, certain listed types of financial undertakings, which are extensively regulated at EU level.

8. Hybrid mismatch rules

The policy aim of the hybrid mismatches rule in the ATAD is to neutralize the tax effects of hybrid arrangements. The first ATAD was later amended by the so-called ATAD 2,[45] which introduced a new article 9, as well as articles 9a and 9b.

Hybrid mismatches were covered by Action 2 of the OECD/G20 BEPS project. They have also been extensively discussed in the EU Code of Conduct Group where guidance on hybrid entities and hybrid permanent establishments was agreed. Finally, hybrids were also discussed in the context of the CCCTB negotiations. The ATAD includes rules to address hybrid mismatches, building on the previous EU and OECD work in this area. In the context of the ATAD, hybrid mismatches cover differences between tax systems that can be exploited to achieve double non-taxation, i.e. double deduction; deduction without inclusion; and non-taxation without inclusion. All of these mismatches can cause base erosion.

The ATAD sets down rules to counteract hybrid mismatches arising between EU Member States, and between Member States and third countries. The types of situations included are imported mismatches, reverse hybrid mismatches and tax residency mismatches. In order to ensure proportionality, the ATAD aims to address only those situations where there is a substantial risk of tax avoidance through the use of hybrid mismatches. The ATAD therefore defines a hybrid mismatch as a situation between a taxpayer in a Member

---

[45]   Council Directive (EU) 2017/952 of 29 May 2017 amending Directive (EU) 2016/1164 as regards hybrid mismatches with third countries, OJ L 144, 7 June 2017, p. 1–11.

State and an associated enterprise in another Member State or a structured arrangement between parties in Member States. The definition includes an entity that is part of the same consolidated group for financial accounting purposes, an enterprise in which the taxpayer has a significant influence in the management and reversely, an enterprise that has a significant influence in the management of the taxpayer.

ATAD 2 allows Member States some optionality as regards the scope of the denial of deduction in certain situations. While the majority of ATAD 2 should be transposed by 1 January 2020, the provisions relating to reverse hybrid mismatches can be applied from 1 January 2022.[46]

9. Country-by-Country Reporting

The minimum standard on Country-by-country Reporting (CbCR) introduced by BEPS Action 13, has been implemented within the EU with Directive 2016/881/EU (DAC4).[47] The reporting obligation and the automatic exchange of CbCR of multinational enterprise groups is governed in article 8aa, with further details on the forms in Annex III. The reporting obligation and the information to be exchanged concerns groups with a consolidated turnover exceeding EUR 750 million.

The CbCR introduces a group approach with respect to reporting. The term "MNE Group" means any group that includes two or more enterprises the tax residence for which is in different jurisdictions, or includes an enterprise that is resident for tax purposes in one jurisdiction and is subject to tax with respect to the business carried out through a permanent establishment in another jurisdiction. The obligation for preparing the CbCR and filing it with the tax authorities of the jurisdiction of tax residence lies with the ultimate parent entity (UPE) of an MNE group or the MNE surrogate parent entity appointed for that purpose. Where the UPE is not resident in an EU Member State or in a country required to provide the same information under the CbCR minimum standard, another constituent entity of the group (which may also be a permanent establishment), may be required to file the report locally.

Member states are required to adopt all the necessary measures to ensure that the reporting obligations of the MNE group are accomplished within 12 months from the last day of the relevant Reporting Fiscal Year. The tax authority to which the MNE reports, shall send the information automatically to the tax authorities of all other relevant Member States. DAC4 exchanges between tax authorities shall take place within 15 months after the end of the fiscal year of the MNE group.

Currently, the OECD Review 2020 of the minimum standard is ongoing. The results of the review will be taken into account in the context of any possible amendment of the DAC framework.

---

[46] Art. 2 of ATAD 2.
[47] Council Directive (EU) 2016/881 of 25 May 2016 amending Directive 2011/16/EU as regards mandatory automatic exchange of information in the field of taxation (OJ L 146, 3 June 2016, p. 8).

10. Digital Services Tax

The Commission proposal for Digital Services Tax (DST)[48] in 2018 is designed as an indirect tax on services. When proposed, the objective of the measure was to introduce a temporary solution to the taxation challenges of the digitalised economy. A more permanent solution was to be addressed with the Commission proposal for Significant Digital Presence (SDP)[49] by establishing a 'digital' nexus and apply the profit split method as a default rule. The taxable person is the person that provided the service. For this reason, the design of the tax looks at the entity that provided the service.[50] Any threshold for exclusion of the scope are thus applied at the entity level as a default rule. However, special rules are set out for entities belonging to a consolidated group for financial accounting purposes. For the purposes of determining whether an entity is above the applicable thresholds and thus qualifies as a taxable person, the thresholds should be applied in respect of total consolidated group revenues.[51] The revenues obtained by an entity from supplies to other entities belonging to the same group for financial accounting purposes should be excluded from the scope of the proposed DST.[52]

If the taxable person is each entity (in scope), it follows that each entity would have to file a separate DST return. In case an entity is a member of a group, the group could nominate a single entity within that group for the purposes of paying the DST and fulfilling the obligations on behalf of each taxable person in that group that is liable to pay the DST. Still, the apportionment of revenues is calculated based on the digital activities provided by the entity in each Member State separately. The proposed DST seems to take a combined approach containing elements of both the entity and the group approach due to the unique nature of such tax and the problem it aims to address.

11. The Two Pillar Solution to address the tax challenges arising from the digitalisation of the economy

The OECD has been working on a global solution articulated around two broad work streams: Pillar One (re-allocation of taxing rights) and Pillar Two (minimum effective taxation). On 8 October 2021, the large majority of the Inclusive Framework agreed on a statement on the principles of the project. This was subsequently endorsed by the G20 Finance Ministers and Governors of Central Banks on 13 October 2021 and G20 Leaders on 31 October 2021.

---

[48] Proposal for a Council Directive on the common system of a digital services tax on revenues resulting from the provision of certain digital services COM(2018) 148 final, available at:
https://ec.europa.eu/taxation_customs/sites/taxation/files/proposal_common_system_digital_services_tax_21032018_en.pdf

[49] Proposal for a Council Directive laying down rules relating to the corporate taxation of a significant digital presence available at: COM(2018) 147 final,
https://ec.europa.eu/taxation_customs/sites/taxation/files/proposal_significant_digital_presence_21032018_en.pdf and its Annexes, available at:
https://ec.europa.eu/taxation_customs/sites/taxation/files/proposal_significant_digital_presence_annex_21032018_en.pdf .

[50] Art. 4 of the DST.

[51] Art. 4(6) of the proposed DST.

[52] Art. 3(7) of the proposed DST.

11.1. Pillar One

The Commission work programme announced a legislative proposal for 2022. Much will depend on a number of elements of the agreement at the international level and the way of proposed implementation. On 22 December 2022, the Commission adopted the Own Resource Package, which proposes to make a certain share of Pillar One revenues a new EU Own Resource.

11.2. Pillar Two

On 22 December 2021, the European Commission proposed a Directive ensuring a minimum effective tax rate for the activities of large groups. The directive provides rules that ensure a minimum level of taxation for large multinational enterprises and large-scale domestic groups. This implements the global agreement reached by the Inclusive Framework on 8 October 2021 and the GloBE (Global Anti-Base Erosion) Model Rules agreed by the Inclusive Framework on 14 December 2021.

The directive implements the GloBE Model Rules in the EU taking into account the specifics of EU law and the Single Market. For this purpose, while the directive closely follows the OECD Model Rules, it extends its scope to domestic situations, by including the subsidiaries in the same Member State as the Parent Entity of the group as well as large-scale purely domestic groups, in order to ensure compliance with the fundamental freedoms. In this context, the directive makes use of an option offered in the Commentary to the GloBE Model Rules whereby in order to ensure effective taxation at the minimum agreed level, the Member State of a Parent Entity is required to apply the primary rule (Income Inclusion Rule – IIR) not only in respect of foreign subsidiaries, but also of all constituent entities resident in that Member State, including permanent establishments in that Member State.

The directive contains two main rules, the Income Inclusion Rule (IIR) and its backstop, the Undertaxed Profits Rule (UTPR), together known as the GloBE Rules. The IIR works by imposing a top-up tax on a parent entity in respect of the low-taxed income of group entities (which are referred to as constituent entities). The UTPR acts as a backstop to the IIR and allocates top-up tax to a jurisdiction to the extent that the low-tax income of a constituent entity is not otherwise subject to tax under the IIR. The UTPR allocates top-up tax to jurisdictions based on a two-factor formula – carrying value of tangible assets in the jurisdiction and number of employees in the jurisdiction.

In addition, the directive allows Member States to introduce a domestic minimum tax, which enables Member States to collect top-up tax with respect to low-taxed constituent entities located in their territory. As a matter of principle, the tax revenues collected locally are offset against the top-up tax liability in the Member State where the parent entity is located. The constituent entities of an MNE group that are located in a Member State which has elected to apply a domestic minimum tax, pay the top-up tax to the tax administration of their own Member State.

The directive applies to groups of multinational enterprises (MNEs) and large-scale domestic groups that have combined annual group revenues of at least EUR 750 million based on consolidated financial statements. This threshold was decided in order to ensure consistency with existing international corporate tax policies such as the rules on Country-by-Country Reporting, which in the EU are reflected in the directive on Administrative

Cooperation. The current Presidency compromise text of the Directive at the time of writing proposes a general application of the IIR on or after 31 December 2023 and 31 December 2024 in respect of the UTPR.

The Pillar Two Directive is an example of a hybrid approach between the separate entity and the group approach. The top up tax is triggered if the effective tax rate of the entities in a given jurisdiction falls below 15%. This suggests a separate entity approach as a starting point. On the other hand, GloBE is to be applied on the basis of the consolidated financial accounting standards. This decides whether the consolidated revenue threshold of EUR 750 million is reached, which leans more towards the group approach. Overall though it can be said that this proposal for a Directive leans more in the direction of the separate entity approach due to the starting point of the ETR test and the general focus of the rules on constituent entities of the group.

12. UNSHELL

The proposal for the UNSHELL Directive has been adopted by the Commission on 22 December 2021.[53] Shell companies are often used for aggressive tax planning or tax evasion purposes. Businesses can direct financial flows through shell entities towards jurisdictions that have no or very low taxes, or where taxes can easily be circumvented. Similarly, some individuals can use shells to shield assets – particularly real estate – from taxes, either in their country of residence or in the country where the property is located.

The initiative is meant to introduce new EU rules in the form of a directive so as to facilitate Member States' tax administrations in identifying entities without a minimum substance which could be used for tax avoidance or evasion. If an entity is found to be a 'shell', it will have to face tax consequences, essentially becoming 'transparent' for tax purposes.

The identification of shell entities will first involve a reporting requirement for entities that are found to be at a high risk of being abusive, i.e. if they cross a 'gateway'. This identification takes into account certain characteristics: mainly passive income, cross-border elements, outsourcing of corporate administration services. Second, reporting entities will have to pass a minimum substance test based on a set of factors (own bank account, premises, directors' or employees' residence and qualifications). Entities that fail even one of these factors will be considered a 'shell' and bear tax consequences. However, entities that fail the test will still be allowed to prove that they have sufficient substance by providing evidence of specific facts and circumstances.

As evident from the test above, the criteria are applied at the entity level. When applying the tax consequences in cases when an entity is considered a shell under the Directive, the approach is broader as it requires the tax administration to apply the prescribed consequences in the source jurisdiction, the jurisdiction of the shell as well as the jurisdiction of the shareholder. The tax consequences impact the taxation of the group as a whole.

---

[53]   Proposal for a COUNCIL DIRECTIVE laying down rules to prevent the misuse of shell entities for tax purposes and amending Directive 2011/16/EU, 2021/0434 (CNS).

List of branch reports Subject 1

Argentina

Australia

Austria

Belgium

Brazil

Canada

Chile

Chinese Taipei

Colombia

Czech Republic

Denmark

Finland

France

Germany

Hong Kong

Hungary

India

Italy

Japan

Korea, Republic of

Luxembourg

Mauritius

Mexico

Netherlands

New Zealand

Norway

Peru

Poland

Portugal

Singapore

South Africa

Spain

Sweden

Switzerland

Turkey

Ukraine

United Kingdom

United States

Uruguay

Summary and conclusions

of all branch reports

**Group approach and separate entity approach
in domestic and international tax law**

Branch reporters
Florencia Fernández Sabella[1]
Mariano Ballone[2]

Summary and conclusions

Despite the globalization of the economy and the application of the principle of worldwide taxation included in the Argentinian Income Tax Law (ITL), groups of companies are not allowed to consolidate their profits and losses. Each legal entity must assess its own income separately from that of its shareholders.

Regarding domestic law, consolidated financial statements are required for groups of companies; this obligation, however, serves mainly an informative purpose and does not create tax effects. Transactions between local corporate entities belonging to the same economically controlled group are not treated differently than those between independent companies, as a rule.

One of the most relevant tax regimes applicable to groups of local companies is ruling business restructuring (*tax-free reorganizations*). This tax regime includes significant restrictions to the transfer of accumulated losses and tax breaks as part of a special regime when there is a change of control in the companies prior to the reorganization date.

There is not any SAAR that allows an economic group to be considered as a unit for tax purposes instead of independent legal entities. In the absence of specific regulations, Argentine case law applied the economic reality principle (Argentina's GAAR) to determine the legitimate taxable event that could arise in transactions between associated companies.

Deduction of intra-group interests arising from financial loans between associated local and international companies are subject to a limitation with a threshold of 30% of taxable EBITDA.

Local tax procedures are carried out considering each company as an independent entity. However, groups of companies must report to tax authorities: (i) any relation they have with other companies, either based in Argentina or abroad; (ii) final beneficiaries of the multinational groups they belong to; and (iii) any local or international tax planning structure.

With regard to international tax law, the ITL taxes non-residents only on their Argentine source income, while it taxes its residents on their worldwide income. Foreign beneficiaries are taxed at source through a final withholding.

Branches (and other PE cases) are considered as independent taxpayers, just like foreign subsidiaries. Taxes are calculated like in any other local corporate entity and each branch must keep its accounting records separate from those of its head office.

The tax credit method is the domestic rule to avoid double taxation. There are no major restrictions regarding the origin of income or losses, the state in which they are created, or segregation of results (except for losses from the sale of shares and other ownership

---

[1]   CPA, partner at Laiún, Fernández Sabella & Smudt, tax specialist and income tax professor at UBA.
[2]   Lawyer, partner at Teijeiro & Ballone Abogados, and post-graduate corporate tax law professor at UCA.

interests). A credit for exempt income in the country of residence of the subsidiaries is not allowed. Credit to be computed is calculated on the tax profit or loss of the PE or with respect to the subsidiary's profit to be attributed to the local controlling company.

Argentina does not impose on its residents a restriction on their ability to become shareholders or controlling shareholders of foreign corporate entities. There is no further limitation either – apart from the GAARs and SAARs (such as the LoB included in some of the latest DTTs signed by Argentina in line with the BEPS actions and the MLI) – preventing a business group from benefiting from a treaty, as long as both contracting parties are subject to the purposes of the DTT and – again – as long as it is not a case of treaty shopping either.

When it comes to transfer pricing in Argentina, the principles of separate accounting and independent operator or arm's length standard prevail. The comparability analysis has been historically implemented considering the local resident as tested party only, except for those cases where the profit split method applied. The comparability analysis based exclusively on the local resident's situation stands against OECD recommendations on comparability.

Argentine CFC rules have a global approach, whereby all the structures located abroad are subject to the transparency standard, even those indirectly owned. Once the CFC rule is applied, the foreign resident legal status for tax purposes is completely disregarded in terms of income imputation, rates and exemptions, so that the treatment here is similar to that given in the case of an Argentine taxpayer who has obtained such income directly. However, this does not mean omitting the foreign entity legally.

As a general rule, intra-group expenses are deductible if they meet a set of requirements published by tax authorities. Additionally, payments made to foreign affiliates generating Argentine source income can only be deducted by the local resident as long as these are paid – and withheld – in the fiscal year in which they accrued or until the deadline for filing the tax return for that year. If the payment is not made within that period, said expenses will only be deductible in the fiscal year in which the payment is made. There are maximum thresholds applicable to royalties and technical services deductions.

Groups of MNEs are required to file the CbCR for revenues above the threshold of EUR 750 million. Requirements concerning CbCR are aligned with those suggested by the OECD.

Regarding digital taxes, they are taxed under VAT. The ITL has not included any specific rule concerning digital services; however, the domestic authority has recently tried to tax the digital economy by expanding the concept of service PE or by trying to generate an Argentine source income. We do not agree with these interpretations.

As explained in the report, a group approach for tax purposes is unlikely to be allowed, at least in the short or medium term, not only because parent companies usually have their headquarters abroad, but also because such consolidation could cause tax collection to drop sharply, something that does not seem to fit with the higher tax revenue goal pursued lately.

Even though Argentina has included in its domestic law several measures recommended by the OECD as part of its project on base erosion and profit shifting (BEPS), the separate entity approach both in domestic and international tax law remains the general rule.

Australia

Branch reporters
Antony Ting[1]
Peter Stinson[2]

Summary and conclusions

Australia's income tax law, in general, treats a company as a separate taxpayer distinct from its shareholders. In response to the rise of corporate groups, various rules and regimes have been enacted reflecting the application of the enterprise doctrine, under which a corporate group is treated – to different extents – as a single taxpayer.

The override of the traditional separate entity doctrine is often driven by the tax policy objective of anti-avoidance. For instance, the Australian Government believed that the strong single entity rule (SER) in the tax consolidation regime would address the dual cost base issue by collapsing multiple levels of ownership in a corporate group into one single level. In particular, the SER in general deems subsidiary members of a tax consolidated group to be parts of the head company for income tax purposes. This strong application of the enterprise doctrine not only creates a uniquely taxpayer-friendly environment for consolidated groups, but also leads to a number of unusual but important implications, including the reset of cost bases of most assets of subsidiary members upon consolidation and the reconstruction of the cost bases of shares in a subsidiary when it leaves a consolidated group. In addition, the interactions between the consolidation regime and other parts of the tax system – which adopts largely the separate entity doctrine – can be difficult.

In general, tax losses of a taxpayer can be carried forward indefinitely to offset against its future taxable income. However, to prevent the trafficking of loss companies by transferring control in those companies away from the original shareholders, Australia has enacted anti-avoidance provisions since 1944 to tackle these arrangements. A company, in general, cannot deduct carried forward losses if there is a major change of shareholdings unless it satisfies the business continuity test.

In respect to cross-border situations, the application of the enterprise doctrine is more prevalent, as anti-BEPS measures tend to be more effective if they recognise that a corporate group operates effectively as one single enterprise, instead of treating each group member as a separate taxpayer. For instance, while the transfer pricing regime adopts largely the separate entity doctrine and the arm's length principle, the ATO has the long-held position that in determining the arm's length conditions, the functional analysis may be performed on a corporate group basis. In the *Chevron* case, the court lent support to the application of the enterprise doctrine in the sense that it rejected the orphan theory put forward by the taxpayer and held that while the arm's length principle required the determination of the interest rate as if the taxpayer borrowed from an independent entity, it did not require assuming away the taxpayer's status as a wholly owned subsidiary of the parent

---

[1]   Associate Professor, University of Sydney Business School, CPA, Chartered Tax Adviser.
[2]   Associate Partner, Ernst & Young, Sydney. B Com, LLB (UNSW), LLM (Syd). Chartered Tax Adviser, Solicitor of the Supreme Court of NSW, PhD candidate, Business School, University of Sydney.

company. The recognition of the taxpayer being a wholly owned subsidiary of the Chevron group ultimately led to the court's conclusion that the arm's length interest rate should be determined based on the hypothesis that the taxpayer would have benefited from a parent guarantee if it were to borrow the money from an independent party.

The CFC regime is a classic example of the application of the enterprise doctrine, as it looks through the separate legal entity principle and attributes certain income of a CFC to its shareholders who are taxed on that income on an accrual basis. It also highlights the constant tension between the tax policy objectives of anti-avoidance and international competitiveness. The Board of Taxation released a report in 2008 with recommendations aimed largely at enhancing the international competitiveness of Australian businesses. The government initially announced in 2009 that it would accept most of the recommendations, but eventually decided in 2013 that it would not proceed with the recommendations.

Australia's thin capitalisation regime is another example illustrating the tension between the tax policy objectives of anti-avoidance and international competitiveness. Most taxpayers rely on an asset-based fixed ratio test to satisfy the thin cap regime. As the test has no link with a corporate group's net third-party interest expense, it is bound to fail to achieve the key objective of the BEPS Project's Action 4, namely, to cap interest deduction of a corporate group to its net third-party interest expense. The Government believed that the current thin capitalisation regime renders the adoption of the Action 4's recommendations unnecessary. However, the *Chevron* case proved that the regime is not effective to deal with tax structures using interest deductions.

Australia's hybrid mismatch rules adopt largely the recommendations in Action 2 of the BEPS Project. They apply primarily to payments between members of a control group, which in general refer to members of a consolidated group for accounting purposes. The hybrid mismatch rules may also apply to unrelated parties if they are parties of a structured arrangement that is designed to engineer a mismatch.

Australia implemented the CbC reporting rules in 2016, which also rely to a large extent on accounting concepts with respect to corporate groups. In particular, the CbC regime applies to resident companies that are significant global entities (SGE), which are either a parent company with annual global income of AUD 1 billion or more, or a member of a consolidated group for accounting purposes where the global parent entity has an annual global income of AUD 1 billion or more.

In response to the international tax avoidance by MNEs, Australia has enacted a couple of unilateral anti-BEPS regimes, namely the Multinational Anti-Avoidance Law (MAAL) and the Diverted Profits Tax (DPT). Both the MAAL and the DPT apply to SGEs, the same group concept as for the CbC reporting rules.

The government has decided against introducing a digital services tax after exploring the idea in 2018. Instead, Australia participates in the search for a multilateral solution to the issues arising from the digital economy through the OECD and the Inclusive Framework.

Branch reporters
Daniela Hohenwarter-Mayr[1]
Stephanie Zolles[2]

Summary and conclusions

Austrian corporate tax law is based on a separate entity approach, according to which corporations are treated as separate taxable subjects. Historically, this approach dates back to the 19th century and ever since has manifested as a pervading element in the Austrian Corporate Income Tax Act (CITA). As a direct consequence, corporations and their shareholders are treated as separate taxpayers. Transactions between them are generally recognized for tax purposes and profit distributions of the corporation are treated as income of the shareholders. From this further follows that benefits granted causa societatis (hidden profit distributions or, vice versa, hidden contributions) are treated like their respective counterparts which are effected openly. Even within a group of companies, every member is generally considered to be a separate taxable subject. However, over the years various measures alleviating the separate entity principle have been implemented. Some of these measures are aimed at providing tax neutrality or tax advantages for the taxpayers concerned. However, the predominant part addresses the need to combat tax avoidance and tax planning structures. Thereby, the separate entity approach is not fully given up. Rather, the separate tax personality of corporations sustains, but circumstances external to the sphere of the entity concerned gain relevance in the assessment of the tax treatment of transactions undertaken or income received.

At the heart of the cross-entity perspective is the optional group taxation regime, which allows members of a group to consolidate profits and losses at the level of the group parent. Under the group taxation regime, the income is attributed up the chain of control, offset against the income of each group member as well as the group parent and finally taxed at the level of the parent. This way, the group taxation regime aims at taking into account the economic reality of groups of companies as units for tax purposes. The group taxation regime has been further supported by economic policy considerations, namely the need to strengthen Austria's attractiveness as a location for group headquarters and the desire to create a regime that is in conformity with EU law. But even though the final tax burden of groups having opted for the group taxation regime approaches the taxation of one entity, the separate tax personality of each group member is preserved. Similarly, the separate entity approach is maintained under the provisions neutralizing inter-company dividends and under the international inter-company participation exemption. Alleviations of the separate entity approach resulting from these schemes are limited to the neutralization of tax effects relating to the specific types of income concerned with a view to eliminate economic double taxation.

A significant number of rules deviating from the separate entity perspective more

---

[1]   Full professor of Tax Law at the University of Vienna.
[2]   Employed in the VAT unit of the Austrian Ministry of Finance.

particularly target tax avoidance and tax planning structures. Despite the recognition of a corporation and its shareholders as distinct taxable subjects, certain changes in the shareholder structure can trigger tax consequences at the level of the corporation in form of a prohibition to deduct losses incurred prior to these changes ("change of control rules"). In other cases, the relation of the entities involved combined with a comparison of similar transactions between unrelated parties are decisive for the tax treatment of the underlying transaction. A variety of measures which more specifically deviate from a strict separate entity perspective by addressing group structures relate to cross-border situations. Among these are the prohibition to exempt inter-company dividends where the dividends are deductible at the level of the foreign distributing company, the ongoing implementation of the OECD's transfer pricing recommendations, the CbC reporting obligations and the transpositions of EU law requirements, including the anti-tax avoidance measures provided for by the Anti-Tax-Avoidance Directive (ATAD).[3] The latter covers CFC and hybrid mismatch rules as well as an interest limitation rule. The need for a cross-entity (i.e., overall) perspective is also addressed in the Digital Advertising Tax introduced in 2020, which was inspired by the EU proposal on a digital service tax; its application being dependent on a certain revenue threshold calculated on a cross-entity basis.

Common elements of the various co-existing measures deviating from the separate entity approach are requirements linked to the "relation" between the corporations concerned. In doing so, Austrian tax law does not provide for one single concept under which corporations are considered to be sufficiently related. Rather, the CITA provides for numerous very similar (but not identical) concepts, sometimes referring to the notion of "group" under corporate law or the Austrian Commercial Code (ACC), sometimes combining aspects of different concepts and sometimes defining affiliated or related corporations autonomously. The common denominator of all these definitions in corporate law, in the ACC as well as in tax law is the financial link between the corporations concerned, mostly in the form of a certain amount of participation held in a corporation. It goes without saying that the coexistence of these concepts and the (partial) overlaps between them add complexity to the legal landscape.

Finally, compared to the above-mentioned alleviations of the separate entity approach in the taxation of corporations, a diametrically opposite development can be noticed when it comes to the taxation of PE income. Even though PEs are generally not considered to be distinct taxable subjects, Austria (partly) applies a separate entity approach to PEs in cross-border situations when it comes to the allocation of profits between states, thereby following the OECD recommendations. The increasing relevance of the separate entity perspective in the taxation of PE income and the deviations from the separate entity approach in the taxation of groups of companies, taken together, result in an approximation of the taxation of PEs and corporations in certain aspects, thus at the end of the day enhancing neutrality of legal forms, particularly in a cross-border context.

---

[3]   Council Directive (EU) 2016/1164 of 12 July 2016 as amended by Council Directive (EU) 2017/952 of 29 May 2017.

Belgium

Branch reporter
Pieter Deré[1]

Summary and conclusions

In this branch report, we address the question of how Belgium taxes Belgian taxpayers and foreign taxpayers with activities in Belgium. We assess whether Belgium applies single entity taxation or rather approaches taxation from a group perspective. More in particular, we investigate to what extent Belgium has moved away from the historical single entity approach and has evolved towards a more group taxation system. In summary, the authors conclude that the Belgian tax system adheres to the principle of single entity taxation, which may create significant policy challenges at the moment Belgium is required to implement a number of the current reforms of the international tax system (such as the OECD Pillar II proposal). There is a momentum for the Belgian government to prepare the Belgian tax system for these upcoming developments and realise a simpler and more transparent tax system in Belgium that is ready for the future (and the anticipated developments).

Belgium historically has applied single entity taxation in its tax system. The entire tax system is strongly organised around the cornerstone principle that each legal entity is taxed on a separate and independent basis. Each legal entity also files a separate tax return.

In the past years, a number of limited steps have been taken to consider certain group effects in the taxation of Belgian taxpayers. One important step is the introduction of a group taxation regime in Belgium as from 2019, which is a truly historical moment as it is the first time in the history of taxation in Belgium that a form of group taxation was effectively introduced. The regime allows taxpayers that are part of a group, to transfer profits from companies with a positive tax base to companies in the same group that have a current year loss via a so-called 'group contribution'. The Belgian regime is inspired by the Scandinavian group contribution regimes. The current group taxation regime is not realising a true system of 'group taxation' as taxpayers still have to file separate tax returns (per entity) and the conditions to qualify for group taxation are very strict (e.g., requiring a direct participation to qualify for group taxation). The group taxation regime in Belgium already considers the current stance of the EU case law and the impact of the freedom of establishment, by allowing group consolidation with foreign subsidiaries that have so-called 'final losses'.

The same limited step towards a more group-wide taxation can also be found in the way that Belgium introduced the EBITDA rule for interest deduction following ATAD I. Indeed, also for the determination of the room for interest deduction, an ad hoc consolidation is required whereby transactions between Belgian related companies are eliminated to determine the EBITDA of the group in Belgium and whereby Belgian group companies can transfer their headroom for interest deduction among the other Belgian group companies

[1] Director at PwC Belgium where he is part of the EU and international tax team. He has almost 15 years of experience and is also a guest lecturer and frequent author on these topics.
     The reporter would like to express his deepest gratitude for the support provided by Jean-Philippe Van West and Gilles Van Hulle regarding the preparation of the report. The Belgian branch report is the result of the work by the branch reporter and Gilles & Jean-Philippe.

that may not have sufficient room for interest deduction. Although this rule results in significant complexity to make the calculations, it is a step towards a more group-level type of taxation.

These developments that indicate small steps towards a group-level taxation are not a general tendency. When looking more profoundly at the Belgian tax system, we conclude in our report that the Belgian tax system is still strongly oriented towards a single entity approach. This can be found, for example, when looking at the Belgian transfer pricing provisions. The Belgian transfer pricing provisions – in principle – only apply in a cross-border context and there are no general transfer pricing provisions between domestic related companies. Thus, the single entity taxation still prevails, even if the transactions are not arm's length and only in cases where there is a risk that the Belgian tax jurisdiction would be eroded by non-arm's length cross-border transactions, Belgian transfer pricing rules kick in to adjust the taxable basis in line with the arm's length principle.

The same is true when looking at the change of control provision. Although, as a general principle, losses and other tax attributes forfeit if the loss company changes owner/control, the loss forfeiture will in practice only apply in case there is a trade in loss companies, in which case the transfer is not substantiated with genuine economic reasons. Again here, we conclude that the losses are attached to the legal entity rather than to the group or the activities developed.

It becomes clear that the individual taxpayer/legal entity is still very much the point of reference for corporate taxation in Belgium. Each legal entity has to file a separate tax return and comply with all relevant formalities. There is no possibility for a group return or simplifications for groups. Of course, certain transfer pricing documentation is provided at group level, which is the immediate consequence of the fact that transfer pricing rules apply to groups of related companies, rather than standalone companies.

The Belgian government indicated in October 2020, as part of the government agreement, to support the introduction of the OECD proposals. We believe that there is a momentum for the government to take an important step forward in creating a simpler and more transparent tax system. One particular idea that could be considered is the introduction of a group tax return. In this summary tax return, Belgian taxpayers could reflect the EBITDA calculation (at Belgian consolidated level), reflect the group contributions and provide an overview of the tax prepayments. Looking ahead at the implementation of the international tax reform in Belgium, there is a momentum for Belgium to ensure that the compliance burden is not increasing further. Based on our assessment, this will require that steps are taken to move away from strict single entity taxation and move towards a more group oriented approach to corporate taxation. The upcoming international tax reform can be a momentum for change. Taking steps towards such a group tax system will be even more important when the OECD Pillar I and Pillar II initiatives crystallize in the next few years. With the current tax system in Belgium and the tax procedures focused on single entities, it will be very complex to introduce the OECD Pillar I and II initiatives in Belgian tax law. Taking the leap forward, with a reform of the Belgian tax procedures, will enable Belgium to make significant administrative wins and prepare the Belgian tax system fit for the future. This approach would seamlessly link in with the broader focus in the EU on digitalization of tax authorities. A digital tax authority should be able to facilitate the increased complexity for companies with multiple individual tax returns and the complexity of group taxation is no longer a valid argument to not implement a more advanced group taxation regime.

Branch reporter
Sergio André Rocha[1]

Summary and conclusions

Brazil's domestic taxation is entirely based on the separate entity approach. This is true for income taxation as well as other taxes levied on legal entities. Assuming a situation in which all group entities are located in Brazil, there are no exceptions to their independent and separate treatment for tax purposes.

Law 11,638 of 2007 initiated the adoption of the International Financial Reporting Standards ("IFRS") as Brazil's generally accepted accounting standards. Since 2007, most of the IFRS standards and Interpretations have been adopted by the country – including IFRS No. 10, which deals with consolidated financial statements.

Brazil's IFRS standards are enacted by the Committee of Accounting Pronouncements. Accounting standards regarding group consolidation are established in Technical Pronouncement No. 36 (R3) – which follow the referenced IFRS No. 10.

In 2014, Law No. 12,973 was enacted. In its articles 2 through 75, rules are established that adapt federal tax regulations to IFRS accounting. Nevertheless, tax legislation did not establish any provisions regarding tax consolidation that follows the accounting consolidation. Therefore, the separate entity approach was not altered for tax purposes.

Brazil's Tax Code does not include a definition of a group of companies. However, it is worth pointing out that there are also some co-liability provisions that apply to shareholders. In addition, tax authorities have been attempting to use article 124, I, of the Code – which establishes a general co-liability rule when there is a common interest in what constitutes the taxable event – to support the co-liability of group companies in some cases.

There are no group taxation regimes in Brazil – with the exception of consolidation in the context of CFC rules.

In fact, the country's CFC rules are currently established in articles 76 through 92 of Law No. 12,973 of 2014. The profits earned by directly or indirectly controlled companies of Brazilian entities must be individually added to the Corporate Income Tax and the Social Contribution Tax calculation at year end. Thus, if a Brazilian company controls a German company, which in turn controls a French company, the profits earned by both the German company and the French company will be added in the calculation of the aforementioned taxes on an individual basis.

Until 2022, a Brazilian company can consolidate the results of all its directly or indirectly controlled companies abroad. However, such consolidation will not be possible when the CFC (i) is located in a low-tax jurisdiction, (ii) is under a preferential tax regime, or (iii) is controlled by an entity that is located in a low-tax jurisdiction or is under preferential tax regime. The same restrictions apply when the country of the CFC taxes income with a nominal rate lower than 20%.

---

[1]   Professor, Director Vice-President at ABDF, Brazil's IFA branch, and tenured professor at the Rio de Janeiro State University (UERJ) in Brazil.

In 2017, Brazil sent a formal request to the Organization for Economic Co-operation and Development ("OECD") to become one of its members.

It was in this context that in an event held on 28 February and 1 March 2018 the joint work of Brazil's Tax Administration and the OECD to review the country's transfer pricing rules started. On 11 July 2019, they presented a partial result of this joint work, and on 18 December of that same year they published the report "Transfer Pricing in Brazil Towards Convergence with the OECD Standard". This report focused on demonstrating the gaps of Brazil's regulations when compared with OECD standards and how such gaps lead to situations of double taxation and double non-taxation.

Therefore, work is currently being done to adapt, to some extent, Brazil's transfer pricing rules to OECD standards. However, at this point there is no public information regarding the draft proposal for change. Hence, there is no indication regarding if or when Brazilian rules will actually be reformed. For the time being, changes in the OECD recommended standards are irrelevant for the application of Brazil's transfer pricing rules.

It is too early to establish whether Brazil is going to apply the new group-related allocation rules for profits as currently discussed under OECD BEPS Pillar 1. It is a known fact that Brazilian authorities are engaged in Pillar 1 discussions. However, there is no concrete indication that the country will actually implement whatever suggestion comes out of Pillar 1 – or Pillar 2 for that matter.

Especially due to the COVID-19 pandemic, several bills have been proposed to create digital services taxes with different scopes. Nevertheless, there is no indication that any of these proposed bills will be approved by Congress.

Even though these proposals have been at least in part justified in the OECD BEPS works, these justifications seem more rhetorical then accurate in reflecting the OECD developments. This is a trend in the current tax policy debate in Brazil probably fostered by the country's intention to become an OECD member. It is noticeable that more and more tax proposals attempt to ground their provisions in alleged OECD recommendations – which, more often than not, is not actually the case.

Branch reporters
Sarah Chiu[1]
Sunita Doobay[2]

Summary and conclusions

Canada does not have a formal group consolidation regime and generally employs the separate entity approach both in domestic and cross-border situations. However, in practice, loss consolidation transactions undertaken by related or affiliated entities to effectively transfer losses from an entity with losses to a profitable entity that is related or affiliated are common and generally accepted by the Canadian federal tax authority, Canada Revenue Agency (CRA). The taxation of dividends received by individuals and other corporations from domestic corporations also deviates somewhat from the strict separate entity approach as taxation depends in part on the activities carried on by and the nature of the paying corporation. Subject to an anti-avoidance rule of potentially broad scope, domestic inter-corporate dividends are effectively subject to no further tax in the hands of the recipient corporation.

Moreover, while adhering to the separate entity approach in form, the relationship between entities is relevant in determining the applicability of certain favourable rules in the *Income Tax Act* (Canada) (Act)[3] and certain anti-deferral and anti-base-erosion rules. The degree of relationship required between entities differs depending on the rule and the effect of certain rules is to set aside the separate entity approach for limited purposes.

For example, in the outbound context, the generally favourable foreign affiliate (FA) surplus regime (applicable when income earned by foreign subsidiaries is returned to Canada) generally applies at a 10% ownership threshold, whereas the passive income CFC rules (which include foreign accrual property income (FAPI) of foreign subsidiaries that are controlled foreign affiliates (CFA) in the income of the Canadian shareholder) applies in most circumstances at a *de jure* control threshold. For purposes of the CFC rules, the *de jure* control threshold is expanded to include circumstances where four or fewer arm's length Canadian persons (together with non-arm's length persons) would have *de jure* control of the foreign corporation. In applying both the FA regime and the CFC rules, the separate entity approach is partially set aside as the nature and location of activities of the foreign subsidiary is relevant to the computation of income of the Canadian shareholder when earned by the foreign subsidiary and when ultimately returned to the Canadian shareholder. In most cases, income that has been subject to foreign tax of 25% or more is not further taxed in Canada. No minimum foreign tax threshold applies for Canada to concede jurisdiction to tax funds repatriated to Canada from certain active business income

---

[1]   Partner, Felesky Flynn LLP, Calgary, Canada and lecturer at the Faculty of Law at the University of Calgary, Canada.

[2]   Partner, Blaney McMurtry LLP, Toronto, Canada and lecturer at the Faculty of Law at Queen's University, Kingston, Canada.

[3]   *Income Tax Act*, RSC 1985, c. 1 [*Act*]. All statutory references are to the Act and *Income Tax Regulations*, CRC, c. 945, [*Regulations*] unless otherwise specified.

earned by certain foreign subsidiaries in countries with which Canada has a tax treaty or tax information exchange agreement.

In the inbound context, the thin capitalization rules which re-characterize (into dividends) interest paid by a Canadian corporation to a non-resident on debts exceeding the specified threshold of 1.5 debt to 1 equity potentially apply when a 25% threshold share ownership is held by the non-resident lender or a related person. The rules applicable to branches of foreign corporations carrying on business in Canada arguably impose a separate entity approach by treating the Canadian branch in a manner similar to a Canadian corporate subsidiary. In contrast, the FA dumping anti-avoidance rules arguably disregard the separate entity principle by requiring examination of the activities of FAs of a Canadian subsidiary of a foreign corporation.

As another example, the cross-border transfer pricing rules and domestic inadequate consideration rules apply between related entities and entities that are factually dealing not at arm's length. In both the cross-border and domestic contexts, the rules generally respect the separate entity approach but make one-sided adjustments to deem arm's length prices or consideration to be paid or received by the Canadian taxpayer, which could result in double taxation.

Administratively, the CRA considers and audits large groups of entities together while the default for smaller groups is to audit entities separately. Canada has also adopted the OECD country-by-country reporting rules which recognizes reports filed by other members of the group.

Canadian corporate law and securities laws applicable to Canadian entities also treat separate corporations as separate entities, although, as under the Act, certain favourable and certain more restrictive rules apply if certain relationships exist between the entities. In contrast, depending on the applicable accounting standard, consolidated reporting for a group of entities is either optional (generally for private enterprises) or mandatory (for publicly-traded groups).

Branch reporter
Darío Romero[1]

Summary and conclusions

It has long been held as an axiomatic truth that Chile has an almost absolute separate entity approach when treating group taxation. This stems from a long tradition of adopting a formalistic view of transactions and a strong protection of the corporate veil, not only in tax law, but also in various other areas of the legal and economic life of businesses.

While on the surface this has been – and continues to be – generally true, as there is no group tax regime as such, it is far from absolute and has been eroded over time by various changes in tax law. Overall, these changes have generally sought to bring Chile closer to the more prevalent opinions held in various international forums on taxation (including the OECD, which Chile joined 10 years ago). It is also interesting to note that if one observes the evolution of the law, while there has been a trend toward adopting a more group-focused approach, recently Chile took a large step in the opposite direction by eliminating a form of consolidation which allowed relief for losses within a group.

On the other hand, Chile has also extended the scope or introduced certain other rules, in which the existence of a group or relationships with related parties is relevant. Most of these rules are not focused on the taxation of the group as a whole in a domestic context, but rather on preventing avoidance at the level of each taxpayer within the group.

While there are no group taxation regimes as such, we can summarize the main features of the Chilean system, as pertains to domestic taxation, as follows:

a. Taxes paid by companies are usable by the shareholders, in general when dividends are paid to the shareholders, which points in the direction of group tax relief. However, if the shareholder is a company in a loss position, the law recently forbade them to recover taxes paid by the distributing entity, which points in the opposite direction.

b. Capital gains (and intercompany transactions more generally) within a group are treated as normal taxable transactions. There are certain preferential treatments for individuals, which are unavailable if they transact with related entities.

c. The tax authority is allowed to assess the prices used in transactions which are the basis for taxation, which is done at the individual level, when these are notoriously inferior to market values. Curiously, the assessment does not result in a readjustment of the taxable base for CIT taxpayers, but rather in a 40% penalty tax.

d. There are reorg provisions which allow for tax-free mergers and spin offs, but contributions are taxable events, which can exceptionally be conducted at zero gain.

e. For the first time in 2020, tax law included a general definition of business groups and related parties, which mostly draws upon established commercial law. For the most part,

[1] Lawyer specializing in the tax aspects of cross-border transactions, partner of EY, and member of its International Tax and Transaction Services practice.
The author wishes to acknowledge and thank the fundamental review of this article made by Juan Pablo Navarrete, as well as the kind contributions made by Jorge Angarita to the transfer pricing sections.

each provision which refers to this definition adds some special feature or additional part to the definition, which limits its usefulness.

f. Chilean law includes change of control rules, which seek to limit the trading of shell companies for the purpose of using tax losses these companies may contain.

g. The definition of being part of a group is also relevant to access special tax regimes (SMEs, presumptive income systems, etc.), so economic groups cannot access preferential tax treatments not aimed at them as a matter of policy.

h. There are also certain anti-avoidance rules aimed at preventing the use of favorable tax rules within an economic group, such as the deduction of ageing debt, the purchase of debt at a discount, use of business assets or loans, or payment of environmental or sustainability fees, for which the law provides stricter requirements or subjects to penalties.

i. While audit activity in general is still directed at individual taxpayers, from a compliance perspective the local tax authority has been requesting more detailed information regarding economic groups and transactions within them. Sworn statement 1913 is the most relevant example of this.

From an international tax perspective, the following aspects are relevant:

a. Non-residents are taxed in Chile on a cash basis for their Chilean source income, generally – in this context, this means that only income arising from activities performed in Chile or assets located in Chile is taxable. There are a few exceptions, such as fees paid from Chile or the indirect disposal of Chilean assets. Normally non-residents are taxed at a fixed rate based on the gross remittance made from Chile.

b. Foreign source income received by Chilean residents is taxed on a cash basis, except when the source of the foreign income is a PE or branch, or a CFC entity.

c. Inbound PEs are treated, generally, as separate taxpayers from their head office, and are subjected to corporate tax on the basis of net profits from activities attributable to them, treated as an entirely separate enterprise from their head office. There is then no branch profits tax, but rather the distribution abroad of local profit is treated as a dividend and taxed accordingly. The local tax authority has held that in certain cases, where there are PEs created under treaty rules which are not PEs under local rules, the foreign taxpayers can be subjected to tax on a gross basis.

d. Outbound PEs are treated as an extension of the local head office, and their results (losses or profits) are recognized in the Chilean company on an accrued basis.

e. Income from foreign subsidiaries is fully taxable, but the local taxpayer is allowed to claim credit for taxes paid abroad, both for corporate tax and dividend tax levied by the source country.

f. Chilean CFC rules are aimed at preventing the deferral of tax on passive income, or certain forms of base erosive payments, from foreign controlled entities. The threshold of control is 50% or more of the shares.

g. Payments made abroad to foreign related entities are controlled mostly through OECD standard transfer pricing – CbC reporting has been enacted, requiring the submission of a local file and master file. Other certain anti-abuse provisions exist, such as limitations on the deduction of related party payments, and thin cap provisions that limit certain advantageous treatments of intercompany debt.

Summary and conclusions

In Chinese Taipei, corporations are taxpayers but partnerships are transparent for tax purposes. On 18 January 2018, Chinese Taipei adopted a new system under which differences exist between individual shareholders and corporate shareholders. Corporate shareholders that are incorporated in Chinese Taipei are tax exempt when receiving dividends paid by other profit-seeking enterprises either incorporated in Chinese Taipei or resident in Chinese Taipei for tax purposes. The exemption does not require a special threshold.

Corporate shareholders that are neither incorporated in Chinese Taipei nor resident in Chinese Taipei for tax purposes, when receiving dividends from profit-seeking enterprises either incorporated in Chinese Taipei or resident in Chinese Taipei for tax purposes, have to pay taxes in the amount of 21% of the dividends. The profit-seeking enterprises paying dividends are responsible for withholding taxes and remitting the amount to the Chinese Taipei government.

In contrast, individual taxpayers (individual recipients of dividend income) are legally obligated to choose between two options. The first option is to include dividend income in the taxpayers' annual taxable income, and then subtract 8.5% of the dividend income. The ceiling of the amount subtracted is NT$ 80,000. The other option is to pay taxes on the dividend income at the rate of 28% separately from other types of income.

Inter-company capital gains and losses have to be realized for the capital gains and losses to be recognized for tax purposes. Article 99 of the Regulations on Auditing Profit-Seeking Enterprises states that the impairment of shares in the invested enterprise is the precondition for the investing enterprise to recognize investment losses for tax purposes. The interest expenses incurred by intra-group loans are subject to thin capitalization rules. Domestic transactions between independent tax entities in Chinese Taipei are also subject to transfer pricing rules. In other words, the arm's length principle applies not only to foreign related transactions, but also to domestic transactions.

In Chinese Taipei, a group taxation system is provided for in article 45 of the Enterprise Mergers and Acquisitions Act. Article 45 provides that a corporation that holds 90% or more of the number of shares, or of the amount of registered capital, of another corporation may, after holding such percentage for 12 months in a fiscal year, elect to file consolidated tax returns on behalf of both the corporation itself and the controlled corporation for both corporate income tax and the income tax on undistributed profits. The election to file consolidated tax returns includes all subsidiaries for which the electing corporation holds 90% or more of the number of shares or of the amount of registered capital. The election to file consolidated tax returns does not require the government's advance approval, but,

[1]   Assistant Professor, Department of Public Finance and Department of Law, National Chengchi University, Taipei. Any views expressed in this report are the reporter's personal views.

once made, the election can be changed only during the last two months of a fiscal year for legitimate reasons and with the approval of the tax authorities.

Therefore, the aforementioned article 45 sets out the requirements to enter into a group for tax purposes. Only corporations that satisfy the statutory requirements can be part of the tax group. Partnerships and other transparent entities do not qualify for the group taxation system. Entities of a group are still considered taxpayers for purposes other than corporate income tax and the income tax on undistributed profits. Intra-group transactions still exist as a matter of contract law. Financial accounting is not itself the basis for taxation. Income is not allocated within a tax group; the group as a whole is taxed by the Chinese Taipei government. Chinese Taipei's group taxation system allows for a full consolidation of profits and losses. The controlling corporation is liable for the taxes of the whole tax group.

Article 14-3 of the Income Tax Act authorizes a tax authority to adjust the tax obligations of a taxpayer, with the approval of the Ministry of Finance, when that taxpayer—whether acting alone or with the help of any other office, organization, or individual—improperly, through sham arrangements, avoids or decreases the amount of its tax obligations.

All those who derive income from Chinese Taipei have to pay taxes on such income (article 8 of the Income Tax Act). Additionally, domestic (resident) corporate taxpayers have to pay taxes to the government of Chinese Taipei on their worldwide income. Profits earned by foreign branches are taxable in Chinese Taipei. Losses made by foreign branches may lower the tax obligations due in Chinese Taipei. The branches that foreign enterprises have in Chinese Taipei are required by its law to maintain separate accounting and pay taxes. Generally, the transactions between a head office and its branch are characterized in Chinese Taipei as ordinary business transactions, rather than tax-exempt dealings. Withholding taxes are therefore due on such transactions. Chinese Taipei does not impose a "branch profit tax."

An exception to the separate entity approach is the option of "sharing management expenses." The option may be chosen by a taxpayer only when the statutory requirements are met. Once chosen, the taxpayer's "management expenses" are apportioned in accordance with the sales revenue of all sales departments and branches, or, in special circumstances, in accordance with a formula approved by Chinese Taipei's tax authority. The sharing of management expenses is not subject to the withholding of income taxes due in Chinese Taipei. Specifically, the branches that foreign corporations have in Chinese Taipei may, when filing their income tax returns, list parts of the management expenses that are incurred by the head office or regional head office, if both of the following two conditions are met: (1) the head office or regional head office itself does not make sales and has a separate sales department, and its sales department lists and shares the management expenses along with its branches elsewhere; (2) the management expenses that are incurred by the head office or regional head office do not include the costs of goods bought, and interest expenses do not accrue for the working capital provided by the head office or regional head office to the branches.

Branch reporters
Juan David Velasco Kerguelen[1]
Andrés González Becerra[2]

Summary and conclusions

The Colombian tax system follows the traditional separate entity approach under which entities are taxed pursuant their individual financial information. Companies and branches located within the country are taxed on their worldwide income whether they belong to a group or not. Taxation of branches of foreign head offices follows the attribution system under the authorized OECD approach considering functions, risks, assets and personnel involved in the activity of the branch.

Group and control situations are relevant for accounting and tax purposes for the application of special provisions. Criteria for determining whether there is a group or control varies in each regime. For accounting purposes, a group of companies is required to present consolidated financial statements whenever any entity exercises control over the other companies. The existence of control under IFRS 10 depends on contractual, operational, administrative and management elements. On the other hand, Colombian tax law contemplates control as a relevant element when applying controlled foreign company rules, country-by-country reporting, and as one of the criteria to determine whether two parties are related for transfer pricing purposes, and application of thin-capitalization rules.

Although tax legislation sets forth the conditions under which a permanent establishment is triggered for tax purposes, corporate legislation requires the incorporation of a subsidiary or a branch to carry out permanent activities in Colombia. Under such approach, as a general rule, companies are considered opaque entities which is coherent with the corporate legislation applicable to companies. However, certain vehicles can be identified as transparent for tax purposes, for instance, trusts and collective investment vehicles, which are deemed transparent for tax purposes, resulting in the obligation for investors to consolidate the corresponding income, costs, and expenses.

The only benefit the tax regime offers for groups of companies is from a dividends tax perspective; dividends distribution between local groups of companies are not subject to dividends tax.

---

[1] President of IFA Colombia and Vice-Chair IFA Central YIN Committee. International Tax Lawyer. J.D, with excellence in honor thesis and LL.M. in Colombian Tax Law, Universidad de los Andes (Colombia). LLM in Taxation. Boston University School of Law (USA). LLM in International Law, The Fletcher School of Law and Diplomacy at Tufts University (USA) and Executive MBA (c), University of Oxford, Exeter College (UK).

[2] Vice-President IFA Colombia. Partner at DLA Piper Martinez Beltrán (Colombia). LLM, International Taxation, Leiden University (The Netherlands) Academic Excellence Award. J.D., Universidad de los Andes (Colombia). Tax Law Specialization, Universidad del Rosario (Colombia). International and European Communitarian Law, Université Robert Schuman.

The separate entity taxation approach is also present in Colombia's taxation rules for cross-border transactions. Thus, this approach can be found in the taxation of both inbound and outbound transactions.

Inbound transactions are taxed on their Colombian source income, and taxation can either be levied through a withholding mechanism, in which case the tax rate will apply depending on the type of income received by the foreign entity, or by filing a tax return under the ordinary income assessment and applying the ordinary income tax rate. If the foreign entity carries out activities through a subsidiary, the subsidiary will be taxed on its worldwide income and any repatriation of resources can potentially be subject to Colombian tax. If, the activities are carried out through a branch, following said separate entity taxation approach, it will be treated for tax purposes as an independent entity from its home office, and in such it must assess its tax based on the worldwide income attributable to it. Moreover, profits transferred from branches to their home office are treated as dividends distribution unless the home office is located in a tax treaty country.

Regarding outbound transactions, Colombian residents are taxed on their worldwide income, and in so Colombian tax law offers a foreign tax credit for taxes paid abroad regarding said foreign source income if all requirements are met, or potentially tax treaty benefits could also apply if income is sourced in a tax treaty jurisdiction. To mitigate potential base erosion or profit shifting situations that could result from outbound transactions, Colombia enacted in 2016 a CFC regime adopting OECD guidelines. This regime is a step taken away from separate entity approach, by including all passive income in the Colombian controlling entity tax assessment. However, there is still no indication of Colombia's intention to extend this regime to other types of income.

As for the transfer pricing scenario, the arm's length principle and separate entity approach are still the observed guidelines to avoid base erosion and profit shifting in transactions between foreign related parties. Locally, there have not been discussions of modifying profit allocation rules as suggested in Pillar 1 and Pillar 2; however, the possibility cannot be fully discarded as Colombia is a country where on average there is a tax reform every two years, and the government is actively participating in the Inclusive Framework on BEPS.

Branch reporter
Viktor Šmejkal[1]

Summary and conclusions

The general rule of domestic tax law is the taxation of each individual corporation.[2] Separate entities are in domestic law defined for tax purposes expressly by special legal provisions.

European Commercial law reflects the phenomenon of the group business by requiring companies to prepare consolidated group accounts as well as stand-alone financial statements imposed by national rules. The corporate individual taxation stays the final objective of the domestic tax law.

A taxable entity is an entity that is designated as a taxable entity by the law, as well as an entity that is designated by the law as a payer or taxpayer.[3]

Taxpayers of corporate income tax are defined by a list. The following are payers: a) a legal entity, b) an organisational component of the state, c) a unit trust in accordance with the act governing investment companies and investment funds, d) a sub-fund of a joint stock company with variable registered capital in accordance with the act governing investment companies and investment funds, e) a pension company fund, which is understood for the purpose of this act as a fund managed by a pension company in accordance with the act governing supplementary pension insurance, f) a trust fund in accordance with the Civil Code, g) a unit that is a payer according to the legal order of the state according to which it was founded or established, h) a fund administered by the Financial Market Guarantee System in accordance with the act governing recovery procedures and crisis resolution on the financial market.[4]

A taxable person becomes a value added taxpayer within the meaning of European law and, in the case of a registered office in the Czech Republic, by exceeding the set turnover or at the moment of effects of tax registration. Natural persons are personal income taxpayers.

The principle is the separate taxation of a payer's income. The tax base of a specific payer is the difference by which the payer's income that is subject to tax exceeds the payer's tax-deductible expenses (costs), while respecting the accrual principle for income and expenses in the relevant fiscal year.

---

[1] Member of the Editorial Board of the journal Dane, a finance (Tax and finances) and member of the Board of IFA Czech Republic; tax lawyer working in the field of private consultancy services for ten years. Prior to that, employed at the Ministry of Finance (CZ).

[2] General evaluation is that any "group taxation is not possible". In SKALICKÁ, H.: Harmonizace zdaňování korporací v EU. Disertační práce. Brno: Vysoké učení technické v Brně, Fakulta podnikatelská, 2008, s. 42.

[3] S. 20 of Act No. 280/2009 Coll., the Tax Code.

[4] S. 17 of Act No. 586/1992 Coll., the Income Taxes Act.

Branch reporters
Katja Dyppel Weber[1]
Michael Tell[2]

Summary and conclusions

The flavor of the Danish tax system is a separate entity approach. As a result, the liability to pay taxes follows other liabilities of the entity, i.e. limited liability companies are considered separate and legal entities for tax purposes. For companies subject to group taxation, the corporate veil is however pierced in regard to liability of paid taxes, including withholding taxes. The purpose of this joint liability of taxes is to ensure an easier administration (the administration company is a "one-stop-shop" for the tax authorities and the other companies subject to group taxation) and to prevent abuse, e.g. by making foreign payments without withholding any taxes followed by liquidation. Besides this, no tendency to (further) pierce the veil of corporations from an overall tax policy perspective seems to exist.

The Danish tax system is based on the separate entity approach and, as such, the Danish rules on transfer pricing apply to all transactions between dependent parties, i.e. also transactions between domestic companies subject to mandatory joint taxation. In addition, the Danish domestic rules on income allocation to foreign and domestic permanent establishments are based on the AOA, where allocation is based on hypothesizing the PE as a separate and independent enterprise.

Under Danish tax law it is however recognized that controlled companies may have different incentives (and planning opportunities) than independent companies. Therefore, most anti-avoidance rules are only applicable for controlled companies, e.g. transfer pricing, CFC legislation, and thin capitalization. In addition, thresholds for being subject to tax benefits or restrictions are applied on a group basis, such thresholds being company size, revenue, asset base, EBITDA, losses etc. The purpose is to ensure that it is not possible to split up entities in order to obtain a tax benefit or avoid being subject to a restriction.

[1]   PhD, Partner at CORIT Advisory.
[2]   PhD, Associate Partner at CORIT Advisory and Associate Professor at Copenhagen Business School.

Summary and conclusions

The Finnish tax system is based on the separate entity approach. Domestic and foreign corporate entities are widely treated as separate corporate entities for tax purposes even though they would not be legal entities or subject to tax treaty benefits. Economic double taxation is eliminated in many group situations by exempting dividend distributions and capital gains from income tax under an applicable income tax treaty or domestic legislation that follows the EU Parent-Subsidiary Directive.

The priority of the separate entity approach is confirmed in preparatory works of the Act on Group Contribution which state that a company is taxed separately irrespective of whether it belongs to a group of companies under the Limited Liability Companies Act. Moreover, the case law confirms the priority of the separate entity approach over the group perspective. In case KHO 2009:70, the Supreme Administrative Court of Finland stated that the Finnish tax system is based on the separate entity approach also in group situations, and therefore profits and expenses must be allocated properly to the right taxpayer.

As an exception to the separate entity approach, since 1987 Finland has applied a group contribution system that allows profit and loss balancing between Finnish entities belonging to the same group of companies. The group contribution is a tax-deductible expense for the paying company and taxable income for the receiving company if the requirements of the Act on Group Contribution are met. The purpose of the group contribution system is to remove tax disadvantages inherent in the structure of a group of companies, when companies are taxed as separate entities, by allowing an offset of tax losses against taxable profits within a group that comprises both profit-making and loss-making companies.

The Finnish group contribution system, enacted before Finland became an EU member state in 1995, was initially applied only to domestic companies owned by another domestic company. However, in case law the scope has been extended to Finnish subsidiaries owned by a foreign parent company and Finnish permanent establishments of foreign companies due to the provisions of EU law and income tax treaties. The compliance of the group contribution system with EU law was tested in case C-231/05 Oy AA, where the Court of Justice of the European Union ruled that the freedom of establishment provided by EU law does not preclude a system instituted by legislation of a member state whereby a subsidiary resident in that member state may not deduct an intra-group financial transfer which it makes in favor of its parent company from its taxable income unless that parent company has its establishment in that same member state.

Even though the scope of the group contribution system has been extended in case law, the tax legislator has remained rather reluctant to amend the wording of the provisions. However, in October 2019 the Ministry of Finance set up a working group inter alia to

[1] Senior tax adviser at Finland Chamber of Commerce. She holds a MSc (economics and business administration) degree from Helsinki School of Economics (2008) and a LLB degree from University of Helsinki (2020).

examine the reform of the group taxation system in order to eliminate the problems found in the system.

In addition, the Finnish parliament enacted a new statute on a group deduction in order to comply with the requirements set by the European Commission in its reasoned opinion. The group deduction system is applicable as from 1 January 2021 and concerns Finnish parent companies whose subsidiaries have incurred final losses within the EU/EEA as defined in the case law of the Court of Justice of the European Union. The amount of final losses incurred by the foreign subsidiary comprises a tax-deductible group deduction for the Finnish parent company in the tax year when the loss-making subsidiary is liquidated up to the amount of taxable income of the parent company for the tax year the group deduction is made.

EU law has increased the impact of the group perspective in Finnish tax legislation also in the field of preventing tax base erosion and profit shifting. For example, the applicability of the interest deduction limitation rules and hybrid mismatch rules deriving from the EU Anti-Tax Avoidance Directive depends largely on whether a corporate entity is a standalone entity or consolidated to a group of companies for accounting purposes. Traditionally, Finnish tax legislation has not made a distinction between standalone entities and entities belonging to a group, and the definition of a group in the tax legislation has been independent from the concept of group for accounting purposes.

Both international and domestic intra-group transactions must be in line with the arm's length principle. Transfer pricing may be adjusted even between group companies that qualify for a tax-deductible group contribution. The arm's length principle is interpreted in line with the OECD TP Guidelines within the limits of the wording of the domestic provision. Case law concerning transfer pricing has been based on the separate entity approach. Some recent changes in the OECD TP Guidelines have increased the weight of the group view in the interpretation of the arm's length principle.

In the future, development of international taxation of the digital economy may shift the foundation of Finnish tax legislation further toward the group approach. Although Finland has not introduced a digital services tax and was hesitant to accept the Commission's proposal on digital services tax in 2016, Finland joined the OECD Statement on a Two–Pillar Solution to Address the Tax Challenges Arising from the Digitalisation of the Economy in 2021. According to the program of Prime Minister Sanna Marin's government for 2019, Finland must participate in ending harmful competition over tax bases with a commitment to common and fair rules within the framework of the OECD, the UN and the European Union, and play an active role in international cooperation for confirming the taxation of platform and digital economy businesses.

Branch reporter
Nicolas Vergnet[1]

Summary and conclusions

The current taxation of corporations in France constitutes an inheritance from a tax system based on the addition of several schedular taxes. Whereas taxation was originally levied on particular kind of income like "business income" or "income from securities", the creation of the corporate income tax at the end of the Second World War made it possible to evolve toward a stronger focus on the legal personality of taxpayers and their effective ability to pay for the purpose of asserting taxation. French corporate taxation therefore adopted the separate entity approach and the arm's length principle, the latter being now the keystone of income allocation within groups of companies, but also between independent entities through the notion of abnormal act of management.

French law has never fully recognized the existence of the "group of companies" as a monolithic concept. The French commercial code provides many definitions of what constitutes a "group of companies" through different criteria identifying the "control" exercised by companies over each other. For instance, the regulation of self-control is based on a strong legal approach focusing on the holding of capital or voting rights in board meetings whereas the accounting consolidation regulation adopts a more economic approach focusing on the effective influence that companies exert over each other. In spite of this, it would be erroneous to assert that French tax law is does not recognize the existence of "groups of companies".

First of all, France implemented a tax consolidation regime in the 80s precisely to enable French groups of companies to be competitive vis-à-vis foreign groups of companies by consolidating the profits and losses generated by all the members of the same group. The French tax consolidation regime, however, does not completely deny the existence of the different members of a tax-consolidated group. Each member of a tax-consolidated group has to file its own tax returns and is subject to tax audit as a separate entity. In addition, transactions performed between members of a tax-consolidated group have to be in line with the interest of each of these members, thus prohibiting a free allocation of income within the group.

Secondly, it has been a long time since France adopted anti-abuse measures to take into account the specific conditions governing relations between related entities. Intra-group transactions are therefore subject to several constraints. For instance, the tax authorities are exempted from having to prove the deliberate nature of an abnormal act of management in cases in which the act takes the form of an advantage granted by a company to another with whom it is in a relationship of interest. The same applies to intra-group financial transactions which are subject to several limitations. As an example, the tax deductibility of intra-group financial expenses incurred by French corporate taxpayers is in principle capped to a rate set by tax regulations, unless the group can provide evidence that the interest rate

---

[1]   Assistant Professor at University of Paris II, Panthéon-Assas.

effectively applied matches the rate that would have been obtained from an independent financial institution or entity in similar circumstances. In this respect, even if it can hardly be doubted that the rate a taxpayer can obtain from an independent lender is influenced by the fact that this taxpayer is a member of a group of companies (e.g., independent lenders obviously take into account the implicit support of the group), French case law rules that the arm's length rate can only be assessed based on the borrowing company's own situation, by disregarding the fact that it belonged to a group.

Thus, in most situations where French tax law takes into account the fact that companies are related, it is only to ensure that the transactions between them do not deviate from those that would exist between independent entities. The separate entities approach is therefore particularly relevant.

When it comes to multinational groups and the tax treatment of cross-border situations, we observe that French tax law provides for a territorial-based system of taxation. As a consequence, both French and foreign companies are solely taxable on their active income from French sources. French companies cannot include in their taxable income the profits and losses incurred by their foreign branches and subsidiaries while foreign companies are only taxable in France if a nexus between their income and the French jurisdiction can be identified. In other words, and as a principle, French tax law only focuses on the existence of business conducted in France to subject foreign companies to corporate income tax. However, this territorial system of taxation is subject to certain exceptions, notably because earnings from any source can be taxed in France when they are attributed for taxation to France by a double tax treaty. In any case, the taxation of a foreign entity is essentially grounded on objective criteria (the taxation of a "business conducted in France") and does not really take the legal personality into account. Despite this objective criteria, the taxation of foreign companies operating in France is still based on a separate entity approach; even if the AOA has not been implemented with regard to foreign or domestic branches and the head office, French case law recognizes to some extent that a foreign branch can be considered as having fiscal personality distinct from the head office and be treated as such for tax purposes, even if branches are not entitled to DTT benefits in their own right on the grounds that they do not have a legal personality distinct from the head office.

The evolution of international taxation toward an increased consideration for the group approach is perceptible in many of the reforms recently adopted by the French tax legislator. Several anti-abuse measures have been introduced over the past several years to ensure that the existence of the group cannot be used to erode the tax base. However, French law is still firmly attached to an approach based on the individual interest of each member of a group: challenging this particularity in the future would undoubtedly constitute a revolution in French tax law.

Summary and conclusions

Since its first practically relevant introduction in 1891 in Prussia, one of the main principles of German corporate income tax has been the separate entity approach. In principle and in contrast to the transparent taxation of partnerships, entities subject to corporate income tax are taxed according to their derived income on a stand-alone basis, i.e., irrespective of the tax regime applicable to their shareholders or other members and their other characteristics as well as other (economic) affiliations to other persons. Thus, transactions between corporations and their members are – except for cases of a violation of the arm's length principle – recognised for tax purposes.

Even the group taxation regime, the *Organschaft*, is widely based on a separate entity approach. In contrast to commercial law, the *Organschaft* does not implement the concept of full consolidation, but is rather confined to an attribution of profits and losses. The taxable income of the parent company is assessed by including the income of the subsidiary – independently assessed at the level of the subsidiary – with the effect that the income is taxed according to the (income or corporate income) tax regime applicable to the parent company. Being confined to the attribution of income, the *Organschaft* has no effect on the status of either the parent or the subsidiary company as tax subjects. As a consequence, both companies have to independently fulfil the tax accounting obligations and file independent tax returns. However, the overall principle of separate tax subjects is derogated to a certain extent as regards the determination of the income of the subsidiary. In particular, the tax exemptions for dividends and capital gains from shares for corporate shareholders are not applicable at the level of the subsidiary. Instead, depending on the tax status of the parent company, such income is subject to the respective relief mechanism applicable at the level of the parent company.

In addition, there are numerous other – more or less comprehensive – deviations from the separate entity approach. Especially, the general change of control rule according to which the carry-forward of losses incurred by a body corporate is no longer deductible in its entirety if more than 50% of the shares (or similar membership rights) are transferred to a single acquirer or to persons affiliated to this acquirer also applies to non-deductible interest expenses. The shareholders of a body corporate and its affiliations to other entities are also taken into account for purposes of the general interest stripping rule. Subject to certain exceptions, the general restriction of the deductibility of interest does not apply if the business does not belong to a consolidated group, or does so only proportionally. But even if the business belongs to a consolidated group, there is an escape clause. The interest stripping rule is not applicable if the equity percentage of the business is equal to or greater than that of the consolidated group (equity percentage comparison).

In principle, the tax regime applicable to international transactions is also based in

---

[1]   Judge at the tax court of Rhineland-Palatinate, Neustadt an der Weinstraße.

the principle of separate entity taxation. Thus, transactions between the head office and branches not being organised as a separate legal entity are not recognised for domestic tax purposes. However, the transfer pricing rules are also applicable to domestic head offices and foreign permanent establishments. As a result, for profit allocation purposes, permanent establishments are – in line with the so-called Authorised OECD Approach – treated as if they were separate legal entities. Concerning the Germany treaty network, neither domestic branches of foreign entities nor branches situated in the other contracting states are entitled to treaty benefits. However, regarding the jurisprudence of the *Bundesfinanzhof* and of regional tax courts, it is yet unclear if this holds true taking into account the German treaty practice regarding non-discrimination clauses similar to article 24 paragraph 3 OECD-MC. Concerning the CFC regime, the fact that the foreign company is a separate legal entity is not fully ignored. Its low-taxed passive income is not attributed to the shareholder as such. Rather, a deemed dividend approach applies: The passive income is deemed income from dividends having been received immediately after the close of the foreign company's relevant fiscal year.

Analysing the scope of these deviations from the traditional separate entity approach both in a purely domestic and an international context, the conventional concept of taxing each corporation on a stand-alone basis – characterising German corporate income tax from its very beginning – has become more and more blurred. The fact that an entity subject to corporate income tax belongs to a corporate group or has a controlling shareholder is taken into account by numerous sets of rules. Nevertheless, German tax law seems to diverge from the concept of separate entity taxation only to the extent necessary. This especially holds true for the group taxation regime and the CFC legislation both not being based on a full consolidation, but rather on an attribution of profits and losses as well as a deemed distribution approach. Consistent with this reluctance to challenge the separate entity approach, the German legislator will most likely refrain from autonomously triggering potential future developments in the taxation of groups of companies. Rather, in this field, German tax law seems to merely react to impulses from the EU and OECD.

Branch reporter
Stefano Mariani[1]

Summary and conclusions

Hong Kong has a conservative approach to tax policy and legislation. As a jurisdiction, it is distinct in a global context for having retained a territorial basis for taxation and for not taxing capital gains. As a broad rule, only Hong Kong source profits are taxable in Hong Kong, irrespective of the jurisdiction of residence of the taxpayer. Hong Kong revenue law is essentially based on early 20th century common law models of taxation and favours a strict, separate-entity basis for taxation. Thus, Hong Kong does not have any group taxation regimes: there is no taxation or loss utilisation on a group basis, and, save for express transfer pricing provisions, Hong Kong tax law is broadly indifferent to group behaviours. Profits are assessed, deductions are claimed, and losses are utilised exclusively on an entity-by-entity basis. That approach was recently reaffirmed by the Court of Final Appeal in CIR v Perfekta Enterprises Ltd.

Nevertheless, there are, at a conceptual level, marked synergies between the principles underpinning BEPS Action Points 8–10 and the juristic notion and application of the territorial principle of taxation in Hong Kong. Jurisprudence in particular suggests that the territorial principle seeks by its very nature to align economic activity and value creation with taxing outcomes.

As Hong Kong does not have any discrete group taxation regimes, and the government and legislature have expressed no interest in changing that state of affairs despite increasing pressure from stakeholders to introduce a group loss regime, it is likely that Hong Kong will continue to conceive of both domestic and international tax essentially on a separate-entity basis. Further, by virtue of the territorial principle of taxation, Hong Kong tax law is in general indifferent to the fiscal position of non-resident entities that do not have a taxable presence in Hong Kong. There are, therefore, no CFC rules in Hong Kong and, in general, profits and gains sourced from outside of Hong Kong are wholly tax neutral, even where they arise to a company that is Hong Kong resident.

Whereas the government of Hong Kong is nominally committed to participating in the BEPS project and so in applying both Pillar 1 and Pillar 2, the peculiarities of Hong Kong's tax system militate against the implementation of certain constituent principles thereof. For example, the tax treatment of intangibles assumes a different, reduced dimension when, generally speaking, gains arising from its disposal are not taxable, and there is no discrete amortisation capital allowance regime.

---

[1]   MA (Oxon), MSc (LSE); head of the tax and trusts practice of Deacons, Hong Kong. He was called to the Bar of England and Wales and is admitted as a solicitor in Hong Kong. He is a member of the Executive Committee of the Hong Kong Branch of IFA.

Branch reporters
Borbála Kolozs[1]
Annamária Kőszegi[2]

Summary and conclusions

Group taxation in the field of corporate income taxation is a relatively new phenomenon in Hungary, as it was introduced in 2018. Earlier the concept of group taxation was recognized in the area of VAT only. As many European countries already have group taxation regimes for corporate income tax purposes, the idea was welcomed by taxpayers and the state budget as well.

The advantages of group taxation (for example, lighter administrative burden, more possibilities to use intra-group tax advantages) are well represented in the Hungarian corporate income tax provisions, too. Countries with a group taxation regime are also more competitive.

Companies may form a tax group with at least two members. The corporate income tax law provides a list of taxpayers that are eligible to create a tax group. These include companies, associations, European companies limited by shares, cooperatives, European cooperatives, incorporated entities of private individuals, foreign persons that have their place of management in Hungary and Hungarian permanent establishment of foreign companies. Partnerships may also be part of a tax group since they are considered as corporate taxpayers and not considered as transparent entities. Eligible companies must submit a request to the tax authorities to form a group but it is also possible for a company to join a group that has already been established. The rules require that members should meet the following conditions:

- Related party relationship between the members where there is at least 75% voting rights as detailed below;
- Members should apply the same tax year;
- Members should prepare their financial statements based on the same accounting rules, i.e., either HAS or IFRS.

Groups may benefit from the overall calculation of the tax base and also enjoy various deductions in the form of tax credits. There has not been any study or research published on the effect of the newly introduced group taxation regime in Hungary but, so far, the rules provided by the regime look promising and economically advantageous.

[1]   Researcher, Budapest, Hungary.
[2]   Director, Deloitte Ltd., Budapest, Hungary.

Branch reporter
P V Srinivasan[1]

Summary and conclusions

Bilateral tax treaties based on Model Conventions, which represent the international tax law, have adopted the separate entity approach. Accordingly, intra-group transactions also trigger taxable income, profits, and losses for the group members. Further, the tax treaties operate on the arm's length standard, acknowledging the fact that associated enterprises are not subject to normal negotiations which would exist between independent parties. The absence of a robust transfer pricing methodology would result in base erosion and profit shifting. That transfer pricing methodologies have remained inadequate is also a concern which is sought to be addressed by Actions 8-10 of the OECD BEPS Project wherein value addition has been emphasized. The separate entity approach also requires several anti-avoidance provisions which find place in the domestic tax laws. The residential status of a corporation determined by considering the place of effective management, is aimed at removing the concerns of residential status based on mere incorporation. The controlled foreign company regulations are intended to curb the practice of deferring income. In a web of companies which develop intangibles together, it is complex to determine the beneficial ownership of royalties and fees for technical services, which are qualifying conditions for higher treaty relief. Countries have also introduced general anti-avoidance regulations to act as a deterrent against transactions without substance. The single entity approach is therefore inherently complex.

Many countries have domestic tax laws based on the group approach following the concept of economic unity. However, not many countries have the concept of a worldwide group. This is possibly because the bilateral tax treaties follow the single entity approach and therefore the alignment of the two approaches requires extant rules. Firstly, treating a country group i.e. domestic group, i.e., a group comprising only resident companies, as a separate taxable unit would pose no difficulty in preserving the arm's length standard of the bilateral tax treaties regarding transactions with non-resident associated enterprises. Secondly, in a country group, it becomes feasible to adopt the group approach under the domestic tax law and still align to the single entity approach in bilateral tax treaties. Thirdly, it will be possible to allow relief by way of foreign tax credit by incorporating suitable provisions in the domestic tax law, dealing with group taxation.

In recent times, there has been a convergence towards the group approach even in international taxation. The country-by-country report is a beginning under the exchange of information protocol. Tax administration of each jurisdiction will have information such as revenue, profit, employees, assets, and tax paid on a country basis. Though the information

---

[1] The author advises large multinational corporates on tax, corporate law matters, and cross-border restructuring. This report discusses the customary separate entity approach in the international tax law and the progressive group approach under the domestic tax laws of countries and as to why the international tax regime must align to the group approach and evolve a framework for fractional apportionment of group profits. The report also discusses the recent developments depicting a gradual shift towards the same.

is for risk assessment, it could lead to having the basis for fractional apportionment of global profits of a group. The Multilateral Convention formulated under article 15 of the OECD BEPS Program includes anti-fragmentation rules in the context of a permanent establishment. Here again, it becomes onerous to avoid the creation of permanent establishment since the rules encompass the activities of closely related enterprises.

A system of group taxation of a worldwide group has many attributes of a sound tax policy. Group taxation allows the tax administration to monitor and assess fewer corporate groups and not focus on base erosion practices of MNEs using pricing in international transactions. The anti-avoidance provisions such as POEM, CFC, transfer pricing, interest deduction limitation, etc. will be academic. Even general anti-avoidance regulations will have a much narrower scope. It only means that a corporate group will be assessed to tax on its global profits in the country in which the parent corporation is resident. All other countries will be entitled to a share of profits based on formulary apportionment. The country in which the parent entity is resident will either not tax the profits which are allocated to other countries or give a credit of the taxes paid in those countries. This is the system of taxation which imparts greater efficiency, transparency, and accountability. Much of the dispute resolution efforts under the Mutual Agreement Procedure will become unnecessary. The businesses will be neutral to the form in which they are organized. Branches and subsidiaries will lose the distinction for tax purposes. It only calls for an international taxation framework that will recognize these benefits.

In fact, very minimal changes will be required in the bilateral treaties. The definition of the term 'person' in article 3(2) of the Model Convention may be expanded to include a group of companies. Article 9 dealing with associated enterprises and transfer pricing will be recast only to ensure that substance is not given a go by altogether. With these changes, the bilateral tax treaties will align to the monism school of thought, which assumes that international law and domestic law are nothing but two components of a single tax system or a body of knowledge.

Branch reporter
Stefano Grilli[1]

Summary and conclusions

The Italian tax system is fairly complex (also) with respect to the approach to the taxation of groups of companies.

The group approach is applied only in a limited number of circumstances and always on an elective basis. In addition, the election for group taxation regimes does not have a permanent effect and it is based on a twofold relationship between consolidating and consolidated companies (in other words, the election may be separately made by the consolidating company together with each consolidated company); it needs to be repeated from time to time and there are several events (mostly corporate restructuring transactions) that trigger the end of such a regime.

Companies that have applied for such a regime are allowed to transfer within the group tax features (such as tax losses, excess passive interest or excess interest capacity and tax deduction for ACE)[2] that would otherwise remain permanently attached to them.

The allocation of tax attributes within the tax group raises several compliance issues, especially when a company enters or exits the regime. Finally, the tax consolidation regime does not actually create a new independent taxpayer (i.e., the group itself) but just allows for the circulation of certain tax attributes among the participating companies.

The Italian income tax system also provides for election for some companies to be treated as transparent for tax purposes; however, in the light of the relevant discipline, it is possible to say that such feature is rarely used within groups especially within groups with a multinational presence.

Certain rules, such as the dividends and capital gains exemption rules, are meant to tackle economic double taxation regardless of whether or not such items of income arise within the context of a group or of a tax consolidation regime.

The change from an imputation system to a classical one triggered the tax irrelevance of the impairment of participations and as a general rule also of the capital losses derived upon their disposal (with some exceptions, namely where the relevant capital gains would be entirely subject to tax, such as in case of real estate companies or companies resident in a low-tax jurisdiction).

With the exception of the tax consolidation regime, the tax provisions that address the existence of a group are relatively few; it can be said that the stand-alone approach is still pivotal to the corporate income tax legislation in Italy. There are, however, some exceptions to such an approach and the main policy reasons behind them have an anti-abuse nature, an anti-deferral nature or anti-profit shifting purposes.

Indeed, with the exception of the rule that under certain circumstances allows the

---

[1]   Tax Partner at Gianni Origoni and Adjunct Professor of International tax law at the University of Milan – Bicocca.
[2]   ACE is equivalent to the so-called Allowance for Growth and Investment – AGI – which basically is a notional interest deduction on the growth of corporate equity.

circulation of tax receivables within the group, the Italian tax system contains some provisions that allow it to "pierce the veil" of corporations, especially in circumstances where a company has control over another. Usually, such rules have an anti-abuse or anti-deferral purpose as, for instance, the Italian anti-interposition rules (which have the effect of allocating the income to a taxpayer different from the one that formally derived it) or general anti-abuse rules (applying in both domestic and cross-border scenarios) and the CFC rules (applying only with respect to foreign controlled entities).

As far as transfer pricing is concerned, Italy has implemented (both through statutes and regulations) a set of rules and regulations which is mostly in line with the one designed by the OECD. Transfer pricing legislation does not apply to purely domestic transactions; however, pursuant to certain jurisprudential doctrine, it is possible to challenge the lawfulness of domestic transactions (mostly those occurring intra-group) carried out at values which drastically deviate from the fair market value.

With respect to pure cross-border situations, besides the CFC rule (implemented by Italy and in line with the OECD and the so-called ATAD provisions) and the transfer pricing regulation, Italy has also implemented the anti-hybrid regulations (in line with the so-called ATAD II) and the reporting rules suggested by the OECD (e.g., country-by-country reporting) and the EU (the process for implemnting DAC6 is about to end).

In conclusion, the Italian tax system is more oriented towards the separate entity approach than the group approach, both with respect to domestic and cross-border scenarios. The few exceptions contemplated (tax consolidation regimes aside) are driven by anti-abuse, anti-deferral or anti-profit shifting reasons.

Japan

Branch reporter
Yuya Suzuki[1]

Summary and conclusions

This report examines Japanese corporate taxation both from the group approach and from the separate entity approach.

The Japanese Corporation Tax Act treats a corporation as a minimum tax unit of corporate income tax. This treatment applies to every aspect of corporate income tax. As a separate entity, each corporation must compute its own taxable profit in accordance with the Corporation Tax Act. If there are some deviations from this basic principle, there is also a group.

What does "group" mean? In other words, by what criteria does the Japanese Corporation Tax Act deviate from the separate entity approach? Fundamentally, the concept of group differs throughout various areas. In general, under accounting principle and commercial law, it is a key factor that one party substantially controls another. However, under the Corporation Tax Act, by and large, it is vital that one party holds shares or any other interest of another. Thus, the meaning of "subsidiary" differs in each area.

Even in the Corporation Tax Act, there are various groups. In other words, requirements of shareholding are not integrated. In this sense, there are various "subsidiaries" for tax purposes, too. For example, dividend payment presupposes some shareholding. However, in relation to exemption of inter-company dividends, there are no specific shareholding requirements among domestic corporations. Adversely, in cross-border situations, there are shareholding requirements of 25 percent or more. In contrast, a consolidated return requires 100 percent shareholding. It is true that an earnings stripping regime covers third party dividends, but it also adopted the group ratio rule as a safe harbor. According to recent reformation on foreign dividend exemption, a counteracting measure requires not only mere shareholding but also decision making on distribution.

Deviating from the separate entity approach, the Corporation Tax Act aims to achieve various goals under the name of the group approach, such as prevention of economic double taxation and anti-abuse. However, two situations can be distinguished. First, belonging to a group itself leads to the application of a measure deviating from the separate entity approach. For example, dividend exemption in a purely domestic situation can be applicable only if there is shareholding in relation to distribution among domestic corporations. A reduced tax rate for SMEs cannot be applicable only if their shares are wholly owned by a large enterprise. Second, in addition to shareholding, it is necessary to meet other requirements. In relation to this majority, belonging to a group is only a trigger of a special measure. For example, CFC regimes presuppose a shareholding requirement between a domestic corporation and CFC. However, in application, there are other requirements, such as activities or effective tax rate of CFC. Dividend exemption in cross-border situations requires shareholding between a domestic corporation and a foreign one. However, in the

---

[1]   Associate Professor of Law, Graduate Institute for Entrepreneurial Studies.

combination of the counteracting measure and hybrid mismatch rule, whether a foreign dividend is exempted is not decided merely by shareholding itself.

The OECD recommendation that originated in the BEPS project affected Japanese corporate income tax. This means that Japan is also moving toward a group approach. However, Action items 8-10 still adhere to separate entity accounting. Thus, in line with the recent reformation, the arm's length standard is still the prevailing principle in Japanese transfer pricing rules. Finally, it should be noted that foreseen reformation on consolidated returns is rather looking toward the separate entity approach.

Republic of Korea

Branch reporters
Ji-Hyun Yoon[1]
Heejeong Cheung[2]
Philje Cho[3]
Ji-Heon Jin[4]

Summary and conclusions

Domestic aspects

The corporate income tax system of the Republic of Korea (hereinafter Korea) may be viewed as firmly rooted in the separate entity approach. The civil-law term of "legal personality" plays an important role also in the tax system, which means that, as a rule of thumb, an entity with legal personality is treated as separate taxpayer for tax purposes. Korean company law or its commercial code regards all the types of companies listed therein as legal persons, so any of these companies is treated as a separate taxpayer that is liable to pay corporate income tax as a matter of principle.

Two limited, but theoretically important, exceptions were however introduced some 10 to 15 years ago, i.e., group taxation and partnership taxation regimes. The group taxation rules constitute a narrow exception that applies only to parent companies and their "100%" subsidiaries for income tax purposes. Initially it started with an expectation that its scope would soon gradually expand, but this prospect has not yet been materialized. Since the usage of this tax regime is very much restricted, gains or losses realized from transactions between associate companies are mostly recognized for income tax purposes. The partnership taxation regime is an optional rule, which allows certain types of companies with legal personality to elect not to pay corporate income tax and attribute their income directly to their shareholders.

On the other hand, the tax authorities widely use the statutory, so-called "repudiation of wrongful act or calculation" provision as a measure against certain problematic transactions effected between distinct but associated entities. This domestic rule is in theory founded on the separate entity approach and relies thereon even more heavily in practice in that it is frequently invoked by the tax authorities even when the total tax burden of the related parties has not been reduced. This often results in an absurd outcome where the tax authorities end up collecting more tax revenue than would have been the case had the transaction in question been carried out at arm's length price.

---

[1]   Professor, Seoul National University School of Law.
[2]   Director, BnH Tax LLC, Seoul.
[3]   Attorney, Lee&Ko's Tax Practice Group, Seoul.
[4]   Legal counsel, Hyundai Motors Company, Seoul.

International aspects

When it comes to international taxation, Korean law deviates little from internationally accepted norms. Its transfer pricing rules faithfully follow the OECD Guidelines including the recent changes added by the outcomes of the BEPS Project. The newly introduced rules connected with limitation on interest deductions are also reflected in Korean tax law, including hybrid mismatch rules and disallowance of excessive interest deduction based on a simple numerical threshold of 30% of taxable income. Korea has also had a rather extensive CFC regime, of which the so-called "deemed-dividend approach" and "entity-based approach" form the backbone. All these features of international taxation have to do, to a certain extent, with the separate entity approach.

Conclusions

To conclude, the Korean income tax system, in terms of both domestic and international taxation, is largely in line with the traditional and conventional separate entity approach. In many areas of tax law, legal personality coincides with separate taxable liability or being treated as a separate and distinct taxable unit. Standard international tax measures such as transfer pricing, CFC rules, etc. are also built upon the premise that each legal entity or company should be considered as a separate taxpayer. In the same vein, Korea has shown no discernible interest in adopting global formulary apportionment. Indeed, the strategic position taken by Korea in this BEPS era appears to be described as prudent and passive, in the sense that Korea is reluctant to experiment with any new radical measures that have not been sufficiently tested in other jurisdictions.

Finally, it should be added that, in the area of anti-avoidance measures, the Korean tax authorities and courts seem to be of the opinion that the separate entity approach should not be abused for the purpose of reducing tax liabilities. It is in this respect that legal personality is often disregarded, and this is so only when it is established that the taxpayer has taken undue advantage thereof, where the outcome is justified by the well-known substance-over-form doctrine.

Branch reporters
Jean-Nicolas Bourtembourg[1]
Aakriti Srivastav[2]
Charlotte Haarsma-den Dekker[3]

Summary and conclusions

In Luxembourg, taxes are assessed on a stand-alone basis for corporate income tax (CIT) purposes unless a fiscal unity has been formed. In line with the separate entity approach, Luxembourg considers all taxpayers on an independent basis and requires each taxpayer to independently determine its tax base. This includes that the arm's length principle, as laid down in the tax laws, applies to any intra-group transaction (both domestic and cross-border). The latest developments of the OECD in the framework of transfer pricing have been implemented into Luxembourg domestic tax law via revised transfer pricing articles as well as an administrative circular letter.

Luxembourg tax laws provide for a fiscal unity regime which was originally introduced in 1981. However, the regime was significantly amended, and more importantly extended, as per 1 January 2016 in accordance with case law from the Court of Justice of the European Union (CJEU) in particular to allow horizontal integration. This resulted in the full re-writing of the article providing for the fiscal unity regime in 2019. The regime does not include any form of consolidation where the intra-group transactions would be cancelled out. Income within the tax group is allocated based on the separate entity approach. If the application of the tax consolidation regime is the source of double taxation or a double deduction, this effect is to be neutralized by an adequate correction of the taxable income of the integrating entity.

Luxembourg tax law does not contain specific change of control regulations.

Luxembourg tax law does not contain any thin capitalisation rules, other than the one specifically applying to companies involved in intra-group financing. In practice, the Luxembourg tax authorities generally accept a debt-to-equity ratio for holding companies of 85:15. However such debt-to-equity ratio is not laid down in any official guidance nor in the Luxembourg tax laws.

In principle, permanent establishments (PEs) of foreign corporate taxpayers in Luxembourg are taxed in a similar manner as Luxembourg corporate resident taxpayers. Further to the implementation of the European Anti-Tax Avoidance Directives 1 and 2, an additional paragraph was added to the Luxembourg tax laws to add certain administrative requirements to avoid a mismatch in recognition of a PE between Luxembourg and a head office or PE jurisdiction.

There are no taxes levied on transactions between PEs and their head office. In those intra-company transactions, Luxembourg follows the legal concept of a PE as a legally

---

[1]   Head of tax and transfer pricing, Grant Thornton Luxembourg.
[2]   Senior Manager Transfer Pricing at Grant Thornton Luxembourg.
[3]   Senior tax associate at Loyens & Loeff Luxembourg.

dependant part of an enterprise with a head office in one state and a PE in another. There are no specific provisions in Luxembourg tax law concerning the allocation of assets and liabilities between a foreign PE and a Luxembourg head office. However, all transactions in Luxembourg must adhere to the arm's length principle.

Luxembourg does not have a history of including income from foreign subsidiaries on a non-remittance basis such as controlled foreign corporation (CFC) legislation. Following the implementation of the European Anti-Tax Avoidance Directive 1 however, Luxembourg has introduced the required minimum standards with regard to such CFC legislation into its domestic laws. From the two options provided by the Directive, Luxembourg adopted option B, which will allow it to tax a CFC's undistributed income that has arisen from non-genuine arrangements, which are put in place essentially for the purpose of obtaining a tax advantage. As yet, there is no tendency outlined by the legislator or the Luxembourg tax authorities towards the full inclusion as proposed by the OECD BEPS Pillar 2 nor is there an intention in the direction of an undertaxed payment rule as discussed in OECD BEPS Pillar 2.

The Luxembourg fiscal unity regime and its application to foreign entities is very much influenced by the case law of the CJEU. Foreign entities cannot participate directly as the controlling entity in a tax group. They can, however, participate as the controlling entity through a Luxembourg PE provided that the foreign entity is in its country of residence fully subject to a tax corresponding to the Luxembourg CIT. Foreign entities can be the non-integrating parent of a horizontal tax group. Each entity that is part of the tax group should be entitled to claim the benefits under a tax treaty to the extent it qualifies, in its own right, as a resident for the purpose of the tax treaty in question. There is no concept in Luxembourg of applying for tax treaty benefits as a fiscal unity per se.

Both the arm's length principle and the separate entity approach have always been implicitly present in Luxembourg's domestic tax legislation. References to article 9 of the OECD MTC by the Administrative Court in its decisions highlight the tendency of the courts, Luxembourg tax authorities and taxpayers to rely on the OECD guidance. The Luxembourg tax laws refer to the use of the five transfer pricing methods described in the OECD Transfer Pricing Guidelines. As yet, neither the courts nor the Luxembourg tax authorities have shown a tendency towards the application of any specific method. Following a consensus on Pillar 1 by the end of 2020, Luxembourg is likely to adopt it into the domestic tax legislation.

Luxembourg entities falling under the country-by-country (CbC) reporting law are required to report economic, financial and tax information in the form of a CbC report to the Luxembourg tax authorities. The Luxembourg tax authorities will subsequently exchange such information per the Multilateral Competent Authority Agreement on the Exchange of CbC reports.

In Luxembourg, there is no tendency to directly implement other national instruments (such as diverted profit taxes, BEAT or GILTI) for cross-border groups. Luxembourg is amongst a few countries that have expressed strong reservations over the EU digital services tax (DST), as it would make the EU less competitive in comparison to non-EU countries, and maintains that profits should be taxed as opposed to turnover. Although Luxembourg remains a supporter of taxing digital companies, it has not announced or shown any intentions towards implementing DST unilaterally on the belief that implementing this without the OECD consensus would harm the EU.

Branch reporters
Heman Jeetun[1]
Oudai Mohun[2]

Summary and conclusions

Tax-resident companies established in Mauritius are regulated by the Mauritius Revenue Authority (MRA) and operate in a harmonised tax environment. Under the Income Tax Act of 1995 (ITA) of Mauritius, a company is tax resident if it is incorporated under the laws of Mauritius or it has its central management and control in Mauritius. The standard headline tax rate is 15% and this is applied uniformly to all companies. However, tax incentives are available to companies, which will reduce their effective tax rate. Chargeable income is the tax-adjusted profit on which the tax liability is calculated. The rationale behind adjusting the profit before tax is to eliminate the effects of accounting entries such as provisions which are based on International Financial Reporting Standards and amend the profit with existing tax rules specified in the ITA.

Sociétés, as defined in the ITA, are not liable to income tax. The associates (ultimate beneficiaries) of the société are liable to income tax on their share of profits which have been distributed or deemed to have been distributed during the accounting year in concern. Whereas a non-resident société shall be liable to corporate tax at the rate of 15% of its chargeable income.

Both individual shareholders and corporate shareholders are exempt from tax on receipt of dividend from a resident company. However, following the amendment in the Solidarity Levy which is effective as from 1 July 2020, resident individual shareholders will be taxed on the excess income if their total leviable income exceeds MUR three million per annum. Leviable income comprises the chargeable income and dividend paid to the individual shareholder. Thus, the dividend paid by the domestic company which was previously exempted from income tax will now be partially or fully taxed up to a maximum rate of 25%.

For non-resident shareholders, the tax treatment of the dividend is dependent on the country of residence which will be applicable.

In contrast, corporate shareholders will always be exempted from income tax on the dividends received from local companies.

---

[1]   Heman Jeetun, tax supervisor of Mazars Mauritius, a leading international audit, tax and advisory firm and chairperson of the Young IFA Network (YIN) of IFA Mauritius.
[2]   Oudai Mohun, assistant manager at KPMG Mauritius, a leading international audit, tax and advisory and Assistant Secretary of IFA Mauritius.
      The authors wish to particularly thank the president of IFA Mauritius, Mr. Rajesh Ramloll, SC and Mr. Roomesh C.P Ramchurn, tax partner at Mazars Mauritius and the Secretary of IFA Mauritius, who have reviewed this paper and have provided their valuable contribution.

In Mauritius, each company is taxed on a stand-alone basis. Thus, each entity is required to calculate its tax liability and file its corporate tax return separately. There is no group taxation regime in the ITA of Mauritius .[3]

Under section 90 of the ITA, provisions for anti-avoidance have been made to address aggressive tax planning to reduce, avoid or defer tax liability. Mauritius introduced the CFC rule in 2019 and it came into effect in respect of the year of assessment commencing on 1 July 2020. A CFC, under the ambit of section 90A of the ITA, is defined as a company which is not resident in Mauritius and in which more than 50 per cent of its total participation rights are held directly or indirectly by the resident company or together with its associated enterprises and includes a permanent establishment of the resident company. The CFC rule is designed to prevent a parent company from artificially moving its profits abroad to a controlled subsidiary in a country with a more favourable or lower tax rate.

With the ongoing work of the OECD/G20 Inclusive Framework on BEPS on taxation issues around the world, Mauritius has a propensity toward changes. Rules are being implemented to deviate fundamentally from the taxation of each separate entity by developing rules for the allocation of group profits and by determining a group's effective tax burden. In Mauritius, there is no legislation for a cross-border group tax approach. Each entity is subject to corporate tax on a stand-alone basis. Nevertheless, the taxation of local branches differs from that of subsidiaries.

Even though there is a need for consolidation at the parent level in Mauritius, income tax is levied at 15% on the parent company only. However, as mentioned above, foreign source dividend, among other specific income, may be subject to partial exemption of 80% provided the company fulfils the prescribed conditions.

On the other hand, a company incorporated in Mauritius that has branches in another jurisdiction will need to consolidate and pay tax at the rate of 15% in Mauritius.

There is no transfer pricing legislation in Mauritius. The domestic legislation only provides for the arm's length principle for any transactions between related parties. Moreover, there is no thin capitalisation requirement in Mauritius.

There is no restriction on outbound payment but a withholding tax is applicable on interest payments, management fees, rental fees, etc. There are no anti-hybrid rules in Mauritius.

Mauritius signed the Multilateral Competent Authority Agreement on the Exchange of Country-by-Country Reports (CbC MCAA) in January 2017 and the CbCR Regulation was proclaimed on 22 February 2018 to be effective for the accounting years beginning on or after 1 July 2018.

The government of Mauritius has implemented a new tax in the form of VAT on digital services provided by non-residents in Mauritius. The standard rate of VAT on the supply of digital services is 15% on providers of digital or electronic services via the internet in Mauritius.

---

[3]   See the case law of *Robert Le Maire Intergraph Co V The Director General MRA* (2011 – Supreme Court) –ANNEX 1.

Branch reporters
Layda Cárcamo Sabido[1]
Jorge García González[2]

Summary and conclusions

It is not news that Mexico has always stood out at the level of international taxation, in general, in a positive way, by adopting and introducing measures or regimes within its tax system, which have largely sought to avoid abuses and, where appropriate, prevent evasion and tax fraud. This has been confirmed by being the first country in the world to adopt BEPS mediated. The latter was very evident with the adoption of additional provisions such as the introduction of measures regarding the deduction of interest in the 2020 tax reform (Action 4 BEPS Plan).

Mexico has traditionally followed the approach of considering the entities that are part of a group of companies as separate entities. In this sense, it is very important to note that although it is true that Mexico maintained a fiscal kind of consolidation regime for many years (introduced for the first time in its fiscal provisions through a decree during the 70-80s), this regime was basically applicable to taxpayers' legal entities resident in Mexico. It is very noteworthy to mention that, at the time, Mexico adopted, at least for a very short period, the possibility of consolidating by levels, allowing the inclusion of foreign resident subsidiaries within the consolidation group. In practice, unfortunately this system did not have the expected results, possibly since Mexico has traditionally been an importer of capital.

The consolidation regime was repealed in 2014, by virtue, according to the federal executive, of abuses in its application. This situation attracted a lot of attention from academics, corporations and civil organizations since it was considered that the consolidation regime was always deferred.

In this same context, we can affirm that Mexico, by adopting measures to inhibit payments to jurisdictions with low taxation, better known as low tax jurisdictions, initially did not recognize fiscal transparency, resulting in payments made abroad always being considered made to an opaque entity.

In this regard, it is important to mention that the agreement entered into by Mexico and the United States has recognized, since its entry into force and applicability (1992), the possibility of considering that an LLC entity or entities that apply the regime known as S-corporation may be subject to the benefits of the agreement to the extent that its members are residents for tax purposes in the latter jurisdiction, thus, giving way to the possibility of recognizing the benefits based on the identity of its members and not on the entity per se.

Considering the above, Mexico evolved significantly in the recognition of the various foreign entities and legal figures to accommodate the new provisions in this matter which

[1]   Tax Partner at Calvo Nicolau y Márquez Cristerna-DFK.
[2]   International Tax Partner at EY Mexico City Office.

are currently in force. We can validly conclude that Mexican provisions, even though they are very complex, allow us to consider and identify the applicable regime to foreign residents, with an approach that is more inclined to recognize separate entities.

Branch reporters
Marlies Baijer[1]
Marius Girolami[2]

Summary and conclusions

Non-transparent entities for Dutch corporate income tax purposes (e.g., public and private limited companies) residing in the Netherlands and defined in the Dutch Corporate Income Tax Act 1969 are in principle separately taxed with CIT on a stand-alone basis. Transparent entities for Dutch tax purposes (e.g., certain partnerships) are not subject to CIT. However, the profits of these entities are taxed at the level of the participants in these entities (e.g., partners) who are either subject to personal income tax (individuals) or CIT (non-transparent entities). All profits of an entity during its total existence – or from the start to the end of being subject to CIT, e.g., as a result of change of tax residence or tax (exempt) regime – should be taxed with CIT (total profit principle). CIT is levied on a yearly basis on the annual profits (annual profit principle). Separate entity taxation is the starting point for CIT purposes. However, for various CIT rules in both domestic and cross-border situations, belonging to a group is of relevance, e.g., for specific interest deduction rules, transfer pricing rules, change of control rules, participation exemption rules, hybrid mismatch rules and CFC rules. Belonging to a group is also relevant for withholding taxes on dividends, interest and royalties.

The optional group regime (fiscal unity regime) is an exception to the separate entity approach. Under the fiscal unity regime, Dutch group entities that are part of a fiscal unity are – on their request – treated as a single taxpayer. The fiscal unity regime aims to reflect the (economic) reality of group formation. Taxation of a group of entities as a single taxpayer is achieved by including the assets, liabilities (capital consolidation) and results (result consolidation) of all fiscal unity members in the consolidated statements. In that respect, the fiscal unity regime is unique compared to other group regimes in the EU, which do not always provide for full consolidation (although result consolidation is quite common). The parent entity of the fiscal unity files one corporate tax return on behalf of all entities that are part of the fiscal unity. During the existence of the fiscal unity, group entities are no longer separately subject to CIT and do not need to file stand-alone CIT returns for the period in which they are included in the fiscal unity. As a result of this full (capital and result) consolidation, all profits and losses (including capital gains and losses) of different entities that originate during the existence of the fiscal unity can be offset against each other. As such, it is possible to "horizontally" offset the losses and profits of the various entities within the same fiscal year. In addition, under certain conditions, it is possible to offset the profit for a previous or subsequent fiscal year ("vertical" loss compensation). Internal transactions, e.g., a transfer of assets or internal reorganizations within the fiscal unity, are in principle

---

[1]   Senior Tax Manager at KPMG Meijburg & Co.
[2]   Head of Unit for Corporate Taxes at the Directorate-General for Tax and Customs Policy and Legislation of the Dutch Ministry of Finance.

non-existent for CIT-purposes (i.e., no profit recognition takes place on these transactions or reorganizations). Within a fiscal unity, legal mergers, business mergers and legal split-offs can take place relatively straightforward in a tax-neutral manner. Despite the fact that there is a fiscal unity, it may also be necessary – e.g., to avoid abuse of the fiscal unity, to offset a pre-fiscal unity loss with a fiscal unity profit or as a result of the emergency response measure as a result of CJEU case-law – to recognize internal transfers of assets between group entities of a fiscal unity or to determine profits of the entities within a fiscal unity on a separate basis.

As a result of CJEU case law, emergency response measures to the fiscal unity regime were introduced with retroactive effect to 1 January 2018. As a result of these emergency response measures, certain CIT rules need to be applied as if there is no fiscal unity in order to establish equal treatment between a cross-border EU-situation and a domestic situation. Although the emergency response measures prevent that the most vulnerable elements of the fiscal unity regime are in breach with EU law as a consequence of the CJEU case law, this does not completely eliminate the risk that other elements may be in breach with EU law. Since the full consolidation of the fiscal unity is unique within the EU and EU vulnerability remains, it has been announced that the emergency response measures in the fiscal unity regime will have to be followed up by a new group regime that is robust and future-proof. Although consultations have started, it is currently unclear when and how a new group regime will be designed.

In our view, the group approach in the CIT is somewhat paradoxical. On the one hand, there is a trend towards more CIT rules where belonging to a group is of relevance, mainly to counter (international) tax avoidance within a group of companies, although separate entity taxation remains the starting point. On the other hand, there is significant pressure on the unique consolidation regime of the fiscal unity in the CIT, resulting in a more separate entity approach for the application of various CIT-rules in the short term and a potential new group regime in the long term.

Branch reporters
Casey Plunket[1]
Sladjana Freakley[2]

Summary and conclusions

As in most countries, the income tax system of New Zealand (hereafter NZ) is based on legal treatment of entities and transactions, rather than treatment based on substance or financial reporting. Accordingly, there is a fundamental bias towards treating group companies as separate fiscal entities.

Domestic aspects of single entity vs group approach

However, NZ tax policy has for many years recognised that good tax rules will often require treating a business conducted through a company as though it were conducted by its shareholders, since the formation of a company to undertake a business or transaction is in many respects a matter of form rather than substance. This is perhaps particularly the case for a group company, and even more so when it is undertaking transactions with other members of its group.

New Zealand's imputation system of corporate taxation, which avoids the double taxation of income earned through companies, is an important manifestation of this policy, as are:

— the exemption for dividends between resident members of a 100% commonly owned group and the participation exemption for inbound dividends received by a company from foreign companies owned more than 10% by the payee;
— the ability to use losses of a company to offset against profits of another company in the same 66% or greater group;
— the tax consolidation regime, available on an elective basis to any members of a wholly owned group.

It is also common, when determining ownership of a company for tax purposes, to look-through holding companies until non-corporate shareholders are identified. Thus, for instance, 100% subsidiaries of a single corporate parent are treated as owned by the same persons.

---

[1] LLB(Hons)/BCA; LLM (Mich.), since 2015 employed by the New Zealand Inland Revenue in its Policy and Strategy team.
[2] LLB(Hons)/BCA – accounting (Victoria University of Wellington), MTAX (Hons) (Auckland University), Bachelor and Solicitor of the High Court of New Zealand. Since mid-2019 working at Ernst & Young based in Auckland, as a senior manager in the Tax Policy team.

International aspects of single entity vs group approach

The treatment of a corporate group as effectively a single entity for tax purposes is also evident in a number of regimes that relate to interest deductions of cross-border groups. The focus on taxation of outbound interest reflects NZ's relatively high corporate tax rate and position as a net capital importer.

Withholding tax on outbound interest

Interest paid by a NZ company to a non-resident group member is generally subject to a much higher rate of tax (up to 15% gross or 28% net) than interest paid to a non-resident third-party lender (generally 2%). This is on the basis that the debt funding on which the interest is paid may reflect equity of the group as a whole. However, this higher rate is imposed on all such interest.

Thin capitalisation

NZ's thin capitalisation rules apply to limit interest deductions on both related and third-party debt. The application of the rules to a company is based on the debt percentage (debt/(assets – non-debt liabilities)) of the NZ group of which the company is a part, not the company's own debt percentage. This group debt percentage must be calculated on a consolidated basis. The thin capitalisation group escape rule allows the usual 60% threshold to be increased to 110% of the worldwide group debt percentage.

Transfer pricing

Transfer pricing related party debt is a significant issue, particularly because NZ uses a balance sheet thin capitalisation rule rather than an EBITDA rule. NZ's approach to transfer pricing on inbound related party debt is particularly interesting in this context.
- First, if the group is a banking or insurance group, for transfer pricing purposes, the borrower is generally treated as having the same credit rating as the member of the worldwide group with the most long-term senior unsecured debt. The borrower can use its own (actual or derived) credit rating for related party debt that is up to four times the amount of the borrower's own third-party borrowing.
- Second, for other groups with a debt percentage over 40%, the pricing of inbound related party debt is amended. For transfer pricing purposes, the borrower is treated as having a credit rating of 1-2 notches less than the member of the worldwide group with the most third-party debt.
- Third, certain borrower-friendly loan terms have to be disregarded in the transfer pricing analysis, unless these are also a feature of third-party borrowing or reflect regulatory capital requirements for bank or insurance companies. Borrower-friendly terms include a term of more than five years, subordination, and convertibility into shares or ability to defer or alter payments where these are within the control of the borrower.

CFC rules

The NZ CFC rules show a more limited acceptance of a group approach. The CFC regime is consistent with OECD Action 3 recommendations. It taxes NZ shareholders on passive and base-eroding income earned by foreign companies which are controlled by five or fewer NZ shareholders. There is a credit for foreign taxes. Both losses and credits are subject to jurisdictional ring-fencing. Australian companies cannot be CFCs.

In the group context in particular, it is significant that this treatment is not the same as that applied to income earned through a foreign branch of a NZ resident, which is taxed directly as it is earned with a credit for foreign taxes paid. This is a deliberate strategy to allow NZ groups to deduct foreign branch losses (often incurred in the establishment phase) against NZ income, while sheltering foreign active income earned through a CFC from NZ tax.

The current treatment is a much more limited application of the group approach than the CFC regime that applied from 1987 to 2008. Under that regime, all income of a CFC (outside a list of six high-tax countries) was taxed to NZ shareholders as it accrued – this was referred to as "branch equivalent" taxation. This approach was abandoned because it was seen as a barrier to offshore investment by NZ companies. A particular concern was the compliance costs involved in recasting financial accounts so that separate companies could be accounted for tax purposes as if they were partnerships.

NZ has implemented an expanded PE definition, which in many respects implements on a unilateral basis changes contained in the MLI in relation to the PE definition.

Branch reporters
Marius Sollund[1]
Morten Platou[2]

Summary and conclusions

The separate entity approach has been a central feature of the Norwegian tax system for more than a century. The tax committee of 1899 continued already existing principles for taxing certain company types as entities separate from the shareholders. The Norwegian Supreme Court confirmed the principle in landmark cases during the 1920s and 1930s, and later during the late 1990s and early 2000s confirmed the separate entity approach in cases that the tax authorities considered as aggressive.

Today, the separate entity approach is in many instances a foundation for Norwegian taxation. Taxation of limited liability companies separate from their owners and other group companies, the arm's length principle and transfer pricing rules, the participation exemption, and several other concepts in Norwegian tax law are considered to embody what could be characterised as a separate entity approach. Even general anti-avoidance rules have not pierced the corporate veil, which is evidence of the principle's strong foothold.

Norway does not have a concept of group taxation as such, which is also a reflection of the separate entity approach. Profits and losses may however be utilised within a tax group by way of group contributions provided certain requirements are met. Perhaps the most important requirement is the minimum ownership requirement of 90%.

Even though the separate entity approach is reflected in many concepts of Norwegian tax law, we have witnessed the introduction of certain sets of rules that deviate from this and which would be considered a reflection of a group approach or piercing the corporate veil. The most notable is the CFC rules, which entail that income in foreign companies etc. in low-tax jurisdictions are taxed in the hands of the Norwegian owners rather than at company level. The rationale for implementing CFC rules, despite the main rule of separate entity taxation, was to ensure capital export neutrality, i.e., that investors in Norwegian companies and companies in low-tax jurisdictions are treated equally.

The Norwegian Ministry of Finance has introduced several measures in order to implement the OECD BEPS Actions, and some of these reflect a group entity approach. Interest deduction limitation rules were implemented in Norway the year before the OECD released the BEPS Action 4 report. The rules have subsequently been amended, latest with effect from 2019 when, inter alia, new group elements were introduced, inter alia, with a group equity escape clause.

As for transfer pricing, the separate entity approach is the prevailing principle in Norway, and the OECD BEPS Action 8-10 has not changed that. Further, we have not observed a wider use of the profit split method as a result of the OECD BEPS Action 8-10. In our opinion, the TNMM method will continue to be the preferred transfer pricing method when it comes

---

[1]   Group Tax Legal Counsel, DNV.
[2]   Senior lawyer, Advokatfirmaet Schjødt.

to transactions involving intangibles. The OECD BEPS Action 8-10 has further resulted in updated transfer pricing guidelines. The arm's length provision in the Norwegian Tax Act contains a direct reference to the guidelines, and the updated guidelines will therefore be an applicable source of law (although not of a binding nature) in transfer pricing cases.

Norway's approach to the current work that is being carried out by the OECD, in order to address the challenges associated with taxing the global players within the digital economy, has been to seek international consensus for a broad, commonly agreed framework. Some countries have taken another approach and introduced unilateral domestic digital tax measures. Norway's official standpoint is to await the results of the work by the OECD in this regard.

In conclusion, the separate entity approach is a prevailing principle in Norway. Even though Norway has introduced certain concepts that embody a group taxation approach or principles that pierce the corporate veil, like the CFC rules, Norway does not have a general group tax system and the transfer pricing rules, the corporate tax system etc. are all based on the separate entity approach. Tax concepts that deviate from the separate entity approach generally seem to have been the result of the need to address specific cross-border challenges, such as base erosion, profit shifting, and capital neutrality.

Branch reporter
Luciana Yañez Salgado[1]

Summary and conclusions

Peru, as a developing country and capital importer, has developed rules focused on the taxation of Peruvian income, under the predominance of the source criterion and the separate entity approach principle. In this sense, the starting point for corporate income taxation is the taxation of each individual entity irrespective of whether it is part of an affiliated group or not.

In addition, as a consequence of the expansion of important Peruvian economic groups to new markets, in various sectors of the economy, some regulations have been approved to promote their growth, such as indirect credit. However, they are still pending specific rules for the determination of foreign income to provide greater legal security, as well as the legislator's decision to deviate from the separate company approach, as a measure to promote Peruvian companies investing abroad to be allowed to recognize profits and losses at a consolidated level.

Entities as one of the central principles affecting the allocation of taxing rights plus the separate entity accounting and the arm's length principle are the cornerstones of the domestic and international approach to inter-company payments for Peruvian tax purposes. Classification of the entities subject to tax is according to the analysis of the Peruvian Income Tax Law (PITL) and the Peruvian Companies Law. A particularity of the Peruvian legislation is that local branches or PEs of non-domiciled taxpayers that carry out their activities in Peru (Peruvian PE of a non-domiciled entity) are treated as legal entities for income tax purposes and only taxed on their Peruvian income.

Peru has developed fairly comprehensive legislation dealing with Peruvian PEs of non-domiciled entities and, to some extent, the attribution of benefits to these PEs. Although some jurisprudence and administrative decisions have been issued, domestic legislation concerning the conditions for considering new types of these PEs and the attribution of profits is pending, especially in certain dealings between the Peruvian PEs and their headquarters abroad.

Unlike a Peruvian PE of a non-domiciled entity, the foreign PE of a domiciled entity is not treated as a different taxpayer and, hence, any dealings between the head office and the PE will not have the status of a transaction. Although the domiciled legal entity must consolidate the results of its foreign PE for the determination of the income tax, a set of rules is pending implementation that will allow the articulation of the taxation of branches located abroad with third parties and with their own head office. There are no specific rules on attributing income to a foreign PE of a domiciled entity; the only rules existing deal with the attribution of income to Peruvian and foreign sources.

[1]   Partner at Zuzunaga, Assereto & Zegarra Abogados. Lawyer from the Pontificia Universidad Católica del Perú. Adv. LLM in international tax law from the International Tax Center Leiden-ITC of the University of Leiden, The Netherlands.

There are no special group taxation regimes, nor special provisions differentiating the taxation between stand-alone companies and companies belonging to a group. In addition, under the PITL, there is no possibility of exemption of capital gains generated between the parent and foreign subsidiaries. Nevertheless, transactions qualifying as corporate reorganizations can be implemented with no significant tax impact if certain conditions are met.

The income tax on dividends does not apply to domiciled companies. Therefore, they are not subject to any kind of withholdings on earned profits and neither should they include them in their taxable income because it will be applied upon redistribution in favour of individuals or non-domiciled companies.

PITL does not have any special rules for intra-group loans like a group ratio or a group-wide allocation. Therefore, the general limitations of deduction of interest are applicable to intra-group loans. These rules also apply to any company regarding loans with related or unrelated parties since in the latter case the legislator considered that business groups could circumvent the limitation, through back-to-back loans.

Unlike in most jurisdictions, transfer pricing rules also apply in a domestic context, as guidance to determining the "fair market value" of the transactions based on the arm's length principle. If a tax prejudice is produced in a transaction between related parties, an adjustment will be made (increase or decrease in income is recognized in one of the related parties, and in the other, an increase or decrease in the cost or expense that would have been recognized). On the other hand, transfer pricing rules apply to transactions which are made from, to or through non-cooperating, low-tax or null-tax countries or those subject to a preferential regime, in order to prevent profit shifting. Secondary adjustments, considering the actual legal framework are inapplicable.

Further, Peruvian transfer pricing obligations reflect in general the OECD standards corresponding to the BEPS Action 13 local file, master file and country-by-country report. Other than the formal obligations' provisions, no further legal provision has been implemented in terms of revising the separate entity approach towards a group view. Peru follows the Actions 8 to 10 with some deviations in the intra-group transactions and commodities.

PITL also provides special rules that consider the specific relationship of companies to their subsidiaries in an international context, such as the CFC regime and indirect credit to certain domiciled legal entities with respect to income tax paid by their first and second level non-domiciled companies.

Under CFC rules, the results of the net passive income of the different CFCs may not be consolidated for the purposes of their attribution to the domiciled taxpayer that owns them.

The Peruvian tax system provides for a GAAR, which grants power to the tax administration to reclassify operations for tax purposes. If it can be proved by the tax administration that the operations are artificial or improper and that the use of said act or acts does not produce legal or economic effects, other than savings or tax benefits, the Peruvian tax administration (SUNAT) will apply to them the tax consequences that have been avoided.

PITL does not contain any provisions that allow a different allocation of income under accepted foreign tax rules to determine compliance with the minimum tax/tax credit threshold.

Finally, there are no legislative moves yet towards further implementation of the OECD BEPS Pillar 1 and 2 recommendations.

Branch reporters
Wojciech Morawski[1]
Adam Zalasiński[2]

Summary and conclusions

The basic principle of the Polish Corporate Income Tax (CIT) is that each legal person is a separate taxpayer. However, that principle is modified in two directions. First, one legal person may theoretically constitute several CIT taxpayers, since entities without legal personality may be CIT taxpayers. Such rare situations may occur when there is legislation providing for an organisational split of a legal person. Second, a group of companies may (optionally) create a so-called tax capital group (*podatkowa grupa kapitałowa*). The election creates the group as a single taxpayer, where the group members appear to lose their distinct tax personality.

The taxation of companies as stand-alone entities is the principal regime of corporate income tax in Poland.

In principle, partnerships are fiscally transparent under the CIT Act. However, there are two exceptions to the rule, where partnerships are fiscally opaque. These are:
- partnerships with limited liability partners (spółka komandytowa, spółka komandytowo-akcyjna and spółka jawna[3])
- foreign partnerships – if they are treated as legal persons and opaque under tax laws of their jurisdictions.

The tax capital group regime was introduced as from 1 January 1996 under article 1a CITA, which has been in force until now with relatively few changes. All the subsequent changes are undoubtedly relaxing the conditions for use of the regime, which make it more attractive.

Currently, the tax capital groups may be set up by Polish resident companies (solely joint-stock, limited liability companies and simple joint-stock companies) with an average share capital of at least PLN 250,000 (approximately EUR 55,500) each. A tax group must be formed for a period of at least three tax years, which is calculated from the date set in a registered notarial agreement.

The following additional requirements apply:
- the controlling company must directly own at least 75% of the shares of the controlled companies;
- the controlled companies may not own shares of the other companies in the group; and
- none of the companies within the group has tax arrears.

The agreement on the group formation (in the form of a notarial deed) must be filed

---

[1] Dr hab. prof. UMK. Head of the Department of Public Financial Law at Nicolaus Copernicus University in Toruń (Poland).
[2] Dr hab. in law, Senior Legal Officer in the Legal Affairs – Direct Taxation Unit of Taxation and Customs Union DG of the European Commission in Brussels. The text represents personal views of the author, which do not purport to represent the views of the European Commission.
[3] *Spółka jawna* is a CIT taxpayer if its partners include persons/entities other than natural persons.

with the tax authorities at least three months before the first tax year of the group. The personal composition of the group cannot be extended after the group agreement is concluded.

In principle, foreign corporate taxpayers are identified and qualified on the basis of the private law of their seat jurisdiction. Corporate income tax taxpayers may also be foreign entities with no legal capacity, provided that they have certain organisational independence. Foreign partnerships are treated as corporate opaque taxpayers if they are treated as opaque in the jurisdictions of their residence.

Non-resident taxpayers are subject to limited tax liability in Poland. Their taxable income is determined under the same rules as applicable to Polish residents, with the exception of certain passive income streams, which are taxed by withholding taxes levied on the gross amounts.

Poland has a relatively extensive network of 90 double taxation conventions. These conventions follow the OECD Model Tax Convention, in particular its article 5 and 7 regarding taxation of inbound and outbound branches. The Polish tax administration officially declares compliance with the OECD Commentary and the Transfer Pricing Guidelines regarding the attribution of profits to the PEs.

The transfer-pricing legislation is provided for in chapter 1a CIT Act. The Polish law-maker and tax authorities tend to strictly follow the OECD Transfer Pricing Guidelines. That approach is even expected to intensify.

The BEPS Actions 8-10 have been or will be implemented in the Polish tax system. The implementation nevertheless shows some differences. For example, it has been noted that the possibility of recharacterization or disregarding of transactions is slightly broader than foreseen in BEPS Actions 8-10.

Poland has implemented the EU Anti-Tax Avoidance Directive (2016/1164) as amended by the Council Directive 2017/952 amending ATAD1 as regards hybrid mismatches with third countries (ATAD2), and applies EU-modelled:
– interest limitation measure,
– CFC regime, and
– anti-hybrid measures.

Branch reporters
Miguel C. Reis[1]
João Velez de Lima[2]
Miguel Gonzalez Amado[3]
Vítor Loureiro e Silva[4]

Summary and conclusions

Tax systems, including that of Portugal, were generally designed and prepared to address a separate entity taxation. Due to numerous factors, such as globalization and the increase in the complexity of business models, most companies are currently organized and carry out their activities as a group.

In Portugal, there is not a standard definition of a group of companies for accounting, corporate or tax purposes. Even from a tax perspective, the definition of a tax group depends on the nature of the taxation under analysis.

In fact, the Portuguese tax law only provides for a detailed special regime to address the corporate income taxation of a group of companies, which is not based on a typical tax consolidation model, being instead a mere tax aggregation by summing-up of each company's individual tax result to obtain the group's aggregate tax result, with specific adjustments and exceptions and allowing under certain conditions the offset of profits and losses recorded at the level of the group and exempting from withholding corporate taxation intra-group income payments.

It should be noted that even though each company within a group's perimeter should prepare and submit its individual IRC return, the aggregated taxable profit or loss is computed and assessed by the so-called dominant company corresponding to the algebraic sum of the taxable profits (losses) individually assessed by each company of the group. Furthermore, municipal and state surcharges are individually assessed and levied over the taxable profit of each entity of the group.

In this context, we can conclude that even in a group context the separate entity taxation principle is still relevant under the Portuguese IRC regime.

Furthermore, as a consequence of the IRC legal reform made in 2014, the Portuguese tax group regime was adapted to the ECJ case law, namely, to enable a non-resident company to be considered as a dominant company of a Portuguese tax group. Additionally, the Portuguese IRC framework has been recently amended in order to introduce in the Portuguese tax system the OECD guidelines as well as the ATAD.

Considering the above, this report aims to analyze in further detail how the Portuguese tax system deals with the separate entity taxation approach and the group approach both in domestic and in cross-border transactions.

[1]   Tax Partner, Vieira de Almeida & Associados – Sociedade de Advogados, SP, RL.
[2]   Tax Partner, Vieira de Almeida & Associados – Sociedade de Advogados, SP, RL.
[3]   Tax Managing Associate, Vieira de Almeida & Associados – Sociedade de Advogados, SP, RL.
[4]   Tax Associate, Vieira de Almeida & Associados – Sociedade de Advogados, SP, RL.

Branch reporters
Barbara Voskamp[1]
Vikna Rajah[2]

Summary and conclusions

Separate entity taxation forms the basis of Singapore's income tax regime. In part one of this report, the implications of the separate entity approach (SEA) in domestic law are examined in relation to groups of companies. Although there is no formal definition of a "group" in Singapore law, this report utilises the equivalent definitions of "related corporation" and "subsidiary".

In section 1.2, a comprehensive overview of the tax implications of various intra-group transactions is considered, including intra-group capital gains, dividends and losses. Also covered in this section are the transfer pricing implications arising from intra-group transactions. By drawing on relevant statutory provisions, case law and tax circulars released by the Inland Revenue Authority of Singapore, section 1.2 demonstrates the implications of the SEA; in particular, individual companies within a group must submit individual tax returns and also transact on an arm's length basis.

Section 1.3 considers the two major exceptions to the SEA, namely the GST group registration system and the group relief system for income tax. Under the group registration system, companies which satisfy certain qualifying criteria may apply to form a GST group and elect a representative member company to submit a single GST return on behalf of the group. More importantly, any intra-group transactions are disregarded for GST purposes, meaning that member companies within the GST group are effectively treated as a single entity. Under the group relief system, qualifying companies are allowed to transfer unabsorbed capital allowances, trade losses and donations from one company to another. Such unabsorbed items can then be deducted against each company's assessable income. The detailed qualifying conditions, mode of operation and policy intention behind these statutory exceptions are considered in detail in the report.

The latter half of part one of this report is devoted to examining the potential abusive tax practices which may arise from the above exceptions to the separate entity approach and the statutory rules designed to mitigate such practices. In particular, section 1.4 considers the shareholding test as a change-of-control rule designed to prevent companies from acquiring loss-making entities to set-off those losses against their assessable income. The circumstances under which a company may apply to waive the test are also examined, affirming that the courts in Singapore adopt a flexible approach in determining when such waivers are appropriate in order to ensure that Singapore's tax regime remains flexible and business-friendly. The role of transfer pricing rules as a specific anti-avoidance rule is also examined in section 1.5, building on the earlier discussion in the report.

---

[1]   LLM, Partner ASEAN, Loyens & Loeff (Singapore) LLP.
[2]   Equity Partner, Head of Tax at Rajah & Tann Singapore LLP, a leading law firm in South-East Asia.

Part two of the report considers the SEA as applied to foreign corporate entities in cross-border situations. In section 2.1, Singapore's modified territorial basis of taxation is explained with reference to the 'source' concept in section 10(1) of the Income Tax Act – i.e., any income accruing in or derived in Singapore, or received in Singapore from outside Singapore, will be subject to tax. Also considered in this section are the 'deeming provisions' – which provide statutory presumptions that income will be deemed to be sourced in Singapore in certain situations – and the caselaw surrounding this area in other common law jurisdictions. In turn, this demonstrates that a wide, purposive approach is generally preferred by the courts as a means of giving effect to the statutory intention behind the 'source' concept.

Section 2.2 examines the treatment of branch profits received from foreign entities by Singapore residents. Generally, such profits received by Singapore residents are covered by the statutory tax exemption in section 13(8) of the ITA, but in the event that they are not, the Singapore resident company may apply to the Inland Revenue Authority of Singapore for a unilateral tax credit or seek relief under the relevant avoidance of a Double Taxation Agreement (DTA).

Unlike the GST group registration system and group relief system which Singapore-incorporated companies may enjoy, foreign companies do not qualify for any group taxation regime in Singapore. However, under the SEA, transfer pricing rules similarly apply to foreign companies as they do to Singapore ones. Singapore does not currently have a CFC regime, nor any intra-group withholding taxes. Neither is there a separate framework for hybrid mismatch rules.

One example of a national special instrument being implemented in Singapore is the recently-introduced 'digital services tax' applicable to cross-border groups. Under this regime, goods and services tax (GST) will apply to imported digital services in the context of business-to-consumer transactions. Notably, overseas suppliers may register to form a group (subject to the qualifying conditions being met) for the purposes of easing compliance with GST reporting and documentation requirements. The meaning of 'digital services' as well as the qualifying conditions are examined in detail in section 2.10. In turn, the analysis confirms that the intention behind the digital services tax is largely to achieve parity in the GST treatment of all digital services consumed in Singapore, regardless of whether the supplier is local or overseas.

Branch reporter
Alta Koekemoer[1]

Summary and conclusions

South Africa adheres to the separate entity principle with regard to corporate groups. No formal group tax system exists. In South Africa each individual corporation is taxed as a separate taxpayer, irrespective of whether it is part of an affiliated group or not. Accordingly, profits and losses of group companies are not consolidated and intra-group dealings, apart from asset transfers under the corporate restructuring rules, trigger taxable income. To avoid double taxation, profit distributions to resident group members are mitigated by tax relief on dividends.

Nonetheless, the South African government introduced a corporate restructuring regime in 2001 to avoid double taxation on capital gains within a corporate group. The corporate restructuring regime applies in limited circumstances and only provides for the tax-free transfer of assets between group members. The corporate restructuring regime does not provide for the offsetting of losses or the consolidation of the income in corporate groups.

Apart from the corporate restructuring regime, there are several other provisions in the South African tax system that recognise the single economic unit or, put differently, that further pierce the veil of corporations. Circumstances where the allocation of income to other taxpayers is accepted include the partnership provisions, the CFC regime and the REIT regime. There are other aspects of the current South African income tax system that also recognise the group as single enterprise. These provisions suggest that, to a certain degree, the South African government wishes to adhere to the single enterprise principle.

Clearly, the separate entity approach still forms the basis of the corporate tax system in South Africa, but an increasing number of rules have been introduced in the last two decades that take into account that group companies operate as a single enterprise. It appears that a tax system that adheres to the single enterprise approach in one respect and the separate entity approach in another respect creates structural weaknesses in the system. Several court decisions have illustrated the challenges caused by these structural flaws. These structural defects in the system were also exploited by tax advisors that devised avoidance schemes.[2] It is submitted that these problems in the system will continue until the current system relating to corporate groups is replaced by a formal group tax regime.

---

[1] Chartered accountant (SA) and associate professor at the School of Accountancy – University of the Free State.
[2] In the past, s. 45 was used in numerous avoidance transactions, including debt push-down schemes that involved claiming substantial interest deductions. These schemes, considered by National Treasury (2011) as unlawful, led to revenue losses for the South African fiscus.

Branch reporter
Roberta Poza Cid[1]

Summary and conclusions

The Spanish Corporate Income Tax has undergone various in-depth reforms, the last of which was carried out with the adoption of Law 27/2014, of 27 November, which currently regulates the tax. The reform then operated had, as guiding principles, both neutrality and competitiveness on the one side, and the fight against fraud and abuse, on the other.

The principle of neutrality, which had already ruled the CIT, was extended, simplifying the rules to eliminate double taxation, by a symmetric application of the participation exemption for domestic and international substantial holdings. Coherent to the exemption of dividends, the exemption regime was foreseen for PEs located outside of Spain. However, a limit was established for the application of these exemptions, linked to the existence of a minimum taxation at source of 10%.

In this sense, the fight against tax fraud and artificial base erosion (BEPS) were also inspiring principles of the reform, limiting the application of the participation exemption in those cases in which there had not been effective taxation at source or including anti-hybrid rules to avoid situations of double non-taxation. In parallel, the law also regulated strict CFC rules, applicable not only to passive income but, when the controlled entity does not carry on an economic activity, to the whole income obtained by the non-resident entity.

In other words, CIT pursued neutrality for all those cases in which it would not lead to double non-taxation, or to taxation below a certain acceptable threshold.

On the other hand, the taxation of non-residents has evolved towards residence taxation with exemption at source. This can be observed in most of the recent Spanish DTT, with a clear tendency to exempt income at source. Similar to what has been described for resident taxpayers, anti-abuse provisions, limit the exemption regime to the cases in which there has been effective taxation, trying not to give rise to cases of double exemption.

It should be noted that neutrality has been achieved to a greater extent for taxpayers' resident of the EU (or the countries of the EEA that have effective exchange of information with Spain), where Spain in the transposition of the Parent-Subsidiary and the Interest and Royalties Directives has gone further than what was required by the EU law. In the case of third countries, there are, on the contrary, relevant differences which in certain cases are far from tax neutral.

This trend towards neutrality has now clearly been altered, by certain legislative changes, recently adopted.

We are referring to the 2021 Budget law, which from 2021 limits in practice, exemption for dividends or capital gains to 95% of the income, resulting in double or multiple taxation, both for domestic and non-resident share holdings.

On the other hand, the CFC regime has also been modified. Spain has modified the CIT to adapt it to ATAD, and it has been chosen to keep the regime as it was in those aspects in

---

[1]   Partner at PwC Spain, responsible for international tax.

which it was stricter than what is required by the directive, as the application of CFC when the taxation of the controlled entity is less than 75% of the tax that would have been applied in Spain (CFC rules are applicable if the tax is below 18.75%).

Last but not least, the draft Budget Bill for 2022, proposes a minimum 15% domestic taxation for entities with a turnover of at least 20 million euros or for entities that belong to a group taxed under the tax consolidation regime.

In summary, there is a tendency, consistent with the principles of Pillar 2, towards the requirement of minimum taxation and on the other hand, following the inspiring principles of Pillar 1, a DST has been adopted, which implies taxation at source, or more concrete where the consumer or user is located, of certain income.

Branch reporters
Roger Persson Österman[1]
Weronica Sjöberg[2]

Summary and conclusions

Sweden applies a classical company tax system. According to the Swedish Income Tax Act (SITA), each and every company is regarded as a separate tax entity and the income of group companies is not aggregated. Taxable income is therefore calculated for each and every company in a group. The concept of consolidated income is not recognised for Swedish tax purposes.

In several aspects, this can of course lead to a disadvantage compared to a single company conducting all business. The overall purpose of Swedish company tax rules is however that the income taxation should, as far as possible, be the same as if all activities had been carried out in one company, i.e., there should be *neutrality* in the choice of company structure for the business.

In the sixties Sweden therefore introduced the still valid rules of "intra-group financial transfers". By using the rules of intra-group financial transfers, it is possible to offset losses incurred In one group company against profits in another group company. Also, Sweden applies participation exemption rules for domestic and international dividends. In addition, Sweden also applies the participation exemption regime on capital gains and losses. In addition to its domestic legislation, Sweden has implemented the EU Parent-Subsidiary Directive. Sweden thus offers a "virtual" group taxation regime.

The most important set of rules of the Swedish "virtual" group taxation regime, i.e., the intra-group financial transfer regime, also applies to foreign companies resident in the EEA, provided that they qualify as a "foreign company" as defined in the SITA.

In Sweden, there is no connection between the earnings or income of the company and the taxation of the corporate distribution.

Companies follow the Annual Accounts Act of 1995 and the Book Keeping Act of 1999 when preparing their financial statements. The Annual Accounts Act is based on the EU Directives. Business income is computed according to generally accepted accounting standards. The connection between tax accounting and the accounting standards is strong. The accounting defines the profits of the company and forms the basis for Swedish taxation. However, the business accounting result is only the starting point, as several tax rules come into play and make necessary adjustments in order to arrive at a taxable result.

Losses incurred by companies are determined on a continuous basis for each tax period

---

[1]   Roger Persson Österman is professor in Tax Law at Stockholm university, Sweden.
[2]   Weronica Sjöberg LLM is tax consultant at PWC Luxembourg.

The intention of the authors is not to provide a detailed technical description of the intricacies of the Swedish tax system. Rather, the intention is to present a high-level overview of the Swedish network of tax rules for the understanding of the general reporters and readers. The information provided in the report cannot provide knowledge for tax planning or be considered as tax consultation.

and are deductible from taxable profits for the following tax period. If the taxable profits are insufficient to cover the losses from the previous year, the excess loss is carried forward to the next year. Losses may be carried forward indefinitely, i.e., without any time limit. However, losses must be deducted from profits as soon as a profit is available. Change of control triggers limitations of the use of tax losses carried forward. First, when a company obtains decisive control of another company with brought forward tax losses, the amount of the losses exceeding 200% of the expenses incurred for obtaining decisive control will be extinguished. Secondly, a change of control triggers a "group contribution limitation". The right to deduct losses carry forward against group contributions from companies within the acquiring group is deferred. Any tax loss carried forward that survives the amount limitation is restricted for five years.

The Swedish income tax system acknowledges the arm's length principle and an adjustment to market value must be made when the result of an enterprise has been reduced in Sweden as a consequence of contractual terms that deviate from those that would have been agreed upon in a similar third-party context. This main provision is however not applicable in domestic situations. Instead, shifting of profits between two Swedish entities is generally accepted under the condition that the companies can exchange tax-deductible group contributions.

As from 2019, general rules have been introduced to cap interest deductions. These rules are rather complicated; their design is in accordance with the EU Anti-Tax Avoidance Directive (Directive (EU) 2016/1164). Interest deductions are limited to 30% of Earnings Before Taxes Interest Depreciation and Amortization (EBTIDA) and apply to internal as well as third-party debt. Special targeted intra-group rules apply against aggressive tax planning.

A company is considered to be tax resident in Sweden if it is registered with the Swedish Companies Registration Office, meaning that non-resident companies are those that are not incorporated in Sweden.

Sweden imposes corporate income tax on foreign legal entities with respect to several types of Swedish-source income, *inter alia*, business income economically connected to immovable properties or permanent establishments (PE) in Sweden, including capital gains derived from the disposal of such immovable property and the disposal of assets allocated to a Swedish PE.

Sweden does not levy any WHT on interest payments. Sweden has no diverted profits taxes and no digital service taxes.

Sweden applies a worldwide tax regime. A foreign branch is normally fully taxed in Sweden. Juridical double taxation is mitigated through applicable tax treaties or by domestic law. The most important domestic law is the unilateral Foreign Tax Credit Act (FTC). Sweden applies an ordinary tax credit regime. An important feature of the ordinary credit is the overall limitation. All income from foreign branches is regarded as one single foreign income. The FTC is not applicable if there is a tax treaty in place. The treaty rules take over. However, the rules of the overall limitation in the FTC are always applied when calculating the credit limitation. As a last resort, it is always possible to deduct foreign tax paid.

A foreign company's branch income is taxed at the ordinary Swedish tax rate. The general company tax rules apply for branch offices in Sweden. Further, no WHT is levied on the outbound repatriation of profits.

The first Swedish CFC rules were introduced in 1990. The objective to protect the tax base has been focused on and further acknowledged during the legislative processes of later amendments of the CFC rules. The latest amendments of the CFC regime are merely an adaptation to the EU Anti-Tax Avoidance Directive and BEPS Action 3 recommendation for the design of more effective CFC rules.

Branch reporter
Floran Ponce[1]

Summary and conclusions

Switzerland takes a strong separate entity approach, although it does not ignore entirely relationships between related entities. The separate entity principle applies domestically, between cantons and communes, and internationally. In particular, Switzerland has no group provisions for corporate income tax purposes, although it does have provisions for participation relief.

The lack of attention placed on group relationships does mean that it can be difficult to define the notions of 'group' or 'related entity', as neither term is defined under Swiss tax law. However, the Swiss Federal Supreme Court has defined 'related entities' as independent entities under a single economic management; under provisions related to tax-neutral group reorganisations, companies are considered to be part of the same group if one company holds the majority of voting rights in, or exercises control over, the other, which is the same as the definition set out in Swiss commercial law.

One area in which the question of whether entities are related is relevant is participation relief. The Swiss tax system provides for participation relief on intra-group dividends and capital gains realised on the sale of qualifying participations; whether a participation qualifies depends on the size of the receiving entities investment in the distributing entity.

There are no statutory provisions permitting groups to consolidate losses. Still, in some cases, groups may be able to achieve the same effect through a group reorganisation, such as a merger with a company with losses. However, these types of transactions are subject to scrutiny from the tax authorities under the general anti-avoidance principle and there is a risk that the tax authorities could consider the transaction to be a form of tax avoidance.

The notion of related entities also comes into play for loans. Companies may not pay interest on loans from shareholders or related parties in excess of what would be paid to an unrelated third party (based on published safe harbour rates). Swiss tax rules also contain thin capitalisation rules and amounts in excess of the maximum allowed debt are requalified as equity. Both interest paid in excess of the safe harbour rates and interest paid on debt requalified as equity under thin capitalisation rules are treated as constructive dividends when paid to a shareholder or related party, resulting in an increased corporate income tax burden for the paying entity and Swiss withholding tax (35%). However, since dividends paid to a parent company benefit from participation relief, no income tax or withholding tax would be due by the parent company in the event of a constructive dividend paid by a subsidiary.

Since Switzerland does not have special transfer pricing rules, the OECD Transfer Pricing Guidelines, which use the separate entity approach, are followed. It should be noted that Switzerland heavily relies on the OECD Transfer Pricing Guidelines, and on numerous occasions the Swiss Federal Supreme Court has affirmed that the transactions must be

---

[1]   Lawyer, certified tax expert, and partner in the Geneva office of Lenz & Staehelin.

commercially justified and that commercially justified must be interpreted using the OECD Transfer Pricing Guidelines. The OECD Transfer Pricing Guidelines are used not only to determine whether international transactions were carried out at arm's length, but also for domestic transactions, which also must be carried out at arm's length.

Switzerland also has implemented, and closely follows, the authorised OECD approach with regard to attribution of business profits between foreign and domestic branches and head offices under article 7 of the OECD MC and Switzerland complies with the BEPS minimum standards.

Additionally, even though Switzerland does not have special anti-avoidance rules, the Swiss Federal Supreme Court's case law, based on a general anti-abuse rule, permits the tax authorities to tax a taxpayer's structure based on its economic substance, rather than its legal structure when there is tax avoidance or abuse of a right. For instance, a foreign entity can be disregarded when a structure is considered abusive in that there is a lack of clear separation between the Swiss company and a foreign subsidiary. In such cases, the foreign entity's income and expenses will be attributed directly to the Swiss taxpayer. In practice, this is rare as there is no real tendency in Switzerland to pierce the corporate veil.

Further, it should be noted that participation relief also applies on the international level. This means that participation income from foreign entities qualifies for participation relief, regardless of the foreign entity's tax rate or of the existence of a double tax treaty between Switzerland and the jurisdiction in which the subsidiary is liable to tax, which is rather generous in comparison to other jurisdictions.

Lastly, Switzerland does not have CFC rules.

In summary, Switzerland's approach to groups can be summed up as an OECD-compliant, separate entity approach that takes into consideration relationships between group entities when necessary, such as for transfer pricing purposes or to prevent tax avoidance or tax evasion, but that places limited importance on groups. Generally, this approach is beneficial for groups, since participation relief provides a formidable exception for participation income, including foreign profits; the major downside is the difficulty of consolidating losses.

Branch reporter
Gülşen Gedik[1]

Summary and conclusions

In the Turkish tax system, there are different legal provisions regarding the taxes on incomes of real persons and the earnings of corporations, and the main reason for these differences is to tax them more effectively. The reason to also consider the corporations, which do not distribute profit, as taxpayers is to ensure that they compete in the market on equal terms.

The profit shares of the partners of simple partnerships, which do not have a separate legal entity, are taxed according to the provisions of the Income Tax Law (ITL) on a partner-by-partner basis, according to the type of the income. The profit shares that the partners of the collective partnership receive from the partnership are taxed according to the provisions on commercial earnings. Since the earnings obtained by the shareholders in limited companies are included within the scope of earnings on the associates' stocks, they will be considered earnings on stocks. Profit shares that the shareholders of joint-stock companies obtain for the shares they own will also be considered earnings on stocks.

Regarding the status of corporations as to whether they are fully or limited taxable, the criterion is if either its registered head office or principal place of business is in Turkey. If both of them are abroad, they will be taxed in Turkey only on the income they obtain in Turkey.

"Group companies / controlling partnerships and subsidiaries" and similar phrases are not included among the taxpayers mentioned in the law, and there is no such provision. Therefore, according to the CTL, in principle, each taxpayer is taxed separately, and in this sense in the corporation tax system of Turkey a "separate entity doctrine" applies and a group taxation system does not exist.

Nor is there any bill pending regarding a separate and special system for group companies. Even if in the Turkish legal system, in the Turkish Commercial Code (TCC), the term "group of companies" is used, controlling companies and the subsidiaries cannot be considered a "group company" within the scope of TCC.

According to the Turkish tax authorities, transfer pricing is defined as the buying or selling goods and services by the owners of corporations and enterprises from and to the related persons, at worth and prices they determine contrary to the arm's length principle.

The transfer pricing rule is based on deeming the persons and corporations that do not apply arm's length prices to have distributed their earnings in a camouflaged way. The earnings that are distributed totally or partially by transfer pricing in a camouflaged way will, according to ITL and CTL, be deemed profit that is distributed as of the last day of the accounting period when the conditions regarding transfer pricing had materialized or, for limited taxable taxpayers, the sum that would be transferred to the head office. Previous taxation transactions of the taxpayer parties will have to be corrected accordingly.

---

[1]   Associate Professor of Tax Law at Marmara University School of Law Tax Law Department. She has two books about Group Taxation and Controlled Foreign Corporations and articles about different topics in tax law.

In the Turkish tax legislation, there is a provision on CFC, according to which a controlled foreign corporation is an association abroad, which real person taxpayers and corporations do control by holding, directly or indirectly, separately, or together, at least 50% of its capital, profit share, or voting rights. Where 25% or more of the total gross proceeds of the associate consists of passive income like interest, profit share, rent, royalty, proceeds from sales of stocks, other than commercial, agricultural, or self-employment activities performed by investing capital, and using an organization, and hiring employees that are proportional in scope to that activity; carries a total burden of tax, like income and corporation tax, of less than 10% of the profit on the balance sheet of the associate abroad and; the total gross proceeds of the associate abroad exceeds the amount of foreign currency that is equal to TRY 100,000, CFC rules will apply.

In the Turkish tax legislation, in the ITL, with the heading "nonallowable expenses," it is provided that in the case of real person businesses, tax rebate on the current account or other claims of the business owner himself/herself, his/her spouse, and children will be considered a nonallowable expense where as in the CTL, it is provided that interests that are calculated and paid on equity capital are not deductible; that the part of the debts the corporations obtain directly or indirectly from their shareholders or from people that are associated with the shareholders, which at any date within the fiscal period exceed three times the amount of the equity capital, will be deemed to be the camouflaged capital for that fiscal period.

A country-by-country reporting requirement for multinational businesses has been introduced and according to the provision in that Communiqué, if the consolidated group income of the multinational businesses' group is 750 million Euro or more, the main business or agents – domiciled in Turkey – of the multinational group will prepare a CbC report and submit it online to the tax administration.

Whereas the Digital Service Tax (DST) that has taken effect in the Turkish tax system is intended for digital platforms and data, the bill on the taxation of major digital assets is intended to cover digital services in the broader sense. According to this legislation, all advertisement services offered in a digital environment; the services offered on a digital environment involving the sale of any audio visual or digital content, and listening, viewing, playing, or recording or using them on electronic devices; the provision and operation of digital media through which the users could interact with one another; and proceeds obtained from these services should they be offered in Turkey, and intermediary services given in association with these services by the digital service providers are subject to DST.

Branch reporters
Tetiana Fedorenko[1]
Oleksandr Markov[2]
Kateryna Kuzmenko[3]

Summary and conclusions

Ukraine does not apply a group approach to domestic or cross-border transactions. Such an approach (taxation of a consolidated tax group at domestic level) was discussed extensively in 2013, and a draft law was even passed, with the first reading in December 2013. The draft law was rather beneficial for big groups and Ukrainian oligarchs and was not adopted. The issue has not been raised since that time. The main concern is the decrease of corporate income tax inflow to the budget, caused by offset of accumulated losses against taxable profit of different entities of one group and adverse social reaction to more benefits for large taxpayers.

Nevertheless, the Ukrainian tax legislation has some rules that can be regarded as belonging to a group approach. Such provisions are non-taxation of dividends received from subsidiaries, absence of separate taxations with corporate income tax and VAT of a Ukrainian company's branches and some restrictions of application of simplified tax regime within a group. From 2020, tax losses accumulated by one entity of a group's can be passed to another group's entity, but only as the result of merger/joining.

Ukraine's efforts to implement international tax control standards are obvious.

With regard to cross-border transactions, Ukraine introduced in 2020 several new concepts: controlled foreign companies, participation exemption for dividends coming into Ukraine and constructive dividends. Thin capitalisation rules will become stricter from 2021, and some changes to the recognition of permanent establishment and permanent establishment taxation have also been introduced.

The Law 466-IX "On amendments to the Tax Code of Ukraine on improvement of taxes administration, elimination of logical and technical inconsistencies in tax legislation" introducing the mentioned changes has come into force on 23 May 2020. The majority of these new concepts apply from 1 January 2021. However, due to ambiguous wording and critics from the business community, CFC rules have been postponed to 2022 and some concepts, e.g., thin capitalisation rules, was softened.

If we take into account the number of changes made to the tax legislation of Ukraine regarding the implementation of the BEPS action plan, we can conclude that Ukraine clearly demonstrates a desire to comply with European and world tax requirements. Moreover, based on the trends in business structuring in the form of groups of companies, certain initiatives concerning the group approach should be expected in Ukraine.

---

[1]   Advocate, International Tax Law, AVIDBIZ.
[2]   Head of Tax, Partner, Redcliffe Partners.
[3]   Tax Consultant, Redcliffe Partners

Branch reporter
Jisun Choi[1]

Summary and conclusions

The concept of a group taxation exists in certain limited contexts in the United Kingdom (UK). The UK's value added tax (VAT) regime operates on a group basis, with a representative member of the group being treated as making and receiving all relevant supplies of goods and services, where an application to HM Revenue & Customs is made by eligible members of a group of companies. The UK's legislative provisions with respect to a VAT group adopts the framework that has been set by the European Union in its directive on the common system of value added tax. The UK digital services tax is a tax that is charged on multinational enterprises (MNEs) by reference to the relevant group's UK digital services revenues. Both VAT and the digital services tax are notably turnover taxes and the respective regimes were of course influenced by international considerations, whether at the European Union or OECD/G20 Inclusive Framework level.

However, the separate entity approach is still very much the prevailing approach applicable to UK corporation tax, which is broadly applicable to UK resident companies and companies carrying on a trade through a UK permanent establishment. This is also the case in respect of other UK taxes on profits, such as the diverted profits tax, and transaction taxes, such as stamp duty and stamp duty land tax.

The UK tax system generally looks to reflect the economic reality of businesses operating through a combination of different companies, or even entities including partnerships – i.e., a 'group' – by providing relevant reliefs or exemptions to companies where the group condition is satisfied. For example, certain trading and non-trading losses or deficits of one company may be surrendered to set against profits of another company in the same group as the first (whether the profits are made in the same accounting period or subsequent accounting periods) and chargeable gains arising on the disposal of (broadly capital) assets may be reallocated to another group company to set against the other group company's losses. Transfers of assets of a company to another company in the same group by and large may be achieved tax neutrally or without significant tax friction.

The belonging to a group in most of these contexts is established through varying percentages of ownership of the relevant companies' 'ordinary share capital' and loans that are not 'normal commercial loans' – i.e., loans that contain equity features, for example, where it is convertible or gives rights to acquire shares or the return is dependent on the results of the relevant company's business. The availability of such group-based reliefs or exemptions is of course subject to a myriad of legislative provisions either denying at the outset or retrospectively withdrawing the relevant relief or exemption in the event of a contemplated or an actual 'degrouping' or other change of ownership or control of the relevant companies.

---

[1]   Counsel, Skadden, Arps, Slate, Meagher & Flom (UK) LLP.

Whilst being eligible to obtain reliefs and exemptions in respect of tax, large groups of companies have additional compliance burdens, such as country-by-country reporting, and are subject to additional tax regimes, such as the corporation tax regimes on transfer pricing, controlled foreign companies and corporate interest restriction rules, each of which either have exemptions made available to SMEs or de minimis thresholds.

Needless to say, the OECD Base Erosion and Profit Shifting (BEPS) project in which the UK was and continues to be an active participant has certainly tested the separate entity approach in many ways and it has brought along significant changes to how governments approach the international system of taxation, in particular as applicable to large multinational groups. As far as BEPS-led changes are concerned, in the author's view, although the UK has been proactive and an early adopter of the OECD recommendations, many of the changes made simply layer on additional group elements to the existing UK corporation tax regime instead of fundamentally shifting the UK corporation tax regime away from an entity-by-entity approach. For example, the anti-hybrid rules still generally look at arrangements on a transaction-by-transaction and entity-by-entity basis albeit in a group context established again through equity ownership or other connection or association. As we await the implementation details of the Two-Pillar Solution, one may question whether Pillar Two, which clearly envisages a group taxation regime in the Income Inclusion Rule, could tip the balance to shift the UK away from a separate entity approach. Given ongoing developments it is difficult to be definitive but the answer is likely to be no. This author anticipates that the Two Pillars will be implemented in the UK as separate regimes applicable to relevant MNEs in line with the internationally agreed scope and that such implementation is unlikely to come together with any radical reform to the UK corporation tax regime, which has the separate entity approach underpinning it.

Branch reporter
Brigitte Muehlmann[1]

Summary and conclusions

Part One: Domestic law

The domestic corporate income tax system treats corporations as independent tax-paying entities, unless they fulfill a tax-exempt purpose, qualify for pass-through treatment as closely held corporations, or have special characteristics. The legal entity can be a domestic corporation or another entity that elects taxation as a corporation using the check-the-box approach. Financial and tax net income or loss are determined separately, and must be reconciled as part of tax reporting. Corporate income is taxed on the corporation and the shareholder levels. The arm's length principle applies to domestic intercompany transactions. Inter-company capital gains are ordinarily recognized, but losses disallowed.

Consolidated financial statements must include all controlled entities worldwide. The objective is the presentation of the economic unit. In contrast, the aim of the elective consolidated tax return group taxation system is neutrality of organization. Consolidated taxable income is determined separate from financial accounting. Affiliated groups have multiple methods available for the allocation of the tax liability. All members are liable for the taxes of the tax group.

The US tax system contains special change of control rules that apply when either an owner shift or an equity structure shift occurred. An extensive list of affected tax attributes includes the carry-forward of losses, the carryover of disallowed interest expense and foreign tax credits. These rules also apply in case of intra-group transfers or re-organizations.

Special avoidance rules limit tax benefits to a group as a whole or deny them altogether, if the principal purpose of acquiring control is evading or avoiding income tax. The economic substance doctrine, which is codified in US tax law, applies more broadly.

Special rules for intra-group interest allow a deduction up to 30 percent of a business' adjusted taxable income, and exceeding amounts to be carried forward. A consolidated group's adjusted taxable income is determined by reference to the group's income.

State corporate income taxes are levied in addition to federal income taxation in 45 states. Formulary apportionment is generally applied. The predominant apportionment factor is based on the destination of sales. States require or permit separate entity or combined reporting. State law may require a consolidated tax return to be based on a federal consolidated return filing.

Coordinated audits are used for groups with substantial operations in more than one IRS district. The instructions to tax auditors include special audit rules for certain cross-border topics. There are special documentation and reporting requirements if corporations

---

[1]   Professor and Research Scholar at Babson College, and an Adjunct Professor at Texas A&M University School of Law.

belong to a multinational group and notice must be given regarding certain transfers to foreign persons.

Part Two: Cross-border situations

The check-the-box classification system is used to determine whether a foreign taxpayer is treated as a corporation or not for US tax purposes. A foreign corporate entity is subject to the same corporate US tax rates on its effectively connected net income as a domestic corporate entity. Treaties generally limit the taxation to US trade or business income that is attributable to a permanent establishment. The receipt of non-business income may be subject to a flat tax on gross income withheld at its source, which may be reduced or exempt by a tax treaty.

Profits from foreign branches are taxed in the US when earned. US tax on foreign branch income can be reduced by foreign income taxes paid by a foreign branch. Losses from a foreign branch flow through to the US taxable entity. If the losses can also be used by a foreign subsidiary to reduce its income under foreign law, dual consolidated loss rules limit the current use in the US.

Any dividend equivalent amount of a domestic branch in the US is subject to a flat rate branch profits tax. The corporation to which the branch belongs is generally entitled to DTT benefits.

Income from foreign subsidiaries is taxed in the year it is earned, either as Subpart F income or GILTI or not at all. Double taxation is avoided through a foreign tax credit. An affiliated group that files a consolidated income tax return may use foreign tax credits at the discretion of the common parent. Losses from the depreciation of shares in a foreign subsidiary are tax deductible if a security becomes worthless during the taxable year, just like a domestic worthless stock loss. Foreign entities are generally excluded from joining in a tax group. Individual member corporations of a group are entitled to claim DTT benefits, not the group.

Separate entity accounting and the arm's length standard are the prevailing transfer pricing principles. The profit split method is available as a transfer pricing method when both parties to a transaction contribute intangibles. The arm's length standard may be overridden by formulary allocations such as in the GILTI rules.

The US was the first country to introduce a CFC regime. The policy rationale was to counter perceived abuses arising from the misuse of the deferral principle by shifting income to foreign subsidiaries in low-tax jurisdictions. The scope of the CFC regime encompasses low taxed passive income, certain illegal income, and income from business with certain ostracized countries. The mechanism is current income inclusion. The deduction for business interest expense is the same as in a domestic context.

Hybrid mismatch-rules provide that no deduction is allowed for certain related party interest or royalty that is not already included as Subpart F income. The treatment in another state is tested on the basis of the abstract application of foreign tax rules. Country-by-country reporting is an annual reporting requirement by the ultimate parent entity of a US multinational enterprise group with a threshold of $850 Million group revenues.

The Tax Reform Act of 2017 introduced a move toward a territorial tax system with a new current inclusion of a controlled foreign corporation's Global Intangible Low-Taxed Income (GILTI) and a Base Erosion and Anti-Abuse Tax (BEAT) in the US. There are no digital service taxes currently implemented or contemplated in Federal US tax law.

Branch reporters
Alejandro Horjales[1]
Fernando Barrios[2]

Summary and conclusions

It is a fact that today a large number of companies – not only multinational ones – are organized as groups of companies. In this context, both corporate and accounting regulations reflect this economic reality by requiring companies to prepare consolidated financial statements for the group as well as individual financial statements.

This increasing phenomenon of groups of companies is an undeniable business reality nowadays and therefore it is contemplated by the law from different angles, including, naturally and necessarily, the tax perspective.

The increasingly frequent existence of groups or conglomerate of entities with different levels of coordination – and which in some cases even reaches hypotheses of subordination – makes the application of tax rules more complex, in many cases necessitating the requalification of the legal forms adopted by the taxpayers, or even a verification of the existence of some indicators which denote the existence of a link or relationship between companies which, depending on the case, could give room to the application of different measures or remedies provided by the rules, with the associated consequences in each case, e.g., joint liability, consolidated tax assessment, among others.

From a domestic standpoint, corporate income taxation in Uruguay has historically adopted an individual or separate entity approach, regardless of whether the entity is part of an economic group. As a rule or general principle, the Uruguayan tax system does not have rules that establish group taxation regimes, i.e., rules which subject to taxation the income generated by a group of companies under a regular and consolidated basis. In this respect, taxation in Uruguay maintains a separate entity imprint or approach, taxing the income generated by each individual entity in its corresponding fiscal year. In addition, and in light of the above, there is no option for entities which are part of an economic group or unit to assess and cancel tax obligations in a consolidated manner and as if it were a single taxpayer.

It is clear in the aforementioned scenario that the existence of a group of companies itself, and the associated intra-group transactions, entail some difficulties and/or distortions in the application of taxes, which are then intended to be contemplated and solved through specific regulations.

In this respect, Uruguayan tax rules provide for certain measures which take as a factual premise the existence of a plurality of entities – either when such plurality responds to a single decision-making center, or when a single business unit actually underlies such plurality – and which are intended to prevent tax avoidance, protect the tax credit and/or also get a better assessment of taxpayers' contributive capacity. These measures – which will

---

[1] Accountant, Universidad de la República (Uruguay). Tax and transfer pricing professor at the Universidad de la República and Universidad de Montevideo.

[2] Attorney-at-law, Universidad de la República (Uruguay). Independent advisor. Specialized in tax and customs law.

be imposed as a result of a reclassification/reassessment of the factual grounds by the tax office or by means of a judgment issued by a competent court – could entail an extension of tax liability to entities which are both legally and functionally independent but in some way linked and/or actually coordinated by a single decision-making center, as well as the assessment and payment of tax debts based on a consolidated balance sheet in those cases where there is a single economic or business unit underlying a plurality of entities. However, and strictly speaking, any of the referred situations entails an actual hypothesis of group taxation based on a regular and standardized group approach.

From an international perspective and in a very simplified way, the separate entity approach and the arm's length principle have been historically the bases of international taxation; therefore, the rules which intend to move forward to a taxation based on a group approach deviate in some manner from such driving principles, whose purpose is to ensure appropriate and effective taxation for each entity individually considered. In this respect, although the recent developments in matters of corporate taxation and transfer pricing still adhere to the separate entity approach, it is a fact that the tax challenges posed by the modern businesses/production schemas and mostly due to the increasing digitalization of the economy have brought into question the current foundational tax concepts and principles, opening a broad discussion on the need and appropriateness of some corrections and/or adjustments with the aim of moving towards to a group approach in the matter of corporate taxation.

Uruguay is not out of touch with this new international context, and in this sense and without prejudice to the general policies which govern taxation based on the source's principle – with few exceptions which allow for taxation abroad – and the separate entity approach, both domestic tax rules and tax treaty provisions executed by Uruguay have been incorporating reporting duties applying to entities which are part of groups of companies with international scope, as well as provisions in the sense of preventing hypotheses of double non-taxation due to hybrid mismatch arrangements in the context of cross-border intra-group transactions or operations.

Following the guidelines provided by the general reporters, the analysis of the subject is carried out considering, firstly, the domestic perspective – particularly regarding potential deviations from the separate entity approach in domestic tax law – and lastly, the international standpoint, focusing on special rules for cross-border groups with the main aim of preventing BEPS and the allocation of profits on a group basis.

General report Subject 2

Big data and tax – domestic and
international taxation of data driven business

Gary D. Sprague (USA)

Big data and tax – domestic and international taxation of data driven business

Table of contents

Summary and conclusions

The topic of Big Data and Tax - Domestic and International Taxation of Data Driven Businesses challenged the branch reporters to apply existing legal principles to new forms of commercial transactions. None of the branch reports disclosed any tax regime specifically legislated or regulated to apply to transactions involving data, except for recent unilateral taxes such as digital services taxes.

The branch reports addressed the topic in the context of four case studies which were designed to raise issues commonly seen in practice. The case studies described business models of (i) a data broker who pays for unprocessed information provided by a third party website host and transfers that data to customers for a fee, (ii) an enterprise which provides processed and structured data to another enterprise for a fee to be displayed on the payor's website, (iii) an enterprise which uses sensors placed on customers' equipment to provide performance analytics and repair services for a fee, and (iv) a consultant who creates a database on which to base its consultancy services and also allows others to access the database for a fee. Thirty-seven IFA branches submitted reports.

The branch reporters generally agreed that the fundamental issue in these transactions is the character of the transaction for tax purposes, both under domestic law and any applicable tax treaty. In many cases, the starting point for the characterization analysis is a review of the commercial law treatment of data transactions. Generally speaking, a copyright or intellectual property right does not exist in raw data, on the basis that data is equivalent to information. In most jurisdictions, there is no specific legal framework applicable to the data itself, other than in the area of regulating data privacy. Nevertheless, it is clear that enterprises can create and control value based on their data analytics functions and contractual restrictions on access to data which they grant to customers.

The branch reports exhibit a significant variety of analytical approaches to the characterization issue. It is not possible to harmonize all of the reports into a single analytical framework. It is possible to draw some general conclusions about tendencies, but it is clear that due to the undeveloped state of national law on this issue, individual circumstances in the national context may result in different analytical approaches and conclusions.

In general, most branch reports identified the principal characterization issue relating to data transfer transactions as the distinction between a payment for the provision of services versus a royalty for the grant of rights in an intangible. In a smaller number of reports, it was also considered possible that the transactions might be considered as a sale of property. The majority view was that the data transfer transactions described in the case studies constituted the provision of services, although the reasoning behind that conclusion differed among the reports.

There was no commonly used point of reference for analogous transactions. The most

---

[1] Gary D. Sprague joined Baker McKenzie in 1985. His practice focuses on advice to software, high technology, and digital enterprise companies.

promising analogy was to national guidance and OECD treaty interpretation regarding the classification of software transactions. The variety of approaches and conclusions expressed in the branch reports raises the question of whether a separate and specific technical framework should be developed to apply to data transactions, or whether existing principles are adequate to produce sensible and economically rational results. In general, at least for those jurisdictions which need to distinguish among the more common categories of sales of property, services, license of intangible property, or transfers of know-how, the prevailing view seems to be that existing analytical approaches can work. That said, the general reporter suspects that many branch reporters would endorse a proposal for international harmonization, perhaps through additions to the OECD MTC Commentary.

An appendix to the general report presents the income characterization conclusions from the branch reporters on the transactions described in the first two case studies.

Regarding transfer pricing, there is little or no precedent in local jurisprudence applying the relevant transfer pricing principles to transactions involving big data. In general, most branch reports referred to the relevant principles, such as the OECD Transfer Pricing Guidelines or domestic legislation, and observed that those principles appeared to be sufficiently robust to apply to big data transactions. There was a difference of views among the reporters on whether residual value in a data enabled transaction should be allocated to the data itself, or to the structuring and analytics functions that allowed the data to be commercialized. The majority pointed to the analytics work as the more significant value creating function under DEMPE concepts.

The most high profile special regime designed to apply to some (but only some) of the big data transactions described in the case studies is the digital services tax. While the tax expressly applies to revenue arising from the transmission of data collected about users and generated from users' activities on digital interfaces, no reporter from a jurisdiction which has enacted a DST reported interpretative issues under this leg of the DST.

A number of the branch reports addressed the challenging question of whether barter principles should be applied to big data transactions of the sort reflected in the case studies. Several branch reports indicated that a barter theory of income and expense recognition might in principle apply, but there is only limited experience of the theory being applied in practice. Many branch reports commented on the perhaps practical impossibility of administering this theory, especially where individuals are involved on one end of the transaction.

Many branch reports described special regimes related to investment incentives which in principle are available to "big data" enterprises, in particular R&D credit or deduction allowances, and in many cases patent or innovation boxes. In general, there is no inherent barrier for big data business enterprises to qualify for the various incentives.

The volume of cross-border "big data" transactions inevitably will increase. Creative entrepreneurs will continue to devise business models that may pose even greater challenges to apply the appropriate tax treatment to novel transactions than the case studies discussed here.

1. Introduction

The topic of Big Data and Tax - Domestic and International Taxation of Data Driven Businesses presents an unusual context for a comparative law analysis of the tax treatment of transactions described by the topic title. The frame of reference for this topic is not a type of transaction (e.g., Sharing and Shifting Losses - the "New" Profit Shifting?; Cancun 2022 Main Subject 1), or a tax policy issue (e.g., Group Approach and Separate Entity Approach in Domestic and International Tax Law; Berlin 2022 Main Subject 1).

Instead, the context for this topic is the growth of technology which both enables new business models and enhances business functionality across many sectors and businesses. This technology enables businesses to access and analyze large amounts of data to develop and offer new goods and services on the market, improve their decision making, and in general capitalize on information technology tools to create value and capture business efficiencies.

The general reporter is not aware of a past IFA main subject or seminar on the specific issue of "big data", although seminars at prior IFA Congresses on software, e-commerce and digital transactions have raised many of the same areas of inquiry, such as the characterization of transactions for both domestic law and treaty purposes.

"Big data" is not a legal or fiscal term in its own right. Rather, the term "big data " usually refers to projects, software, services or business functions that involve collecting, aggregating, structuring, and analyzing large information sets, often unstructured data or information that was originally collected for different purposes, which can lead to direct or indirect commercialization. A critical element of big data commercialization is the development and deployment of sophisticated data analytics tools, including algorithms, which allow an enterprise to determine relationships and tendencies within very large data sets and derive insights therefrom. This subject addresses tax issues arising from commercial transactions in which businesses aggregate, process, and analyze large data sets in order to create and provide new forms of goods or services or to improve the utility of goods or services already existing in the market.

Using data analytics to collect, aggregate, structure, and analyze large data sets has become an increasingly significant business function in the global marketplace. A large variety of businesses - not only or even primarily digital services providers - make use of big data techniques. Businesses implement big data analytics for many purposes, including to boost customer acquisition and retention, identify potential business risks, develop risk management solutions, innovate and develop new products, and manage supply chains.

Some business models which are based on big data analytics are very visible in the public eye, most notably those businesses which are able to aggregate and structure personal data. Those business models have received attention from regulators, as governments around the world have moved to protect personal privacy through regulatory limits on the use of personally identifiable information.[2]

Those business models also have attracted attention in the international tax arena, as the original impetus for the digital services tax initially proposed by the European Commission was based at least in part on the concept that companies which are able to collect and structure data from individual users for commercial benefit should be subject to tax in the user jurisdiction on revenues connected to that user data.

Big data business applications, however, extend far beyond those transactions subject to digital services taxes. Other emerging and foreseeable business applications of big data

---

[2]   See, e.g., the General Data Protection Regulation in the EU (Regulation (EU) 2016/679 of the European Parliament and of the Council of 27 April 2016, and the California Consumer Privacy Act of 2018 (Cal. Civ. Code §§ 1798.100 - 1798.199.100).

technologies include, among others, the following: connected and autonomous vehicles; medical research; remote equipment monitoring; machine learning; predictive and prescriptive analytics; and an increasingly interconnected "Internet of Things."

The relationship between big data and taxation involves both domestic and international aspects. Branch reporters were encouraged to consider tax issues that may arise across the larger spectrum of data enhanced businesses. In particular, branch reporters were asked to consider how their jurisdictions treat payments to nonresident firms that use big data to provide goods or services to their residents.

Thirty-seven IFA branches submitted branch reports on the topic.[3] In all cases, the reports were of high quality, and reflected thoughtful consideration of these challenging issues. The general reporter was gratified to see many contributions from younger IFA members; clearly the topic resonated with those who have grown up in an intensely digital environment.

2. Legal framework

Many of the issues arising from transactions involving big data require a consideration of the relevant property or commercial law aspects of data and of transactions in which data are used or conveyed. The legal framework relating to collection of, use of, and transactions in data is highly undeveloped around the world and the application of general legal principles to big data and related transactions may vary from jurisdiction to jurisdiction. Generally speaking, in most jurisdictions a copyright or intellectual property right does not exist in raw data, on the basis that data is equivalent to information. However, some jurisdictions are considering the creation of *sui generis* ownership rights in data, in some cases drawing fine distinctions between various types of data, including raw data, personal data, machine data, etc. The EU has for some time had a *sui generis* database right, which does not create property in the data itself, but in the economic investment in collecting and organizing the data in a database. In most jurisdictions, however, there is no specific legal framework applicable to the data itself, other than in the area of regulating data privacy.

In order to provide the branch reporters with a background of generally applicable legal principles that determine rights in data, the general reporter provided a summary of prevailing academic commentary relating to legal principles that normally apply to the collection of or transactions in data.[4] Branch reporters also were asked to consider their own country's legal framework in order to confirm or elaborate on this general description.

---

[3]   The following Branches submitted reports: Argentina, Australia, Austria, Belgium, Brazil, Canada, Chile, Chinese Taipei, Colombia, Czech Republic, Denmark, Finland, France, Germany, India, Italy, Japan, Republic of Korea, Liechtenstein, Luxembourg, Malaysia, Mauritius, Mexico, Netherlands, Norway, Peru, Poland, Portugal, Russia, Singapore, South Africa, Spain, Sweden, Switzerland, Turkey, United States, and Uruguay. The general reporter thanks all of the branch reporters for their hard work and insightful observations.

[4]   I would like to express my appreciation to Lothar Determann, partner resident in the Baker McKenzie Palo Alto office, for his assistance in preparing this summary of the international legal framework.

2.1. General property law:

- In general, academics tend to agree that there is no property right in data *per se*, even when that data has been aggregated in a database.
- The general reporter is not aware of any general "data property statute" providing for a generalized property right in data.
- Various property law concepts might apply to protect against access to data and information by third parties. For example, data sets might be subject to access rights and restrictions.

2.2. Copyright:

- There is a general consensus among academics that there can be no copyright protection in data, as data are not the expression of an original creation; data exist separately from works of authorship, databases, and media.
- However, jurisdictions differ in the copyright protection given to databases.
  - US copyright law distinguishes between the substance of the data or information and the particular form or collection of words in which the writer communicates that data or information. *See* Int'l News Serv. v. Associated Press, 248 U.S. 215, 234 (1918).
  - US law does provide copyright ownership rights for compilations of data, so long as that compilation of data is creative in nature. See Feist Publ'ns, Inc. v. Rural Tel. Serv. Co., Inc , 499 U.S. 340, (1991).
  - EU copyright law recognizes that copyright can exist in a database if the database meets the subsistence requirements of copyright at the member state level. Such rights would exist independent of the EU's sui generis database right.

2.3. Sui Generis Rights:

- Some jurisdictions afford limited sui generis protection for collections of valuable data sets.
- For example, European database laws offer copyright-like protection to creators of valuable databases. See Directive 96/9/EC of the European Parliament and of the Council of 11 March 1996 on the Legal Protection of Databases, 1996 O.J. (L 77) 20.

2.4. Trade Secret / Confidential Information:

- The law of trade secret / confidential information can protect information that is held secret, has value due to that secrecy, and steps are taken to maintain secrecy.
- These principles can apply to transactions in data depending on the circumstances.
- Device manufacturers generally cannot claim trade secret ownership rights in data and information collected by the devices they sell to customers.
- Similarly, consumers typically cannot claim trade secret rights in the data collected by the devices they own because normally consumers cannot claim a competitive advantage from keeping such data secret.

2.5. Contract law:

- Parties are free to regulate the use of data provided under contract per the terms of the contract.
- Contract law creates rights and obligations between the contracting parties and named beneficiaries, i.e., these agreements bind the other contracting parties but do not convey actual property rights.

2.6. Regulatory restrictions:

- Government regulation could impose obligations on those who acquire and process data, particularly personal data.
- For example, EU lawmakers have taken broad action to promote data privacy with the General Data Protection Regulation, which prohibits companies from processing any personal data unless there is a statutory exception.

2.7. Control:

- The fact of unique control over specific data sets may allow some enterprises to commercialize that data as a practical matter.
- Control may be exercised by not allowing others to access the data, or by transferring data only under limitations provided by contract.

3. Case Studies

Given the variety of transactions that could involve the use, transfer or other commercial exploitation of big data and big data analytics tools, the branch reporters were given a set of four representative case studies, which were designed to illustrate different tax issues that could arise in the very broad category of "big data transactions". In some cases, branch reporters provided a specific analysis for each of the case studies; in others the branch report referred to a subset of those cases.

In most cases, the branch reports did not reproduce the facts of the case studies. Accordingly, the case studies are reproduced here to assist the reader of those branch reports which included an analysis of the case study without describing the assumed facts.

3.1. Data Brokers / Information Resellers

An enterprise is in the business of gathering data from various sources in order to build profiles of consumer behavior ("Broker Co."). Broker Co gathers some information through application program interfaces ("APIs") which a website owner ("Website Co.") may allow to provide access to information generated through traffic on Website Co.'s website. Broker Co. also may separately contract with other suppliers to acquire information though loyalty cards, user-contributed data from social media websites, and various other sources. Broker

Co. makes an annual payment to Website Co. for access to user generated data through the API.

Broker Co. invests in engineering personnel who develop data analytics software which organizes and structures the data. Data retained in Broker Co.'s structured database may persist for several years. Broker Co. sells copies of data sets to Customers. Customers may set parameters to define the data sets they purchase. Customers may purchase the data sets for purposes of targeted advertising, fraud detection, marketing analysis, insurance risk analysis, or similar purposes. Broker Co. charges Customer fees based on the size of data sets supplied and the degree of analytics which it had applied to that data set. Broker Co. by contract prohibits Customers from on-selling the data. Customers may use the purchased data sets for as long as they wish, although the value of a static data set decreases rapidly over time.

Most Customers are located outside Broker Co.'s country of residence, and typically will download the data sets from Broker Co.'s servers. The data relates to persons resident inside and outside the residence jurisdictions of Website Co., Broker Co., and Customer.

3.1.1. *Issues raised*

This example was designed to raise the following issues.

i.   character: this example describes two payments that must be characterized for tax purposes, payments (i) by Customer to Broker Co., and (ii) by Broker Co. to Website Co. Does the character of these payments depend on the nature of data or Broker Co.'s structured database as property under applicable law? Does the lack of ownership of a property interest in the data itself signify something other than a sale? Under what circumstances could these transactions be characterized as a lease or license? If the data transferred is not property, should the transaction be characterized as a provision of service? Do the differences in the commercial relationships between Website Co. and Broker Co., and between Broker Co. and Customer, indicate a different character of the two transactions?

ii. source: should the source of the income be at the place of business of Website Co., Broker Co., Customer, or the location of the persons who are the data sources? Does the source differ between the two transactions? Does it differ depending on the character of the transactions? How does the determination of source affect the tax treatment of the relevant income item?

iii. nexus: could direct tax nexus exist for Website Co. or Broker Co. outside their countries of residence?

iv. transfer pricing: assume that Website Co. and Broker Co. are related parties. What would be the most appropriate transfer pricing method to determine the price paid by Broker Co. to Website Co. for access to the user generated data? What facts particular to this business arrangement are most significant in making that determination? How would the different contributions to value of Website Co. and Broker Co. be evaluated?

v.   deduction vs capitalization and amortization: are Broker Co.'s data acquisition costs and software development expenses currently deductible expenses? If they must be capitalized, can those costs be deducted through amortization expenses? Over what period?

vi. DST: if the jurisdiction has imposed a DST, could the DST apply to the revenue of Website Co., Broker Co. or both derived from selling the data sets?

3.2. Data Feeds

An enterprise is in the business of predicting animal migration ("Animal Data Co."). The enterprise gathers data on weather forecasts, food supply, predator density, urban development, climate change, and other elements. The enterprise has developed data analytics tools which it uses to create maps of predicted animal density at various future points of time. Another enterprise operates a website whose viewers would be interested in animal migration information ("Information Site Co."). Information Site Co. contracts with Animal Data Co. to provide a continuous feed showing migration patterns and predictions for a monthly fee. For the fee, Information Site Co. receives the data feed and is entitled to display the information to all viewers on its website. Information Site Co. receives no rights to use Animal Data Co.'s data analytics software and algorithms, except as may be necessary to allow display of the output on Information Site Co.'s website. Information Site Co. does not charge its users a fee to view the information. Information Site Co. is located in a different jurisdiction than Animal Data Co.

As an alternative, Animal Data Co. is a not for profit NGO formed for the purpose of supporting wildlife conservation. Animal Data Co. does not charge Information Site Co. a fee for the data feed, but it requires Information Site Co. to prominently indicate on its website that Animal Data Co. is the source of the information and to include a link to Animal Data Co.'s website. Information Site Co. supplies Animal Data Co. with personally identifiable data relating to visitors to the website who view the animal migration information. The NGO actively solicits donations from users who click through to its website using data received from Information Site Co. to target solicitation requests.

3.2.1. *Issues raised*

This example was designed to raise the following issues.
i.   character: in contrast to the data broker case, Information Site Co. does not sell the information received from Animal Data Co. Animal Data Co. does not transfer the underlying data items; it transfers the output produced through application of its data analytics software to the underlying data. Do these differences affect the character of the payments by Information Site Co. to Animal Data Co.?
ii. source: the data is gathered from many places on earth. The data analytics tools are developed in Animal Data Co.'s jurisdiction, while Information Site Co. makes the information available to viewers throughout the world via its website. Is source of income determined by the location of the origin of the data, the place of operations of Animal Data Co., the place of operations of Information Site Co., the location of viewers of Information Site Co.'s website, or some other place?
iii. nexus: Animal Data Co. is willing to sell access to its data feed to any person. Animal Data Co.'s sales model is based on advertising the availability of contracts through its website and then entering into contracts online. Assuming that Animal Data Co. has no physical presence outside its jurisdiction of operation, could this remote sales model

give Animal Data Co. nexus in the Information Site Co. jurisdiction under the branch reporter jurisdiction's law?

iv. treaty application: should these payments be treated as business profits? Under what circumstances might they be treated as payments for know-how, for the use of industrial, commercial or scientific equipment, or for services of a technical, managerial or consultancy nature?

v. VAT: could the exchange of access to the data feed for personal data generated from click-throughs be seen as an exchange for value between Animal Data Co. and Information Site Co.? If so, should that barter exchange be recognized as a transaction subject to VAT? Similarly, a viewer of Information Site Co.'s website allows its data to be transferred to Animal Data Co. in exchange for viewing the information feeds on animal migration. Should that exchange be treated as a barter exchange and recognized for VAT purposes (or any other tax purpose)?

vi. DST: if the jurisdiction has imposed a DST, could the DST apply to the revenue of Animal Data Co. if the viewers of Information Site Co.'s website are located in the taxing jurisdiction?

3.3. Performance Data Analytics

An enterprise is engaged in the business of designing, selling, and servicing complex equipment ("Equipment Co."). An affiliate of Equipment Co. resident in a different jurisdiction ("Service Co.") enters into after-sales service contracts with equipment purchasers. An important part of the service contract is the provision of performance monitoring and failure prediction services to equipment users. Service Co. performs those monitoring and prediction services by obtaining real time performance data from the manufacturer's equipment over time, both the equipment purchased by the customer which has entered into the service contract and equipment purchased by other equipment owners. Service Co. has developed data analytics tools which are essential to its ability to perform these services. Those tools analyze data received from the equipment while in operation in combination with data derived from other machines over time to provide information to the equipment owner and Service Co. employees relating to early warnings of failure, risk prediction, suggested preventive maintenance, and needed repairs.

For a heavy equipment product line, Equipment Co. installs sensors in the equipment which it sells to customers. Equipment normally is sold on a bundled basis with a one-year service contract. Data collected by the sensors is used to develop performance analytics which enhance the services provided to all equipment owners purchasing a service contract. Most, but not all, equipment purchasers also purchase additional terms of the service contract after the first year.

For a consumer appliance product line, Service Co. provides sensor equipment for free to consumers who purchase an after-sales service contract. Some of this equipment is located at consumer locations outside of Service Co.'s jurisdiction of residence. Service Co. uses data derived from the sensors as well as accumulated data to remotely adjust the equipment and to recommend preventive maintenance.

The remote monitoring and failure prediction services are provided through a data center located outside the jurisdiction of the customer. The data center equipment hosts the data base that stores the historic data and captures real time performance data, and hosts the analytics software that predicts failures and proposes remedies. In many cases, the repair services consist of adjustments to software or other equipment controls which can be implemented through communications from the data center without human participation. The data center assets might be owned by Service Co. directly, or through a separately incorporated affiliate. Data centers are located in several jurisdictions in order to reduce latency between the equipment being monitored and the data center.

Service Co. also provides consumer behavior consulting services to third parties for a fee based on information received from the consumer appliance user data. The data itself is not transferred to the consulting contract customer.

3.3.1. *Issues raised*

This example was designed to raise the following issues.

i.   character: in all three of these cases, a large part of the value provided by Service Co. derives from Service Co.'s data collection and data analytics capabilities. The automatic software corrections happen without human involvement at the time of delivery. Do these facts affect the characterization analysis?

ii. source: this case includes a remote delivery of automated services from a data center without direct human involvement in the service delivery at the time of delivery. What is the source of services income in this case? Should the source determination be different if Service Co.'s analytics software is hosted on equipment owned by a third-party cloud service hosting provider?

iii. nexus - sensors: in both the heavy equipment and consumer appliance cases, data is captured through sensors installed on equipment operating outside the residence state of Service Co. In the case of the heavy equipment, the sensor is installed by Equipment Co. as original equipment, and therefore is owned by the equipment owner. In contrast, the sensors installed on consumer appliances are acquired only by those customers desiring to purchase a service contract, and the sensors remain the property of Service Co. Could those equipment items in either case create direct tax nexus or a PE in the jurisdiction where the equipment is located?

iv. nexus - data centers: the data centers which host the software necessary to provide the remote diagnostics and repair services are located near customers, outside the country of residence of Service Co. Under what circumstances could those data centers create taxable nexus for Service Co. in the other state? The data center assets alternatively could be owned directly by Service Co., by a separately incorporated affiliate of Service Co., or an unrelated party cloud hosting services provider.

V.   treaty application: should these payments be treated as business profits? Under what circumstances might they be treated as payments for know-how, for the use of industrial, commercial or scientific equipment, or for services of a technical, managerial or consultancy nature?

vi. transfer pricing: in any of these cases, is there a transaction between Equipment Co. and Service Co. which must be assessed under the arm's length principle? If so, what factors in this transaction determine which method is the most appropriate method? How would the different contributions to value of Equipment Co. and Service Co. be valued?

3.4. Analytics Based Consultancies

An enterprise is engaged in the business of providing consulting services to educational institutions to improve student results ("Consultant Co."). Consultant Co. has accumulated a database designed to capture and analyze data that predicts educational performance, career choice, and earnings potential. The database includes data spanning many years of student test scores, background factors including socio-economic background, residence addresses, ethnicity, language capabilities, parents' education levels and occupations, and similar factors, and post-graduation employment history. The data is derived from subjects located throughout the world. Consultant Co. uses that database to support its consultancy work with educational institutions to improve the likelihood of successful career outcomes through improved educational methods. Consultant Co. charges fees on a negotiated project basis for its consulting services.

Consultant Co. also allows third party researchers to access its database for a fee to engage in their own research projects. The access agreement does not allow the researcher to further disseminate the data, but does allow the researcher to commercialize the results of its research.

3.4.1. Issues raised

This example was designed to raise the following issues.

i.   character: Consultant Co. commercializes its structured database through different commercialization models. Are the two revenue streams characterized differently, and if so, why?

ii. treaty application: should these payments be treated as business profits? Under what circumstances might they be treated as payments for know-how, for the use of industrial, commercial or scientific equipment, or for services of a technical, managerial or consultancy nature?

iii. deduction vs capitalization and amortization: how should the costs of data acquisition, software development, and creation and maintenance of the searchable database be treated?

iv. DST: if the jurisdiction has imposed a DST, could the DST apply to either type of revenue derived from commercializing the student information database?

4. Outline of Topics

The branch reporters were requested to address the following topics, to the extent relevant in their jurisdiction, as applied to specific or generalized big data transactions:

1. Basic principles: character, source and nexus
2. Application of tax treaty principles
3. Transfer pricing
4. Special regimes, including digital services taxes (DSTs), incentives, and barter reporting regimes
5. Indirect tax
6. Tax accounting

In general, the branch reports follow that outline, which will assist the reader to compare discussions of those topics across jurisdictions.

5. Synthesis of branch reports

This general report addresses those technical issues which received the most attention in the branch reports, and which posed the most challenging technical analyses. No branch reporter described a domestic statute or regulation which comprehensively addresses data transactions,[5] although several jurisdictions noted that the jurisdiction has imposed a DST or similar tax. Further, very little judicial or administrative guidance exists directly addressing data transfer transactions, or applying a technical analysis to "big data" transactions where the nature of the transaction as involving big data was an element in the case. Accordingly, in all cases, the branch reports principally operated from the basis that the technical analysis of a big data transaction would proceed by applying general principles of domestic law. In many cases, the reports illustrated the application of those general principles by applying those principles to the facts of the representative case studies.

Indirect tax and tax accounting, including deductions and amortization for the development of data based assets, are not discussed in the general report; readers interested in those topics can consult the branch reports directly.

5.1. Property law

Several branch reports provided detailed statements of legal principles in their jurisdiction relevant to big data transactions.[6] Readers are referred to the reports themselves for the detail. Readers who appreciate the long view of legal history will note the Czech Republic report which connects current property rights relevant to data transactions with Roman law antecedents.

5.2. Character

By far the topic that engendered the most discussion in the branch reports was the characterization of the transaction under domestic law or by reference to the terms of tax treaties. In general, the analysis of character is the essential first step before applying other elements of tax law to the transaction, such as potentially withholding tax on cross-border payments. The Malaysia branch report, for example, presents a useful table that demonstrates the tax consequences of a transaction being determined to have a particular character.

---

[5]   See the Germany branch report, discussing a 2017 Federal Ministry of Finance circular which addresses data access transactions and tangentially refers to transfers of data, and the United States branch report which describes proposed regulations that cover data access transactions, but not cases of transfers of possession of the data.

[6]   See, in particular, branch reports from Czech Republic, Finland, Japan, Republic of Korea, Liechtenstein, Mauritius, Netherlands, Portugal, Spain, Switzerland, Turkey, and the United States.

This section reviews the analysis conducted for direct tax purposes. Several of the reports include additional descriptions of the distinction between a transfer of goods or a service for purposes of VAT law.[7] Given that the indirect tax characterization distinction creates fewer classification issues, this general report does not summarize the indirect tax analyses.

The most challenging transactions, and the ones which gave rise to the greatest divergence of views among the branch reports, were transactions in which data alone is made available by one party to another. The "data broker" and the "data feed" case studies present those transactions. Those two case studies present different facts relating to the party in the transaction chain which applies data analytics tools to organize and structure the data in a way that would be useful to the person acquiring the data. In the data broker case, the entity which acquires raw data supplies the data to another enterprise that applies data analytics tools to structure and organize the data for further sale, while in the data feed case, the enterprise which collects the data also organizes and structures the data through its own tools in order to provide the data output to the recipient enterprise for display on the recipient's website. Accordingly, the two examples gave the branch reporters an opportunity to compare a payment for an acquisition of raw data prior to the application of big data analytics tools to a payment for an acquisition of processed data which is an output of the application of those tools.

The branch reports exhibit a significant variety of analytical approaches. It is not possible to harmonize all of the reports into a single analytical framework. It is possible to draw some general conclusions about tendencies, but it is clear that due to the undeveloped state of national law on this issue, individual circumstances in the national context may result in different analytical approaches and conclusions.

In the cross-border context, the most significant consequence of the characterization analysis is whether a payment by a resident of the state to a nonresident supplier could be subject to withholding tax. In very broad terms, many jurisdictions approached that characterization issue by endeavoring to apply familiar classification categories: a purchase of property (i.e. the data); provision of a service; license of intangible property; lease of property; or transfer of know-how. Many jurisdictions do not have all of those distinctions in their domestic law, so that a jurisdiction which distinguishes only between "professional income" and "moveable income", for example, would not need under domestic law to distinguish sales of property from the provision of a service.[8] The laws of many jurisdictions which have emphasized source-based taxation rights impose tax on payments for various types of technical service fees.[9] In a few jurisdictions, special categories which apply to digital transactions of various sorts also might apply to "big data" transactions.[10]

In general, most branch reports identified the principal characterization issue relating to data transfer transactions as the distinction between a payment for the provision of services versus a royalty for the grant of rights in an intangible. In a smaller number of reports, it was also considered possible that the transactions might be considered as a sale of property. The majority view was that the data transfer transactions described in the case studies constituted the provision of services, although the reasoning behind that conclusion differed among the reports.

---

[7]   See, e.g., Korean report.
[8]   See, e.g., Belgium report.
[9]   See, e.g., India, Colombia reports.
[10]   See, e.g., Chinese Taipei report.

In most cases, the branch reports commenced the characterization analysis by reviewing the copyright and property law treatment of the transaction. The reports confirmed that most national copyright and property laws conform to the general statement of law above on the point that there is no property right in data *per se*, and that copyright is not granted in the data itself. In many of the reports, the authors concluded that the absence of a property right in data suggested that a transaction in which data is transferred could not be characterized as a transfer of property. In the absence of a transfer of property, that analytical approach suggested that the most appropriate classification would be that of providing a service or other relevant form of business income.[11] This was the most common conclusion.

This conclusion was most widely adopted for transactions in unprocessed data. Where the provider had structured and analyzed the data, and then granted access to that data for a fee, there was more room to consider whether that transaction involved the grant of a right to use an intangible asset. Even in that case, however, the more common conclusion was that the nature of that data provision transaction is a service.

In other cases, the branch reports concluded that even if no ownership interest exists in the data under property law, tax law still might recognize an asset for tax purposes.[12] In that case, a classification analysis analogous to transfers of other assets might apply, leading to the possibility that the data could be sold or leased for tax purposes. From that perspective, contractual restrictions on further use frequently included in data transfer transactions could be seen as analogous to similar restrictions imposed on other transfers of property, supporting the use of property analogues.

In some cases, the reports suggested that a classification distinction could be based on a multi-factor analysis of economic or commercial elements of the transaction, including factors such as the payment structure, whether confidentiality restrictions were imposed on the user, the legal form of the transaction, and other circumstances.[13]

Those jurisdictions which concluded that any of the data transfer transactions was subject to withholding tax generally did so on the basis that domestic law would classify the transaction as a royalty for the use of intangible property, a payment for the transfer of know-how, or a technical service fee.

There was no commonly used point of reference of analogous transactions. The most promising analogy was to national guidance and the OECD model treaty commentary regarding the classification of software transactions.[14] While these analogous sources of guidance were not necessarily controlling authority (the US regulations, for example, are expressly limited to transfers of computer programs), the software guidance referred to in the branch reports generally endeavor to distinguish between a software transaction which is analogous to an article of property passing in commerce (i.e. the sale of a copyrighted article), and a transaction that transfers to the transferee the rights to exploit the software copyright (i.e. an exploitation license). For jurisdictions that are inclined to regard a data transfer transaction as at least analogous to a property transaction, the software precedents could be useful in both the data broker and the data feed case studies to support the view that the data itself is more like a copyrighted article passing in commerce, so that its on-sale is not the exploitation of a protected right on the market. Even for those jurisdictions which

---

[11]   See, e.g., Italy, Liechtenstein reports.
[12]   See, e.g., Denmark report.
[13]   See, e.g., Mexico report.
[14]   Commentary to OECD MTC art. 12, paras 12 - 17.4; Germany, Norway and United States reports.

regard the provisions of data as a service rather than a transfer of property, the software authorities may be useful to demonstrate by analogy that a data transfer transaction does not constitute the transfer to the purchaser of a commercial exploitation right in the property itself.

5.2.1. *Example of analysis starting with property law*

For many branch reports, an important first step in the characterization analysis was to address the nature of data under local property law. For example, the Australian branch report described the general classification analysis as follows:

> The key differentiating characteristic is that royalties are connected to an underlying capital asset (e.g., property or rights), whereas sales and services are not. ... In differentiating sales transactions from royalty transactions, it is important to recall that raw data cannot, without more, be described as property. Therefore, payments for the granting of a licence which allows only simple access to raw data is likely to be characterized as ordinary business income (i.e., a sale). Similarly, where a taxpayer is in the business of providing access to aggregated data for a fee (and the aggregated data does not amount to knowhow), the transaction is likely to be characterized as ordinary business income (i.e., a sale). This is the case regardless of whether the transaction is described as a 'sale', a 'licence', or otherwise.

The Australian report considered that existing domestic principles that distinguish sales from royalty transactions could be applied to data transfer transactions:

> In differentiating services transactions from royalty transactions, the Commissioner has provided helpful guidance. Key differentiating characteristics of a service transaction include the following:[15]
>
> — The contractor performs services (that may result in the creation, development or bringing into existence of property);
> — The contractor applies existing knowledge, skill and expertise (i.e., there is not a transfer of pre-existing property, but a use by the contractor of the pre-existing property); and
> — Any property created by the service belongs to the buyer without having to obtain any further rights in respect of the property.

One factor emphasized by the Australian report is the cost to provide the service:[16]

> Although not conclusive, a common differentiating characteristic is cost. Whereas the provision of access to intellectual property (i.e., a royalty transaction) is unlikely to involve much beyond the copying of existing material, the provision of services is

---

[15] Reference as cited in branch report: IT 2660, [29].
[16] This factor was not unique to the Australian report.

likely to involve a much greater level of expenditure.[17] Big data analytics, such as the interpretation or interpolation of big data or the identification or analysis of trends in datasets, would likely be treated as services. However, each case will be determined on its facts and, in certain cases, apportionment may be required.

5.2.2. Examples of analysis supporting services classification

The France branch report presented an analytical framework that placed the services classification category as a residual, if none of the other alternatives based on property concepts was more appropriate. Like most jurisdictions, the French report first analyzed whether a data transfer would constitute a property transaction:

> As the French tax law does not provide for any specific definitions, French legal definitions should be used. In this respect, the transfer of data could be considered as a sale of intangibles when there is a transfer of ownership of the data. When there is no transfer of ownership but a right to use the intellectual property rights, the remuneration of such right should be considered as a royalty. Finally, if none of the previous characterizations is retained, the transfer of data should be considered as a provision of service.

Applying that construct to the data broker case study, the French report concluded that the sale of processed data transaction might be characterized differently depending on the commercial terms with the customer. The report notes that under applicable law, it is possible to transfer ownership of anonymized and structured data. In that case, the transaction in which the customer acquires a data set from the broker could be regarded as a sale of property. The report notes that if the data sets transferred had been structured in accordance with the needs of a specific customer, that factor supports sale characterization. While not expressly explained in the French report, the idea seems to be that in that case, the customized data set transferred was sufficiently distinct from other possible transactions arising from the same data pool that the particular data set transferred could be regarded as an item of property for tax purposes.

In contrast, the French report noted that the transaction between Animal Data Co. and Information Site Co. in the second case study does not transfer the ownership of data, but instead entitles Information Site Co. to display the data structured through data analytics tools developed by Animal Data Co. Applying French principles, the "transfer of data" by Animal Data Co. to Information Site Co. should be considered as a provision of service.

The Germany branch report notes that relevant guidance exists for the classification of some payments for the use of a database, in guidelines issued principally to address software transactions (principally software-as-a-service transactions). In the German context, the most significant distinction for purposes of the case studies is between transactions where the taxpayer is being paid to perform a certain activity, which would be characterized as a service fee, compared to a payment for a transfer of rights, which could be characterized as a royalty subject to withholding tax. For purposes of determining when a royalty may exist, a Federal Ministry of Finance circular issued in 2017 concludes that a tax liability on

---

[17]   Reference as cited in branch report: IT 2660, [30]-[32].

royalties is triggered only if the transferee is granted the right to commercially exploit the copyright. This approach is based on domestic copyright law and in principle is largely consistent with the OECD Commentary on article. 12, which also differentiates between the mere use of a copyrighted article by an end user and the right to commercially exploit a copyright.[18] Applying that concept to data access transactions, the circular provides that royalty character is appropriate only where the user has been provided with comprehensive rights of use for commercial exploitation of the database, but not where the user is only granted rights required to conventionally using the different elements of the database (access, read and print functions).[19]

The analytical focus on whether the transferee has obtained rights to exploit the protected database thus produces the following results. Payments for access to and retrieval of data by end users from a database operated by a foreign taxpayer should not constitute an exploitation royalty subject to withholding tax, even if the customer uses the retrieved data in its domestic business. In contrast, granting the right to reproduce the database for distribution or the right to make the database publicly available for download would trigger a tax liability for the foreign licensor.

The German report was one of the few to expressly address streaming transactions in the framework of a copyright law based analysis. On that business model, the report notes:

> The guidelines do not mention the supply of streaming data for display on a customer's website. While it could be argued that the customer has been granted a right to publicly display the content of the database, which might trigger a tax liability (similar to a license to show a movie to an audience in a cinema), the customer neither reproduces nor sublicenses the data. In addition, the data streaming contract may be classified as a "data delivery contract", under which the database owner is required to perform services which include frequent updates and reliable transmission of the data to the customer.[20]

Applying these principles to the case studies, this copyright law influenced approach would conclude that neither payment in the Data Broker case study would qualify as a royalty. Payments by customers of Data Broker Co. do not constitute royalties on the basis that the users do not obtain the right to commercially exploit the data sets. The payment by Data Broker Co. to Website Co. would be more properly characterized a payment for permission to collect user data on its website, apparently on the basis that Data Broker Co. is not obtaining the use of a copyright protected database nor is acquiring know-how from Website Co.

The payment received by Animal Data Co. in the second case study presents a more challenging characterization analysis under this copyright law oriented approach. One view of the transaction is that the payment is subject to withholding tax on the basis that Information Site Co. is entitled to publicly display major parts of a database owned by Animal Data Co. and protected by copyright. The opposite view would be that the payment is not subject to withholding tax on the basis that Animal Data Co. is merely providing a service to Information Site Co. consisting of the timely and uninterrupted delivery of animal migration data and forecasts of migration patterns. An important part of the analysis would be a close review of the copyright law aspects of the transaction, raising questions of which copyright

---

[18]   OECD MTC art. 12 Commentary, paras. 13, 14.1 and 17.1 through 17.5.
[19]   BMF, 27 October 2017, BStBl. I 2017.
[20]   FG Niedersachsen, 6 December 2018, BeckRS 2018, 42909.

law would be the controlling reference. Relevant points would be whether Animal Data Co. in fact holds copyright protection over its data or the way its reports are formatted, and if so, whether Information Site Co. commercially exploits that copyright.

The United States branch reporters note that there is no explicit guidance under US tax law as to the classification of data transfer transactions, but also point to two regulatory frameworks that could provide points of reference. The first set of regulations applies to transfers of software programs. Those regulations generally apply a copyright law based analysis to distinguish between transactions in copyright rights and transactions in copyrighted articles.[21] While the regulation is limited by its terms to transfers of computer software programs, like the German Circular referenced above they provide useful analogous guidance by distinguishing between transactions in digital items that are treated as sales of goods versus the grant of a right of a commercial exploitation right in IP. Those regulations do not provide an analytical framework to distinguish services from property transactions in the data transfer context.

The second possible source of guidance is a set of proposed regulations which distinguish service from lease characterization for "cloud transactions", defined as "obtaining on-demand network access to computer hardware, digital content or other similar resources".[22] In contrast to the software classification regulations, the cloud regulations do distinguish between transactions in services (providing a hosted computing environment) from transactions in property (leasing the computer infrastructure or the digital content), by applying rules traditionally applied to distinguish equipment leasing transactions from services arrangements.[23] Notably, the preamble to the cloud regulations explains that the drafters intended the regulation to apply to transactions that "share characteristics of on-demand network access to technological resources such as *access to information in certain databases*".[24] There is no indication, however, whether the Treasury intended this reference to apply to data transfer transactions, as opposed to only transactions where users may access data but not acquire control over the data as in the case studies discussed here.

Ultimately, the United States report concluded that services classification generally would be a residual category, likely to apply if the transaction did not constitute a transaction in property that could be addressed as either a sale or lease of that property:

> As noted, in a variety of contexts in the Code, the taxpayer must determine whether an item of income is considered compensation for personal services, or some other form of income. There is no specific test for this inquiry, and so general principles of US federal taxation apply. Stated simply, personal services income exists when the income is not better treated as another kind of income; in this sense, to characterize income as arising from services is in essence to prove a negative. Given the extent to which the Code defines intangible property by reference to statutory property rights,[25] and the general inapplicability of property rights to data, it seems that many data transactions (particularly, some aggregated data and most, if not all data analytics transactions), could give rise to services income, at least under existing rules.

---

[21] Treas. Reg. § 1.861-18.
[22] Prop. Treas. Reg. § 1.861-19(b).
[23] Prop. Treas. Reg. § 1.861-19(c)(2), listing the factors to distinguish provision of services from a lease of property. See also I.R.C. § 7701(e).
[24] Fed. Reg. Vol. 84, No. 157 (emphasis added).
[25] But see the catch-all provisions in the definitions in section 367(d) and Treas. Reg. § 1.482-4.

Several reports expressed at a high level the distinction between a services and a property transaction as the difference between the obligation to do something vs. the obligation to give something.[26] The concept of a service characterization being something of a residual category in the absence of a clear property transaction was not a commonly expressed approach, but it does provide a useful dividing line in principle.

5.2.3. *Example of a several factor analysis*

The Mexico branch report describes a multi-factor analysis to determine the character of a transaction. The reporters note that Mexico has enacted a data protection law that imposes responsibilities on persons who collect personal data from users and provides users with several protection rights. That law, however, doesn't create legal ownership rights *per se* over the data. Further, under Mexican law even aggregated data generally would not be protected by copyright law, as the collection and aggregation does not constitute an original creation as understood by the copyright law.

With that as the property law background, the report notes several possible characterization categories:

> In our view, raw data, structured data and big data analytics transactions can be characterized in three different types of transactions: (i) the sale or exchange of property, (ii) granting the temporary use of intangible property or, (iii) the provision of a service. Since each data transaction is unique there isn't a rule of thumb to characterize them and the determination would greatly depend on the specific facts and circumstances.

The report then mentions several facts and circumstances which could be relevant. One interesting factor which could distinguish between a property transaction and a services transaction is the relative value inherent to the data itself as opposed to the value created by the work to aggregate and structure that data.

> Under the sale of property construct, the consideration would need to be determined on the value of the data itself and not by any added value that may be created by the provider by aggregating data through an algorithm. This construct would be particularly difficult to sustain in the case of structured data and big data analytics transactions, as most of the value paid by customers in these cases derives from the aggregation and analysis performed rather than the data itself. This is strengthened by the fact that the value of raw data from each individual user is substantially less than the value of the data once it has been aggregated and analyzed by the provider.

Another important factor is based on property and data privacy law concepts. Under those laws, persons collecting and aggregating data generally are not considered to have legal ownership in the data and the data itself generally would not be protected under copyright law. That consideration would support characterizing the data transfer transactions as service transactions for tax purposes, and not as sales of the data or a license of intangible property.

---

[26]   See, e.g., Brazil report.

The Mexican report lists other factors that could be relevant to classify the transaction:

— whether even in the absence of a property right under commercial or property law, the aggregated data is akin to a self-created intangible, like a customer list, goodwill or ongoing concern;

— whether the provider's participation is limited to providing access to data as opposed to aggregating and analyzing the data it then transfers (this consideration could create characterization distinctions between a raw data transfer and a processed data transaction);

— whether consideration is based on a fixed or a periodic fee, the amount of work performed, the value of the data, or some other factor (payment based on the amount of work performed is considered to indicate a service, while a fee paid simply as a matter of passage of time indicates a property transaction);

— whether the purchaser is restricted from further transferring the data (which would preclude a sale of property characterization); and

— the legal form of the commercialization agreement.

5.2.4. Possible theory of payment for use of equipment

The Austria branch report raised the possibility that payments for the use of data could be regarded as payments for the use of "industrial, commercial or scientific equipment." The Austrian tax authorities take the view that "equipment" is not necessarily limited to tangible assets, but may also include intangibles, such as software. Applying such a broad interpretation of the term "equipment" could allow withholding tax on payments for access to data under treaties that allow withholding on payment for the use of equipment, such as those which follow the UN Model.

That said, the Austrian report nevertheless concludes that both the payment by Broker Co. to Website Co. for access to information gathered through website traffic and payments by customers to Broker Co. for acquisition of specific data sets would not be regarded as a royalty on the basis that in neither case does the transaction constitute the use of or a right to use a copyright. Whether the payments could be regarded as for the right to use equipment is left as an open question.

The Italy branch report, in contrast, disagreed with the suggestion that payments for data or access to a database could be regarded as a lease of equipment. That position is based on the view that data or a database cannot constitute equipment. Web hosting is seen as an analogous case. The provision of web hosting services normally would constitute the provision of a service, where the service provider simply makes space available on a server. That analogy supports the conclusion that data transfer transactions cannot be regarded as a lease of equipment.

5.2.5. Theories supporting royalty treatment for license or know-how transfer

Several of the branch reporters concluded that one or more of the case study transactions should be characterized as a license, giving rise to royalties, rather than as a form of business profits. The theories differed for that conclusion. The most commonly expressed theory was that the data being transferred was an intangible asset, and the payment was made to acquire the use of that asset. In some cases, the payment was conceptualized as akin to a payment for the use of copyright.

The Republic of Korea Branch report, for example, notes that under domestic law applicable to cross-border transactions, data likely would be treated as an intangible asset. Data is analogous to other assets similarly treated as intangible property, such as copyrights, trade secrets, customer information and customer networks. Accordingly, data transactions potentially could be characterized as the provision of services, the license of intangible assets, the leasing of information, or the sale or exchange of property. The Korean National Tax Service has published guidance distinguishing personal services income from a know-how royalty as follows:

> According to the Korean National Tax Service's authoritative interpretation, 'consideration for information that a foreign corporation provides to a domestic corporation by collecting and compiling publicly available data constitutes personal service income, whereas it constitutes royalty income if it is consideration for provision of unpublished technical information related to industrial, commercial or scientific knowledge and experience'.[27]

The Finland branch report also addresses the circumstances in which the payment might be regarded as a payment for know-how. As is the case in most countries, the Finnish report first notes that a payment for the use or the right to use a copyright is classified as royalty. For the payment to be considered as compensation for the use or the right to use a copyright, it must be, in private law terms, remuneration for partial alienation of the copyright. Partial alienation of copyright means giving the other party a permit (license) to reproduce copies of the copyrighted work, for example a software master copy, or to make the copyrighted content available to the public either in the original form or in an altered form.

The same analysis should apply to payments made for the use of the *sui generis* right protecting databases or the similar right protecting certain catalogues. Two cases can be distinguished. A payment would be classified as a royalty if it is for the right to reproduce or make available to the public a *sui generis* protected database, or substantial parts of the database, either as such or in modified form. In contrast, a payment would be business income, and not a royalty, if it is only for the use of the database in the customer's own business operations.

The Finnish report also notes that concepts of know-how may apply to distinguish between payments which constitute royalties from those which constitute business income in the context of data transactions.

> Different from products that are protected by copyright or a copyright-like property right, a payment for the right to use information or material that is not subject to any such right may constitute royalties even if it is simply for the acquiror's own use. This is because ... [the Finnish law on nonresident taxation] also covers remuneration for the use of technical and commercial information or know-how. In the context of big data this means that also a payment for the right to use an undisclosed algorithm or a programming technique, for example, may be classified as royalty. However, for such

---

[27]   Written/Internet/Onsite Counseling Team II-1547, 27 September 2005.

payment to qualify as royalty the information must be provided with the condition that the customer will not disclose it without authorisation.

Applying these principles to the reference case studies, the Finnish reporter apparently inclines towards business income (i.e. not a royalty) for all payments in the data broker and data feed case studies, but noting that with respect to payments by customers to Data Broker Co., it would have to be explored whether the structured database created by Broker Co. constitutes protectable property under the relevant *sui generis* right. If the agreement with the customer includes a confidentiality agreement, that provision might indicate the presence of a know-how transfer.

The Liechtenstein branch report draws several distinctions between types of data as relevant for the characterization question. Based on the fundamental principle that there is no right of ownership in raw data, raw data can neither be leased nor sold. In contrast, structured or aggregated data, as well as analytics based on that data, are regarded as imbued with sufficient property rights so as to enable persons creating those works to sell or exchange the property rights. In the case of access to the data of a weather forecast for a periodic payment, however, the nature of that delivery of data possibly could be regarded as a license of intangible property.

While the Italy branch reporter concluded that a services characterization would be more appropriate in the data broker and data feed case studies, the report addresses in detail the circumstances under which a data transaction could be regarded as a transfer of know-how, thereby giving rise to royalty income. Know-how, along with use of copyright, were regarded as the possible bases for data transfer payments to be characterized as royalties under Italian law.

Know-how is defined in Italian law as follows:

Know-how is defined in the law as "information concerning industrial, commercial or scientific experience". In line with international consensus, Tax Authorities defined know-how as an "undivulged complex of technical information, that may be patented or not, needed for the industrial reproduction of a product or a process, which constitutes a complement of what a manufacturer cannot know through the analysis of a product or the general knowledge of the progress of a technique".

In applying this concept to the cases of data transfers, the Italian report emphasizes the distinction between using one's own know-how in the business versus transferring that know-how to another. As applied to data transfer transactions, the Italian report commented as follows in support of the conclusion that these case studies did not constitute the transfer of know-how:

As to know-how, while certain skills constituting know-how are certainly applied in order to collect, organize and analyze data, the output of these actions does not appear to constitute know-how in itself, in light of the fact that the skills needed to provide such output are not transferred; also, a specific activity may be put in place to provide structured data or data analytics targeted for the client, which confirms the application of skills which are already available and are not transferred.

As for the question of whether a data access payment could be regarded as a copyright royalty, the report noted that copyright does not apply to the data *per se*, but only to the relational model of a database. Under these principles, the report concluded that the payments in both the data broker case study and the data feed case study should be characterized as service fees.

5.2.6. Examples of other classification categories

The classification analysis in some countries is based on categories other than the sale of property, provision of services or license of rights or know-how as generally described above. In these other jurisdictions, complex questions of classification can arise, with little possible recourse to precedents from other jurisdictions because the relevant classification categories are unusual.

In Colombia, for example, the most relevant classification categories are technical assistance, technical services, consultancy, and royalties. Of these categories, technical services and royalties appear to be the most likely categories to classify big data transactions.

The tax system of Chinese Taipei largely relies on source concepts to determine what payments to nonresidents without a fixed place of business in the country are subject to withholding tax. Different withholding rates apply to different types of payments, so a determination of the character of the payment is necessary to conclude whether the payment is subject to tax, and at what rate. The four relevant categories are licensing activity, provision of e-services, provision of (other) services, and provision of goods.

The distinction between a license and a service transaction is not clear. Intangible assets are defined broadly and while the definition does not expressly refer to data, possibly analogous intangible assets such as "client information" suggest that data could be treated as an intangible asset. While there are no prescribed factors to distinguish data transfers which are characterized as a license of an intangible asset from those that are treated as services, factors likely will include whether the service is tailor-made (a service factor) and whether the price is structured as a periodic payment (a license factor). Thus, the provider of access to a data feed likely is granting access to that data under a licensing arrangement, while if the provider customizes the data transfer output for the customer, that transaction is more like a service.[28]

Chinese Taipei law also includes a special category of "e-services", which are subject to their own withholding tax. This law is more recent, so its classification categories exist in parallel with the normal classification rules. This category was designed to address a much wider range of digital transactions than data transfers, such as digital deliveries of content, online games, and the like. The definition is based more on delivery methods than the type of value being transferred, but its scope apparently can encompass big data transactions such as weather predictions, mapping services, and the like. Transactions falling in this category are subject to withholding tax (at different rates) even if the service is carried out entirely outside Chinese Taipei. The withholding tax rate levied on payments for e-services is lower than the 20% rate applied to royalties.

Applying these principles to the reference case studies, payments for transfers of data sets by the data broker in the first case study likely would be characterized as a royalty. The data broker might be able to avoid royalty classification and qualify the payment as for

---

[28]   Compare the France report, where customization of the data set transferred might indicate a property transaction instead of a service.

services if it customized the data sets for each user. Similarly, payment for the data feed provided by Animal Data Co. likely would be classified as a royalty based on the periodic nature of the payment.

5.2.7. Characterization aspects of the Performance Data Analytics and Analytics Based Consultancy case studies

The other two case studies, namely the Performance Data Analytics case and the Analytics Based Consultancies case, raised far fewer complex characterization issues, or at least inspired much less discussion in the branch reports. While the value of both businesses was considerably enhanced by big data inputs of capturing, structuring and analyzing information, the commercial transaction in both cases generally was regarded as the provision of a service. Even if classified as the provision of a service, different tax treatments could arise if the service were regarded as a technical service or a transaction which conveyed know-how, or if the service was deemed performed in the taxing jurisdiction.

The more common view was that the service provided in these two cases studies did not constitute the transfer of know-how. While valuable business information undoubtedly was used to perform the service, the output of the service did not constitute a transfer of that proprietary information to the customer. In contrast, for those jurisdictions whose domestic law or treaties allowed for source based taxation of technical service fees, these transactions were potentially subject to withholding tax on the basis that the service constituted a technical service.

For example, the Peru branch report noted that the principal classification distinction in these two cases would be between technical assistance and digital services. In either case, the payment abroad would be subject to withholding tax, although at a lower rate for technical assistance.

The Chinese Taipei report concludes that whether the offering is customized for the user is a critical character determinant in these two cases. The services provided in the Performance Data Analytics and Analytics Based Consultancies case studies both should be characterized as services rather than royalties despite the fact that the value of the service is greatly enhanced by reliance on big data collection, aggregation and analytics capabilities. Payments for those services would not be subject to withholding tax if the service is performed entirely outside of the jurisdiction. In contrast, if the same taxpayer in the Analytics Based Consultancy offers access rights to its database, the lack of customization for that user likely will cause those payments to be classified as a royalty.

5.2.8. Summary of characterization discussions

The variety of approaches and conclusions expressed in the branch reports raises the question of whether a separate and specific technical framework should apply to transactions in data, or whether existing principles are adequate to produce sensible and economically rational results. In general, at least for those jurisdictions which need to distinguish among the more common categories of sales of property, services, license of intangible property, or transfers of know-how, the prevailing view seems to be that existing analytical approaches can work. That said, the branch reporters were asked only to apply their jurisdiction's existing law to the transactions at issue, and were not asked whether a separate regime should be designed, either through national statutory or administrative law, or through international harmonization. The general reporter suspects that the branch reporters would endorse a proposal for international harmonization, perhaps through additions to the OECD MTC Commentary.

The most common approach among the branch reports was to commence the analysis with an application of the copyright or other property law to the data transaction. The absence of copyright or property law protection for data *per se* in many cases led to and supported the conclusion that data transfer transactions should not be characterized as licenses of intangible property rights.

In some transactions, there may be uses of statutorily protected rights which are ancillary to the main purpose of the transaction. In those cases, a *de minimis* transfer of rights should not preclude the classification of the main transaction as a sale of property or a service. This concept forms a critical part of the OECD article 12 Commentary on software and the US regulations classifying software transactions. A *de minimis* rule will prevent incidental uses of IP rights to inappropriately characterize a transaction as a license when the main purpose of the transaction is the provision of services or a transaction analogous to the sale of copyrighted articles.

A data transfer transaction without more normally should not be classified as a know-how transfer. The elements that makes the provision of structured and analyzed data valuable to the purchaser beyond the inherent value of the individual data points are the software and algorithms which the enterprise uses to create the valuable structured database. In the case where the purchaser acquires only access to the structured data, the proprietary know-how embedded in that software or algorithms is not transferred to the purchaser, even if the user is willing the pay a high price for access to structured or even customized data. Accordingly, existing principles that distinguish between the transfer of know-how versus the use of proprietary techniques to provide technology enabled services should be sufficient in the normal case to conclude that data transfer transactions do not constitute the transfer of know-how.[29]

Cases involving payments for access to or transfer of structured and analyzed data are more challenging than cases of the transfer of raw data. In those cases, the purchaser is paying for the work performed by the supplier to acquire and structure the data to make the output useful to the purchaser. In the commercial context, the purchaser normally will use that data in some productive way in its own business. The absence of distinct statutory property rights even in the structured data, however, would point to a classification as either a service or a sale or lease of property, but not as a license.

Even if a data transfer transaction would be regarded as giving rise to business profits rather than a royalty under a tax treaty, it may be necessary under domestic law to distinguish between sales of property or the provision of services. This distinction can be very challenging, as the purchaser normally will acquire the data under a contract which allows the purchaser to possess the data and to use that data as long as it wishes. The object of many data acquisition transactions, however, is to obtain current business information, such that in many cases the value of the data set delivered to the purchaser will dissipate quickly over time. In these cases, even if the transaction allows the purchaser to retain the data transferred, the principal business activity of the provider creating value in the market may be to continuously enhance the database. These factors, in addition to the point

---

[29]   See, e.g., definition of know-how transactions in OECD MTC (2017). Art. 12 Commentary, paras 11 - 11.6.

that there is no property right in the data itself, would suggest that the most reasonable classification for data transfer transactions of the types described in the case studies should be that of providing a service.

In considering whether a withholding tax should be imposed on data transfer transactions as a matter of foundational tax policy, it is worth noting that income from allowing access to or transferring data sets will constitute the normal business income of an operating enterprise. Revenue from these transactions will be burdened by all the normal development and operating expenses of other businesses. A comparable industry might be enterprises that produce and distribute digital content, as the value of their product or service is created through a large expenditure of operating expense, but does not depend on any tangible elements.

As such, the economics of payments for data access or data transfers are unlike the pure profit payments that typically are subject to withholding tax. For example, these payments are very different from payments for the use of capital such as dividends or interest. Payments for the use of equipment or existing IP rights also are fundamentally different, in that an item of equipment or an IP right (such as a patent) are capital assets which in principle can be commercialized over their useful lives without further enhancement. In contrast, an enterprise based on collecting, structuring and analyzing data most likely establishes its market value through constant collection and transmission of new or refreshed data.

Policy considerations in many countries, of course, dictate that source based taxation should exist on a wider variety of cross-border payments, such as payments for technical services. In those cases, withholding tax might be imposed on payments for the transfer of data even if the underlying nature of the transaction is that of the provision of a service. It may make a difference in this analysis whether the technical service is one provided through the provision of human expertise, or is an automated service provided through computer interaction.

An appendix to this general report presents the income characterization conclusions from the branch reporters on the four transactions described in the Data Broker and Data Feed case studies. The conclusions were based solely on the facts as stated in the reference case studies, and thus would need to be reexamined in the context of any actual case.

5.3. Tax Treaty Principles - Permanent Establishment

All data is collected and stored through a physical apparatus of some sort. The Performance Data Analytics case study gave the branch reporters an opportunity to comment on whether either the collection devices or the data centers which store the data could create income tax nexus for the service supplier resident in a different jurisdiction. While not every branch report addressed the issue, several did include useful discussions as to whether the sensors or data center could constitute a permanent establishment ("PE") of the nonresident.

The Performance Data Analytics case study presented three different scenarios:

i.   sensors installed on equipment which then is sold (including the sensor) to the customer; the sensors collect and transmit data to be used by a separate legal entity providing services which are enhanced by access to that data;

ii. sensors delivered separately to consumers who purchase an after sales service contract for their connected device; ownership of the sensor is retained by the service provider; and

198

iii. data centers located outside the residence state of the service provider; the data center equipment hosts the database that stores historic data and captures real time performance data, and hosts the analytics software which is used to provide remote services to customers; the data center assets could be owned by the nonresident service provider or a separately incorporated affiliate.

The Denmark branch report provided the most complete exposition of these issues, as both scenarios have been addressed recently by the Danish Tax Assessment Board.

The first ruling addressed an equipment manufacturer that installed certain hardware and software in all equipment that it sold into Denmark.[30] The purchaser could activate certain services which were delivered through the hardware and software installed on the equipment. Noting that the basic test was whether the nonresident had the equipment at its disposal, the Board concluded that the nonresident taxpayer did not have a PE in Denmark as the equipment was at the disposal of the equipment owner, and the equipment owner is the one who could activate and deactivate the features.[31]

In a second ruling, the Board addressed the question of whether a nonresident could have a "fixed place of business" PE if the nonresident contracted with a related Danish entity for data center hosting services.[32] The Danish entity owned the data center equipment, and its employees were responsible for maintaining the equipment. As with the equipment manufacturer case, the technical issue was whether the nonresident had the equipment located in the data center "at its disposal" within the meaning of the PE article of the relevant treaty. The Board concluded that the use of the data center by the nonresident did not create a PE, while expressly addressing the practical realities of how groups manage their software and data from remote locations. The Board came to its conclusion while recognizing the following facts:

The parent company and a small group of its employees would be granted permission to visit the datacenter but only if accompanied by employees of the Danish subsidiary. The parent company's own employees – located outside Denmark – would handle the webpage through remote access. Such employees would have the possibility to monitor the efficiency of the hardware and software installed in the datacenter as well as to install and uninstall applications, to carry out maintenance of the hosted applications and finally to handle the software and data stored on the servers In case a server would not work correctly (or in other situation of emergencies), this server could be shut down using the remote access, which also enabled redirecting the data to other servers.

This ruling provides a compelling analysis to reach its conclusion under a PE provision conforming to OECD MTC article 5 relating to a fixed place of business. As this case dealt with a related party owning the data center assets, profits arising from the data center activity itself would be allocated to the host jurisdiction pursuant to the intercompany services fee paid to the associated enterprise. The opposite conclusion would have produced a burdensome result for groups endeavoring to reduce latency and improve the

[30] Tax Assessment Board, SKM 2019.643.SR.
[31] The Board also concluded that the payments for the features did not constitute a royalty, on the basis that the equipment owner paid for the use of the features, but not for any right to use patents, trademarks or other assets included in the royalty definition.
[32] Tax Assessment Board, SKM2016.188.SR.

user experience by locating hardware to host their websites and data at locations close to users.

The Canada branch report also observes that for both the sensor and data center cases, the issue is whether the nonresident has control over the equipment, whether it is legal or physical control.[33] This is regarded as consistent with the OECD MTC article 5 Commentary, which mandates that the nonresident must have the premises or equipment "at its disposal". The Canadian report distinguishes between the cases of data center equipment owned directly by the nonresident versus equipment owned by a separate Canadian entity, even if a related party. In the former case, the principal issue regarding PE status would be whether the activity conducted through the data center assets could be regarded as preparatory or auxiliary. This necessarily would be a factual exercise based on the nature of the information gathering or hosting process and the relationship of that activity to the core business of the enterprise. In the case of data center assets owned by a related entity, the Canada Revenue Agency has issued a technical interpretation in a case very similar to the Danish ruling that the provision of data hosting services to a nonresident does not create a PE, even when personnel of the nonresident have the ability to monitor traffic through the data center from remote locations.[34] With respect to sensors installed on equipment owned by third parties, as in the Performance Data Analytics case study, the Canadian reporter concluded "it is difficult to argue that the non-resident has control over the sensors."

The India branch report presents a different view on both the sensors and the data center assets. For the sensors, the Indian reporters conclude that there is little doubt under the OECD Commentary to article 5 that the sensors constitute a fixed place of business of the nonresident obtaining data through the sensors (apparently concluding that the same analysis applies both to the sensors installed by the manufacturer on equipment and sold to the equipment purchaser and those delivered to consumers who purchase service contracts with title to the sensor remaining in the nonresident). The Indian reporters thus frame the critical interpretative issue as whether those sensors are at the disposal of the nonresident. Based on the facts stated in the Performance Data Analytics case, the Indian reporters conclude that the sensors were at the disposal of the nonresident entity providing the data analytics services and thus create a fixed place of business for the nonresident.[35] On the data center case, the reporters conclude that whether the assets are owned by the nonresident or by a locally incorporated affiliate is not important. Under the facts as presented in the Performance Data Analytics case study, the reporters conclude that it appears that the data center assets are at the disposal of the nonresident, and thus create nexus for the nonresident at the data center location.

Several branch reports addressed the case of server equipment located in the country and directly owned by the nonresident.[36] In these cases, the reporters generally referred to the relevant OECD MTC Commentary relating to electronic commerce for guidance when activity conducted through servers can be regarded as preparatory or auxiliary.[37] In practice, however, the more common issue arises when the data center assets are owned by

---

[33]   CRA, Income Tax Technical News #22, 1 November 2002 and CRA, Income Tax Technical News #33, 16 September 2005.

[34]   CRA, Technical Interpretation 2012-0432141R3, 2012.

[35]   Citing to the decision of the Authority for Advance Rulings, in the case of MasterCard Asia Pacific Pte Limited (2018) 406 ITR 0043.

[36]   See, e.g., Luxembourg report.

[37]   OECD MTC art. 5 Commentary, paras. 122-131.

an associated enterprise, which makes the Danish and Canadian rulings described above the more significant interpretative statements in this area.

The Switzerland branch report emphasized that several analytical steps may be required to determine whether sensors could constitute a PE. Under Swiss domestic law, whether a sensor could be regarded as a fixed place of business mainly depends on its nature and purpose. Sensors attached to mobile equipment would not create a PE as they lack the requirement of being fixed. Fixed sensors, however, may constitute a PE if the data extracted from them is part of the core business of the enterprise and not just of an insignificant nature. In the treaty content, the issue arises whether the activity conducted through the sensor is solely for the purpose of collecting information for the enterprise, or is otherwise preparatory or auxiliary. As the Swiss reporter explained:

> Whether or not collection of data qualifies as a preparatory or auxiliary activity needs to be determined taking the specific corporate purpose and business model into account. For data-driven corporations whose core purpose consists of collecting and selling raw data, data collection normally will not qualify as preparatory or auxiliary. A different view may be taken if a company collects data in its raw form so that it can convert or process them into a more readable format. If data processing is the main business purpose, collection of raw data may qualify as preparatory. In this writer's opinion, collection of data should qualify as an auxiliary activity if a company's value chain is mainly a physical one and data analytics are used as a tool to improve efficiency or reduce costs. In such a case, the captured information will be integrated in a physical value chain, which makes the data as a supporting element. The same holds true for corporations collecting data through a fixed place for the purpose of market research or the like. In this context, it may make sense to distinguish between external and internal data. External data provided to data consumers may indicate that the data themselves are the business asset and, thus, collecting them is not only a preparatory activity as long as they do not need to be significantly processed further (directly consumable information). These data are the service. When leveraging internal data, however, often another product or service is in the foreground. The question is, therefore, whether the business is built around data or data around the business.

Even if the sensors did constitute a fixed place of business PE, there would be a question whether any material income could be attributable to that PE, given the absence of activity by the taxpayer's personnel at the sensor location. This point would be particularly relevant for those jurisdictions which follow the Authorized OECD Approach for attributing profits to a PE.

5.4. Transfer Pricing

By far the most frequent response from the branch reporters on the transfer pricing topic is that there is little or no precedent in their jurisprudence applying transfer pricing principles to transactions involving big data. In general, most branch reports pointed to the relevant principles, such as the OECD Transfer Pricing Guidelines ("TPG") or domestic legislation, and observed that those principles appeared to be sufficiently robust to apply to big data transactions.

The Performance Data Analytics case study was designed to present an opportunity for transfer pricing analysis. In that case, one member of the group designed, manufactured and sold equipment (Equipment Co.), while a different member of the group entered into after-sale service contracts with equipment purchasers (Service Co.). Equipment Co. installs sensors on the equipment at the time of sale, which transmit data to Service Co. Service Co. developed the data analytics tools which aggregated the performance history of the equipment, monitored current performance, and used that analyzed data to provide after sales service. Service Co. also made the benefit of its analytics available to Equipment Co. to allow Equipment Co. to improve its designs and manufacturing techniques. The principal issues raised by this case study is the division of value between the entity that controls the acquisition of the data (Equipment Co.) and the one which creates the data analytics (Service Co.), plus the allocation of value between the equipment sale and the bundled service contract.

The facts and circumstances nature of transfer pricing analysis presumably inhibited the branch reporters from analyzing this case in detail. Nevertheless, the reports did include several interesting observations on aspects of the transfer pricing analysis that would apply to data intensive transactions generally, including the relative value of raw data compared to the analytics process, the application of a DEMPE analysis to data intensive businesses, and the possible application of the residual profit split method to data intensive transactions.

Perhaps the first question is how to place data into the transfer pricing analytical framework, given that data themselves are not property under legal concepts. The Netherlands branch report addresses this issue. The report first notes in the legal discussion that ownership of data is not possible in Dutch property law, as data are not tangible assets. Software which is used to process data can be protected by copyright law, and the report further notes that "[d]ata of a commercial value, which has been processed by means of having been subject to reasonable steps to keep it secret, may be protected as a trade secret under the Netherlands Trade Secrets Act (*Wet bescherming bedrijfsgeheimen* 2018)." That said, the Dutch report concludes that "it seems to be generally accepted in international literature and at the OECD level that data may, given the circumstances, qualify as an intangible asset within the notion of chapter 6 OECD Guidelines 2017." Indeed, after the revisions introduced as part of the BEPS project, the definition of "intangible" in the OECD TPG does not limit the scope of possible intangibles to items protected by property law. The TPG define intangibles as follows:

> In these Guidelines, therefore, the word "intangible" is intended to address something which is not a physical asset or a financial asset, which is capable of being owned or controlled for use in commercial activities, and whose use or transfer would be compensated had it occurred in a transaction between independent parties in comparable circumstances. Rather than focusing on accounting or legal definitions, the thrust of a transfer pricing analysis in a case involving intangibles should be the determination of the conditions that would be agreed upon between independent parties for a comparable transaction.[38]

The TPG include an example that assumes data can be regarded as an intangible used in a controlled transaction. That example describes an exploration company that "has acquired or developed valuable geological data and analysis, and sophisticated exploratory

---

[38]   TPG, para 6.6.

software and know-how", all of which it uses to provide exploration services to an associated enterprise.[39]

Accepting that data could fall within the TPG definition of "intangible", the Dutch reporters note that it is not clear how the value of data should be determined and attributed to an asset, as not all data would have the same value to a business. Recognizing the difference between raw data and data which has been structured and analysed, the Dutch reporters address that distinction as follows:

> An additional item to consider is how any additional value and hence profits generated by digitalising business models can be allocated to the different members of a multinational enterprise. As per chapters 1-3 OECD Guidelines 2017, functions performed, risks assumed, and assets used by the involved members of a multinational enterprise remain pivotal for any transfer pricing analysis; hence also in relation to big data transactions. Against this background, it could be argued that data collection and storage could be considered low-value activities, especially if no (substantial) risks are being borne in this respect and any assets used are of (comparatively) low value. Further processing of the data, such as the interpretation and analysis thereof, and the control over the development and maintenance of relevant data processing software and other technology, are more likely to contribute to unfolding the value of data. It is therefore the member(s) of the multinational enterprise that perform these activities that would typically be allocated the largest portion of the profits.

Several branch reports emphasized the contributions of the analytics functions to the creation of value in any big data asset. The Singapore branch report analysed typical group functions which could create value in a big data intangible through a DEMPE analysis:

> Using the DEMPE analysis one can factor in the role of multiple group entities in the creation of an intangible. In the context of big data, the key functions may include design of the database, software platform, algorithms and APIs, ongoing research and development including enhancements to the platform, strategic decisions and creative direction in relation to the database and product offering, decisions and actions to protect the intangible and ensure quality control, marketing functions that enhance the brand value of the intangible product, routine functions such as maintenance of server, troubleshooting and customer support. All these functions and services provided by related entities in the group can be compensated on an arm's length basis.

Similarly, the Switzerland branch report presented a useful classification of functions relating to the collection, structuring and exploitation of big data assets through the lens of DEMPE functions. The Swiss reporter presented her conclusions in the following chart:

---

[39]   TPG, para. 6.106.

Functions	Activities

Development	• Research activities, such as:
	  • Definition of big data strategy
	  • Analysis how to digitalize value chain
	  • Search fot data sources and systems for data collection
	  • Drafts in connection with IT architecture or cloud computing
	
	• Development activities, such as:
	  • Implementation of big data strategy including cloud computing services
	  • Construction of IT architecture
	  • Data collection

Enhancement	• Test runs in connection with IT architecture and data processing • Search for alternatives
Maintenance	• Measures for keeping data pool up to date • Application management
Protection	• Draft and implementation IT security concept • Implementation of data security measures • Licensing or accessing rights
Exploitation	• Decision making process regarding data exploitation (e.g., sale, licensing, processing data)

This analysis emphasizes that value is created where these business functions are performed, as opposed to the location of origin of the data or the location of the customer for the data-enhanced service.

A significantly different view is presented in the Italy branch report. The Italian reporter notes a view that the value attributable to processing activity conducted through software operating on a hardware platform could be compensated according to a cost-plus mark-up, with the data itself being attributed the residual value. This view would become significant, for example, if in the case of a significant economic presence PE, the user contributed data were to be treated as an asset allocated to the PE even if the analytics work was performed elsewhere.

The German report also addressed the issue of the relative value contribution of the data collection function compared to the aggregation, structuring and processing functions, identifying the arguments on both sides of the issue. As expressed in the German report:

Some practitioners have argued that collection of data could be treated as a routine function of an associated enterprise, whereas the associated enterprise that aggregates or processes the data into a database should be entitled to residual profits. [footnote omitted] ... No official guidance has been published by the German tax authorities on this issue, but high-ranking members of the federal tax administration have indicated that they do not agree with this analysis. [footnote omitted] In their view, an enterprise that collects data and then transfers it to another enterprise within the group should receive compensation that reflects its value (as opposed to merely being compensated for the performance of collection services to the transferee).

In the view of the German reporter, however, the data collection function normally should be treated as a routine activity. At least in the case of non-personal data, the mere collection of data does not result in the creation of anything new or unique. A different result might arise where personal data subject to GDPR is collected, due to the greater legal liability risks assumed and control responsibilities performed by the entity acting as data controller.

The German reporter also surveyed recent German scholarly literature on the transfer pricing implications of data transactions in the context of value creation. Conclusions expressed in the literature included the following:

- It is very difficult to tie income from data transactions to a geographical location.
- Raw data as such has only little value because monetization requires the data to be processed first. As a result, there is virtually no value creation in the country of residence of users.
- Data from clinical trials is different in that it is considered to be quite valuable within the pharmaceutical industry. However, value creation is attributable to the companies that generate the data and not to the patients.
- Traditional TP methods can also be applied to digital transactions, but there should be a re-evaluation of the transactional profit split method.
- Profit splits should not be based on sales but on R&D expenses.

The view that the principal value creation in a data intensive business happens through the development and application of the software and hardware tools that perform the structuring and analytics function is clearly the majority view of branch reporters who commented on the point. On the point whether the data collection function relating to personal data might contribute more value due to the assumption of GDPR risks and responsibilities, it also could be argued that enterprises manage that legal risk simply by properly complying with legal requirements as opposed to creating value. Under that view, even for transactions involving personal data, the entrepreneurial value of the enterprise arises through the subsequent stages of the data management process, namely the aggregation, structuring and analytics which turn the collected data into a valuable resource for the enterprise.

While the performance analytics case study presented a relatively simple two-party arrangement, the Norway branch report notes that data can be shared within groups in many more complex ways. In many cases, including the performance analytics example, the data is not shared outside the group in either raw or processed form. Accordingly, there likely will be no market benchmarks for transactions in the data itself. The report emphasizes that the variety of possible uses of data within the group leads to the possibility of many different ways that the group could organize its intragroup relationships regarding the development and use of data, including in relationships without cash consideration:

> Accordingly, we would expect to see arrangements that range from bartering arrangements to cost contribution arrangements with shared ownership, to licensing arrangements with one owner of the data, with many internal users. For the latter we can expect that some companies will charge a license fee, while others may provide the data for free. ...
>
> If we look at the example of sharing of data within a group, this can be organized in many ways as described above, and will most likely depend on the underlying nature of the data, how it is collected, the use and application of the data, and the perceived benefit of the data to all users. Typically, many companies, by sharing data within the

group, will perceive that the benefit of accessing global data from all other group companies outweighs the value of their own contribution of data, and as such see that it is commercially rational to share the data for free as long as they receive access to the global data. Whether this perception is correct, will have to be considered from situation to situation, as it will be very fact specific.

It is also easy to see that you can have situations where you can organize the ownership of data in one or a couple of legal entities, for gathering, processing and analytics, and where processed data or analytics are provided to group entities. That use of the data needs to be compensated.

Assuming that the aggregated and structured data is considered to be an intangible under tax law, even if not property under property law, tax concepts specific to the transfer of intangibles will need to be considered. For example, in the case of a transfer of a database of aggregated and processed data, the TPG treatment of hard-to-value intangibles conceivably could be relevant.[40] In practice, however, the much larger number of intercompany transactions involving the use of valuable data arise in the context of the provision of services or the sale of goods by entities which use data to enhance the value of their commercial activities. For those cases, the TPG note that data held by the tested party enterprise may be a comparability factor which must be considered in performing a comparability analysis with uncontrolled entities engaging in similar transactions.[41]

Even though transfer pricing analysis is intensely fact dependent, the Poland branch report did make some useful observations on how normal transfer pricing principles would apply in some of the case studies. In the Data Broker case study, if Website Co. and Data Broker Co. were related parties, Website Co. likely would be regarded as the tested party, with a cost plus method as the most reliable transfer pricing method. The report noted the reasons for that conclusion as follows:

> Key assumptions and pricing method determination factors are: the key value driver is the data analytics software developed by Broker Co and that the big data collected by Website Co is rapidly losing its value for the Customers, depending on the nature of the big data collected. Also, the GDPR should be taken into account, limiting the time and scope of data usability.

Under the same logic, focusing just on the creation of the valuable data feed in the Data Feeds case, Information Site Co. could be the tested party, as it has no involvement in the software and algorithms which create the animal migration data feed. Animal Data Co. in that case is the enterprise that not only collected the data, but processes it to create a feed that is useful for Information Site Co. to display. On the other hand, Information Site Co. may have developed an extensive viewer base, and will bring that intangible element to the table for purposes of transfer pricing analysis.

The Poland branch report also analyzes the Performance Analytics case, pointing out that in an affiliated group, the delineation of the value adding components of data may not be easily separated and valued:

40   TPG, para 6.186 et seq.
41   TPG, para 6.199 and 6.200.

Both Equipment Co and Service Co give access to the other party to big data – Equipment Co shares their client database with Service Co, whereas Service Co may share the data with Equipment Co from sensors and data analytics tools for analysis of the raw data from the sensors installed in the equipment. Both sides benefit from the big data selected from the sensors – Service Co optimizes their costs of providing the services, whereas Equipment Co is able to improve their products. Depending on how other transactions between Equipment Co and Service Co are set (if any), and the mutual benefits from the big data extracted from the sensors, there might be a transaction set between the two parties. There are, however, too many variables to determine the most appropriate method based on the background set in the case.

5.5. Data Specific Taxes - DSTs and the Significant Economic Presence PE

5.5.1. DST

The most high profile special regime designed to apply to some (but only some) of the big data transactions described in the case studies is the digital services tax (DST), as originally proposed by the European Commission for introduction as an EU Directive. Several reports noted the fact that a DST or similar tax (like the Equalisation Levy in India) had been introduced or was under consideration in that jurisdiction.

In the form originally proposed by the European Commission, the DST would apply a 3% tax on gross revenue derived by groups exceeding certain revenue thresholds for three specifically defined categories of transactions. The policy basis for specifying those three categories of transactions was to isolate those commercial transactions characterized by "user value creation". As explained by the Commission, the proposed tax rests on the proposition that "the input obtained by a business from users ... actually constitutes the creation of value for the company."[42] The explanation posits that this requires a new taxation right because: (i) current tax rules do not create jurisdiction to tax based on this value creation theory; and (ii) even if a permanent establishment is found and tax jurisdiction exists over an enterprise with such a business model, the value created by user participation is not taken into account when profits are allocated to the PE and taxed.[43] The stated justification for the tax is that there is a gap between the place where profits are taxed and the place where value is created.

The original proposal stated that the revenues resulting from the provision of each of the following services by an entity qualify as "taxable revenues" for the purposes of the Directive:[44]

(a) the placing on a digital interface of advertising targeted at users of that interface;
(b) the making available to users of a multi-sided digital interface which allows users to find other users and to interact with them, and which may also facilitate the provision of underlying supplies of goods or services directly between users;

---

[42]   European Commission, *Proposal on the Common system of a digital services tax on revenues resulting from the provision of certain digital services*, COM (2018) 148 final, 21 March 2018, 2. Documents relating to the EC Directives on digital taxation can be found here: https://ec.europa.eu/taxation_customs/business/Company-tax/fair-taxation-digital-economy_en.
[43]   *Id.*
[44]   DST Proposal, 24.

(c) the transmission of data collected about users and generated from users' activities on digital interfaces.

In large part, the DST seeks to tax certain transactions which capitalize on big data technologies. The first category is based on the assumption that the advertising service provider aggregates and organizes data in order to target digital advertising. The third category describes data transfer transactions. The second category, relating to multi-sided user interfaces, is focused more on digitally enabled businesses which are able to provide certain intermediation services that enable commercial transactions across borders, but the utility of those intermediation services frequently is enhanced through the application of big data technologies.

The Commission's explanatory materials regarding revenues arising from the transmission of data expressly exclude from its scope data generated by sensors or other means, and only include data generated from users' activities on digital interfaces.[45] That distinction would seem to exclude all data gathered through "internet of things" devices, such as sensors installed in automobiles. As a matter of tax policy, it is hard to see material distinctions among data commercialization models based on the collection mechanism.

Several branch reports note that the jurisdiction has either introduced a DST (France, Italy, Spain, Turkey) or at some point had the tax under active consideration (Czech Republic). In these cases, the tax has been modeled on the original EC proposal, although with some national variants. The Turkish DST, for example, encompasses a notably wider scope of transactions than the (e.g.) French DST. The Equalisation Levy ("EL") in India, as recently expanded in 2020, also applies to a notably broader scope of transactions than the DST. In the case of the Indian EL, the scope is not defined by reference to three specified types of commercial transactions, but by more general references to transactions conducted through internet communications.

Of the four case studies, the DST is of most direct relevance for the data broker case study, as in that case an enterprise operating a website sells access to data generated from user traffic on the website. That data is transferred to Broker Co. which creates its own structured data sets, and then Broker Co. sells copies of customized data sets to customers. It would seem that both transactions could be considered a "transmission of data" collected about users.

The data feed supplied by Animal Data Co. relates to data about animal behavior, and thus presumably would be out of scope on the basis that the data transferred to Information Site Co. deals with animals, not users on an interface. In the variation where Animal Data Co. is an NGO, however, Information Site Co. expressly transfers personally identifiable information about visitors to its site which the NGO then uses to target solicitations to support Animal Data Co.'s wildlife prevention activity. That transaction would seem to raise interesting issues involving both the DST and the application of barter concepts; if Information Site Co. is regarded as a digital interface, its collection and transfer of information about its users could fall within the category of user data transmission for DST purposes. If so, the question arises whether the provision of the data feed on animal migration which Animal Data Co. provides to Information Site Co. in exchange for that personally identifiable information could be regarded under barter principles as a payment for the user data and therefore be subject to DST.

---

[45]   DST Proposal, 18, para. 12.

The case studies regarding performance data analytics and analytics based consultancies both describe situations where a significant part of the value of the business derives from the acquisition and structuring of data regarding activity and even personal characteristics of individual users. Nevertheless, at least the performance based analytics case falls outside the three defined transactions subject to DST on the basis that the data was collected by sensors. The analytics based consultancy case facts noted that the data was collected from many sources, so it is unclear whether some part of its acquired data could be regarded as generated through user activity on a digital interface. Further, while the consultant enterprise allows third parties to access its database for a fee, merely allowing access would not seem to constitute the "transmission" of data to bring that fee within scope of DST.

The DST, by its nature, applies unique principles in substitution for the traditional character, nexus, source, net income, and profit allocation concepts. In scope revenues are defined according to a type of business activity, not according to a classification of an item of income. Nexus thresholds are replaced by the concept that the location of users of a digital interface give the state the right to tax. The number of users in the country generally acts as the source determinant through an allocation of in scope revenue to the jurisdiction based on relative presence of users accessing a site. There is an asserted connection to the concept of value creation, in that one element of the policy argument justifying a DST is that enterprises create value through the interaction by users with the platform. There is no element of a net income or transfer pricing analysis which would assess the amount of such value creation, however, as the tax is a flat percentage of revenue, without regard to what actual value might be generated though user engagement.

The European national DSTs enacted to date have generally followed the EC model in terms of their definition of data transfer transactions that would be in scope of the tax. The France branch report, for example, provides a detailed description of the terms of the French DST.[46] The Czech Republic branch report describes some of the policy reasons for imposing a DST, and also notes some of the practical implementation challenges, such as possible inaccuracies created in relying on IP addresses to determine user location.[47]

The Italy branch report illustrates the complexities which can arise in applying the "transmission of data" category to transactions in the "big data" ecosystem. With reference to the first case study dealing with Broker Co., the Italian report noted that it would need to be carefully examined whether the source of the data constituted a "digital interface". Accordingly, if the data collected through Website Co. did not constitute data from users of a digital interface, then neither the payment by Broker Co. to Website Co. nor the payment by customers to Broker Co. would be subject to DST. On the other hand, if the source of the data, i.e. Website Co., constituted a social media website, the transfer by that social media website operator would be subject to the DST, but in that case the onward transfer by Broker Co. would be outside the scope of the Italian DST.[48]

Of the countries with an enacted or proposed DST discussed in their reports, the Spanish branch report contains the most detailed analysis of the "transmission of data" category of in-scope transactions. The report points out that the tax seems to be focused on the transfer of raw data, while the higher value transactions in the "big data" ecosystem relate

---

[46]   The French DST was the first to be enacted, effective 1 January 2019.
[47]   At the moment, the Czech parliament has suspended its review of a possible DST.
[48]   Not all DST statutes have an exemption to exclude double taxation on subsequent transfers.

to commercial exploitation of aggregated, structured and processed data. To that point, the Spanish report comments:

[For the DST,] the taxable event is the transfer of data collected, once that they have been generated by the users' activities on digital interfaces. There is a potential problem with the wording, as it is intended to cover only the transmission of user data, i.e. raw data. These data are often of scarce value if compared to the ones available after refining processes. Consequently, the most lucrative options (e.g. the analysis and exploitation, or obtaining any conclusions drawn from those data) are excluded. The new tax does not impose a levy on the real economic benefit arising from the exploitation of refined data.

The Spanish report also contains a description of some of the political issues which have affected the timing of the introduction of the DST in Spain, along with some of the technical issues created by this unique tax, such as the issue whether this tax is compatible with Spain's double tax conventions.

The Turkish DST applies to a wider scope of digital services, including audio, visual or digital content streaming services. At 7.5%, its rate is the highest of any of the enacted DSTs, and includes the unique enforcement mechanism that a digital service provider which does not comply with its DST obligations can suffer the sanction of having access to its site blocked in Turkey.

The Equalisation Levy in India was the first DST-type tax to be focused on digital services transactions. The original EL was brought into law in the Finance Act 2016, and imposed a 6% tax on payments for online advertisements. The Finance Act 2020 considerably expanded the scope of the EL effective 1 April 2020. As described in the Indian report, the transactions subject to the expanded EL are as follows:

The expanded levy is @ 2% of the consideration received or receivable by an e-commerce operator from e-commerce supply of goods or services made or provided or facilitated by it to an Indian resident, or to a nonresident in specified circumstances, or to a person who buys such goods or services or both using IP address located in India.

In a recent development, the Finance Act 2021 amended the EL to expand coverage to include any transaction if any of the following takes place on-line: (i) acceptance of offer for sale; (ii) placing the purchase order; (iii) acceptance of the purchase order; (iv) payment of consideration; or (v) supply of goods or provision of services, partly or wholly.

These amendments will take effect retrospectively from 1 April 2020, i.e. the date from which the original provisions were introduced.

Due to the extremely broad scope of the expanded EL, it is not surprising to note that many of the transactions described in the case studies would be subject to the EL. In the first reference case study involving the data broker, the Indian report noted that the EL apparently could apply in that case study to a payment by Broker Co. to Website Co. for access to date derived from Indian users (even if both Broker Co. and Website Co. are nonresidents of India), as well as to payments by Indian persons to Broker Co.:

As regards Equalisation Levy, the same is to be paid on consideration received or receivable by an e-commerce operator from e-commerce supply of services made or provided or facilitated by it, inter alia, to a nonresident in the specified circumstances. These circumstances include sale of data collected from a person who is resident in

India or from a person who uses internet protocol address located in India. If there is a customer resident in India who is buying data from B [defined as an Indian nonresident which acquired data from Website Co.], one would assume that the said data is in the nature of data collected from Indian residents, or from a person who uses internet protocol address located in India. On that basis, if the total payment for the same exceeds the threshold of INR 20 million, equalization levy @ 2% would be payable.

The Indian report also referred to theories under domestic law that customized data should be treated as computer software. If so, and if the payment is regarded as a royalty, then payments by customers to the data broker would be subject to the higher withholding tax on royalties for software as opposed to the lower 2% EL. Regarding that theory, the Indian report noted the recent decision of the Indian Supreme Court in *Engineering Analysis Centre of Excellence Pvt. Limited v. CIT*.[49] In that case, decided 2 March 2021, the Court held that payments for licensing and distributing computer software are not subject to tax as royalties in India under India's various tax treaties unless an interest in one or more of the rights contained in section 14(b) of the Indian Copyright Act were transferred in the transaction. Under that decision, it would seem that transfers of data such as those in the case studies would not be subject to withholding tax under a copyright theory. Even if that decision were to apply to a payment to the data broker by the customer, however, presumably the EL still could apply to that transaction if the data was transferred in digital form, or the transaction otherwise fits within the scope of the EL. The Income tax Department has filed a review petition before the Supreme Court in the *Engineering Analysis* case, so the final chapter on the characterization of payments for software in India may not yet have been written.

With respect to the information supplied by Animal Data Co. to Information Site Co., the payment would be subject to EL if Information Site Co. were a resident of India, but not if it were a nonresident. While the EL can apply in certain circumstances to payments between two nonresidents, in particular payments for the provision of advertising services targeting Indian users, or users with Indian IP addresses, those circumstances do not exist in this case.

The analysis of all four case studies is made more complex in the case of India since India also imposes tax at source on fees for technical services and for the provision of know-how. As alluded to in the reference above to the litigation over the characterization of software payments, Indian tax authorities also take an expansive view of what payments related to software can be taxed at source as copyright royalties. The Indian report analyses each of the possible bases to impose tax at source in the context of the reference case studies, along with the possible application of the EL where any payment by an Indian customer falls outside the scope of the other charging provisions.

5.5.2. *Significant Economic Presence PE*

Proposals to create a new nexus for an in-country "significant digital presence" or a "significant economic presence" also have a policy foundation in part as an effort to tax big data transactions as commercialized through cross-border remote sales. The proposed EC Directive regarding the DST was intended to be a temporary first step in advance of a Directive establishing a "significant digital presence" nexus threshold in the EU. Of the

---

[49]   Civil Appeal No. 8733 of 2018; Civil Appeal No. 8734 of 2018.

branch reporters responding to this topic, only India and Italy reported an actual enactment of such a standard (the Italian standard was effective from 2018 and the Indian one from 1 April 2020). The branch reports do not, however, address the question of how income would be attributed to those deemed PEs.

The concept of deemed a PE through a "significant economic presence" as enacted by India has a significant component which focuses on transactions in data. In summary, the new law expands the concept of "business connection" under Indian domestic law by inserting the following "Explanation" to cause the nonresident to have an Indian tax nexus if the nonresident supplies certain services:

Explanation 2A.—For the removal of doubts, it is hereby declared that the significant economic presence of a non-resident in India shall constitute "business connection" in India and "significant economic presence" for this purpose, shall mean—

(a) transaction in respect of any goods, services or property carried out by a non-resident with any person in India including provision of download of data or software in India, if the aggregate of payments arising from such transaction or transactions during the previous year exceeds such amount as may be prescribed;

The Explanation also causes a business connection to arise if the nonresident engages in sufficient solicitation or engages in interactions with sufficient users in India. Further, the law notes that several types of income involving the commercialization of data are expressly included as income attributable to the SEP PE:

Explanation 3A.—For the removal of doubts, it is hereby declared that the income attributable to the operations carried out in India, as referred to in Explanation 1, shall include income from—

(i)   such advertisement which targets a customer who resides in India or a customer who accesses the advertisement through internet protocol address located in India;
(ii) sale of data collected from a person who resides in India or from a person who uses internet protocol address located in India; and
(iii) sale of goods or services using data collected from a person who resides in India or from a person who uses internet protocol address located in India.

The India branch reporters point out that this tax will have considerable extraterritorial effect. Income attributable to the SEP PE includes income from targeted advertisements and sale of data even though the actual business activities may have happened outside India. The reference to data apparently is intended to include all data, whether raw, aggregated or analyzed. Prior to this expansion of the "business connection" concept, only income which could be attributed to operations carried out in India was deemed to accrue or arise in India.

This expansion of the business connection rule creates domestic tax liability expressly tied to data of Indian residents, or from persons using an Indian IP address. Even transactions between two non-residents that fall in these categories will be attributed to the SEP PE. The general reporter notes that applying these rules to transactions between two non-Indian parties could create some unexpected extraterritorial claims of tax nexus.

As part of domestic taxing provisions, the SEP PE could not be asserted against a supplier resident in a treaty country unless the treaty had been amended to allow the tax.

5.6. Barter

A number of the branch reports addressed the challenging question of whether barter principles should apply to big data transactions of the sort described in the representative case studies. Several branch reports indicated that a barter theory of income and expense recognition might in principle apply,[50] in particular for VAT purposes, but only the German report noted a case raising this theory in practice. Many branch reports commented on the perhaps practical impossibility of administering this theory, especially where individuals were involved on one end of the transaction.

The Data Feed case study raises the issue of a possible barter transaction between two businesses. In that case study, Animal Data Co., as an NGO, agreed to provide a data feed showing animal migration patterns to Information Site Co., in exchange for Information Site Co. linking to Animal Data Co. on its site and providing user e-mail addresses and profiles to Animal Site Co., which the latter enterprise then uses to solicit contributions.

The issue of applying barter treatment to data transactions apparently first arose in Germany in the VAT context. The German report notes that two members of the tax administration, acting in their individual capacities, published two articles in 2015 claiming that advertising business models such as internet search engines and social media platforms are not free of charge for the users but, rather, are based on barter transactions between the platform operator and their users. That view of the transaction led to the conclusion that the provider had made a taxable supply of services within the meaning of the VAT law, and the tax base should be determined by looking at the expenses the platform operator incurs for obtaining consent from each user (referred to as "subjective value").

This issue also has appeared in court litigation in Germany, but there has been no clear resolution on the merits. The German report describes the litigation as follows:

> The same argument was put forward by the local tax office in a recent court case which was decided by the Federal Tax Court on 16 January 2020.[51] However, the court was able to dodge the contested barter issue based on the specific facts of the case. The court analyzed the taxpayer's terms of service and found that even though obtaining user data clearly was one of the taxpayer's motives for offering the services, there was no language in the terms of service that would have created a contractual link between a user's permission to use the data and the supply of services by the taxpayer to this user. The lack of specific contractual provisions on personal data can be explained by the fact that the case dates back to 2008 when businesses used much simpler terms of service and did not have to comply with the GDPR. Today's environment is entirely different, also taking into account that supply of services to a consumer is treated as a barter transaction under private law if the consumer has to consent to the processing of his data if he wants to receive the service "for free". It remains to be seen how the tax courts will decide similar cases that involve more up-to-date terms of service. Finally, it should be mentioned that the German Ministry of Finance also submitted several questions to the EU VAT Committee under article 398 VAT Directive aiming to clarify the application of the VAT Directive to possible barter transactions between platform operators and internet users. While the EU VAT Committee laid down some useful guidelines on 3

---

[50]   See, for example, the Japan branch report.
[51]   BFH, DStR 2020, 713.

November 2018, the German tax authorities do not feel bound by these guidelines as the EU VAT Committee has a strictly advisory function.

The German reporter expects that there will be more litigation in the future on this issue, and that the controversy likely will ultimately come before the European Court of Justice (CJEU).

The Netherlands branch report provides some more detail on guidance on this issue at the EU level:

> The EU Value Added Tax ("VAT") Committee unanimously agreed that there is no taxable transaction for VAT purposes when internet services are provided in exchange of user data, without requesting monetary consideration, as long as those services are offered under the same conditions to all users of the internet, irrespective of the quantity and quality of the personal data they provide individually, in such a way that no direct link can be established between the services provided and the consideration in the form of personal data received.[52]

The current state of this issue, therefore, seems to be that in principle a VAT obligation might arise, but only if there is a direct link between a supply and the consideration, which implies an agreed reciprocal performance based on a legal relationship, and the consideration must be capable of being expressed in money terms. It would seem that in cases under GDPR or similar regulations, a user who declines to share certain information yet still receives the service, an argument exists that no such contractual link between the supply and the consideration exists. In any event, the requirement that a monetary value be set on the value of the service received will be extremely challenging.

The fact that the valuation issue may be challenging, however, may not put this issue to rest in the case of data transfers. In a case decided after the VAT Committee guidelines were issued, the CJEU addressed a case in which a demolition company, in addition to receiving monetary payments from its client for carrying out demolition works, acquired, pursuant to the demolition contract, recyclable scrap metal that it could then sell to third parties.[53] The Court concluded that the taxable base of the supply of demolition services must include both the price actually paid and "the value attributed by the service provider to the recyclable scrap metal, as reflected in the amount of the reduction of the price charged for the supply of services." Importantly for the data exchange context, the Court addressed the value of the scrap metal from the perspective of the service provider (i.e. the enterprise collecting the data) and not from the party asking for demolition (i.e. the user). The CJEU also noted that "any technical difficulties which exist in determining the amount of the consideration cannot by themselves justify the conclusion that no consideration exists".

There are some obvious distinctions between this case and the case of data transfers, in particular on the basis that data is non-rivalrous, i.e. that a person may acquire or consume the data without precluding others from possessing or consuming that same data. In contrast, the scrap metal in the CJEU case mentioned above may be a commodity, but no two persons could own the same piece of scrap metal. That said, the question of whether

---

[52]   VAT Committee Guidelines of the 111th meeting of 30 November 2018, Document B – taxud.c.1(2019)3722302 – 967.

[53]   A Oy (Judgment of 10 January 2019, A Oy, C-410/17, ECLI:EU:C:2019:12).

a "direct link" between the service provided and the data received may remain a topic for future controversy, especially if the immense challenges of setting an appropriate value are given little weight.

The Austria branch reporter notes that an "intensive academic discussion" is underway in Austria on this issue. Those who oppose recognizing a taxable supply for VAT purposes argue that from the user's perspective, the user does not regard the transmission of data as in exchange for a service. From that perspective, taxation of this transaction would conflict with the purpose of the VAT to be a general consumption tax. The opponents also note that analogous business models such as loyalty programs do not trigger VAT consequences.

The issue of indirect tax being imposed on a barter exchange involving data is not limited to the European reporters. The branch reporters in Canada, Chinese Taipei and Mauritius all concluded that indirect tax could apply to the exchange of animal migration data for user data in the Data Feeds case study. The Canadian reporter expressly notes that in the Data Feed case, there are two distinct supplies of data between the parties but in opposite directions, so that both parties to that transaction could be required to collect and remit GST/HST.

The concept of a barter exchange exists not only in the VAT law, but also for income tax purposes generally. In the case described above where individual users exchange data for "free" services, the natural consequence of applying a barter theory for income tax purposes is that the individual user must recognize income in the value of the services received. For that reason, it can be safely assumed that popular satisfaction with free internet services will constrain tax administrations from pursuing the barter exchange theory for individual income tax purposes.

A few branch reports discussed the possible application of the barter theory for income tax purposes between taxable parties. The India branch report, in addressing the Animal Data Co. case, concluded that if Animal Data Co. supplies the information on animal migration not for a fee, but in exchange for information on visitors visiting the Information Site Co. website, that exchange will result in income imputation as a payment in kind. Further, it will be subject to transfer pricing review if the parties are associated enterprises. From a different perspective, the Uruguay branch report noted the extreme complexity that would arise in valuing data transfers in relationships such as the Data Feed case. The German report notes that the Federal Ministry of Finance recently circulated draft regulations on the income tax treatment of cryptocurrency transactions in which it seemed to take the position that the provision of personal data by an individual taxpayer in exchange for virtual currency tokens is a barter transaction that may give rise to taxable income in the amount of the fair market value of the tokens. In that case, however, one side of the transaction presumably can be valued, reducing the uncertainty noted by the Uruguayan reporter.

Given that in transactions between taxable persons, a deemed income recognition on a barter transaction would be followed at some point with an expense deduction, either an operating expense or a cost of goods sold deduction, there seems to be little practical purpose for a tax administration to pursue the barter theory between business entities. A different case may arise in jurisdictions which classify the data transaction as the acquisition of a license to use an intangible asset, as in that case the imputed value of the consideration could be subject to withholding tax.

In the big data ecosystem, one can expect that numerous examples exist where data exchanges are common. The Belgian reporter noted that uncompensated (at least not compensated with money) data exchanges might exist in the Performance Data Analytics case, as Service Co. and Equipment Co. exchange data with each other to improve the performance of their particular business activities. As the Austrian reporter noted, this issue has inspired an intense "academic" discussion, probably in no small part because the issue is intrinsically interesting to academics. From a practical perspective, however, there would seem to be little benefit to efficient tax administration to apply this theory to the myriad instances of uncompensated data transmission in the data enabled economy. One hopes that this does not become an area of controversy in the future.

5.7. Special Incentive Regimes

Many branch reports described special regimes related to investment incentives which in principle are available to "big data" enterprises, in particular R&D credit or deduction allowances, and patent or innovation boxes. These incentives are available in a remarkable number of jurisdictions contributing branch reports, which shows the persistence of national efforts to provide a tax benefit for home grown innovators and well as to provide an incentive for foreign groups to locate innovative activity in the jurisdiction.

In general, there is no inherent barrier for big data enterprises to qualify for the various incentives. The issue in most cases is whether the definition of the activity covered by the incentive encompasses the software development or other innovative work necessary to create or deliver the product or service offered by the taxpayer. In many cases, the incentives are fairly narrowly tailored to particular types of activity, raising questions as to what part of the R&D investment would be eligible.

As an example, a 150% deduction is allowed in Russia for R&D activities appearing on a list published by the government, which includes "development of technology of storing, providing and processing of information on computer systems." Poland offers two incentives, an enhanced deduction of R&D activity and an innovation box which allows a 5% corporate income tax rate on qualified income derived from qualified rights. Private rulings have been issued confirming that some data processing activity has qualified for the enhanced deduction. The United States, in contrast, allows a credit for certain research or experimental expenditures. Innovative work to design and develop the software and algorithms to perform big data analytics would be the sort of activity that normally qualifies for the US R&D credit.

Given the variety of approaches and the different qualification standards in each country, an investor seeking the most attractive regime for their circumstances will need to read each of the branch reports.

6. Conclusion

The volume of cross-border "big data" transactions inevitably will increase. Creative entrepreneurs will continue to devise business models that may pose even greater challenges to apply the appropriate tax treatment to novel transactions than the four case studies presented here. At the moment, no reporting jurisdiction has noted a comprehensive domestic tax regime specifically designed to address big data transactions. While normal classification principles may be difficult to apply in some cases, the available tools and concepts dealing with transactions in copyrighted articles, IP rights and know-how transfers provide a useful framework to analyze these transactions under domestic law.

Given the lack of existing domestic law precedent, however, the classification of data transfer transactions is an area that would benefit from international harmonization. For example, an analysis could be added to the OECD Model Convention commentary to article 12 to encourage uniform treatment and reduce controversies.[54]

Transfer pricing analysis always depends on the facts and circumstances of the particular case, but the essential step in the functional analysis should be to assess the relative value creation arising from the development and application of the software and algorithms necessary to capture and structure the data in a way that creates the valuable data enabled offering. Overall, the principal effect of big data technologies will be to improve business efficiencies across the global economy, contributing to overall economic growth.

[54] Since the most common data transfer transactions presumably would be classified as business profits and not as royalties, the art. 7 commentary also would be a logical place to confirm that treatment. Given that the software commentary appears in the art. 12 commentary, however, the commentary on data transfer transactions also could be placed there, even though the main point of the commentary would be to confirm circumstances under which the transaction is not treated as a royalty.

Appendix general report Subject 2

Big data and tax – domestic and international taxation of data driven business

Country	Data Brokers/Information Resellers	
	Payment by Broker Co. to Website Co.	Payment by Customer to Broker Co.
Argentina	Provision of a service. Ordinary business income. Assessed if there is Argentinean source income. Unlikely to be considered a royalty. Not a capital transaction.	Provision of a service.
Australia	Ordinary business income. Unlikely to be considered a royalty. Not a capital transaction. Under OECD MTC, would likely be treated as Other Income: Art 21.	Ordinary business income. Unlikely to be considered a royalty or capital transaction. Under OECD MTC, would likely be treated as Other Income: Art 21.
Austria	Domestic: (ordinary) business income; DTC: business profits, possibly royalties under Art 12 UN MC.	Domestic: (ordinary) business income; DTC: business profits, possibly royalties under Art 12 UN MC.
Belgium	under domestic law: arguably 'professional income' (~service); under tax treaty usually business profits	under domestic law arguably 'movable income' (~royalties based on trade secret and/or database right) *Except for withholding tax purposes, movable income is generally re-characterized in professional income if the underlying assets are used for the income recipient's professional activity.*; under tax treaty arguably business profits
Brazil	Service Provision - depending on the structured database and analysis performed, the service might be configured as a technical service with withholding tax and CIDE taxation being levied (apart from PIS/COFINS, ISS and IOF - indirect and financial tax)	Service Provision - depending on the structured database and analysis performed, the service might be configured as a technical service with withholding tax and CIDE taxation being levied (apart from PIS/COFINS, ISS and IOF - indirect and financial tax)

Data Feeds	
Payment by Information Site Co. to Animal Data Co.	**No cash consideration, but visitor information transferred**
Provision of a service. Ordinary business income. Assessed if there is Argentinean source income. Unlikely to be considered a royalty. Not a capital transaction.	Not applicable.
Likely to be considered a royalty, although more information required. Not a capital transaction. Under OECD MTC, would likely be treated as a Royalty: Art 12.	Assuming Animal Data Co is a registered charity, any income (in money or in kind) will be exempt. Assuming Animal Data Co is not a registered charity, this is likely to be considered a barter transaction giving rise to taxable ordinary business income. Unlikely to be considered a royalty. Not a capital transaction. Under the OECD MTC, would likely be treated as Other Income: Art 21.
Domestic: (ordinary) business income DTC: business profits, possibly royalties under Art 12 UN MC	Domestic: (ordinary) business income DTC: business profits, possibly royalties under Art 12 UN MC
under domestic law 'movable income' (~royalties) *Except for withholding tax purposes, movable income is generally re-characterized in professional income if the underlying assets are used for the income recipient's professional activity.*; under tax treaties royalties (copyright)	not clear that taxable income arises; if so, arguably same treatment as for cash consideration
Service Provision - the tax character of the transaction will not be affected because there is an automatization. The analysis performed by the software in a customized perspective and which results in the creation of value via data analysis, will continue to be considered as a service.	Service Provision - independently of Consultant Co commercialization models.

	Data Brokers/Information Resellers	
Country	Payment by Broker Co. to Website Co.	Payment by Customer to Broker Co.
Canada	The transaction could be viewed as a contractual arrangement (akin to a license agreement) pursuant to which Website Co. grants to Broker Co. certain limited rights to use its website infrastructure to gather website generated data. Depending on the level of activity involved, this could generate property income or business income under domestic law and for DTC purposes.	Depending on the nature of the rights granted and possessed by Broker Co. into such data sets, the transaction could be viewed as akin to the (perpetual) licensing of an intangible property. It may be that the provision of the data set could also qualify as the provision of a service if Broker Co. develops data analytics tools to better its services and perform specific work made to measure based on the Customer's specific requests. Depending on the nature and tailoring of the rights granted by Broker Co. to Customer, this could generate property income or business income under domestic law and for DTC purposes.
Chile	No guidance in Chile, most likely licence of an intangible asset.	No guidance in Chile, most likely provision of service given the relevance of the analytics applied.
Chinese Taipei	Although it should very depend on the forms of the transaction, the payment in relation to the data would be more likely to be deemed as royalty and in that case a 20% WHT would be levied as default, which could be further reduced by the applicable tax treaty provided that the payment is cross-border.	Although it should very depend on the forms of the transaction, the payment in relation to the data would be more likely to be deemed as royalty and in that case a 20% WHT would be levied as default, which could be further reduced by the applicable tax treaty provided that the payment is cross-border.
Colombia	The transaction between Broker Co. and Website Co. is considered a payment to a foreign entity as operating costs.	The transaction between Broker Co. and Website Co. is considered a payment to a foreign entity as operating costs.

Data Feeds	
Payment by Information Site Co. to Animal Data Co.	**No cash consideration, but visitor information transferred**
The transaction could be viewed as the licensing of the right to reproduce a data feed (which right may arguably be protected under the Copyright Act). It may be that the provision of the data feed could also qualify as the provision of a service if the data feed is highly customized and if the payment made by Information Site Co. to Animal Data Co. is made in consideration for the process by which the data feed is created and delivered. Depending on the level of activity involved, a royalty could be generating property income or business income under domestic law and for DTC purposes. A service fee would likely generate business income.	The fact that the consideration paid for the data feed is cash or something else (such as advertising) should not change the intrinsic nature of the transaction (i.e. a licensing or the provision of a service, depending on the surrounding circumstances).
No guidance in Chile, most likely licence of an intangible asset.	No guidance in Chile, most likely licence of an intangible asset.
Although it should very depend on the forms of the transaction, the payment in relation to the data would be more likely to be deemed as royalty and in that case a 20% WHT would be levied as default, which could be further reduced by the applicable tax treaty provided that the payment is cross-border.	The provision/exchange of data shall be deemed as sales of goods/service, and the revenue shall be the fair value of the personally identifiable data provided by the Chinese Taipei company, which is subject to a 20% CIT in Taiwan.
To determine the source of the payment, regardless of which of the two companies is domiciled in Colombia, we will consider that such payment is made within the country. For the income tax purposes of Information Site Co., this payment could be considered to establish the taxable base provided that it is directly related to the income obtained. In any case, a withholding tax must be applied to the payment made to Animal Data Co. in the event that the latter does not have a permanent establishment in Colombia; otherwise, the latter must declare the income tax, and the payment made by Information Site Co. is part of the taxable base as it constitutes ordinary income.	The exchange of information of both Animal Data Co. and Information Site Co. with the website's users is not subject to taxation. It is only necessary to specify that, in accordance with the regulations on personal data protection, Information Site Co. should guarantee that the owners of the information give their express authorization for the data to be processed.

Country	Data Brokers/Information Resellers	
	Payment by Broker Co. to Website Co.	Payment by Customer to Broker Co.
Czech Republic	Determination according to a concrete real nature of the transaction: License/royalty or the provision of a service.	Determination according to a concrete real nature of the transaction: License/royalty or the provision of a service.
Denmark	Under domestic law: Ordinary business income; Under tax treaty: Usually business profits.	Under domestic law: Ordinary business income; Under tax treaty: Usually business profit, possibly royalties (based on database right).
Finland	Likely business income.	Likely business income.
France	The "transfer of data" by Website Co to Broker Co should be considered as a provision of services and not a sale of goods.	It is unclear : − if the service does not meet the specific needs of each customer customers (the original structured data sets themselves are not transferred) and Broker Co sells only copies to different customers, the "transfer of data" sets could be considered as a provision of services (i.e., access to the data). − if Broker Co had transferred specific data structured in accordance with needs of a specific customer, the transfer of those structured data could have been considered as a sale of goods, from a legal standpoint, and treated as such for tax purposes.
Germany	Business profits (services).	Business profits (services).
India	Royalty under domestic law. Under the treaty it would be royalty if it involves transfer of interest in any of rights under Indian copyrights Act. Not covered as Fees for Technical Services. May trigger business connection in case engaged in systematic and continuous soliciting of business activities or engaging in interaction with such number of users in India. Exposure also to Equalisation Levy, if not taxed as royalty.	Royalty under domestic law. Under the treaty it would be royalty if it involves transfer of interest in any of rights under Indian copyrights Act. Not covered as Fees for Technical Services. If data collected from Indian resident or from person using Indian IP address, would give rise to Significant Economic Presence and hence business connection under domestic law. Exposure also to Equalisation Levy, if not taxed as royalty.

Data Feeds	
Payment by Information Site Co. to Animal Data Co.	**No cash consideration, but visitor information transferred**
Determination according to a concrete real nature of the transaction: License/royalty or the provision of a service.	No taxes if no money-valued consideration.
Under domestic law: Ordinary business income; Under tax treaty: Usually business profits.	Not clear that taxable income arises; if so, arguably same treatment as for cash consideration; Under domestic law: Ordinary business income; Under tax treaty: Usually business profits.
Likely business income.	No taxable income arises.
The "transfer of data" by Animal Data Co to Information Site Co should be considered as a provision of service.	For the time being, this characterization is irrelevant from a French tax law standpoint because the French tax authorities have not attempted to consider the exchange of data for free services as a barter transaction.
Not clear, tax authorities may characterize payments as royalty income (right to publicly display major parts of protected database).	Income tax: not clear; VAT: taxable barter transaction.
There are two possible views. If it involves transfer of interest in any of the rights under Indian copyrights Act, It can be royalty. It is not FTS. Equalisation Levy attracted if Information Supply Co is resident in India, not otherwise	Income will need to be imputed on the barter transaction as a payment in kind. If the parties are Associated Enterprises, income will need to be demonstrated to be at arm's length

	Data Brokers/Information Resellers	
Country	Payment by Broker Co. to Website Co.	Payment by Customer to Broker Co.
Italy	Provision of a service giving rise to business profit	Provision of a service giving rise to business profit
Japan	No conclusion in the report.	Royalty (if it is paid for the use of data that is treated as a kind of work under the Copyright Law), not Capital Gains (given that it is difficult to presume a complete transfer of ownership of big data), or Business Profit (if Broker Co. has a PE and the income is attributable to it)
Korea, Republic of	Business profits (Income tax or Corporate tax) + VAT	Business profits (Income tax or Corporate tax) + VAT
Liechtenstein	Business profits (as it is a service fee) --> Income tax or Corporate tax + VAT	Business profits (as it is a service fee) --> Income tax or Corporate tax + VAT
Luxembourg	Business income since it involves collection and access to raw data	Business income since it involves collection and access to raw data
Malaysia	–*	–*
Mauritius	It will depend on the contractual obligation between the parties. Given that it is a transfer of property, the nature of the transfer will determine the taxation.	When Broker Co. is selling the data to the customer , those data are already its property. If the payment is for a structured database, it will amount to property.
Mexico	Mexico lacks guidance as to how to characterize this transaction. However, our view is that the payment is more akin to consideration paid for a license of property.	Mexico lacks guidance as to how to characterize this transaction. However, our view is that the payment is more akin to consideration paid for the provision of services.
Netherlands	For (tax treaty) provisions dealing with royalties, this is likely business income and not a royalty.	For (tax treaty) provisions dealing with royalties, this is likely business income and not a royalty.

Data Feeds	
Payment by Information Site Co. to Animal Data Co.	**No cash consideration, but visitor information transferred**
Provision of a service giving rise to business profit	Provision of a service giving rise to business profit, in kind transaction: barter treatment cannot be excluded, also in light of the fact that both data feeds and making space available on the website are commercial activities
Royalty (if it is paid for the use of data that is treated as a kind of work under the Copyright Law)	No conclusion for corporate tax purposes in the report. However, any delivery of assets that does not involve a monetary payment but has some kind of counter-benefit, is subject to taxation under consumption tax law.
Royalty income (right to publicly display major parts of protected database)	No taxes
Business profits --> Income tax or Corporate tax + VAT; it is likely to be classified as royalty income	No taxes
Royalty income to the extent it involves the developing and exploitation of an intangible and not merely an execution of a task requested by a third/ affiliated party	The character of the activity should in principle be the same.
_*	_*
There is no transfer of ownership rights at the end of every transaction.	Yes, only if the concerned party is registered for VAT. Further the barter exchange should also be able to quantify the value addition accruing to the individual, i.e., the open market value of such services to the individual.
Mexico lacks guidance as to how to characterize this transaction. However, our view is that the payment could potentially be characterized as consideration for a license of property or the provision of services.	Mexico lacks guidance as to how to characterize this transaction. In our view, data should not be treated as property for tax purposes and thus, our view is that the characterization of a barter transaction where property is exchanged for a service is unlikely.
For (tax treaty) provisions dealing with royalties, this is likely business income and not a royalty.	For (tax treaty) provisions dealing with royalties, this is likely business income and not a royalty.

Country	Data Brokers/Information Resellers	
	Payment by Broker Co. to Website Co.	**Payment by Customer to Broker Co.**
Norway	Transfer of data, recognized as ordinary business income for Website Co.	The payment should not be considered a royalty, and would likely be considered ordinary business income.
Peru	Provision of a service.	Provision of a service.
Poland	Likely a service payment.	Likely a service payment, but other classifications cannot be excluded.
Portugal	Provision of a service.	Provision of a service.
Russia	Most likely to be considered as a consideration paid for provision of a service (classification as royalty can't be excluded).	Most likely to be considered as a consideration paid for provision of a service (classification as royalty can't be excluded).
Singapore	This payment is possibly in the nature of ordinary service income and not royalties or technical service fees. Website Co may not have any copyrights in the raw data shared with Broker Co. The access to the raw data also does not involve any application or use scientific or technical knowledge.	This payment may also be viewed as ordinary service income and not royalties or technical service fees. Even if it is argued that Broker Co has some IP in the unique structure or manner of compiling data, the sale of customized data sets does not seem to involve any license of the IP. It also does not seem to involve the application or use any scientific or technical knowledge.
South Africa	No specific guidance issued by the South African government nor case studies or court cases to classify transactions of this nature for tax purposes.	No specific guidance issued by the South African government nor case studies or court cases to classify transactions of this nature for tax purposes.
Spain	Business profits (services)	Spanish DST and business profit
Sweden	An intangible protected by sui generis	Provision of a service

Data Feeds	
Payment by Information Site Co. to Animal Data Co.	**No cash consideration, but visitor information transferred**
Even though the payment may have characteristics of both business income and royalty, we assume that this will likely be treated as a royalty in Norway.	In principle, no royalty WHT would be levied in Norway under this arrangement. However, transferred information could in theory be characterized as royalty income to the extent it constitutes value for the recipient which is transferred in return for the copyright. However, since no payment is made, we assume no WHT should be "deemed" to arise in this case.
Provision of a service.	
Likely a service payment.	Classification not clear, potentially barter transaction (exchange of services).
Provision of a service.	Provision of a service. Potential barter transaction.
Most likely to be considered as a consideration paid for provision of a service (classification as royalty can't be excluded).	Not clear, however, likely considered as a barter transaction regarding the provision of a service.
It is possible that the payments may be viewed as royalty. This assumes that copyrights vest in the unique maps, predictions and outputs created through the data analytics tools. Information Site Co is not only getting access to live feed but also product of data analytics which are being used to provide services to the website visitors. It does not seem that Information Site Co is merely getting access to raw unstructured data. The conclusion may be different if the predictions are done by AI software which analyses data and makes predictions without any human involvement.	The characterization of income earned by Animal Data Co would not be impacted by payment of non-cash consideration by Information Site Co.
No specific guidance issued by the South African government nor case studies or court cases to classify transactions of this nature for tax purposes.	No specific guidance issued by the South African government nor case studies or court cases to classify transactions of this nature for tax purposes.
Business profits	Unclear. It could be a provision of a service, but not Spanish DST
Provision of a service	Provision of a service, that will be taxed, if the NGO as such is not tax exempt.

	Data Brokers/Information Resellers	
Country	Payment by Broker Co. to Website Co.	Payment by Customer to Broker Co.
Switzerland	Not clear from a tax treaty perspective (payment could be qualified as a licence fee or provision of services)	Not clear from a tax treaty perspective (payment could be qualified as a licence fee or provision of services)
Turkey	Provision of a service	There may be a 15 % WHT on payments made to the providers of online services. Depending upon the conditions of DTCs, there may not be a WHT on payments that are part of a commercial income, If Broker Co doesn't have a permanent establishment or representative in Turkey. If the income is part of a royalty income, there might be a reduced rate of WHT on payments. Meeting the required; these payments also may be subjected to DST.
United States	Likely payment for provision of services. License fee/royalty is possible too depending on the terms of the arrangement whereby Website Co. agrees to allow the use of APIs to provide access to user information.	Depending on the terms of the customer agreement, the payment could be qualified as consideration for services provided or a license fee. License characterization would be appropriate only if the arrangement indicated that Broker Co. had transferred or made available "intangibles" or "intangible property" or rights to same.
Uruguay	Likely to be considered as a license/ authorization to use	Service fee

* readers are referred to the Branch report for a detailed analysis.

Data Feeds	
Payment by Information Site Co. to Animal Data Co.	**No cash consideration, but visitor information transferred**
Not clear from a tax treaty perspective (payment could be qualified as a licence fee or provision of services)	Not clear from a tax treaty perspective (payment could be qualified as a licence fee or provision of services in case the value of the proceeds can be determined)
Likely to be considered a service.	For both parties (if Animal Data Co is an NGO, in this case, part of its presumed commercial enterprise), the value of the transaction must be determined and accepted as income. Calculating the tax base may be difficult.
Likely payment for provision of services (assuming the digital information is hosted by Animal Data Co., and is not transferred to Information Site Co).	US tax does not have a uniform approach to addressing a supply without consideration. This could be a barter transaction (animal migration data in exchange for advertising services and/or customer information). There may be sales and use tax consequences under state law.
Likely to be considered a service	Barter transaction regarding the provision of a service

List of branch reports Subject 2

Argentina	Luxembourg
Australia	Malaysia
Austria	Mauritius
Belgium	Mexico
Brazil	Netherlands
Canada	Norway
Chile	Peru
Chinese Taipei	Poland
Colombia	Portugal
Czech Republic	Russia
Denmark	Singapore
Finland	South Africa
France	Spain
Germany	Sweden
India	Switzerland
Italy	Turkey
Japan	United States
Korea, Republic of	Uruguay
Liechtenstein	

Summary and conclusions

of all branch reports

Big data and tax – domestic and international taxation of data driven business

Branch reporters
Mariano F. Braccia[1]
Jorge E. Prats Vuotto[2]

Summary and conclusions

In recent years Argentina has taken a step forward in taxing the digital economy, especially by taxing digital services under sales-related taxes such as VAT and turnover tax. It is still not clear what will happen when the courts evaluate the constitutionality of using the turnover tax in this manner.

Argentina has not adopted substantial modifications to the income tax for the digital economy, and it appears to be waiting for the final outcome of discussions that are already underway at a supranational level. Today, foreign beneficiaries furnishing digital services from abroad to resident recipients do not generate taxable Argentine-source income unless they provide those services through a PE in Argentina or the digital services involve the furnishing of technical or another kind of assistance. In terms of streaming services rendered by foreign beneficiaries from abroad, a recent amendment to an old provision within the ITL could be construed as establishing that part of the income obtained from streaming services is from an Argentine source if the services are exploited in Argentina, but that position has not been advanced by the tax authorities so far.

Thus, as a general principle, the furnishing of digital services by foreign beneficiaries does not involve income derived from an Argentine source, and thus income tax is not triggered. However, exceptions to this general principle exist and may include cases involving:
– the existence of a PE in Argentina;
– the transmission or broadcast of images and sound through streaming platforms; and
– the provision of digital services involving the furnishing of technical assistance.

In a recent ruling, the Argentine tax authority (Administración Federal de Ingresos Públicos, or AFIP) concluded that online advertising services rendered by foreign beneficiaries from abroad are not subject to income tax. The AFIP found that the income derived from the services was foreign source because it did not involve technical or other assistance, and there were no servers in Argentina. We believe that the existence of servers in Argentina does not necessarily mean that services are rendered in Argentina, but it is not clear if the tax authorities would agree. The AFIP might find that the existence of servers in Argentina means that the service is rendered in Argentina and gives rise to Argentine-source income.

In another ruling, the tax authorities concluded that cloud computing services do not derive Argentine-source income. The AFIP asserted that those services did not involve the

---

[1]   Law clerk of the Supreme Court of Argentina. LLM in Taxation (NYU) and in International Tax (KCL).
[2]   Transfer Pricing Senior Manager at Deloitte Argentina. MSC in Economics (UPF), MSC in Finance (UCEMA) and in International Tax (UBA).

transmission of intangible property or goods and no technical or other kind of assistance was provided.

PAIS is also levied on digital services, but it will only be in force temporarily.

Therefore, the furnishing of digital services to Argentine residents is subject to a total tax burden in Argentina of 31 percent – that is, 21 percent of VAT, 8 percent of PAIS, and 2 percent of turnover tax.

Branch reporter
Thomas Ickeringill[1]

Summary and conclusions

In Australia, there are no property rights in data per se. In certain circumstances, however, there may be property rights in the presentation of data (in the form of copyright) or contractual rights in confidential data (in the form of confidential information). Moreover, data may attach itself to a capital asset, such as knowhow, a database, a customer or supplier list, a server or software.

For Australian income tax purposes, a data transaction may be characterised as a royalty, a service, a sale (on income account) or a capital transaction. As leasing arrangements are intimately connected with real property in Australia, a data transaction will not be characterised as such.

The characterisation of the data transaction, coupled with traditional concepts of residence and source, will largely inform the income tax consequences. An inbound royalty is taxable in the hands of the Australian payee. An outbound royalty is taxable in the hands of the Australian payer (i.e., subject to withholding tax), but the rate may be reduced if Australia has a double tax agreement with the jurisdiction of the payee. A royalty between two non-resident taxpayers is unlikely to be subject to Australian tax unless it has an Australian source. Complexities may arise where, for example, the property to which the royalty relates, is located in Australia (e.g., data stored in an Australian server).

Inbound service fees and sales receipts are taxable in the hands of the Australian payee. Outbound service fees, and service fees between two non-resident taxpayers, are unlikely to be taxable in Australia unless they have an Australian source. Complexities may arise where, for example, the service is performed in Australia. Similarly, sales payments, and sales between two non-resident taxpayers, are unlikely to be taxable in Australia unless they have an Australian source. Complexities may arise where, for example, the sales are negotiated and concluded in Australia.

Where a data transaction is on capital account, Australia's capital gains tax provisions may apply if a so-called 'CGT event' (e.g., disposal of capital asset) has occurred. Australia's ordinary residence and source rules apply to determine whether, and the circumstances in which, tax is payable in Australia. Key considerations may include, but are not necessarily limited to, where any underlying capital asset is owned, how it came into existence and where any contracts were negotiated or concluded.

Australia has domestic permanent establishment rules that are arguably broader than those provided by article 5(1) of the OECD Model Tax Convention, with no requirement that any permanent establishment is *fixed*. This may be modified by any double tax agreement that may apply to a particular data transaction. It is important to note that many of Australia's double tax agreements contain uncommon or unique permanent establishment rules, including services permanent establishments, substantial equipment permanent

---

[1]   Senior Associate in the Tax Practice at Allens, member of the Linklaters Alliance.

establishments and manufacturing or processing permanent establishments. Many of these rules exist to protect Australia's sovereign interest in taxing activities connected with its natural resources sector, although they may have broader application and need to be consulted in each case. In attributing profits to permanent establishments, Australia has not adopted the Authorised OECD Approach contained in its *Report on the Attribution of Profits to Permanent Establishments* (2010). Instead, it applies the so-called 'Relevant Business Activity' approach, which attributes profits between a head office and its permanent establishment by only allocating third party income and expenses.

Australia's domestic transfer pricing provisions are broadly aligned with article 9 of the OECD Model Tax Convention and the OECD Transfer Pricing Guidelines, although there are a number of subtle differences that may need to be considered in certain circumstances. Importantly, Australia's domestic transfer pricing provisions are not restricted in their application to associated enterprises (although, in practice, they are rarely invoked outside an associated enterprises context). In addition, this reporter notes the potential emergence of a unique 'commercial rationality' principle in domestic Australian law. Although such a principle may be found in the reconstruction guidance contained in the 2017 version of the OECD Transfer Pricing Guidelines, it appears to be applied more widely in Australia, arguably differing from transfer pricing orthodoxy that acknowledges the fact that just because a transaction cannot be observed at arm's length, does not mean that it is not arm's length. Australia also contains two targeted anti-avoidance rules that may be relevant in transfer pricing / permanent establishment profit attribution disputes, namely the multinational anti-avoidance law (loosely based on the 'avoided permanent establishment' limb of the UK's diverted profits tax) and the diverted profits tax (loosely based on the 'insufficient economic substance' limb of the UK's diverted profits tax).

Australia does not have any special tax regimes that are uniquely relevant to data transactions. However, Australia has a general research and development tax incentive regime that may be of relevance to particular data transactions.

Australia imposes a goods and services tax, commonly referred to as the 'GST'. Given the broad-based nature of the Australian GST regime, it is likely to apply to most data transactions between independent entities involving an Australian recipient. It is important that entities within a multinational group give consideration to forming a so-called 'GST group' to ensure that such transactions between related parties are disregarded for GST purposes.

In general, assessable income and allowable deductions are determined on an accruals basis in Australia. There is, therefore, a reasonable degree of alignment between tax and accounting outcomes. Where there is a difference between tax and accounting outcomes, a deferred tax asset or liability may arise. In Australia, these rules are governed by AASB 112 *Income Taxes* (which is aligned with IAS 12).

Branch reporters
Veronika Daurer[1]
Georg Kofler[2]
Gunter Mayr[3]

Summary and conclusions

- As for the relevant legal background applicable to big data transactions, Austria has implemented EU legislation, including the EU Database Directive, the Trade Secrets Directive and General Data Protection Regulation (GDPR). However, the Austrian legal system does not recognize a property right in data *per se*, and contractual agreement dominates the "market for data".
- In Austria, there is no specific (direct) tax legislation relating to data transactions such as "raw data transactions", "aggregated data transactions", and "big data analytics". Instead, the general rules of the Austrian Income Tax Act (*Einkommensteuergesetz*, "EStG") and the Corporate Income Tax Act (*Körperschaftsteuergesetz*, "KStG") apply. This means that the income from such transactions derived by resident taxpayers will usually qualify as ordinary business income. If the income is derived by a non-resident, it also qualifies as business income which is only subject to limited tax liability in Austria, if it is derived through a permanent establishment in Austria. Income from data transactions does not qualify as royalty income which could be taxed in Austria irrespective of a permanent establishment. This is because raw data and aggregated data do not constitute rights under copyright law, commercial know-how or other rights; consequently, payments for the use of them are not considered as royalties in terms of the EStG.
- Generally, Austria's treaty practice follows the OECD Model, so that line-drawing between business profits (articles 7), royalties (article 12), capital gains (article 13) and other income (article 21) is relevant. The UN Model, which sometimes forms a foundation for bilateral treaties, includes further provisions that may apply in the context of data transactions: technical services (article 12A) and, prospectively, automated digital services (article 12B). There is very little domestic guidance on the application of these treaty provisions to data transaction. Arguably, however, (1) the mere fact that the relevant data is collected from a particular state or the data is bought and/or used by a taxpayer in a particular state would not create nexus under existing treaty rules; (2) the mere use of server capacity does not create a permanent establishment, implying that infrastructure-as-a-service (IaaS) transactions will be treated as services (so that they are characterised as business profits for treaty purposes); (3) the Austrian tax authorities may treat user data as "equipment" in terms of article 12 UN Model; and (4) collecting,

---

[1]   International tax expert at the Austrian Ministry of Finance; lecturer at the Institute for Austrian and International Tax Law (WU Vienna).
[2]   Professor of International Taxation at the Vienna University of Economics and Business (WU Vienna), Austria.
[3]   Director General at the Austrian Ministry of Finance and Professor of Tax Law at the University of Vienna, Faculty of Law.

    organizing and structuring data may be qualified as a "technical service" within the meaning of specific royalty articles in the Austrian treaty network.

- In Austria, no specific transfer pricing guidance applies for the transfer of data or for the provision of goods or services where the value or efficiency has been enhanced by an enterprise's use of big data. Instead, the application of the arm's length principle to such transactions has to be based on the general guidance provided in the OECD Transfer Pricing Guidelines (TPG). The Austrian tax authorities take the position that tax treaties in general are interpreted dynamically and that the OECD TPG in their latest version have to be applied. This means that currently, the OECD TPG 2017 are applicable in Austria, including the latest guidance for intangibles.

- In 2020, Austria introduced new legislation which provides for a revenue-based digital business tax of 5% on online advertising, i.e., the Digital Tax Act 2020 (*Digitalsteuergesetz 2020*). From an Austrian perspective this act is viewed primarily as an addition to the existing tax regime and not as a special tax for digital corporations, as Austria already has a corresponding "traditional" advertising tax for print, broadcasting etc. since 2000. The Digital Tax Act applies to online advertising services with effect from 1 January 2020. However, the digital tax must be regularly evaluated starting on 31 December 2021 in terms of uniformity of taxation and implementation, as well as its impact on business entities in the light of any more comprehensive measures for taxation of the digital economy at EU or OECD level. With global consensus reached, Austria has agreed to remove the digital tax; further modalities are yet to be coordinated.

- Austrian tax law provides for different tax incentives related to research and development potentially relevant in the context of big data, amongst others the research premium and relocation tax benefits. Data collection does not constitute research or experimental development for the purpose of these incentives. In contrast, software development (including data analytics tools) can qualify as research and experimental development, but only if it contributes to problem solutions that represent scientific and/or technological progress.

- There has been an intensive academic discussion in Austria if a user's enjoyment of free digital services (e.g., use of a social media platform, a search engine, a message service, a free e-mail service etc.) in cases where the provider is able to collect user data, constitutes a barter transaction that could be recognized for Value Added Tax (VAT) purposes *de lege lata* (in light of the harmonized EU VAT regime and the respective case law of the CJEU) or should be so *de lege ferenda*. One core issue of this discussion is whether mere agreement to agreeing to a service provider's terms and conditions results in the transmission of data being not in exchange for a service (or in lieu of monetary compensation). However, to date no court decision on that issue has been rendered and no legislative action *de lege ferenda* has been announced.

- For Austrian tax accounting purposes, expenses for internally developing intangible assets are immediately deductible and no asset is capitalised. Up to now the question if acquired "big data" qualifies as an (intangible) asset has not been discussed in Austria. However, following Austrian case law by analogy, in our opinion acquired "big data" has to be capitalised as an asset with its acquisition costs. If "big data" is transferred to a foreign permanent establishment, the hidden reserves are taxed irrespective of the data being capitalised or not (within the EU/EEA in instalments) because the Austrian exit tax rules comprise the transfer of assets and "other services".

Branch reporters
Wolfgang Oepen[1]
Jos Goubert[2]

Summary and conclusions

Belgium is striving for a data-driven economy. Research & development is encouraged by tax incentives, which may benefit data-driven business, e.g. the innovation income deduction. As in all EU member states, protection of personal data against abuse is of great concern in Belgium.

So far, hardly any legislative reaction is noticeable to the 'big data' phenomenon, i.e. the less and less expensive possibility to create value by gathering massive volumes of data (individually of little or no value) from varied sources and gaining insights from them through data analytics. A law proposal for a Belgian Digital Services Tax has been submitted. However, Belgium prefers participation in international initiatives (OECD and EU) and will not introduce such a tax alone before 2023.

As elsewhere, the legal status of data is partly uncertain and developing. Arguably, neither an *in rem* property right to data of the person holding or controlling it, is recognised, nor data ownership of individuals of personal data relating to them. No clear contract law framework exists for enterprises trading in data. Intellectual property (IP) legislation is important. Whilst raw data is generally unprotected, both aggregated data and fruits of data analytics (e.g. insights, algorithms, software and IT tools, databases) may entitle to protection of copyright, *sui generis* database producer right, and trade secrets, depending on the circumstances.

Belgian tax laws generally rely on notions of civil law – and thus incorporate some of its uncertainties about data. In any case, VAT does have some – EU-harmonised – specific rules for data transactions, especially for 'electronically supplied services'.

In Belgian income taxation, data transactions result either in "professional income" or "income from movable assets and capital" (hereafter movable income) – the term 'royalties' is not used for such income in the Belgian Income Tax Code (ITC). Whilst professional income is a broad, residual category, movable income relevant for data transactions is covered by two sub-categories of article 17, § 1 ITC (i.e. 3° and 5°). Data transactions trigger movable income if they involve a concession, use rental or lease of a movable asset or of a movable

[1]   Executive Director Corporate Tax, KPMG Tax, Legal & Accountancy, Belgium; Rechtsanwalt, Steuerberater, LLM Internat. Taxation (Leiden, NL). He advises multinationals, medium-sized enterprises, and investment funds on national, international and EU tax law.

[2]   Director Knowledge and Research Center, KPMG Tax, Legal & Accountancy, Belgium; Certified Tax Adviser ITAA; Master of Law KU Leuven. Focusing on national and international taxation (EU, OECD, UN). Chair of the Direct Tax Subcommittee, CFE Tax Advisers Europe.

The authors would like to thank their colleagues Peter Van den Spiegel of Technology Advisory, Yves de Groote, Robrecht Tits, Jeroen Gobbin, Sofie Vandermarliere and Maximiliaan Geeroms of KPMG Tax, Legal & Accountancy as well as Tim Fransen of KPMG Law for their valuable support.

right. The latter term links to civil law, including IP law with the three relevant IP rights addressed earlier. In our understanding, concession is a rather broad concept and may include 'end-user licenses' (which the OECD seeks to eliminate from the application of the royalties article in treaties). In the case of copyright, not only concessions result in movable income, but also the alienation of the right itself (cf. article 17, § 1, 5° ITC).

Domestic tax law provides for a Belgian source of professional income by application of the permanent establishment (PE) principle. Exceptionally, though, also non-PE income may have Belgian source ("catch-all clause"). Movable income is Belgian-sourced if either the debtor is a Belgian resident, or the expense is borne by the Belgian PE of a non-resident. Under Belgian tax treaties in line with the OECD Model Convention (OECD MC) / Belgian standard model, the application of article 7(1), 12(1), 13(5) or 21(1), depending on the circumstances, usually means no taxation is allocated to Belgium as source country. This may be different under treaties following the UN Model Convention (UN MC) pursuant to article 12 royalties, article 12A technical services – and in the future article 12B for automated digital services (2021 UN Model update – not yet available).

If movable income arises from data transactions, the law requires a Belgian debtor (including private individuals) to duly perform withholding tax (WHT) compliance – even if a tax treaty excludes Belgian taxation (nil return). The income debtor may encounter difficulties ascertaining whether the other party indeed holds relevant IP-protected rights. Moreover, multitude and speed of data transactions as well as valuation uncertainties sow doubt whether the existing WHT compliance framework – rather tailored to infrequent transactions – is adequate. Belgian tax authorities ease the WHT compliance burden by waiving it for intra-Belgian transactions ('unconditional exemption') – but data transactions are often cross-border.

A distinct feature of big data business is the collection of (typically raw) data provided by third parties who do not receive a monetary remuneration. "Free" internet services are usually "paid for" by users through the disclosure of personal data to the service provider (and often its "partners"). In our view, the provision of data in such situations does not usually constitute a barter exchange for tax purposes. Another common feature of big data is that physical devices (e.g. sensors) for the data collection are present at premises of (third-party) users / customers. In our understanding, these devices generally do not fulfil the conditions under Belgian domestic law and treaties for a PE of the data-collecting enterprise. PE income allocation would in any case be challenging.

The data value chain of data collection, data aggregation, data analysis, and data use / monetisation can take place within a single company but will often be accomplished within a group of companies with several contributors. This is true not only for data-enabled business (fully reliant on data for revenue generation, and would not exist without access to large data amounts and advanced data analytics), but also for data-enhanced business (data is used to improve existing products or overall capacities and business efficiency). For multinational enterprises (MNE), the internationally recognised OECD Transfer Pricing Guidelines (2022) are fully applicable in Belgium. Absent data-specific guidance in these Guidelines, the relevant key principles are those for intangibles. In our understanding, data (even raw data) can generally be characterised as intangible for TP purposes. Data sharing within an MNE seems possible without remuneration if the sharing entity can expect a benefit – which can be either data sharing by other entities or another benefit, e.g. the use of data analytics products / tools that another entity develops from centrally collected data. Where several group entities are involved, the DEMPE Guidelines (development, enhancement, maintenance, protection, exploitation) for intangibles apply for determining the economic owner(-s). The economic owner(-s) are entitled to the intangibles' proceeds but also bear the losses in case of failure. Instead of a central developer, data analytics intangibles can be created also by several group members under a cost contribution agreement.

Branch reporters
Tathiane dos Santos Piscitelli[1]
Bruna Camargo Ferrari[2]

Summary and conclusions

The following branch report aims at establishing the main legal, regulatory and jurisprudential framework that needs to be analyzed in order to define the tax character of "big data" in Brazil and the controversies regarding its direct and indirect taxation on domestic and international transactions.

Once defined that collecting, aggregating, structuring, and analyzing large information sets, in order to generate value, will be considered under domestic tax legislation and jurisprudence as a service provision activity, the main issue, regarding direct taxation on cross border transactions, arises from its tax treatment as a technical (specialized) service, as detailed in the report. Brazilian tax authorities' unique approach towards the interpretation and application of tax treaties' articles, results in different taxation scenarios depending on how the specific service income is treated.

Considering the vast majority of tax treaties concluded by Brazil, big data transactions will normally be taxed according to article 12. Only residually, income will be treated under article 7, resulting in a non-taxation (no withholding tax) scenario. In practice, foreign enterprise' business profit related to services provision will normally be subject to withholding taxation in Brazil.

Technical services will also be subject to the Contribution for Intervention in the Economic Domain (CIDE), which is levied on the remittance of resources, as payment for royalties and technical services taken. Not just the incidence of withholding tax, but also CIDE is questionable, especially considering the non-transference of technology in big data operations. The Superior Court of Justice has already ruled in several technical services provision cases, that they should not be levied in such circumstances.

From an indirect perspective, the main controversy relates to the concept of result, for purposes of defining if the service provision should be subject to the services tax (ISS), either in exportations or importations, and social contributions on importation (PIS and COFINS – importation). The main question mark is whether the "result" of the service is verified in the Brazilian territory.

There are two opposite perspectives: i) The utility theory according to which the result is where it is possible to identify the fruition of the service, and ii) the completion theory, which states that the result of the service is at the place where it is consummated, regardless of the place where the beneficiary and utility of the service is taken.

Considering cross border operations, should there be an importation of "big data" services, depending on the mentioned controversial analysis, the operation will be subject

[1] Professor of tax law at Fundação Getulio Vargas' São Paulo Law School. Co-director of the Tax Law Center of Fundação Getulio Vargas' São Paulo Law School. PhD and LLM in Tax Law at University of São Paulo.
[2] Legal, Tax Planning and Tax Corporate Affairs and Government Relations Manager in Brazil. Tax Courses Coordinator and Professor in Brazil. International Tax Researcher at IBFD and FGV São Paulo Law School.

to ISS, PIS and COFINS on importation, withholding tax and CIDE taxation. Over the foreign exchange operation, it will also be levied a federal tax on financial operations (IOF). In case of exportations, as there is no remittance made abroad (CIDE taxable basis) and no indirect taxation (immune), the revenue will just be subject to Corporate Income Tax (CIT) and Social Contribution Tax (SCT), which has an almost identical tax basis as the CIT.

In purely domestic operations, big data transactions will be subject to ISS, PIS and COFINS (from an indirect tax perspective), CIT and SCT (from a direct perspective), considering the specific tax rates and taxable basis to be further detailed in this report.

Branch reporters
Mathieu Champagne[1]
Marie-Emmanuelle Vaillancourt[2]

Summary and conclusions

The objective of this report is to provide an overview of the Canadian taxation regime applicable to big data by addressing the following two main components: (1) the taxation of big data under domestic rules from an income and sales tax perspective, and (2) the application of Canada's tax treaties to big data.

Canadian tax law has left the explicit question of big data unaddressed and taxpayers must therefore rely on general principles to determine the income and sales tax consequences of big data transactions.

Income Tax

From an income tax standpoint, the first step is to ascertain the nature of, and circumstances surrounding, a transaction to identify the "source" of the income arising therefrom, namely business, property or capital gain. In the context of big data, the most likely scenarios are the sale of data or rights in respect thereto, the licensing of data or rights in respect thereto and the provision of data as a service.

In the case of a sale of data or rights in respect thereto, the income derived therefrom can be on capital or income account. For non-residents, if on income account it would be subject to tax in Canada only to the extent that the income is *arising* from a business carried on in Canada. As for a sale on capital account, it will be subject to tax only if it can be established that the data or the rights in respect thereto are *used in and form part of a business* carried on in Canada. While the threshold to be considered to carry on a business is quite low under the *Income Tax Act*, one must also carry on the business "in Canada," which generally means that profits must arise from the activities taking place in Canada. It should also be noted that business income is fully taxable, whereas only fifty percent of any capital gain is taxable.

Licensing can give rise to business or property income, depending on the circumstances. Royalties and other-like payments (the taxing provision is extremely broad) received by a non-resident of Canada are generally subject to withholding tax at the rate of 25% unless the non-resident carries on a business in Canada through a permanent establishment (such that the royalties are therefore already subject to Canadian taxation). Various exceptions

[1] Tax partner at Deloitte LLP
[2] Tax partner at Davies Ward Phillips & Vineberg LLP

The authors would like to thank Thierry Morin-Cloutier (Deloitte Legal Canada LLP) and Ariane Hunter-Meunier (Davies Ward Phillips & Vineberg LLP) for their invaluable support in the preparation of this report. They would also like to thank Nathan Boidman (Davies Ward Phillips & Vineberg LLP), Bruno De Camargo (Deloitte LLP) and Frédéric Langlois (Deloitte LLP) for their reviews and insight.

apply to the 25% withholding tax, notably for copyrights in respect of the production or reproduction of any literary, dramatic, musical or artistic work, which could include datasets. Certain payments can be subject to withholding tax even if the property in respect of which the payment is made is not used in Canada, as long as there is an element of dependency.

As for data as a service, it would generally be treated as business income and, in the case of a non-resident service provider, would be subject to tax if the activities of the non-resident amount to a business being carried on in Canada, as highlighted above. Services rendered in Canada by a non-resident are subject to deductions at source that may be refunded if the non-resident can demonstrate that it is not otherwise subject to tax in Canada.

Treaty Provisions

The income taxation of non-residents can be modified by one of Canada's 94 tax treaties. To benefit from a tax treaty, a non-resident seeking its application must be a "resident" of the relevant country and, as a result of the recent enactment of the OECD multilateral convention, must generally satisfy the "principle purpose test."

Where a treaty applies, a non-resident carrying on business in Canada will not be subject to tax in Canada unless it has a permanent establishment in Canada. Based on current case law and the OECD Commentary, big data transactions are unlikely to give rise to a permanent establishment in Canada unless the non-resident has a server at its disposal in Canada and the activities carried out through such server are not preparatory or auxiliary. Even if the non-resident has a permanent establishment in Canada, allocating income to it might prove difficult. As for the sale of data on capital account, it could only be subject to tax in Canada if the data is considered personal property and forms part of the business property of a permanent establishment in Canada.

Finally, and contrary to the OECD Model, Canada's treaties generally preserve Canada's right to tax Canadian-sourced royalties, subject to specific exemptions or rate reductions. Particularly relevant to data transactions are the exemptions for copyright royalties (and other like payments) in respect of the production or reproduction of any literary, dramatic, musical or artistic work, payment for the use of computer software and payments for the use of patent and information concerning industrial, commercial or scientific experience. It should also be noted that the royalty article in Canada's treaties is generally narrower in its application than the domestic charging provision, resulting in various payments that would otherwise be subject to withholding tax under the *Income Tax Act* being exempt under an applicable treaty (if a payment is not a royalty for the purposes of the relevant treaty, it will only be subject to tax in Canada if it pertains to a business carried on in Canada by the non-resident through a permanent establishment).

Sales Taxes

From a sales tax perspective, most data transactions should be subject to the federal goods and services tax (GST), which is a value-added tax. GST applies to supplies of services, as well as intangible and tangible property. Distinguishing services, intangible property and tangible property is particularly relevant for non-residents of Canada as the "place of supply" rules, which determine whether a particular supply is made in Canada and therefore subject to GST, vary from one type to another.

Other

The authors also briefly address transfer pricing, tax accounting and special regimes (including the newly announced digital service tax) that could be relevant to big data transactions.

Branch reporters
Sandra Benedetto[1]
Jonatan Israel[2]

Summary and conclusions

The legal nature of data in Chile is complex considering the existing provisions within Chilean Civil and Commercial rules. The main distinction that Civil law makes, considers a duality of things, corporeal and incorporeal things, although incorporeal things are only rights. Data, and its current status as an asset that may derive significant value, does not properly fit within this duality and therefore its legal standing pursuant to the rights and obligations that may be created or transferred in a big data transaction exceed any potential property consideration that may be held in Chile.

Considering the lack of regulation regarding the legal standing of data in Chile, the legal nature of the three kinds of big data transactions, namely (i) Transfer of raw data; (ii) Transfer of or access to aggregated data; and (iii) Big data analytics, requires a separate analysis from a Chilean legal standpoint, and this becomes an exercise of trying to fit these new developments into old legal institutions.

The three main kinds of legal nature classifications described in this report address these big data transactions as: (i) the creation or transference of rights different than ownership; (ii) the transference of an intellectual property or copyright in the transaction; and (iii) the rendering of a service.

Besides the above, special considerations need to be given with respect to personal data. In this sense, when a big data transaction involves personal data, its legal nature may be better defined than in those cases where it involves data that is not personal, since it is clear that there is no property over personal data in Chile. In this sense, when bringing together the big data transactions legal analysis and the protection of personal data in Chile, some different conclusions may be reached. In the case of raw data transactions that involve personal data, it is clear that these would not mean a transference of a property right in Chile. An aggregated data set containing personal data may be considered the creation of the intelligence or talent of the author, and therefore be under the scope of Chilean Copyright Law. This is under the provision that certain regulatory restrains imposed by Chilean Law no. 19.628 would be applicable.

Moving forward to taxation, the identification of the legal nature of the transactions is highly relevant to characterize the transaction itself for tax purposes, and as such, this report addresses the cases where big data transactions are characterized as services, transactions that involve the transference or creation of a right different than copyrights, and transactions that are characterized as payment for a license.

The domestic taxation of all three kinds of big data transactions, whether they are

---

[1] Bachelor of Law from Universidad de Chile, Master in law (LLM) and Certificate on International Taxation (ITP), Harvard University; partner at PwC Chile.
[2] Bachelor of Law and Master of Tax Law from Universidad de Chile, Master in law (LLM) from the London School of Economics; manager at PwC Chile.

characterized as services or as transference or creation of rights or copyrights, may be affected by the application of tax treaties. Chile has sustained a coherent tax treaty policy when negotiating with its different counterparties. Indeed, no major differences are included from one country to another, maintaining a uniform policy when establishing income that is subject to withholding, limited rates, etc. This coherent tax treaty policy has been kept up to date also considering the adoption by Chile of post-BEPS tax treaty provisions.

In the case of big data transactions that would be characterized as a service, the permanent establishment analysis should be performed to determine whether Chile's taxing rights would be limited in the case of the remunerations in consideration for big data transactions that are characterized as services. In this sense, the newly enacted domestic concept of permanent establishment set forth by Chile's most recent tax reform becomes highly relevant.

In the case of royalties, Chile's tax treaties allow for the taxation both by the state of residence and the state of source, however the taxation at the state of source is commonly capped on a maximum applicable tax rate. Chile has included a most favorable nation clause with respect to royalties in most of its tax treaties to allow for certain uniformity in the application of Additional Tax. In the case of royalties, Chile departs slightly from the OECD Model, since in its tax treaties Chile refers to the rights that would be deemed as royalties. In this sense, Chile includes a reference to "other intangible property" when defining the concept of royalties in article 12 of its tax treaties. This would mean that any big data transaction that covers the right to use, access or even distribute a given data set, should be understood as a royalty. This would be the case for the license of use or access to an aggregated or structured data set.

Another relevant aspect to consider, is the recent legal enactment of Chile's Digital Services Tax. In the most recent Chilean tax reform set forth by Law No. 21.210, Chile has included new taxable events within its VAT law that intend to cover the provision of digital services by foreign enterprises. This has been Chile's option to implement a digital service tax within its tax system, but the resulting rules and the taxable events included by the tax reform are much broader than solely digital services.

Chilean VAT on digital services was included within the scope of the services that are subject to VAT. For this purpose, the tax reform included four specific taxable events within the scope of Chilean VAT Law.

The main policy considerations that were given to enact such VAT on digital services were to set a level playing field for foreign and local services providers, to increase revenue collection and to do so by following the recommendations on the matter that the OECD had issued.

As it can be observed, Chile's legal landscape on the taxation of big data transactions has a bit of both worlds. On the one hand, Chile's legal system does not easily fit these new kinds of big data transactions within its existing provisions, and that leaves doubts on their actual characterization for tax purposes. On the other hand, Chile is very up to date in the tax developments that have derived since BEPS and has even recently established a form of Digital Services Tax on its VAT Law.

Branch reporter
Sophie Chou[1]

Summary and conclusions

From a legal perspective, there is no specific law/regulation governing the transaction in relation to big data, and thus the transaction on big data is regulated by a combination of existing laws including the Civil Code, the Trade Secrets Act, the Personal Data Protection Act and the Copyright Act. Relevant regulation requirements should be satisfied when conducting the transactions on big data in Chinese Taipei.

On the other hand, from a Chinese Taipei direct tax perspective, similar to a legal standpoint, there is no specific tax law or ruling addressing "data transaction", or a legislated classification of "raw data transactions", "aggregated data transactions", and "big data analytics" in Chinese Taipei. The tax treatment of the transactions on big data should depend on the terms and conditions specified in the agreement of the transaction and how the data is packaged to be sold therein. Nevertheless, as Chinese Taipei uses sourcing rule to determine a foreign company's tax obligation in Chinese Taipei, the transaction on big data could be captured and taxed under the current sourcing rule. In summary, from a Chinese Taipei tax perspective there are four types of transactions that are related to big data, namely (1) licensing activity, (2) provision of e-services, (3) provision of services and (4) provision of goods. According to the sourcing rule, the nature of the income deriving from licensing activities is royalty and it would be business income for other services.

For a foreign company without a fixed place of business, a business agent in Chinese Taipei conducts transaction on big data, if the income generated therein is royalty, the default statutory withholding tax for the royalty payment is 20% on the gross royalty payment. The 20% default withholding tax rate could be further reduced if an applicable bilateral tax treaty or other tax regime exists provided that relevant requirements are met.

For a foreign company providing services and e-services to its customers in Chinese Taipei, it would be very difficult to justify that the income generated therein is not Chinese Taipei sourced income and is exempt from corporate income tax as a result, unless certain requirements are met. Only when the transaction is all rendered outside Chinese Taipei and without the assistance of an entity or individual in Chinese Taipei, could the income generated be deemed as non-Chinese Taipei sourced income. Otherwise, the income derived from big data transactions in relation to e-services is considered as other income from a domestic tax perspective and would be subject to WHT at a default rate of 20% with a 30% deemed profit rate and a 50% contribution ratio provided that there is no relevant evidence justifying the deemed profit rate and the contribution ratio. The income derived from services is subject to a default withholding tax rate at 20% with a deemed profit rate by the profit standard of the same trade concerned published by the tax authority. Both

---

[1]   Partner of EY Chinese Taipei, Master's degree in accounting of National Taiwan University, and Certified Public Accountant of Chinese Taipei.

abovementioned income could be further exempt/reduced under applicable bilateral tax treaty if certain requirements are met.

For big data transactions in relation to the provision of goods, provided that a foreign company sells data to a buyer by means that the buyer imports the goods embedded with result of analytics, such transactions shall be recognized as the import of goods qualifying the international trade rules and are exempt from CIT.

As there is no determinative factor separating the transaction into licensing activity and provision of services, the nature of the transaction should very much be subject to the terms and conditions under the applicable transaction agreement.

From a bilateral tax treaty perspective, given big data transactions, the OECD Model and the UN Model differ in article 12. Both the OECD Model and the UN Model treat royalties the same as passive income (e.g. dividend and interest) which the sourcing country has the right to tax and a reduced WHT rate could be applied once certain requirements are met. However, under article 12A of the UN Model, for e-services and services in relation to big data transactions, if the e-services and services in question are considered as technical services, the UN Model also treats such income therefrom as royalty and a reduced WHT rate could be applied accordingly.

On the other hand, for services not qualified as technical services under the UN Model as well as both e-services and services under the OECD Model, article 7 – business profit of the bilateral tax treaty should apply. If the services in question are carried out without a permanent establishment in another country, that county should not have the taxing right regarding the income derived.

Any data transaction, regardless of nature, shall be subject to transfer pricing regulations in Chinese Taipei. As data transaction is a relatively new way of transaction, in the absence of comparable transactions, the comparable uncontrolled transaction method may be difficult to apply. When determining relevant revenues of the transaction, the DEMPE (Development, Enhancement, Maintenance, Protection, Exploitation and Promotion) function the foreign company performs, should be considered.

Given indirect tax in Chinese Taipei regarding transactions on big data, unlike the ambiguity of definition under direct tax, data transaction by a foreign company to a buyer in Chinese Taipei is generally accepted to be regarded as a service provision and is therefore subject to business tax under the current VAT regulation at a rate of 5%.

Lastly, Chinese Taipei provides certain incentives to transactions on big data such as Grants or Guidance for Innovation Activities of the Statute for Industrial Innovation, when certain conditions are met, and approval is received from the relevant authorities. Companies in Chinese Taipei could enjoy either that (1) up to 5% of the annual spending sum may be credited against the profit-seeking enterprise income tax payable by it in the then-current year; or (2) up to 3% of the annual spending sum may be credited against the profit-seeking enterprise's income tax payable in each of the three years from the then-current year.

Colombia

Branch reporters
Eleonora Lozano Rodríguez[1]
Francisco Soler-Peña[2]

Summary and conclusions[3]

The report reveals an important restriction to the treatment of personal data, from both a legal perspective and a jurisprudential one. In addition, the property rights related to data processing (storage and processing) are regulated only by intellectual property protection laws. It can be said that there is no specific regulation on big data.

Attempts at tax regulation are minimal. One of these, of national application, regulates the cloud computing service. This service has several uses but can be implemented as a mechanism for transactions with big data to the extent that it would facilitate the collection and storage of unstructured information and the availability of databases. The Colombian Tax Statute (TS) includes regulations on the orange economy and on technological, scientific and innovation development projects. These could be applied to transactions with big data, although this is not their specific purpose.

The other attempt at regulating big data in Colombia has been implemented at municipal level, specifically in Medellin, which has focused on obtaining, storing, and processing data. This regulatory model is the only one in Colombia specifically designed for transactions involving data.

This report consists of six parts, which make up a proposed tax framework applicable to big data transactions in Colombia. This is only a proposal, since Colombian regulations in this area are only incipient, and the existing ones predate the tensions and problems caused by the issue.

In the first part, we explain how operations with big data can be understood; that is, we attempt to identify their nature and to determine the source of the payments in these operations and whether there are any instruments that enable the establishment of the link between these. The main conclusion is that, strictly speaking, these operations would be classified either as a cloud computing service (national)—whose source of payment would always be the national territory regardless of where the user is located—or as data collection, storage, and processing operations (municipal), whose source of payment would be Medellin, provided that the user is domiciled or makes use of the service through an Internet Protocol address (hereafter IP) there. Furthermore, the regime of permanent establishment in Colombia does not include "virtual" or "digital" concepts.

In the second part, we describe how the concepts of nexus, source, and permanent

[1]   Graduated in Law and Economics and holds a Master's Degree in Economics from Universidad de los Andes. Doctor of Law from Universidad de Salamanca. Law School Dean, Universidad de los Andes (Bogotá, Colombia).
[2]   PhD student at Universidad de los Andes. His main area of research is the macroeconomic analysis of law, which in his thesis project he applies to the study of the challenges of Action 1 of the OECD BEPS Project. Currently, working for Seguros Suramericana S.A.
[3]   We extend a special and heartfelt thanks to the members of Semillero de Estudios Interdisciplinarios de la Tributación, Isabel Gaviria and David Ulloa, for their determined collaboration and research support.

establishment are regulated in international treaties, as well as the treatment of operations that could catalogue transactions with big data. We highlight that the only possible way to address the issue of big data in light of the treaties is through the concept of royalty, as it includes all payments generated by intellectual property rights, as well as those pertaining to technical assistance, consulting, and technical service.

We address transfer pricing in the third part. In 2012, Colombia implemented a general pricing regime that has not been updated to address transactions with big data. The TS establishes that transfer prices will fail to apply only when some type of subordination is configured (subordinates, subsidiaries, agencies, branches, among others), but it also includes, within the same regime, business collaboration contracts, which are free of structural subordination.

In the fourth part, we develop the incentives for operations with big data and the special municipal regime of the industry and commerce tax. In particular, we analyse income tax exemption for activities in the orange economy. It also explains the tax credit in favour of scientific, and technological development and innovation projects, recently regulated by the national government.

In relation to indirect taxes, in part five, we refer to the treatment of sales tax (VAT) for cloud computing and digital services provided from abroad. In particular, we explore the regulatory framework that determines the requirements for collecting VAT, as well as the mechanisms that have been established so that the tax is withheld by national companies for payments made by Colombian residents to providers that are not domiciled in the country.

In the last part, we discuss the rules for the accounting record of transactions with big data, as well as the journal entry for depreciation. Colombia is governed by the International Financial Reporting Standards (IFRS), which do not establish a special treatment for such records.

The above is preceded by an introduction in which we present the commercial regulatory framework related to transactions with big data, as well as the way in which personal data is protected in Colombia. Also, given that information is collected, stored, structured and used through computer components (hardware and software), we also discuss how the creation of these media is protected by intellectual property law. We conclude that these regulatory frameworks are insufficient for the treatment of big data because their enactment precedes the difficulties and tensions that arise.

Finally, we present three of the hypothetical cases suggested by the general reporter for the application of the big data tax regulatory framework in Colombia explained in this report.

Branch reporters
Viktor Šmejkal[1]
Linda Kolaříková[2]

Summary and conclusions

Czech law does not have a legal definition of data in general. Even further, their legal nature is not clear as there is no conclusive opinion, whether data should be considered a thing under Czech law or not. The biggest challenge in this context is the ubiquity of data, the unlimited potential to be duplicate (unless consistently attached to a tangible data medium) and therefore insufficient controllability, which leads to the conclusion that data are not a thing.

The character (size) of big data compared with data of regular size is not relevant for a legal assessment. In both cases the types of data involved in relevant datasets must be assessed in order to determine whether there is a special regulation of such type. The most strict regime is established for the personal data, other specific regimes include open data, data related to the environment, certain public sector data, if requested by a citizen, etc.

Further, certain data might be protected on the basis of specific legal institute, if they are considered to be a part of e.g. a trade secret, databases, etc. Use of others might be subject to special relative rights established by a contract. In some cases, such as personal data, it might be even questionable if such data are tradeable at all.

The biggest challenge in determining their character as outlined above and possible legal disposal of data, is their dynamics. In order to utilize data which are not considered as a thing, the way of their utilization and not data themselves must be the subject of a contract.

The tax law tries to apply a general fiscal regime to the specific described situations as to other similar business operations. From the tax perspective, data are generally intangible assets.

---

[1] Member of the Editorial Board of the journal Dane a finance (Tax and finances) and member of the Board of International Fiscal Association Czech Republic. He has been tax lawyer working in the field of private consultancy services for ten years. Prior to that, he was employed at Ministry of Finance (CZ).

[2] Czech based attorney at law. She mainly focuses on new technologies, data and financial services.

Branch reporters
Jakob Bundgaard[1]
Louise Fjord Kjærsgaard[2]

Summary and conclusions

Big data and data driven businesses have not yet given rise to any specific legislation or case law in Danish law. Consequently, the below overview to a large extent expresses the view of the authors on how data will likely be treated for Danish tax purposes in an international context. However, as no authoritative sources and guidelines exist, the below is based on generally applicable tax principles, and it is needless to say that the views presented are surrounded by great uncertainty as it is the first attempt to analyze big data and data driven businesses from a Danish tax perspective.

In a legal setting over the past decades a new discipline called "IT law" has been developed, being a cross-disciplinary legal discipline covering the legal aspects related to information technology where the facts (i.e. technologies) determine the scope of the discipline and where the topics, in principle, are handled by existing well established legal disciplines, e.g. copyright law, patent law, the law of domain names, liability for intermediaries, data protection law, market law, contract law and software licensing law.

Raw data (understood as units of information) which is not part of a work, a structured database etc. is not covered by copyright protection and it is our understanding that in this respect Denmark is in line with most jurisdictions.

While data seemingly is not reflected on the balance sheet, it is relevant to consider whether data should still be considered an intangible asset for Danish tax purposes. This is primarily of relevance with respect to tax depreciation, which is inter alia available to know-how, patents, copyrights and trademarks.[3] Tax depreciation requires that the intangible asset has been acquired, i.e., not built up internally. The definition of depreciable intangible is broad and may according to the wording also include other intangible assets, "such as" the intangible assets explicitly mentioned in the provision. While there is very little guidance on how to delineate the definition, it has previously been argued in the tax literature that only intangible assets "similar" to the listed assets may be within the scope[4] but the exact scope is uncertain and could also develop over time in line with societal and technical developments.

In the context of big data transactions, we consider it most likely that tax depreciations will not be available to raw data. On the other hand, copyright protected databases should

---

[1]   PhD, Managing Director of CORIT Advisory, and the chairman of the Danish IFA branch.
[2]   PhD scholar at Copenhagen Business School, Senior Associate at CORIT Advisory, and Danish member of YIN.
[3]   S. 40(2) of the Danish Tax Depreciation Act [DK: Afskrivningsloven] (unofficial translation): In the case of acquisition of other intangible assets such as special manufacturing method or similar (know-how), patent right, author and artist right and the right to a design or trademark or in the case of acquisition of the right under a yield contract, lease or rental contract.
[4]   Louise Fjord Kjærsgaard and Jakob Bundgaard, *Afståelsesbeskatning ved flytning af DEMPE-funktioner?* Tidskrift for skatter og afgifter, TfS 2017, 668, pp. 668-672.

be within the scope. The above uncertainty with respect to the exact scope of depreciable intangible assets is then of primary relevance in other data-driven businesses including aggregated and structured data sets not being a copyright protected database and algorithm.

If covered by the Danish tax Depreciation Act, the acquisition price of the intangible asset can be depreciated 1/7 for seven years.

The most predominant tax consequences involving big data transactions seem to be whether the income generated is considered taxable income and whether the expenses connected with big data transactions are considered deductible business expenses. We consider it likely that any income arising from business transactions involving data, may be regarded as taxable income and should be computed in accordance with the net principle. The eligibility of deduction requires that the relevant costs are incurred for the purpose of acquiring, securing or maintain taxable income. In addition, deductibility requires that the cost in question is not used to broaden the income base, including start-up costs and establishment costs.

From an international perspective, the term 'permanent establishment' under Danish domestic tax law should be interpreted according to the definition in the 2017-OECD Model Tax Convention and its Commentary.

There is no provision on imposing source taxation specifically on payments for digital product or services. However, payment classified as royalties are subject to Danish withholding tax. Notably, if comparing the domestic definition of royalty with the definition included in article 12 (2) of the 2017-OECD Model Tax Convention, the definition excludes *payments of any kind received as a consideration for the use of, or the right to use, any copyright of literary, artistic or scientific work including cinematograph films.* This is of great importance, since EDB[5] including software is categorised as literary work.[6] Therefore, if software is not protected by a patent, payments for the right to use software should *not* be classified as royalties for Danish domestic tax purposes.

Denmark has a rather extensive tax treaty network comprising more than 70 applicable tax treaties. In general, Denmark adheres to the OECD Model Convention as a basis for negotiating bilateral tax treaties and relies heavily on the OECD Commentaries when formulating and interpreting tax treaty provisions. However, approximately 40% of the Danish tax treaties provides for shared taxing rights on payments classified as royalties.

The arm's length principle is a fixed part of Danish tax law and should be interpreted in accordance with the OECD Transfer Pricing Guidelines (2017) which are considered a crucial source of interpretation guidance. Currently, no official guidance from the Danish legislator or the Danish tax authorities exists with respect to the transfer pricing treatment of data and data driven transactions.

With respect to special regimes, Denmark has currently not introduced any digital services tax regime or other taxes targeting digital business models. Similarly, no specific tax incentives with respect to data driven business models have been introduced. However, a generally applicable rule exists regarding deduction for trial and research costs beyond the scope of deductibility for ordinary business costs (due to COVID-19 temporarily increased to a 130% deduction). Despite a narrow wording of the provision, in our view, the development of software, the structuring of data and the development of algorithms could fall within the scope.

---

[5]   Danish abbreviation for a group of assets equal to those covered by "Information Technology".
[6]   S. 1 (3) of the Danish Copyright Act [DK: Ophavsretsloven].

Finally, the current international debate on potential barter transactions and the tax implication of such transactions has not been considered in a Danish tax law context. However, since all economic benefits, in principle, are subject to tax in Denmark, it cannot be precluded that certain data transactions could be subject to tax on this basis.

Branch reporter
Martti Nieminen[1]

Summary and conclusions

Despite the major societal benefits that arise from the data sector, there is no comprehensive approach adopted in Finland to ensure the legal protection of private investments made in data. There are legal tools that safeguard the investor, but these instruments are not arranged to constitute an all-encompassing system with a clear underlying principle, such as the protection of economic investment by itself. One likely reason for this is that the data sector is not particularly dependent on legal protection because, among other things, data can also be made excludable through technical protection. Also maximizing the social wellbeing from data requires not only incentives for data businesses but also, and perhaps foremost, access rights for the public.

The relevant legal instruments that protect investments made in data vary from ownership-like property rights to regulation concerning trade secrets as well as contract law. All of them are also relevant when assessing the tax treatment of data related payments. Copyright safeguards creative human effort by granting the author exclusive rights to dispose of his/her original work, for example a computer program. In some cases, software may also be patented. Copyright does not, however, protect mere ideas, including mathematical concepts such as algorithms, or efforts that require money, time and expertise but not much creativity. To also protect the labour and skill required for putting the product together, the Finnish copyright law provides for so-called neighbouring rights. The producer of a database is protected by the EU law based *sui generis* right and the producer of a catalogue containing large amount of information is protected by the catalogue right, which is a domestic law concept that is based on Nordic copyright tradition. Further protection to safeguard valuable business information is provided by legislation that concerns so-called trade secrets. Protection of data is routinely strengthened beyond statutory protection by concluding non-disclosure agreements.

There are no specific laws in Finland concerning the income taxation of data transactions. Accordingly, there are, for example, no special nexus rules that would apply. When a Finnish resident company receives income from a data transaction from Finland or elsewhere, in Finnish domestic tax law it does not matter much what the precise character of that income is. In any case it is income that is taxable in Finland. The possible tax paid in the source state for the same income is usually creditable in Finland even if there is no tax treaty. When a non-resident company receives income from a data transaction, the classification of that income does matter also in domestic law because it depends on the income type what kind of connection to Finland is required for the income to be taxable in Finland. The importance of the classification of the data payment, in general terms, is in that if the payment qualifies as royalty it may be taxed in Finland without the non-resident having physical business presence here. Instead, if the payment qualifies as business income or capital gain it cannot

[1]   University Lecturer (Tax Law), Faculty of Management and Business, Tampere University.

be taxed in Finland unless it is connected to a physical business presence in Finland. the definition of royalty in Finnish domestic tax law is virtually like the definition of royalty in article 12(2) of the OECD Model. Accordingly, and because there is not much domestic guidance available, the OECD Commentaries are an important source of interpretation regarding the concept of royalty, also in Finnish domestic law.

Finland has an income tax treaty with close to 80 countries including all major trading partners except for Portugal. The provisions in Finland's tax treaties concerning the taxing rights over business income and capital gains from movable property are essentially like the provisions in the OECD Model. Accordingly, in a tax treaty situation business income and capital gain from movable property is taxable only in the residence state of the recipient unless the income is connected to a permanent establishment in the paying state. The provisions in Finland's tax treaties concerning the taxing rights over royalties are not uniform. Some treaties follow the OECD Model in that exclusive taxing rights are given to the residence state. Most treaties, however, also assign taxing rights to the source country. Those taxing rights are usually limited to 5, 10 or 15 percent of the gross amount of the royalty but there may be different rates in individual treaties. The definition of royalty in Finland's tax treaties is generally like in article 12(2) of the OECD Model. There are, however, some specific features in the royalty definition of Finland's tax treaties compared to the OECD Model and Finnish domestic law that are relevant in the context of big data.

In the transfer pricing rules of Finnish domestic law and tax treaties, there is no definition of an intangible or a data transaction or any other special provision that would apply in the context of big data. There is also no published case law in Finland concerning the transfer pricing of data transactions or any other relevant intangible. Accordingly, the OECD guidelines are in practice the most important and, in most cases, the only available source of interpretation of the arm's length principle with respect to tax treaties as well as domestic law.

There are no special regimes that might apply to the development and sale of big data enabled goods or services. Research and development costs are deductible as current expenses unless the taxpayer wishes to capitalize them, in which case the taxpayer may also choose the applicable amortization period. Data acquisition costs, unless considered as research and development costs, are deductible either as current expenses or capital expenditures depending on whether they are expected to generate income for more than three years.

The VAT treatment of data transactions in Finland is based on the VAT Directive of the European Union. For VAT purposes, data transaction is a supply of service notwithstanding whether the supplied material and information is subject to any intellectual property right or not. There are no special rules or case law in Finland concerning the VAT treatment of data transactions.

Branch reporter
Xenia Legendre[1]

Summary and conclusions

In the rapidly changing world, France tried to adapt its tax rules to the digital economy.

France implemented several incentive measures designed to attract and retain high value-added R&D in the digital sphere in France (*i.e.*, so-called "IP box" for the software, specific depreciation rules, R&D tax credit etc.).

In parallel, France tried to capture into its tax net, a portion of profits generated by digital platforms on the basis of users located in France. France has been one of the pioneer countries in introducing a digital services tax in July 2019, applicable to digital intermediation and targeted advertising services which costs it the risk of retaliation measures from the United States in the form of customs duties on certain typical French non digital products. France authorised the access of the tax authorities to the social networks with the objective to track fraudsters.

From the corporate income tax perspective, France continues to apply a strict territoriality regime (*i.e.*, only profits resulting from a business carried on in France are subject to corporate income tax in France) and does not take into account significant digital presence: the French courts apply the traditional permanent establishment definition implying physical presence and human involvement to digital companies. French tax law has no specific rules for the transfer of data. In particular, no tax rule indicates if the transfer of "raw data" or "structured/aggregated data" should be treated as sale of goods, provision of services or license for royalties. This distinction is particularly relevant from an international tax law perspective, where taxation is different for each of these categories. In this respect, the approach taken by other branches of law should be used. As a result, in most cases, the transfer of data should be considered as a provision of services. France withholds tax on payments for provision of services if there is no tax treaty with the recipient's jurisdiction. If there is a tax treaty, the income will in most cases be taxable in the state where the service provider is established unless the service provider has a traditional permanent establishment in France.

Finally, when the transfer of data is carried out in exchange of a fee, the transaction falls within the scope of VAT as a provision of services. Moreover, specific rules exist for services provided by electronic means. As a result, VAT rules applicable to such services apply to big data transactions. The concept of barter transaction has not been applied to exchanges of personal data for free services.

---

[1]   Tax partner with Hogan Lovells Paris office. She leads the French tax practice of Hogan Lovells and is managing partner of the Paris office. For the purposes of this report Xenia coordinated the group of lawyers from Hogan Lovells from the tax practice (Maryll Pizzetta) and the data practice (Patrice Navarro, Charlotte Le Roux).

Branch reporter
Reimar Pinkernell[1]

Summary and conclusions

There are no specific substantive tax laws in Germany relating to data transactions. As a result, the tax consequences of any given transaction must be determined by applying the pertinent sections of the Income Tax Act (ITA – Einkommensteuergesetz), the VAT Act (Umsatzsteuergesetz) and the Foreign Tax Act (FTA – Außensteuergesetz), which contains Germany's transfer pricing and CFC rules. In a purely domestic setting, all income from commercial data transactions carried out for profit would be characterized as "business income" under section 15 ITA. Income from services arises if the taxpayer is paid to perform a certain activity (contract for services under section 611 of the Civil Code (CC) – Buergerliches Gesetzbuch) or to supply a pre-defined non-tangible work result such as performing a test and reporting the results thereof (contract for work results under section 631 CC). For example, a contract under which the taxpayer is required to use his own expertise to deliver results or data without having to also divulge his methods would not be classified as a know-how license agreement but as "knowledge-based services". A contractual "license to use and access the services" granted by the operator of an electronic platform to his customers will be treated as a contract for services even though the parties use the term "license" to describe the services. It does not matter in this regard that the platform incorporates a self-service interface and that transactions are carried out automatically without human intervention. More specifically, it is not possible to treat this type of automated service as a lease of tangible property or a license for the use of an intangible such as a computer program. The same analysis applies with respect to fully automated online advertising services even if the provider's business model requires large amounts of personal data to target advertising to specific audiences and utilizes advanced algorithms to maximize conversions. Transactions of this type are services and not licensing transactions.

Germany imposes tax on certain items of income derived by foreign taxpayers under section 49 ITA. With respect to data transactions, however, only three income categories of section 49 ITA need to be discussed: The first potentially relevant category is domestic business income, which includes income from a domestic permanent establishment and income derived through a domestic permanent agent under section. 49(1) no. 2a ITA. Germany's permanent establishment concept is fairly similar to article 5 of the OECD Model Convention (OECD MC), so there are no surprises to be expected. In particular, an automated server that is at the disposal of – and operated by – the foreign taxpayer will create a server permanent establishment under sections 49(1) no. 2a ITA and 12 of the General Tax Code (GTC – Abgabenordnung). The concept of permanent agent, however, is much broader than even the recently expanded concept of agency permanent establishment under article 5 OECD MC. It includes not only brokers but also unrelated internet marketing affiliates that

---

[1] Dr., LLM International Taxation (NYU) lawyer, tax advisor, and associated partner with Flick Gocke Schaumburg, Germany's leading tax firm.

(i) solicit business for the foreign taxpayer regularly and (ii) are paid on a contingent basis (e.g., pay-per-sale model, revenue sharing). The second potentially applicable category of income includes royalty income of foreign corporations and income from the transfer of rights by foreign corporations under section 49(1) no. 2a ITA. Fortunately, the German Federal Ministry of Finance issued guidelines in 2017 that favor a narrow interpretation so that a tax liability is triggered only if the licensee is granted the right to commercially exploit the copyright in a database. The guidelines do not mention the supply of streaming data for display on a customer's website. While the customer has arguably been granted a right to publicly display the content of the database, which might trigger a tax liability (similar to a license to show a movie to a cinema audience), the customer neither reproduces nor sublicences the data. In addition, the data streaming contract may be classified as a "data delivery contract", under which the database owner is required to perform services that include frequent updates and reliable transmission of the data to the customer. The third potentially relevant category of income is royalty income from know-how under section 49(1) no. 9 ITA. Provided that the transaction does not involve the licensing or sale of a database protected under copyright law, payments for the collection and transfer of raw data can be characterized as income from services, which is not taxable in Germany. The same analysis applies to "knowledge-based services" such as targeted online advertising and big data analyses prepared by a foreign taxpayer for use by a customer in Germany.

The issue of barter transactions involving user data has come up in Germany in a VAT context. While the EU VAT Committee laid down some useful guidelines on 3 November 2018, the German tax authorities do not feel bound by these guidelines as the EU VAT Committee has a strictly advisory function. It is likely that there will be more cases in the future and that the controversy will ultimately come before the ECJ. No official guidance has been published by the German tax authorities on transfer pricing issues resulting from intragroup transfers of data. In particular, it is not clear whether an enterprise that collects data for other associated enterprises that process and monetize the data should be entitled to a share of the group's residual profits. There are also cases in which two associated enterprises have joint controllership of personal data. So, the outcome of the analysis would depend on the facts and circumstances of each case.

Branch reporters
Kamlesh Varshney[1]
Nilesh M Kapadia[2]

Summary and conclusions

The 21st century is known as "the information age" and its digital revolution has permeated India as well. With nearly 450 million Internet users and a growth rate of 7-8%, India is well on the path to becoming a digital economy, which has a large market for global players. At the same time, the unregulated and arbitrary use of data, especially personal data, has raised concerns regarding the privacy and autonomy of an individual. This was also the subject matter of the landmark judgment of the Supreme Court, which recognized the right to privacy as a fundamental right. Following this, Justice B. N. Srikrishna committee was entrusted with the responsibility of identifying lapses in the present data protection regulations and preparing more robust and comprehensive data protection laws. Based on this committee report and responses from stakeholders, a revised Personal Data Protection Bill, 2019 (Draft Bill), has been cleared by the Union Cabinet on 4 December 2019, which was examined by the Joint Parliament Committee which gave its report in December 2021, and is pending enactment.

The tax implications of data in India have been analysed in detail in the paper. Summarised these are:

(i) If the non-resident has stored the data on the server in India whether owned or otherwise at its disposal, it could create its permanent establishment.

(ii) India has introduced the concept of significant economic presence in its domestic legislation widening the source based taxation based on business connection. The SEP can be created based on transaction in goods, service or property in India (including downloading of data or software) or through systematic and continuous soliciting of business activities or engaging in interaction with Indian users, above a threshold. This would come into effect from Financial Year 2021-22. It would generally not have any effect in treaty situations.

(iii) India has also widened the scope of income attributable (and hence taxable) to operations in India by including targeted advertisement, sale of Indian data and sale of goods or services using Indian data. This has already come into force from the financial year 2020-21.

(iv) Transfer of all or any right in data could also result in its taxation as royalty in India. Data could represent Industrial, Commercial or Scientific information, information concerning the working or use of patent, invention etc, or it could represent right in copyright. Under Indian domestic law customized electronic data is included in the definition of computer software. Whether use of computer software amounts to use

---

[1] Officer of Indian Revenue Service who has worked in tax administrations of India and Papua New Guinea. He is currently Joint Secretary Tax Policy with Indian Ministry of Finance.
[2] Partner of N M K & Co LLP, Chartered Accountants.

of right in copyright (hence royalty) or use of copyrighted article (hence not royalty) was an issue before the Indian apex court[3] as different High courts have given different judgments. With respect to access to data base or furnishing of report based on data access, Indian courts have held it as royalty where the information is not public and have held it as not royalty if it is publicly available information. Under the treaty, the definition of royalty could be narrower.

(v) The source rule of taxation is payment based. Payment made by the government is sourced in India. Payment made by a resident is sourced in India unless it is for business or profession outside India or for earning income from source outside India. Payment made by a non-resident is sourced in India only when it is for business or profession in India or for earning income from source in India.

(vi) There could also be an issue of taxation of payment for use of data as Fees for Technical Services (FTS). The Indian apex court has made an important distinction between a facility and service. The presence of human element in rendering of service is held to be no longer relevant. A standard facility has been held to be not in the nature of FTS. Most of the Indian tax treaties contain an article on FTS giving source country the limited right to tax FTS on gross basis unless effectively connected with a PE. In most cases the definition of FTS is the same as in domestic law. However, some of the Indian treaties also contain a requirement of "make available". In those treaties the scope of FTS is narrower, as in addition the test of "make available" is required to be satisfied.

(vii) The provisions of transfer pricing would come into play if there are transactions between two Associated Enterprises(Aes). The Indian TP regime is generally modelled on internationally accepted norms laid down in OECD/UN guidelines.

(viii) India has also introduced the Equalisation Levy (EL) and it applies   at the rate of 6% on online advertisements (from April 2016) and 2% on online supply of goods or services (from April 2020). The 2020 EL also covers transactions between two non-residents, if for targeted Indian advertisements and for sale of Indian data.

(ix) India provides tax incentives to start ups and also taxes barter transactions.

(x) Under the GST law, there is a specific provision for inclusion of barter within the definition of supplies liable to GST. The outward supply of data will be taxed, as the inward supply of services will also be taxed, the latter on a reverse charge basis. One of the items liable to GST, is Online Information Database Access and Retrieval services (OIDAR) a category of services provided through the medium of internet and received by the recipient online without having any physical interface with the supplier of such services. This covers all types of data accessed by the users.

(xi) In order for a database to be treated as Intangible asset in accounts, the entity owning the same should comply with the recognition criterion laid down in the relevant Accounting Standards on Intangible Assets (AS-26, Ind-AS 38). These standards require the entity to consider certain recognition criteria before capitalizing such as identifiability, measurability of cost, control over a resource and expectation of future economic benefits flowing to the enterprise etc. There are rules for revenue recognition on monetizing the same.

---

[3] The Supreme Court has in Civil Appeal Nos 8733-8734 of 2018 decided on March 2, 2021 held that. unless an interest in all or any of the rights contained in section 14(b), read with section 14(a), of the Indian Copyright Act is transferred through a license, it would not amount to use of right in copyright and hence it cannot be characterised as royalty. Income-tax Department has filed a review petition before the Supreme Court

Branch reporter
Carlomaria Setti della Volta[1,2]

Summary and conclusions

Certain IP rights may apply to a database, if creativity or substantial investment occurs, and law of trade secret may provide an *erga omnes* protection of data, if information is secret, protected through adequate arrangements and with business value, leading to an intellectual property of data and databases. IP rights may apply to big data, depending upon the circumstances, among which whether data are raw, structured, or analyzed.

Various aspects of big data, such as transfer, analysis and sharing, may be governed by contractual arrangements. From a legal perspective, in principle data are not sold, but rather made available to the other party of the agreements through the performance of a service. Contractual restrictions on the use of data may lead to a *de facto* property right.

Italian tax laws do not specifically regulate data transaction income, which thus needs to be characterized by interpreting existing rules and principles.

In particular, income character and source of data transactions may be addressed by leveraging – where appropriate – on existing interpretation with regard to software, database, know-how and lease of equipment, to be distinguished from general provision of services. This leads to consider whether data transactions may give rise to royalty income, gains or business profits.

With regard to character, and in particular to royalty income, while copyright generally applies to software, an important aspect is whether data may *inter alia* qualify as secret business information or know-how, and exploitation of such data occurs.

Further, although data, a database and software may – under certain circumstances – constitute IP, income arising therefrom qualifies as royalty only to the extent that it constitutes consideration for commercial exploitation, rather than for personal or commercial use. This principle, which has been stated with regard to software, should be applied to data and databases.

Beside royalties, data transaction may give rise also to gains or business profits.

In this context, two recent private rulings qualified income from the sale of databases as gain; on the other hand, where a business – as a core activity – collects, organizes and/or analyzes data, in order to provide raw/structured data and data analytics, the most appropriate character is business profits: these activities require material investments, R&D and specialistic skills, which are applied to provide a service.

Against this background, in most cases source taxation should apply only if an Italian permanent establishment occurs. However, should data transaction income characterize as royalty, a withholding tax will apply, unless an exemption is available.

[1]   Avvocato, MA in Taxation, Chiomenti – Milan.
[2]   The author would like to thank Andrea Alcara, Giammarco Cottani, Paolo Giacometti, Antonino Guida, Alessandro Turina and Antonio Zambon for their insights; the author is grateful to Paolo Bertoni, Sara Molina and Jacopo Baieri for their support on IP law profiles, and to Fabio Dotti on technical matters. Contents and views expressed in this report are those of the author.

With regard to permanent establishment, two aspects are worth mentioning. First, effective from 2018, Italy enacted a "significant economic presence" threshold. The relevant provision is extremely vague and is expected to give rise to uncertainties, especially in relation to treaty provisions. Second, for a long time the Italian Tax Authorities have been assessing undisclosed permanent establishments in a quite aggressive and "novel" manner. This intertwines with issues that are posed by purely digital businesses, among which whether there may be a physical presence in Italy, constituted by servers and fiber optic cables. This is an update of the issue whether, and at what conditions, a server may constitute a permanent establishment, with certain innovative traits.

Double Tax Treaties encompass various wordings to define "software", but it is reasonable to conclude that all definitions point to the same concept.

Among special regimes provided by the Italian tax system, the Digital Service Tax, certain incentives, and the barter theory are worth mentioning.

Effective from 2020, Italy enacted a Digital Service Tax, which is largely aligned with the Proposal for a Directive by the EU Commission; the threshold of local qualifying revenue is set at Euro 5.500.000,00. Among qualifying digital services, there is the transmission of data collected, which must be from users and generated through the use of a digital interface. The DST will be repealed as of 2023 following consensus reached at the OECD G-20 Inclusive Framework level.

Further, the Italian tax system currently encompasses certain incentives which may relate to data.

No official guidelines support the barter theory, under which free digital services would be rendered in exchange of data from the users. Academic works report a general consensus on the difficulties to identify a sufficiently direct link between the supply and its consideration.

Finally, the report addresses the case studies set out in the general report, with particular regard to income character and source.

Branch reporters
Mari Takahashi[1]
Atsushi Onishi[2]

Summary and conclusions

Japan is losing tax revenue on income derived from big data transactions because of traditional tax rules on new e-commerce business models, such as big data, which produces more profits without physical or human capital in a source state. Despite Japan's active contributions to Base Erosion and Profit Shifting (BEPS) Projects, this challenge has not yet been solved.

In principle, big data transactions require a platform providing the information technology (IT) infrastructure for their sales or services. Generally, the more significant in scale they are, the more profit they gain. Although there is no established definition of big data and its market size remains unknown, Japan does not have platforms comparable to the so-called Big Tech, which consists of the largest dominant companies in the IT industry. In this way, Japan may have assumed the position of a source state for most big data transactions.

This report provides an in-depth analysis of the existing Japanese tax system relating to big data transactions. It mainly explores taxation for corporations at the national level. The introduction covers the background of big data. It delves into the legal classification of big data and examines data protection techniques, which are crucial in ascertaining how the Japanese tax system treats big data.

Part one explains the basic principles of tax treatment on the legal character of income. The highlight is the existence of a permanent establishment (PE) and the attributed income. There have been several amendments to PE-related articles in the past, and important guidance has been provided in advanced rulings.

Part two reviews the application of tax treaties. In the Japanese legal hierarchy, treaties take precedence over domestic law, and consequently, the application of each treaty changes legal classifications and source rules under domestic law.

Part three examines transfer pricing taxation on big data transactions. The application of the transfer pricing rule depends on the facts and circumstances of each case. Since it is impossible to determine a calculation method for the cases provided, this section discusses the specific issues affecting intangible transactions, including big data.

Part four reconfirms that Japanese tax law does not have any particular provisions that apply to the development and sale of big data. It also notes that Japan has not enacted a

[1]   LLM in Taxation (Georgetown University Law Center), National Tax Agency of Japan (on Leave).
[2]   Deputy Director of Economic Treaty Division, International Law Bureau, Ministry of Foreign Affairs of Japan, LLM (Vienna University of Economics and Business (WU)).

The reporters would like to thank the IFA Japan Branch colleagues for their valuable comments in preparing this report. All views expressed are solely those of the reporters, and errors and omissions remain their sole responsibilities. The opinions expressed herein do not necessarily reflect organizational or state positions.

digital services tax or any similar tax on the acquisition and use of data.

Part five describes how the 2015 tax reform altered the Japanese consumption tax's criterion for determining the place of supply of specific electronic services to the "address of the service recipient" (destination principle). Even foreign platformers, like Big Tech, can be registered taxpayers under this system. Accordingly, the potential of consumption tax on new electronic transactions needs to be explored.

Part six analyzes basic rules of recognition standards and capital amortization of tax accounting regarding data transactions, including updates of current recognition standards and capital amortization rules for software essential for data transactions. There are no specific regulations for data transactions themselves.

In conclusion, the current Japanese tax system may not accommodate new businesses, such as big data transactions, which affects the amount of tax revenue collected from such companies. More specifically, corporation tax, withholding tax, and transfer pricing rules cannot fully encapsulate big data transactions. First, for corporation tax, it is difficult to find a PE in data transactions. Even if a source state successfully identifies a PE, the attributed income may be insignificant due to their limited human functions, as most data transactions are automated, and no human labor is required. In addition, the corporate tax rate has been reduced in recent years,[3] resulting in a further decline in the amount of tax. Second, withholding tax on royalties has been exempted under several tax treaties since the 2004 revision of the Japan-US tax treaty. Third, transfer pricing taxation faces difficulties in transactions involving intangible assets. Whatever method is selected, it is challenging to find a comparable transaction and adjust the differences. On the other hand, consumption tax on specific cross-border services can barely catch big data transactions by foreign businesses, but unanswered questions remain regarding the extent of their compliance.

Fundamental reforms are needed to address these issues. However, the authors of this report choose to respect the global tax certainty reaffirmed in the 2019 G20 Osaka Declaration and do not seek unilateral measures for big data taxation in Japan. By coincidence, we came to the same conclusion as the Japanese branch report written twenty years ago. The report states that "(t)he discussion on the taxation of electronic commerce should proceed with due consideration to the development of new business models. At the same time, it should aim at a balanced revenue sharing in this diversified and pluralistic world."[4] We hope that a new framework for digital taxation will be designed through international cooperation.

---

[3] The 2016 amendments reduced the effective corporate tax rate for national and local governments to below 30%; the current effective tax rate is 29.74%.
[4] Y. Masui, Japan Branch Report, IFA Cahiers (2001).

Republic of Korea

Branch reporters
Sun Young (Sunny) Kim[1]
Hyun Seok Yoon[2]

Summary and conclusions

With the advent of the Fourth Industrial Revolution, people are constantly absorbing an immense amount of data by using intelligence as well as information and communication technology on a daily basis. The use of such data accumulation has triggered unprecedented changes in every aspect of our society including the economic industry and medical services. Far more data encompassing numerical, textual and visual data are generated in shorter cycles than in a past analogue setting, which is referred to as "big data".[3]

Big data is created by developing and analyzing a large volume of valuable data using basic data sets, often in combination with new technologies such as artificial intelligence and the Internet of Things (IoT). Unlike data that was available at the early stages of the Internet, big data as of today contains information on almost every aspect of our daily life, and effective analysis thereof can produce information of immense value.[4] In the global market, it has become an increasingly important business function to collect, aggregate, structure and analyze large sets of data. Not only IT companies, but also companies adopting diverse business models utilize big data technology. For instance, corporate entities utilize such big data technology to facilitate customer acquisition and retention, detect potential business risks at an early phase, develop risk management solutions, innovate and develop new products, and manage supply chains.

Under these circumstances, how much data can be collected and how elaborately can such data be analyzed and utilized, is what builds competitiveness not only on a corporate level, but also on a national level. In other words, data increasingly becomes resources for business and administrations, where individuals, companies and countries will take advantage of big data by retaining and utilizing high-quality data in large quantities in the era of the Fourth Industrial Revolution.[5]

This report seeks to address the tax implications of transactions where big data is accumulated, processed, and analyzed in a domestic and international context. First, this report intends to introduce legal issues in the Republic of Korea (hereafter Korea)that are

---

[1]   Partner (US attorney and AICPA) at Shin & Kim LLC leading the International Tax Team. Prior to joining Shin & Kim LLC, she led the Global Tax Team at Deloitte Anjin LLC.

[2]   Director of the Wonkwang University Research Institute and currently teaching tax law at Wonkwang University Law School. Mr. Yoon is also a member of the International Fiscal Association of the Republic of Korea and a member of the National Tax Review Committee of the National Tax Service of the Republic of Korea.

[3]   Naver encyclopedia of knowledge:
(https://terms.naver.com/entry.nhn?docId=1691554&cid=42171&categoryId=42183)

[4]   Jun-seok Park, "The protectability of new data such as big data and etc. from the perspective of intellectual property law", Journal of Industrial Property Vol. 58, 2019. 1, p.81.

[5]   Bang, Dong Hee, "A Study on Enactment of Data Legislation for Activating the Data Economy", LAW REVIEW Institute of Law Studies PUSAN NATIONAL UNIVERSITY Vol.59, No.1, February 2018, p.6.

associated with big data development and commercialization by companies. Then, it will examine how foreign companies, supplying goods or services to residents by using big data, are subject to taxation under Korean tax laws and international tax treaties.

Liechtenstein

Branch reporters
Matthias Langer[1]
Lara Olms[2]

Summary and conclusions

The legal analysis in the report finds that Liechtenstein does not have any special regulations that are exclusively limited to big data and its applications. Instead, several laws of different areas are to be applied, which state that no right and therefore no ownership can be acquired in digital data. Nevertheless, there is a distinction to intellectual property rights. The Liechtenstein copyright law protects computer programs, databases and data files as they are considered to be works of literature and art and are therefore protected. This does not hold for individual data and information. Data can be classified among others by their form: raw data, structured and aggregated data and the analysis of them. None of them when being transferred for free, qualify as a service. They only do if they are transferred in exchange for a payment according to the law on VAT (MWSTG). Also, data transactions may qualify as a license but that data cannot be leased. As a further result due to the possibility that data files qualify as intellectual creations, the creator of structured or aggregated data and their analysis owns the property rights and is therefore also able to sell or exchange them.

Additionally, by regarding the source of income, it is determined that data do not qualify as asset and are therefore not subject to asset-based tax. With regard to income tax, the income from data and data transactions may derive from self-employment or from legal entities that generate income from data usage, sales and transactions. However, as data itself is neither money nor has monetary value, it is not subjected to income tax. As one of the last results, it is also found that servers and websites usually do not qualify as permanent establishments and are therefore not subject to taxes in Liechtenstein. Nevertheless, in some very specific circumstances they may still qualify as taxable. This is further examined in the context of treaty principles that are based on the OECD guidelines. By answering the question of qualification of a server in another country as a permanent establishment that justifies the taxation of the payments attributable to that permanent establishment, the server characteristics are further examined. In addition to the significant functions and business activities that have to be performed at that place to qualify as a permanent establishment, the server has to be fixed locally, has to have a specific degree of independence and the possible power of disposition.

---

[1] Certified Tax Consultant, Dipl.-Kauf., LLM, Partner of the tax consultancy actus ag and lecturer at the University of Liechtenstein. He is focused on Liechtenstein and German tax law as well as cross-border tax structuring. He also advises blockchain and crypto driven businesses and accompanied the first STO in the EEA. In addition to providing tax advice regarding new technologies, he also provides his own IT services within actus ag.
[2] Tax Engineer, MSc, at actus ag in Liechtenstein. She has a background in taxes, accounting and commercial law, studied her Master of Finance in Liechtenstein and is a current Master student of US Tax Law in San Francisco as well as a current LLM student of Digitalization & Tax Law in Vienna. Her main focus within actus is acting as an interface between the IT and tax department i.e. dealing with technological innovations such as crypto and blockchain in the tax sector.

In the context of transfer pricing, the arm's length principle as well as the latest version of the OECD Transfer Pricing Guidelines (TPG) are to be applied in Liechtenstein. The approach when data are transferred does not differ from the approach of a normal transaction. In both cases: If the conditions of a transaction between two related parties differ from the usual conditions of two non-related parties, the suitable transfer pricing method with regard to the specific circumstances has to be determined and the firms have to be taxed based on the conditions between two non-related parties. Furthermore, it is stated that there is no Digital Service Tax (DST) or barter treatment in Liechtenstein. However, the Blockchain Act ensures legal security for business models using DLT. Liechtenstein additionally provides checks to support innovation and strengthen the development of digitalization. As the IP-Box regime was abolished in 2016, incentives that grant specific tax credits in relation to the development and exploitation of big data no longer exist.

Regarding VAT, it is found that if data or data products are sold, the selling company has to include VAT, because it qualifies as a service against payment. Furthermore, when studying the subscription tax, it is concluded that if a foreign or domestic company receives imported data carriers without market value that are not already exempt from VAT and either obtains such services for more than CHF 10,000 a year or has a company or permanent establishment in Liechtenstein that makes profits of more than CHF 100,000 a year, it is liable to subscription tax. This also results in the fact that he has to be registered for the purpose of subscription tax and VAT in Liechtenstein.

With regard to tax accounting, the expenses and revenues in relation to data have to be included in the balance sheet and the financial statements leading to the net income that is the starting point for taxational adaptions and corrections before calculating the tax liability. Furthermore, if data would be understood as an intangible asset, it has to be carried on in the balance sheet, which is uncertain up to now. Expenses for establishing databases and analytic tools, maintaining datasets and for collecting raw data would be considered as development expenses or expenses for the expansion of business operations and would be capitalized and amortized.

Finally, some issues that could arise if data transactions are liable to taxation are addressed. These are issues concerning documentation, monitoring and traceability as well as concerning the very individual value of data that can change with the data owner.

To summarize, as long as there are no payments related to data transactions or income, there are no taxes. As soon as a company generates income in providing, selling or transferring data, this income is subject to income tax. Furthermore, as there is a payment for a service, VAT is incurred in this context. Same holds for tax deductibility. If the data transactions are part of the business activity of that operating business the taxable net income is reduced by the expenses justified by the business activity and therefore also by the data transactions. As pointed out in some of the sections, often no clear regulations are yet in place, but as data will become even more valuable for companies the discussions about how to include them in the balance sheet and how to treat them for the purpose of taxation will go on and will introduce new approaches and regulations. Until then the standard principle "substance over form" applies.

Branch reporters
Christian Schlesser[1]
Hermann Schomakers[2]

Summary and conclusions

Thanks to the steady increase of computing hardware capabilities in line with Moore´s law, the phenomenon of big data emerged in recent years. The current legislative frameworks can hardly keep up with the pace of technological developments. There is no legal framework for data transactions and the definitions of property and ownership in the Luxembourg civil code date back to the times of Napoleon Bonaparte. In 2013, though, Luxembourg introduced an action for data recovery in insolvency proceedings of cloud providers. In addition, the protection of personal data was improved on 25 May 2018 with the implementation of the General Data Protection Regulation. Data protection officers warn that the collection of big data may violate the principles of transparency, of purpose limitation and of data minimization.

There are no specific tax laws in Luxembourg relating to data transactions. For income tax purposes, the business income and rental income categories are the most relevant. Here, the Luxembourg sourcing rules provide that business income must be earned by non-resident taxpayers through a domestic permanent establishment, which requires a fixed piece of equipment or fixed place of business. However, big data, APIs, databases and websites are not tangible properties that could be linked to a specific geographical point and thus cannot constitute a permanent establishment. The remote delivery of automated digital services from a self-owned Luxembourg server without human involvement could however give rise to a permanent establishment. Still, the profits attributable to such a server-PE should be low in absence of significant people functions. Physical presence remains the major nexus for direct taxes in Luxembourg.

Most of the 83 double taxation treaties applicable in Luxembourg follow the OECD Model Tax Convention. Some 68 treaties are amended by the multilateral instrument. However, there is no specific clause in the tax treaties that deals with the different types of data transactions. Data driven businesses are free to choose the location of their operations. In light of the principal purpose test of the MLI, multinationals are encouraged to produce robust business documentation explaining the role of the subsidiaries involved in data transactions.

In the absence of specific guidance, the three tax treaty provisions that are relevant for data transactions are article 7 on business profits, article 12 on royalties and article 12A regarding technical fees. As regards business profits, the definition of a permanent establishment is paramount and still very much dependent on a given degree of physical presence. In most cross-border transactions involving the collection and access to raw data, the income to be derived from such transaction should qualify as a business income and not

---

[1]   Partner, International Tax Services, EY Luxembourg.
[2]   Director, Tax Dispute Resolution, KPMG Luxembourg.

as a royalty. Only a few tax treaties signed by Luxembourg include a provision applicable to technical services' transactions. This provision should generally not be applicable to raw data transactions, as they are not meant to embed a material added value, but it may cover big data analytics that require specialized knowledge, skill or expertise. It is noteworthy that Luxembourg is not levying any withholding tax on royalty payments.

Luxembourg transfer pricing rules do not provide specific guidance on the treatment of data transactions. In the absence of reliable information on comparable uncontrolled transactions, the transfer pricing method most likely to be used in transactions involving big data is the transactional profit split method, which considers the relative value of the functions performed by the contributors. The significant functions associated to big data would be identified by reference to each activity in the big data life cycle. Raw data itself should have limited value. Like oil, data is raw until its intrinsic value is unlocked in a process where the information is extracted from data. In most cases, data would need to be combined with a platform, people or algorithms to create and amplify value.

Luxembourg is currently not offering any special tax regimes for the development and sale of big data enabled goods or services. Luxembourg has not introduced any digital service tax and has no plans to do so on a unilateral basis. The IP tax regime is focused on patents and copyrighted software and thus not directly applicable to big data transactions. Still, taxpayers are eligible for an 80% tax exemption to the extent that they can establish a direct nexus between the qualifying income, assets and expenditures. For VAT purposes, data transactions are generally classified as a service.

Luxembourg accounting principles do not provide specific provisions in relation to data transactions. When companies own or internally generate data which they can exploit economically, those expenses can most of the time not be capitalized as intangibles but must be deducted the same year. However, the expenses incurred to develop and maintain data-analytics tools could qualify as tangible or intangible assets. Provided that it can be reliably measured, the development costs of a data-analytics tool can be capitalized, to the extent it supports a business. Research costs can however not be capitalized.

Finally, data transactions may constitute a reportable cross-border arrangement under the mandatory disclosure rules of DAC 6, if the transaction involves the transfer of hard-to-value intangibles or an intragroup cross-border transfer of functions, risks or assets.

Malaysia

Branch reporters
Anand Raj[1]
Thenesh Kannaa[2]

Summary and conclusions

Character, Source & Nexus – Recipient's perspective

The tax laws of Malaysia do not have any specific provisions pertaining to the taxation of data transactions.

The general principles of tax are to be applied to establish whether any receipt or transaction is of an income or capital character, the type of income, the tax rate and mechanism for payment of tax. For completeness, Malaysia has an income tax but no capital gains tax.

The character of a transaction plays an important role in determining the source of income. Each source has its own derivation scope, i.e. nexus rule, hence the character of a transaction often influences the taxability of that transaction, especially in cross-border cases.

Data driven transactions may involve a one-time non-exclusive transfer of data/ information or a continuous non-exclusive transfer of data/information via a subscription model. These may be associated with the character of a license of intangible property.

Other types of data driven transactions may involve the transfer of data/information which involves alienation of the transferor's ownership of such data/information (i.e. transfer on an exclusive basis). Such transactions may be viewed as a sale of intangible property. On the other hand, a commitment to collect, aggregate and/or analyse a certain amount of data over a period of time may be regarded as either a service or a sale of intangible property, depending upon the terms of the transaction.

In some service organisations, data may be heavily used by the service providers. In such cases a distinction must be made between the provision of data and the provision of a service whereby the provider merely uses the data in the course of providing the service. The character of a data-driven service should not be any different from a conventional service, merely due to the involvement or use of data in the performance of the data-driven service.

As for the source, Malaysia has specific provisions to deal with Special Classes of Income, which include technical and other services provided by non-residents. The royalty source in the domestic tax law also has a wider scope than that of the OECD recommendation as it includes payments for the use of software and payments for the alienation of certain intangible property. Incidentally, the scope of terms such as 'copyright' in the DTA is interpreted widely by including software-related payments.

---

[1]   Partner of Shearn Delamore & Co. and recognised as one of Malaysia's Top 100 Lawyers Asia Business Law Journal (2020 & 2021) and is recognised in tier 1 of tax and competition law counsel by the International Tax Review, Chambers, Asia Pacific Legal 500, Asialaw Profiles and other legal directories over decades.
[2]   Partner of TraTax, an independent tax advisory firm that is the sole member firm of WTS Global in Malaysia.

Malaysian law provides for taxation on a 'derived or remittance' basis, but a 'territorial scope' is practised due to a wide exemption for foreign source income. The application of the territorial scope is subject to deeming provisions that dictate the nexus for certain income to be deemed to be derived from Malaysia. These are summarised in Table 1 (see section 1.4).

The link between character, source and nexus is vital, and is summarised in Table 2 (see section 1.5). It is interesting to see how subtle differences may render certain transactions as taxable or non-taxable, particularly in cross-border situations.

Character – Payer's perspective

The perspective of the person who earns the income is not necessarily important for the payer. The key concern for the payer is to establish whether the payment is a revenue expense (which is normally a tax-deductible expense) or a capital expenditure – for which the key criterion is whether or not the payment leads to creation of an enduring benefit.

Where the payment is taken as a capital expenditure, the character of the payment is examined to establish whether the payment constitutes expenditure on 'plant', which is a vital qualification to claim tax depreciation known as capital allowance on such costs. This was tested in a landmark decision of the Malaysian Court of Appeal in the case of *CIMB Bank Berhad* that affirmed that "plant" could also include intangible assets like databases.

However, the tax statue was amended effective 1 January 2021 to curtail the scope of 'plant' by excluding intangible assets – this was done to reverse the effect of the *CIMB* case prospectively.

Transfer Pricing

The local tax rules and guidelines are broadly consistent with that of the OECD; hence it is expected that future OECD developments would also be generally (albeit not invariably or completely) adopted by Malaysia.

The authors are of the view that, in principle, the value of data does not solely rest in the jurisdiction from which the raw data is collected. Say, a multinational enterprise collects data and sells the data, including data from the Malaysian market via its Malaysian subsidiary (say, Company A) globally. The aggregation and analysis of the data is done in another jurisdiction by another entity (say, Company B). Say, Company B is responsible for the Development, Enhancement, Maintenance and Protection (i.e. four out of the five DEMPE criteria) hence is the owner of the intangible property, the question arises as to what should be the arm's length compensation by Company B to Company A in respect of the provision / right to use the raw data provided and collected. This question should be addressed in conjunction with the question whether such provision should be evaluated on a separate basis, or on an aggregated or bundled basis with other transactions (such as the provision of platform/software or provision of analysed information by Company B to Company A).

Digital Tax (SToDS)

As part of the indirect tax regime, Malaysia introduced a digital service tax regime which is formally referred to as the Service Tax on Digital Services ("SToDS"). Foreign businesses that provide digital services to Malaysian customers exceeding MYR 500,000 per annum are required to register for SToDS in Malaysia and collect a 6% tax from its Malaysian customers.

Digital service is statutorily defined as a service that:

(i) is to be delivered through an information technology medium or any other electronic network;

(ii) cannot be delivered without the use of Internet technology; and

(iii) the delivery to the consumer is essentially automated.

In practical terms, the third criterion is interpreted to mean service delivery with minimal or no human intervention from the service provider.

Data-driven transactions that do not satisfy the definition of digital services above, may fall within the scope of other taxable services within the service tax regime, which in inbound cross-border scenarios require the Malaysian business customer to self-account for the 6% service tax under a reverse charge mechanism albeit without any input tax credit.

Summary and conclusions

Data has been said to be the "New Oil". This is the way in which data is being treated around the world. The present report will assess the legal basis on which data is treated as well as its treatment. It suffices to say that data in Mauritius has not reached the level which has been reached in other countries but the amount of work that has been put in Mauritius is certainly of interest. This report will look at data and its processing, as well as the other elements of data protection and privacy, and will conclude that the treaty-based assessment on the processing of data will have to be mirrored in relation to how the law will see the processing of data. The various algorithms and the intellectual property will guide the manner in which taxation will apply. Where the traditional aspects of property will apply, there shall be taxation.

To start with, ownership of data related to specific individuals has been subject to serious debate. In the past few years, the extent of data processing as well as the extent of data collection has increased considerably. At present, the manner in which data has been transferred is also essential. Further, data exchange at the level of European laws (GDPR) and the Privacy Shield at the level of EU and US for the purposes of CRS and FATCA has also been deemed to be an essential component that determines the level of exchange of information. However, what this report is not about, is the interaction and exchange of data at that level.

The report will consider the following principles:
1. It will consider the laws associated with the ownership of data and the manner in which it is exchanged in Mauritius. Initially, it will look at the legal perspective of data. Data belongs to the data subject; only the right to process it can be obtained by the data subject. It will argue that the property rights and commercial laws in Mauritius will be followed in relation to the Mauritian Civil code and the Mauritian Commercial code. Further, in relation to the various methods of provision of digital services, the extent of value creation and the source and nexus have to be established. In Mauritius, it will be argued that the nexus and source will be determined by the manner in which the Income-tax act determines the source of the services.
2. The various methods of provision of digital services are nascent in Mauritius and therefore, the government is first trying to develop the industry by giving incentives. Initially, the government did not even have legislative frameworks for many of the

[1] Barrister-at-Law of Lincolns Inn, also called to the Bar in Mauritius and duly qualified to practise before the courts in Mauritius. He heads the KL Chambers and is the Chair of the Technical Committee of the Mauritian Branch of IFA.

The author wishes to particularly thank the president of IFA Mauritius, Mr. Rajesh Ramloll, SC and Mr. Roomesh C.P Ramchurn, Tax Partner at Mazars Mauritius and the Secretary of IFA Mauritius who have reviewed this paper and have provided their valuable contribution.

projects and decided to come up with regulatory sandbox licences. After legislative frameworks have been put into place for the purposes of regulating the business, the government has introduced the regulation for Fintech. The Mauritian parliament has recently passed the Virtual Asset And Initial Token Offering Services Act 2021 which is meant to regulate the various methods of regulating this industry and definition of the Virtual assets and how can they be regulated

3. The property laws, the confidentiality and other laws related to trade secrets will be essential in determining the value addition for taxation. The other question is whether the data gathered from API and other analytics software would be taxable in the source country or the country where the digital company is headquartered. However, there are interesting features in the Mauritian Data Protection laws which make Mauritius a jurisdiction safeguarding the data rights of data subjects and control the manner in which the data is sourced, processed, subjected to automated processing and transferred outside Mauritius. The mass transfer of data is surely subjected to a Data Privacy Impact Assessment and therefore requires the consent of the Data Protection Office before its transfer outside Mauritius. As a result, for a proper application of the laws, especially if the data being analysed or collected arise from Mauritius, there needs to be a trail.

4. The context of data exchange or raw data sales ought to be considered in line with the Data Protection Act in relation to the collection of data for the purposes of direct marketing. Data can be collected for the purposes of direct marketing in line with the Data Protection Act. On 4 September 2020, Mauritius agreed to sign the Protocol amending the Convention for the Protection of Individuals with regard to the Automatic Processing of Personal data. The convention is important in various respects, namely, the right not to be subject to a decision which affects the data subject, which is based solely on automated processing, without the data subject having his/her views taken into consideration. Therefore, ownership remains, together with the human rights considerations of privacy, with the data subject.

5. It will also be argued that the use of the Data Protection Act as a basis for the starting point for the taxation of personal data will be suitable to establish the right of the individuals to their personal data. The value attached to the processing of said personal data, insofar as it concerns the person, would be ascertainable in relation to the property rights and the patents that may be attached to it.

6. The position of Mauritius is unique in its approach. First, it has been involved in the inclusive framework and therefore, has shown a commitment to the application of BEPS in Mauritius. Second, it has been a jurisdiction of rather simple taxes and has chosen, as per its taxation model, to keep taxes simple. This ambivalence is what makes it unique. In relation to Pillar Two, keeping a minimum tax might be the approach taken ultimately. In relation to the taxation, in that case, it is argued that the Mauritian authorities would rather favour the return of the tax base to the country where a value was created rather than engaging into the debate on source and nexus.

It will be concluded that the data protection laws in Mauritius are good indicators of the PE regime and of how the Mauritian laws in relation to the Data Protection Act will apply on data collection, processing and other operations, done with the data. Mauritian property laws will still apply.

Branch reporters
Eduardo Brandt[1]
Yair Kershenovich Tavel[2]

Summary and conclusions

With the digitalization of the economy, we have seen the proliferation of multi-sided businesses that are able to derive value from user contributions. MNEs have been able to create value by interacting with users in a particular jurisdiction, collect their information and find a secondary market that is willing to purchase the data once It has been aggregated and analyzed.

The digitalization of the economy and the proliferation of big data transactions have created significant challenges for international tax policy. Jurisdictions have often taken the view that they should hold taxing rights with respect to an item of income derived by a non-resident when such income is derived from sources in that country or by maintaining a taxable presence. The premise behind this view is that value is created in their jurisdiction by taking advantage of the economic conditions in a jurisdiction (i.e., roads, infrastructure, legal system, etc.).

Current sourcing rules are based on more traditional brick and mortar businesses and are not really tailored to heavily digitalized businesses without any physical presence. Nexus rules are also based under the faulted notion that a MNE needs a physical presence to derive value from a particular jurisdiction. In the context of big data transactions, MNEs are able to monetize user contributions by transferring structured data to other customers. While MNEs are able to do so without generally triggering taxes in the jurisdiction of the users, this raises the question of whether the jurisdiction of the users should have taxing rights over a portion of the income received by the MNEs. After all, MNEs are able to derive value by taking advantage of user contributions in a particular jurisdiction.

OECD member states as Mexico are well aware of how international tax rules have fallen behind with the economic reality of the digital economy. In an unprecedented effort, OECD member states have discussed in the context of the Pillar One framework, the possibility of establishing a particular nexus rule for these types of businesses and the allocation of certain non-routine profits under a formulaic approach (i.e., Amount A). As it has been the case for most of the OECD BEPS related measures, we would expect Mexico to adopt most of the recommendations under the Pillar One framework. In fact, Mexico has taken a step forward and in 2020 it updated its VAT and Income Tax laws to provide an effective mechanism to collect: (i) VAT triggered in the context of certain automated services that are provided by foreign digital platforms and, (ii) VAT and Income Tax triggered in connection to individuals providing services and selling goods through a digital platform that provides intermediation services.

[1] Partner at Creel, García-Cuéllar, Aiza y Enríquez, S.C. ('Creel') in Mexico City.
[2] Partner in Despacho Tavel, S.C. which is an accounting firm in Mexico. He has a Master degree in taxes and a tax specialization and is part of committees in IFA and the Mexican School of Accountancy.

Despite Mexico's efforts, there are several issues outstanding in the context of big data transactions. The proliferation of big data transactions and the amount of value they can create raise the question as to how these transactions should be characterized for Mexican tax purposes. Clearly these should be a facts and circumstances analysis that may vary depending on the specifics of a particular arrangement, but Mexico lacks guidance as to which factors should be taken into account to characterize the transaction in a particular manner.

The characterization of these transactions under domestic law is important as it could determine how items of income are sourced for Mexican tax purposes. Absent a specific sourcing rule dealing with big data transactions, taxpayers need to rely on existing sourcing rules that were not drafted with the aim of dealing with these type of business models. In most instances, given the fact that sourcing rules were not drafted under the notion of a digitalized business, the existing sourcing rules raise the issue of whether the parameters used, are appropriate.

Further, Mexico relies on the PE concept to determine whether a non-resident should be subject to net basis taxation. The PE concept is based under the faulted notion that an MNE needs to have a physical presence to derive value from Mexico. Therefore, currently, it is hard to imagine that big data transactions entered into by foreign MNEs give rise to net basis Mexican taxation. This result is expected to be modified prospectively once a new nexus rule and a methodology to attribute profits that deviates from the arm's length standard, are established. These changes to domestic law would presumably need to be accompanied by modifications to Mexico's existing treaty network, given that article 5 and article 7 of Mexico's existing treaties would prevent taxation on these types of transactions.

As big data transactions continue to proliferate, the issues raised with respect to character, source and nexus will become more and more common. MNE's collecting and aggregating data of Mexican users should remain close observants of the policy developments on the Pillar One Framework and the route Mexico decides to take, as the treatment of these transactions under current rules is arguably going to be modified in the near future.

Netherlands

Branch reporters
Alexia Kardachaki[1]
Marcel Schaper[2]

Summary and conclusions

This report outlines the legal background and tax treatment of big data transactions in the Netherlands. The term big data transactions covers various commercial transactions and applications, including the development, deployment and exploitation of relevant technology, such as algorithms and software. Throughout the report, the term 'data processing', as set out in article 4(2) of the General Data Protection Regulation ("GDPR"),[3] is used to refer to any operation or set of operations which is performed on (raw) data or on sets of data, whether or not by automated means.

Legal background

Ownership of data is not possible in Dutch property law, as data is not a tangible object. Data could be the object of other property rights, if this is provided by law or agreed contractually between parties. Contract parties could agree by private deed to transfer the right to use certain data. Depending on circumstances, the Dutch Databases Act (*Databankenwet* 1999) could provide a *sui generis* right to a systematically or methodically structured collection of data – but not data *sec* – which has required substantial investment specifically in relation to obtaining, verifying and presenting the data. Data processing software and data (as a collection of data/database or if the data is an original intellectual creation) could enjoy copyright protection by the Dutch Copyright Act (*Auteurswet* 1912). Data of a commercial value, which has been processed by means of having been subject to reasonable steps to keep it secret, may be protected as a trade secret under the Dutch Trade Secrets Act (*Wet bescherming bedrijfsgeheimen* 2018). Personal data and its processing are protected under the GDPR and the Dutch Data Protection Act (*Uitvoeringswet Algemene Verordening Gegevensbescherming* 2018).

Basic (domestic) and treaty principles on taxation of big data transactions

The character of a big data transaction is in principle not relevant for the purposes of Dutch direct taxation. The Netherlands does not have any special (nexus) rules that explicitly address taxation of big data transactions. The provisions of the Income Tax Act (*Wet*

---

[1]   LLM, Associate at Lubbers, Boer & Douma.
[2]   Associate Professor of International Taxation and Tax Technology at Maastricht University.
[3]   Regulation (EU) 2016/679, OJ L 119, 4 May 2016.

Inkomstenbelasting 2001) and Corporate Income Tax Act (*Wet op de Vennootschapsbelasting* 1969) are generally applicable to big data transactions.

Unless income arising from big data transactions can be attributed to a foreign permanent establishment ("PE"), in which case it is treated as exempt foreign sourced business income, income from big data transactions will be taxable in the Netherlands under the ordinary corporate income tax rules. The Netherlands avoids double taxation in non-treaty situations, where income is sourced and subject to tax in a developing state, through a unilateral credit pursuant to the Decree for the Avoidance of Double Taxation 2001 (*Besluit voorkoming dubbele belasting* 2001, "ADT Decree"). Depending on circumstances, income from certain big data transactions could fall within the ambit of the royalty definition contained in the ADT Decree, which corresponds to the one included in the Organisation for Economic Cooperation and Development ("OECD") Model Tax Convention 1977.

Income earned by non-residents will be subject to corporate income tax, if it can be attributed to a PE in the Netherlands. The Netherlands has introduced a source tax on interest and royalty payments to low-tax jurisdictions and non-cooperative jurisdictions on the list of the European Union ("EU") as from 1 January 2021. Accordingly, the Withholding Tax Act (*Wet bronbelasting* 2021) may result in income from certain big data transactions qualifying as royalties, corresponding to the term in the OECD Model Tax Convention 2017, becoming subject to tax in the Netherlands.

The Netherlands strives to follow the OECD Model Tax Convention for purposes of defining a PE and royalties in tax treaties. However, in the context of tax treaties with (certain) developing states, the Netherlands might be open to negotiate a services PE or include payments for technical services in the royalty definition. Unless income from big data transactions falls within the ambit of a different tax treaty provision (e.g. royalties or technical services), it will typically be considered business income under the Dutch tax treaties.

Transfer pricing

The Dutch transfer pricing rules are aligned with the OECD Transfer Pricing Guidelines 2017. Neither the domestic nor the OECD guidance, however, explicitly addresses (all) issues arising in the context of big data transactions and consequently the (increasingly) digitalising business models. The Netherlands is committed to contribute to a speedy and smooth implementation of the agreement achieved on 1 July 2021 amongst the Inclusive Framework ("IF") members on Pillar 1 and 2 of the OECD Base Erosion and Profit Shifting 2.0 project.

Special regimes

There is no digital services tax or similar tax in the Netherlands, and, following the IF agreement, no such unilateral tax is expected to be implemented in the Netherlands. Income from big data transactions could, under specific circumstances, be eligible for preferential corporate income tax treatment under the innovation box regime. Certain activities relating to the development of data processing software may be eligible for a wage tax credit.

Value added tax ("VAT")

Any big data transaction would be considered a supply of services for VAT purposes and be taxed accordingly. The view that user data can be treated as consideration for a supply for VAT purposes has been expressed in the Dutch literature, contrary to EU VAT Committee guidance on barter transactions.

Tax accounting

The annual business profit for Dutch tax purposes is computed according to the principle of sound business practice (*'goed koopmansgebruik'*), which has been interpreted in extensive case law of the Supreme Court. Accordingly, income and corresponding expenses relating to big data transactions are in principle realised at the moment the taxpayer has completed her performance. Acquisition or self-development expenses relating to data processing software could be considered a depreciable fixed asset. In the case of self-developed software, the taxpayer also has the choice of deducting the development expenses in the year in which they incurred. The treatment of the acquisition costs of data might differ depending on the facts and circumstances.

Branch reporters
Gjert Melsom[1]
Anton Baumann[2]

Summary and conclusions

Norway does not have rules which are specific to data transactions. Until 2021, such rules have not been strictly required under Norwegian domestic taxation, as Norway generally treats income derived from data transactions in the same manner as income derived from other sources. Where it has been necessary to make such distinctions (e.g. in the context of an applicable double tax treaty giving rise to royalty WHT), Norway has mainly relied on the OECD Model Tax Convention and its Commentary in order to ascertain the applicability of such taxes.

In July 2021, new rules on WHT on royalty payments entered into effect, and the determination of royalty vs. other income will be of greater importance. However, since the WHT will only be applicable to payments made to related entities resident in a low tax jurisdiction, the application of the WHT is somewhat limited.

Further, Norway has not yet implemented any nexus threshold (digital PE or digital services tax) on digital transactions which do not have a physical connection to Norwegian taxable territory. On this topic, the Norwegian government is awaiting a unified solution on OECD/G20 or potentially EU level.

Transactions that involve structured data (use of databases or software) raise a number of potentially challenging tax questions. As a consequence of the new WHT rules that entered into force in 2021, the main focus of this report has been to determine when a data transaction may give rise to a royalty payment.

As a starting point, there is the distinction of making a copy of the database for internal use in the business of the acquirer, which should not be considered a licensing arrangement giving rise to a royalty payment. On the other hand, if the purchaser pays for the right to use the significant underlying copyright, this would be royalty subject to royalty WHT (even if the full copyright is not transferred).

For software distributors, the right to access a database and make a certain number of copies for distribution should not be considered a licensing arrangement (provided that the distributor does not have the right to reproduce the software).

However, where the database owner transfers the right to make essential parts of the database available to the public and/or to repeated and systematic make insignificant parts of the database available to the public (e.g. copies), then this would be considered a licensing arrangement for Norwegian tax purposes.

---

[1] International tax partner at EY Norway; graduated from University of Oslo in 1992 with the degree of candidatus juris and holds a licentiate degree in Law from the University of Oslo from 2000 on Taxation of Software.
[2] Master's degree in Law from the University of Oslo in 2017; associate attorney in CMS Kluge in Oslo, Norway.

Any payment made for the full ownership rights to the database should not be considered a royalty payment. However, this starting point gives rise to several grey areas, which are addressed in this report.

The utilization of structured data by the owner itself when providing services to another taxpayer, should not lead to the payment being considered a royalty. However, in practice, the line may be hard to draw in cases where a contract consists of several elements.

Under Norwegian tax law, the determination of the source of an income stream must be made based on the underlying economic reality. Any proforma arrangements would potentially be subject to the general anti-abuse rule.

The main nexus factors under Norwegian tax law are the tax residency rule, the domestic permanent establishment rules and the rules for taxation of foreigners. None of these rules provide taxation rights in Norway based solely on the digital economic presence of a foreign resident enterprise. Further, in order for Norway to impose royalty WHT on any enterprise, this payment must be attributable to a Norwegian tax resident enterprise, or a Norwegian permanent establishment of a foreign enterprise.

From a tax treaty perspective, Norway has entered into almost 100 double tax treaties. However, very few of these treaties provide Norway with a right to impose WHT on royalty payments. Thus, this further limits the application of the royalty WHT rules. Further, Norway will not be levying any WHT on payments made for "technical services", in accordance with the OECD approach. However, Norway will be imposing a WHT on "industrial, commercial or scientific equipment" effective from October 2021.

The transfer pricing aspects in this report are limited to a few comments on the intercompany dealings which may take place in relation to data transactions. Norway generally follows the OECD transfer pricing guidelines, and an in-depth analysis is not included in the report.

Branch reporter
José Barja Quispe[1]

Summary and conclusions

In accordance with the megatrends and the changes generated by the technological disruption, economic agents in our country have been adapting their way of doing business and carrying out their activities, noting an increase in the flow of cross-border operations, mainly those related to e-commerce and digital services, including big data transactions.

Regulatorily, there is no legal framework that specifically deals with this type of transactions. As initial reference points for the analysis, the provisions contained in the rules on copyright, industrial property and, recently, the law on personal data are considered. Following this line, this report evaluates the various legal businesses that could arise around big data transactions, initially identifying the sale of intangibles, temporary transfer of rights, the transfer in use, as well as digital services and technical assistance, among others.

From the local tax perspective, the legislation does not have specific provisions applicable to define the nature of big data transactions, resulting in one of the most complex tax matters. This aspect is especially addressed in this report.

Due to the unique characteristics that big data transactions may involve, the identification of the obligations assumed by the parties as well as the aim of the transaction will constitute the first step in order to have the transactions duly characterized, which will determine various tax consequences, with particular attention to those related to the withholding of taxes on Peruvian source income generated by non-domiciled subjects. In this sense, the report emphasizes the problem in defining whether a service is digital or technical assistance (applicable withholding rate of 30% and 15%, respectively).

At the local legislation level, there are pronouncements from the Tax Administration and jurisprudence from the Tax Court covering the criteria for determining the qualification of services as digital, technical assistance or other related services.

Another point of analysis is the application of the provisions contained in the Double Taxation Conventions signed by Peru, in particular the application of the article related to royalties since, in some conventions, the definition for royalties includes the digital services and the technical assistance (in other agreements, only the technical assistance) which could determine the tax levy without exceeding 10% or 15%.

It should be added that some controversy has arisen in relation to transactions that involve the transfer of databases. Their classification as intangibles, if their transfer constitutes a sale or provision of service, and the amortization of the investment have also been the subject of pronouncements by the Tax Administration and the Tax Court. Although the tax legislation does not have a definition of intangibles, accounting standards

---

[1] Currently tax partner of EY Peru. He leads the provision of tax compliance services to local and multinational companies and projects aimed to the technological transformation for tax departments
The Peruvian branch report has been prepared with the great contribution of Victor Mora, a talented tax professional.

are used, which in the author's opinion is reasonable, despite the suggestion of inclusion of a definition in the tax legislation.

Another area where controversy can arise is transfer pricing. To make big data transactions possible, it is common to appreciate a significant contribution or intensive use of intangibles and, in more than one case, new ones could be generated. Our tax legislation, in this case, follows the guidelines of the OECD, as it does not establish a priority or hierarchy in the choice of the applicable valuation method, since, on the contrary, it must reflect the economic reality of the transaction, which must be evaluated as appropriate in each case.

In the last part, the report presents comments referring to the treatment of cross-border services, especially digital services that could derive from data transactions, for the purposes of the General Sales Tax, as well as tax incentives in relation to research and development projects that may be applicable in certain circumstances.

Based on the above, the definition of the tax effects derived from big data transactions requires, as occurs with other tax topics, a careful analysis for each case.

Branch reporter
Monika Lewandowska[1]

Summary and conclusions

Polish law does not provide for a separate big data legal concept or definition. Also, Poland has so far not developed any specific tax provisions that would relate to big data transactions as such, nor to digital economy taxation. Thus, in practice an analysis of the tax consequences of big data transactions would have to be made on a case-by-case basis and by an analysis of the general rules.

Polish income tax law includes a few provisions that may be useful to determine the tax consequences of the underlying big data operations. These refer, in principle, to operations on certain forms of intangible properties, such as copyrights, know-how or licenses. Where cross-border operations are concerned, the Corporate Income Tax Act[2] (further: *CITA*) contains certain provisions which may be relevant from the perspective of big data transactions, such as taxation at source of intangible services, such as, inter alia, data processing, consulting or advertising services, if they are paid out by the Polish tax resident. It seems though, that at this stage application of all of the above rules to the specifics of big data operations, has not been widely tested in the case law.

Moreover, one of the obstacles that tax practitioners and taxpayers may face when trying to determine tax consequences of big data transactions is variability of their forms and frequently – their complexity. It seems inevitable that big data operations will bring many discussions on what exactly the scope of the transaction is. Lack of developed tax practice, case law and uncertainties regarding the character of big data operations may sometimes hamper assessment of the application of the general rules, and the possibility to draw the line in which cases lack, e.g. human involvement, changes the ultimate tax conclusion. The same issue concerns the discussion on the source of income, where case law is moderately rich from the perspective of, i.e., intangible services, but has no developed approach to more digital business, where a value can be derived from data collected or generated by users located in Poland.

It should also be noted that Poland is a party to nearly 90 Double Tax Treaties (further: *DTTs*). This means that in case of cross-border transactions, often tax conclusions will be based on the wording of the relevant DTT interpreted with the use of the Commentary to the OECD Model Convention (further: *OECD MC*), or UN Model. DTTs concluded by Poland provide for some dissimilarity from the OECD MC, which might be interesting in terms of big data transactions, e.g. Poland made a reservation for withholding tax collection for royalties payment. Also, in several DTTs concluded by Poland, technical services are subject to withholding tax next to royalties. Of course, Poland is highly interested in discussions regarding taxation of a broadly understood "digital economy". In February 2021 the

---

[1]   Lawyer, graduate of the Warsaw University and a tax advisor in Crido Taxand. The author would like to thank Anna Wcisło, Filip Łajkowski, Martyna Gałdecka-Karpińska and Joanna Ciołko-Wąsowicz from Crido for the exchange of views and experience on the reports' topic.
[2]   Corporate Income Tax Act of 15 February 1992.

Polish Ministry of Finance presented for public consultation a draft law introducing a so called "contribution on advertisement". The bill assumed imposing new contributions on advertising revenues that taxpayers engaged in certain types of business activities, would be required to pay. The proposed contributions include contributions from i.a online advertising revenues. The taxation base for the latter was supposed to be calculated as the percentage of the revenue from online advertising, regardless of where it is earned, corresponding to the percentage of advertising recipients located in the territory of Poland. Nevertheless – at this point no further works concerning the draft are conducted and Poland is watching the discussion conducted at the international level.

Polish transfer pricing regulations do not address any specific regulations related to big data or even, more general, to digital data transactions. However, they do follow the OECD Guidelines for Multinational Enterprises and Tax Administrations quite accurately. Also, more often than not, the reference to the OECD Guidelines is used as an interpretation of the transfer pricing rules in developed tax practice and case law. There is also a very general mentioning of DEMPE functions with respect to comparability analysis of intangible properties, though no details of how to interpret the DEMPE functions are given, as well as a very brief summary of how intangibles difficult to value should be tested against the arm's length principle (following the OECD approach, without any detailed comments).

In terms of VAT, dynamic development of the digital market, as well as big data collection and analytics creates completely new challenges in the area of VAT taxation. Although it seems doubtless that if there is a big data transaction that is to be assessed from the VAT perspective, it would be a provision of a service, the main problems may especially concentrate on the definition of "economic activity", "taxable person", as well as on determination of the value of services, in particular in case of data exchange operations.

Lastly, the Polish CITA provides for certain incentives, such as R&D relief or the IP Box regime, application of which to some of the big data developments or exploitations seems to be possible.

Branch reporter
José Maria Pires[1]

Summary and conclusions

Big data consists of the exploitation of information and knowledge contained in electronic media for several purposes, especially on research and economic activity. The calculation capacity and processing speed that technological developments are providing, allow computer systems to carry out procedures that humans did not perform. As a result, the ability to obtain information and to produce knowledge has become faster, deeper and more comprehensive. Knowledge is the basis of value generation, economic growth and well-being, where big data plays a central role.

The recursive procedures, making endless attempts of data combinations until finding a possibility to produce a certain result, as well as the possibility of algorithms to determine historical trends and cause-effect relationships in the past, allow the development of predictive systems, which can be improved successively. These possibilities have created the concept of artificial intelligence.

Both concepts are challenges for law, especially in what concerns copyright protection.[2] If there is artificial intelligence, a computer can operate creatively, generating original works. But who would be the copyright holder?

The Portuguese law protects six rights:

1. Copyright in favour of creators of original databases;
2. The *sui generis* right of investors and database manufacturers, even when they do not meet the requirements of protection as originals. Three forms of their profitability and negotiation are identified:
   2.1. The final transmission of the right, either in physical form or by making full copy available online;
   2.2. The availability through licensing, on a mandatory and temporary basis;
   2.3. The performance of identical business operations of the database manufacturer in the acquisition of the data necessary for its construction, maintenance and updating.
3. On software operating data, which is likely to be protected by copyright;
4. On the works and data constituting the content of databases, including copyright and its ownership;
5. With regard to artificial intelligence, Portuguese law attributes the ownership of the rights to the authors of the algorithms and programs;
6. The rights of creators and software producers.

---

[1] Jurist at the center for tax studies, in the Portuguese finance ministry; professor and international tax consultant.

[2] According to the EC "Like the steam engine or electricity in the past, AI is transforming our world, our society and our industry". SWD (2018)137final.

In Portuguese tax law, the income associated with big data may be classified as i) copyright, ii) royalties, iii) provision of services, iv) profit of a company, or v) capital gains. The first two categories include income arising from the use or concession of use, as well as the granting of rights protected by copyright or industrial property, respectively. This is where the income from databases protected by copyright and industrial property law, previously referenced, are included.

But the characterization as royalties extends to situations when, in the absence of those immaterial rights, a previously acquired knowledge is available, bearing in mind the two following clarifications:

i)   This knowledge must have been acquired outside the scope of the contractual relationship and must be prior to it;

ii) To be framed in this category of income, the object of the contractual relationship must be the mere provision of knowledge and not its practical application within the activity of the acquirer.

In general, there is a provision of services in the case of technical assistance resulting from knowledge acquired in the context of the contractual relationship, or when there is an acquisition of a service execution involving not only the provision of knowledge, but also its practical application or incorporation into the acquirer's procedures.

Branch reporters
Alexandra Berger[1]
Nikolai Milogolov[2]

Summary and conclusions

Big data transactions in Russia are taxed on the same basic tax law principles as any other business transactions both in domestic and in international context. Regulation of big data businesses is more developed in other areas of law covering data protection and privacy than in tax law. In tax law regulation is more developed in VAT than in corporate income tax.

Application of the basic tax law methodology to big data transactions can in some cases lead to legal uncertainty, especially in relation to the characterization of supply as provision of services or as licensing of intellectual property. There is very little specific guidance addressing such kind of uncertainty, which results in growing tax risks for taxpayers. Certain characterization of big data transactions is important both for direct tax (CIT) and indirect tax (VAT) consequences. Uncertainty in the characterization is not a unique issue for transfer of data but rather a broader problem of characterization of supplies of digitized products for tax purposes. Recharacterization of non-exclusive license contract arrangements into services arrangements for tax purposes is a potentially anticipated area of tax audit and tax disputes in Russia.

The delineation between licensing and provision of services is especially a critical issue for tax planning because of indirect tax (VAT) implications. There is currently VAT exemption of IP licensing under article 149 (2(26)) of Tax Code which includes provision of software, databases and rights for their use under licensing contracts. This exemption was reformed significantly effective from 1 January 2021 and also includes updates and provisions of the remote access to software, databases, and rights for their use. However, as follows from VAT tax case law and administrative guidelines an emerging trend can currently be observed in case law towards the treatment of data transactions (especially "raw data transactions" and "aggregated data transactions") as supplies of services. In case of mixed contracts providing for both licensing and for other supplies (for example, supply of equipment or supply of services) the whole contract can be regarded for tax purposes as a provision of services.

The most critical issues for corporate income tax include income characterization and status of PE. For CIT purposes income arising from cross-border big data transactions will likely be characterized either as provision of services or as licensing of IP rights. Such characterization is also relevant for tax treaty purposes and some uncertainty is present

---

[1]   PhD candidate in Economics, LLM International Tax Law, YIN Representative in Russia, Senior consultant at EY Russia.
[2]   ADIT, Cand. of Sc. (econ.), Head of Laboratory of Tax policy research at the Institute of Applied Economic Research of the RANEPA and principal academic researcher at the Tax Policy Center at the Financial Research Institute under the Ministry of Finance of the Russian Federation, PhD candidate in Tax Law at Erasmus University Rotterdam.

Note IFA: This report was prepared by the authors for the Russian Branch of IFA and was submitted to the general reporter on 6 December 2021.

because dividing criteria between provision of services and licensing are not yet explicitly formulated in legislation nor in practice. However, the approach towards this issue developed in the Commentaries to article 12 of OECD MC (2010) is generally followed by the Russian Ministry of Finance in its guidelines. Outbound royalties are taxed at source and tax can be significantly reduced or even eliminated under tax treaties. A PE can arise resulting from compliance with non-tax legislation (the Federal Law on Information) which implies that all personal data of Russian citizens shall be carried out on servers located in Russia. Even in case such a server is serviced by a third party and remuneration is at arm's length, this server can constitute a PE for a foreign company since such a server shall be at the disposal of a foreign company.

Current Russian practice demonstrates that the following methods are the most suitable for performing transfer pricing analysis in transactions involving intangible assets (including transfer of big data) between related parties: the CUP method, the TNMM, the profit split method and non-transfer pricing valuation techniques. However, the selection and application of the method for determination of market prices depends on contractual arrangements.

When a company provides services that allow access to the user data for its related party the CPM and the TNMM methods are typically used. Considering the sale of access to a database containing raw data prices can be tested with the application of the CPM method. In case of a license agreement between parties, the CUP method (provided information on comparable royalty rates is available) or the TNMM/PSM for evaluation of post-royalty profitability are more relevant. Valuation techniques are mainly used in case of a sale of property rights on hard to value intangibles provided such sale is a one-time transaction.

In recent years, the Russian government has paid greater attention to tax preferences for innovation activity. From 2005 there have been special zones available with attractive tax regimes for their residents and from 2021 the Tax Maneuver significantly reduced applicable corporate profits tax and social contribution rates for eligible Russian IT companies. In addition, Russian tax legislation provides tax allowances, tax credit, and other incentives for the IT industry which can be applicable to big data transactions.

Non-resident providers of electronic services to customers in Russia shall register for, and to charge VAT. Currently, in case of no presence in Russia companies do not require to pay corporate income tax from such services (until they do not fall into scope of withholding tax) since Russian tax legislation does not contain concepts of DST, digital PE etc. However, the Russian Federation participates in the framework of Pillar 1 and considers codifying approaches enshrined therein. Moreover, the concept of "digital residence" for foreign IT companies and individuals engaged in IT – activities without a physical presence in Russia, is under discussion.

Russia is consistently implementing the outcomes of the BEPS Project into its domestic legislation and has already joined a two-pillar plan to reform international taxation rules.

Branch reporter
Mahesh Kumar[1]

Summary and conclusions

Singapore has emerged as a technology and big data hub which complements its position as a major international financial center and Asia-Pacific headquarters for several MNCs. In addition to the competitive tax regime, MNCs are attracted by a number of strategic advantages offered by the business-friendly ecosystem in Singapore.

The tax issues surrounding data transactions are impacted by the status of data and databases under intellectual property law. In Singapore, the law of copyrights and patents are the primary tools to protect rights in a database including the software, algorithms and application programming interface. However, as a general principle copyright protection is not available with respect to the data itself. Singapore law does not recognize *sui generis* database rights as accepted in the European Union.

Singapore has a territorial based tax system which taxes income that accrues in or is derived from Singapore or received in Singapore from outside Singapore. A rights-based approach is used for characterizing payments for software and use of information or digitized goods. It recognizes the difference between transfer of a 'copyright' and a 'copyrighted article'. A transfer of copyright typically allows the payer to commercially exploit the copyright. This is different from the transfer of a copyrighted article which only contemplates a limited right to enable the payer to operate the software or to use the information or digitized goods, for personal consumption or for use within business operations. Payments for transfer or license of a copyright may be characterized as royalty triggering deemed source rules and withholding tax obligations if the recipient is a non-resident.

In the case of a data broker who sells raw or aggregated data to a customer who redistributes the data to other persons, one could argue that although the customer is commercially exploiting the data, the data broker did not have a copyright in the data and hence the payments may not be in the nature of royalty.

In several data transactions, it is possible to take a view that supply of data is either a non-technical service or a sale of goods. In Singapore, the source rules applicable to trading or business income would apply in both cases.

Different source rules apply depending on how a transaction is characterized for tax purposes. Trading or business income is taxable if the trade or business is carried out within Singapore. Deemed source rules apply to royalty or payments for the use of or the right to use any movable property. They also apply to payments for the use of or the right to use scientific, technical, industrial or commercial knowledge or information or for the rendering of assistance or service in connection with the application or use of such knowledge or information. The deemed source rules do not apply to payments for the right to use software, information or digitized goods, not being a right to commercially exploit the copyright in the software, information or digitized goods.

[1]   Tax Partner, Withers KhattarWong LLP, Singapore.

The presence of a server in Singapore which merely acts as a tool of communication usually does not result in the conduct of business or trade. In the context of data transactions, a key consideration is the place where the business is carried out and not where the database and software platform are hosted. However, if advanced and automated functions are performed by the server, this could be viewed as carrying on business in Singapore.

These outcomes also apply when viewed in the context of most of Singapore's treaties, which are broadly consistent with the OECD Model Convention with some exceptions. Payments for data transactions or services are likely to be treated as royalty only if there is a transfer of the copyright allowing the recipient to commercially exploit the data. A sever is generally not a permanent establishment unless it performs core business functions.

Singapore's transfer pricing regime permits adjustments to transactions between related parties that are not at arm's length. The transfer pricing guidelines in Singapore broadly align with the OECD guidelines and also take into account various BEPS related recommendations. CUP, cost plus or TNMM methods are often considered to be the most appropriate choice for related party services. The guidelines specifically comment on pass-through costs, routine support services and cost pooling arrangements. While database administration is a routine service, data analytics is not considered routine. In the functional analysis one can consider contributions by group entities in the development, enhancement, maintenance, protection and exploitation of intangibles such as the database, software, algorithms and APIs.

A number of tax incentives and concessions are available in Singapore which makes it attractive for tech companies including big data players to establish operations in Singapore.

GST is generally chargeable at the rate of 7% on the supply of goods or services in Singapore. The charge of GST applies irrespective of the medium of transfer, and electronic supplies of goods or services in Singapore may also attract GST. From 1 January 2020, the GST regime has been expanded to cover digital services rendered by an overseas supplier or an electronic marketplace supplying digital services on behalf of overseas suppliers to end customers in Singapore (on a business-to-customer basis). Whether a service provider or customer 'belongs to Singapore' can impact the obligation to charge GST. A foreign company with a business establishment or fixed establishment in Singapore is said to belong to Singapore. Overseas service providers who provide digital services through a server in Singapore may not have a fixed establishment in the absence of employees on the ground for a significant period of time. It is debatable whether this conclusion will change if the server and software platform are sufficiently automated and carry out core business activities in Singapore.

Branch reporter
Helena Strauss[1]

Summary and conclusions

South Africa's legislative and policy response to the digitalization of the economy has been limited to date. South Africa currently thus applies its existing income tax legislation to tax domestic and international data driven businesses and other business models associated with the digitalized economy. South Africa follows a residence-based tax system and the taxation of highly digitalized domestic businesses are of a lesser concern than that of highly digitalized multinational entities (MNEs) that create value within South African borders. This is mainly due to the risks associated with the business models within the digitalized economy and base erosion and profit shifting that is further enabled by these business models.

The indirect tax legislation was amended in 2013 in to include digital services, as defined, by both domestic and international suppliers. This enables South Africa to levy Value Added Tax (VAT) of 15% on digital services supplied by foreign suppliers such as data driven businesses if all conditions are met as set out in this report. The enforcement of this legislation does, however, remain a challenge due to various factors but mainly due to the intangible nature of digital suppliers such as data driven businesses which requires further reform in the tax risk management and the assurance process. The mere legislative and policy amendments do thus not guarantee the reduction of BEPS associated with highly digitalized MNEs.

In summary significant scope exists in South Africa for further tax reform in response to the digitalization of the economy and the associated business models such as data driven businesses.

---

[1] PhD in Accountancy with focused on international tax, technology, and assurance. Strauss further holds a Master's in international taxation and a Bachelor's in Finance and Assurance. She a specialist and national consulting lead in the field of tax administration within the digitalized economy. She is currently responsible for audit, consulting, and organizational development within an international organization. She is a member of SAICA, ISACA, IIA and an affiliate member of the ACFE.

Branch reporters
María Amparo Grau Ruiz[1]
Guillermo Sánchez-Archidona Hidalgo[2]

Summary and conclusions

Big data is a polyvalent concept. Data influence entrepreneurial decisions and are the object of transactions, that may be taxed, respecting data protection and digital rights. Debates on the distinction between open data or secrets, or the configuration as work vs. capital have tax consequences. There are no specific laws relating to data transactions in Spain. Principles on responsible use of AI-related technologies should be considered (prudence, proportionality, transparency), moving from ethical to legal control (non-discrimination). Valuation techniques should be improved.

In Spain, the relevant factors for determining the tax character of a data transaction are the general ones. The Tax on Certain Digital Services (DST) has been introduced by Act 4/2020 of 15 October. It includes as a third taxable event, specifically, the transfer or sale of data. This has been presented by the government as a transitional tax, that will be in force only until reaching more advanced agreements in the EU or multilaterally. It is justified to face financial needs in the midst of the pandemic in line with unilateral reactions in neighboring countries. For the legitimacy of any fiscal policy that tries to subject to tax the income derived from new business models in a digital society, the Spanish Supreme Court has stressed the important administrative requirements in the EU framework.

Due to the fact that the tax on certain digital services has been configured as indirect, the typical treaty provisions in Spain cannot have a clear impact on the taxation of these data transactions. The Spanish Double Taxation Conventions currently in force do not mention data transactions explicitly. Spanish transfer pricing rules do not take data transactions particularly into account.

The transfer or sale of collected data on the users (that have been generated by their activities on the digital interfaces in the area of application of the tax) is subject to the DST. There are two thresholds: the annual turnover exceeding 750 million euros and the income generated in Spain exceeding 3 million euros. The electronic commerce is explicitly not subject to tax, among other. The tax base is the amount of income obtained in Spain and the tax rate is 3%. The tax is borne with each transaction. There are some procedural obligations, such as the geo-localization of the devices. Some difficulties are expected in

---

[1]   Full Professor of Financial and Tax Law, Universidad Complutense de Madrid. Visiting Professor of Transnational Taxation, Northwestern University. Principal investigator WP2 INBOTS EU H2020 project, Grant Agreement No. 780073; AudIT-S project, PID2019-105959RB-I00.
[2]   Assistant Professor of Financial and Tax Law, Universidad de Málaga. AudIT-S project PID2019-105959RB-I00 (researcher).

The authors thank Mabel López Medina, Eduardo Merino, Elisa García Jara, Roma Asumadu, Tom Gaylord, Jesse Bowman and Leah Karchmer for their help when searching some materials.

its application and control by the tax administration. Secondary regulation develops the declarations to file, the sanctions, etc.

There is no mention to the nature of the data transferred. The new tax does not impose a levy on the real economic benefit arising from the exploitation of refined data, and it does not solve the problem of ascertaining how much data are worth.

There are general tax benefits for research, development and innovation activities in the Corporate Income Tax Act, that can be also applied to big data. The Spanish Independent Authority for Fiscal Responsibility has conducted a review of their effectiveness and it has proposed changes to increase their efficacy and transparency.

To date, in Spain, user's enjoyment of free digital services in cases where the provider is able to collect user data, does not constitute a barter transaction. Theoretically some possibilities could be further explored.

In principle, the present Spanish DST would be compatible with VAT, because its tax base is specific and it does not tax general consumption. The taxation of data transactions for VAT purposes may somehow raise the definitional challenge of goods vs. services, as happened when characterizing cloud computing transactions. A similar solution could be envisaged in EU law.

Spain basically follows the International Financial Reporting Standards. The tax principles governing the recognition of revenues and expenses generally coincide with accounting principles, although special tax rules do exist.

In the Tax Control plans there are recent uses of big data by different levels of government to carry on audits and fight fraud. The tax authorities tend to increase duties and exploit opportunities to provide and get information (e.g. chatbots). The Spanish General Tax Act has been reformed to allow digital procedures, which obviously generate new data. In this context, some risks of discrimination through permanent access to big data and profiling may exist. The use of big data is common in several areas of tax administration. Data governance has become strategic. The architecture to integrate and exploit big data is being developed progressively in the Spanish Tax Agency. One may wonder if a continuous flux of information between taxpayers and the tax administration can really reduce the indirect tax pressure but increase the direct one.

Branch reporter
Eleonor Kristoffersson[1]

Summary and conclusions

Data is either proprietary data or public data. Public data is free for everybody to use and exploit. Proprietary data is protected, either by law or by contractual terms. Data as such is not subject to copy right. They only are if they are an original work. If a database is a result of financial or professional investment it is subject to the sui generis protection. This protection is similar to copyright and applies for a period of 15 years. When data is protected by contractual terms, it is a trade secret. For tax purposes, data is classified as an intangible. The accrual and valuation of assets follow, as a main rule, business accounting. The accounting principles that apply on each taxpayer governs the taxation. Thus, the accrual may vary depending on if a company applies for example national or international accounting standards.

The Swedish tax system is based on a broad tax basis with few special regimes. Thus, there is no such thing as DST or patent boxes, or similar special schemes that apply on data transactions. The general laws apply, such as the Income Tax Act and the VAT Act (VATA). Whereas the VATA has special regimes for electronically supplied services, such as transactions with data, the ITA does not contain any such rules. Sweden has concluded 106 tax treaties, 16 treaties on tax liability in certain situations and 28 tax information exchange agreements. Swedish tax treaties are based on the OECD Model Tax Convention. The relevant income types in the Swedish tax treaties for data transactions are business income and royalty income.

As in many other countries, a server may constitute a permanent establishment. The concept of permanent establishment in national law is adapted to the OECD Model Tax Convention. According to the Swedish Tax Agency, a permanent establishment may entail a foreign company having one or more servers placed in Sweden and the activities consisting of providing storage and data capacity at the server facility to customers. There is no permanent establishment if the foreign company leases the server in its entirety to another company which uses it in its business activities.

For transfer pricing purposes, there is no specific Swedish regime. According to the Swedish Supreme Administrative Court cases RÅ 1991 ref. 107 and HFD 2016 ref. 45, Sweden follows the transfer pricing guidelines also when applying its domestic transfer pricing rules. Setting the arm's length price on intangibles, the use of aggregated data is not easy, since all data sets are unique. The comparable uncontrolled price (CUP) is seldom available. Other methods are adjusted CUP/CUT, which entail a comparison with similar but not identical data transactions, return on research and development, residual profit method, and profit available method. In the event that the intangible is only partly developed at the time of the transfer, it may be a so-called "hard to value intangible". Where big data is integrated in an asset, for example, a self-driving car, the car as such qualifies as tangible goods for

---

[1]   Dr, professor in tax law at Örebro University and visiting professor at Linköping University and Gävle University.

transfer pricing purposes. For the self-driving car as such, there may well be a CUP available.

The general consumption tax in Sweden is, as indicated above, VAT. There are no excise duties or other special consumption taxes that apply to data transactions. Since Sweden is a member of the EU, VAT is EU harmonized. There are special rules for electronically supplied services. According to the EU Implementing Regulation, which is directly applicable in all member states, electronically supplied services are "services which are delivered over the Internet or an electronic network and the nature of which renders their supply essentially automated, involving minimal human intervention, and impossible to ensure in the absence of information technology. In Annex II of the VAT Directive electronically supplied services are listed. The provision of raw data and aggregated data would normally be electronically supplied services. Data analysis, which is integrated in an asset, constitutes goods, from a VAT perspective.

As mentioned above, the main rule regarding the valuation of assets and debts, and accrual of income and expenditures is that taxation follows business accounting. This may be considered as special, but there is not anything anomalous in relation to big data transactions.

Branch reporter
Angelica Maria Schwarz[1]

Summary and conclusions

The term *"big data"* has been in use since the early 1990s. Thus, big data is not something that is completely new. What has changed within the last three decades, however, is the development of technology that allows higher volumes of data to be processed in a shorter time. Data-driven business models have become increasingly important in order to maintain critical competitive advantages and market shares. True to the motto "knowledge is power", the aim today is to gather more information, which will provide ready-to-use insights for business decisions.

For the legal environment, the challenge is to keep up with the technological developments and the digital transformation. The following analysis shows that Switzerland is not only an attractive location for innovation, but also offers an interesting tax and legal framework that allows data-driven corporations to conduct their business under favourable conditions. Especially the patent box and the R&D super-deduction that were implemented in the last tax reform, have shown that Switzerland is not too late in entering the digital age and providing for sustainable tax models that are particularly attractive to data-driven corporations.

---

[1] Attorney-at-law at Bär & Karrer AG. Her practice focuses on all aspects of national and international corporate tax law and tax planning for Swiss and foreign private clients. She regularly publishes on tax matters with a special focus on topics dealing with data, digitalization, innovation and technology.

Branch reporter
N. Semih ÖZ[1]

Summary and conclusions

Article 20 of the Constitution of 1982 is related to the privacy of private life. In this article, there has been an amendment with the Constitutional Referendum in 2010, and this amendment was going to constitute the basis for some regulations to come into force later.

Regulations about fundamental rights and freedoms and protection of private life, as well as big databases, are mainly related to Turkish Civil Code No. 4741, Obligations Law No. 6098, The Turkish Commercial Law No. 6102, The Protection of Personal Data Law No. 6698, Intellectual and Artistic Works Law No. 5846, The Industrial Property Law No. 6769, Electronic Communications Law No. 5809, Electronic Commerce Law No. 6563, Internet Law of Turkey, Law No. 5651, and the Turkish Criminal Law No. 5237.

The rules of these regulations regarding databases will be briefly explained. The subject is handled together with the regulations on personal data, their protection, transfer, commercialization, and the penalty to be applied in case of failure to comply with the rules. According to article 9 of Law No.6698, personal data cannot be transferred abroad without the explicit consent of the data subject. Thus, relevant social network providers are obliged to store data of their Turkish users in Turkey.

The primary regulation related to copyright in Turkey is the Law on Intellectual and Artistic Works No. 5846. In terms of international agreements and arrangements related to databases and their protection in Turkey, two types of legal databases are foreseen in Law No. 5846. One of them, also regulated in TRIPS, article.10(2) and WCT. article 5, is the original database. The other, defined in article 7 of EU Directive and article 8 of Law No. 5846 is the sui generis database.

In addition to national laws, international agreements are also regulations related to databases. The Convention for the Protection of Individuals with regard to Automatic Processing of Personal Data of 28 January 1981, known as Treaty 108 of the Council of Europe, entered into force on 1 October 1985 and was ratified by Turkey with Law No. 6669 on 30 January 2016. The Convention entered into force on 1 September 2016.

The new digitalized type of international trade has enabled companies to generate a considerable profit without a physical presence in a country. However, in conventional regulation, domestic tax laws require the physical presence of taxpayers.

Income from data transfers as part of commercial activity constitutes the subject of income tax, while gross revenue is subject to value-added tax. The taxation of incomes from big data transfers contains problems related to the taxation of e-commerce. If transactions involve cross-border businesses, they become a concern for more than one government.

As a general rule, income obtained from data transfer as part of commercial activity is taxed according to the Income Tax Law No.193 when the real persons obtain it. If legal entities obtain that income, they are subject to Corporate Income Tax No. 5520. Gross sales

---

[1] Professor, Faculty of Political Science at the Ankara University, Turkey.

revenue from data transfer is also subject to value-added tax according to Law No. 3065.

Payments for big data transfers within the scope of commercial activity are subject to VAT. It can be questioned whether the data transfer is a good or service delivery. However, data transfers cannot be accepted as the delivery of goods under the VAT Law. Data transfers may be considered service delivery.

Turkey has signed agreements on the prevention of double taxation on income with 85 countries so far. In general, article 6 of these agreements is on income from immovable property, article 7 on business profits, article 9 on associated enterprises, and article 12 on royalties.

In the agreements in question, in principle, there is no specific provision regarding how the income derived from the transfer of information obtained from databases would be taxed. It should be taken into account that most of these agreements are outdated. At the time these agreements were signed, databases did not exist or were not commercialized as they are today. In the current form of the agreements, the issue that needs to be addressed is which agreement clause would be considered for taxation of the income derived from the sale of the information obtained from big databases. In this context, the income derived from big databases should be considered as a business profit.

Specific transfer pricing rules are valid in Turkey as of 1 January 2007, under article 13 of the CIT Law No. 5520. According to the Communique, in determining the comparable value for intangible rights, the transferee of the intangible right and the assignee must be evaluated separately. However, from the point of DEMPE functions, there is no definition of the transferee who is creating the intangibles that do not receive their fair share of income in the Communique. Arms-length prices might be available if an abundance of data is used, and for intangibles, it is almost impossible to find any similar data for comparison.

As of 1 January 2018, persons who do not have residency, nor legal center or business center in Turkey, that provide services electronically to a real person who is not a VAT taxpayer, shall declare and pay VAT of this transaction in Turkey. As of 1 January 2019, a withholding tax rate of 15% was introduced for payments made to real persons regardless of whether they are taxpayers or not, and payments made to non-resident entities in Turkey. As effective 1 March 2020, a digital services tax came into force in Turkey with Law No. 7194. Companies may be subject to double taxation on digital advertising services' revenues with an overlapping scope between the withholding tax and the digital service tax.

The economic assets used for commercial activities are subject to depreciation, and their depreciation periods are determined in accordance with the Communique numbered 333 of Law No. 213. Those related to databases can be envisioned as data communication systems, intangible assets, or computer software. According to the regulations, it is not clear to what extent databases will be subject to depreciation.

United States

Branch reporters
Erik Christenson[1]
Grace Meador[2]

Summary and conclusions

The commercial use of data (that is, digital information) has been transformed by modern technology. The ubiquity and accessibility of the internet alongside technological advancements in computing power and algorithmic processing, have made it easier and more useful to collect and analyze unprecedented volumes of data. In turn, this has made it possible to transact in a variety of complex commercial offerings involving data. Various new rules have been proposed and adopted at the state and local tax ("SALT") level, including sales taxes on "data processing transactions" (broadly similar to the "digital services taxes" proposed and enacted by numerous countries around the world).

At the federal level, there are no special regimes or cohesive rules in the United States Internal Revenue Code ("Code") or otherwise that are explicitly applicable to data transactions. The rules that could be applied to determine the tax consequences of a data transaction are based on commercial and tax law concepts that long predate the modern leaps in technology that have made today's data transactions possible. Accordingly, it is difficult to ascertain with certainty the US federal income tax treatment of the innovative business models described in this branch report.

The US federal income tax consequences for a taxpayer often depend, in the first instance, on the character of income derived by the taxpayer. In this framework, the threshold question is whether a transaction involving data should be considered a property transaction or a services transaction. The "income characterization" rules in the Code refer to various key words, including property, intangible property, intangibles, and services, and then provide the rules for determining the type of income derived from transactions involving these things, including but not necessarily limited to "gain", "rents", "royalties"

[1]   Tax partner at Baker McKenzie San Francisco, whose practice focuses on advising multinational corporations in various industries, including online services and e-commerce, software, payments and fintech, and life sciences.
[2]   Formerly an associate of Baker McKenzie and now works in the tax department at Twitch Interactive, Inc. Any views expressed herein are her own, and not the views of Twitch Interactive, Inc. and/or its affiliates.

The US branch reporters would like to extend their sincere gratitude to Shree Sharma for her keen insights and her never-ending willingness to contribute to the drafting of this document. Thanks also to Gene Tien, Eric Torrey and Amanda Worcester-Martin for contributions on transfer pricing, Lindsay LaCava, Stephen Long and Mike Shaikh for input on state and local tax issues, and Jonathan Tam for guidance on commercial and data privacy law.

and "services income".[3] Transactions in data might fall within any one of these categories, depending on the commercial realities of a given offering or exchange. Even though "data" can be collected, archived, processed, and analyzed – and even though it can be held, stored, and transferred from one party to another – traditional notions of property law do not apply. Rather, in most cases, the commercial and legal consequences of transaction involving data are derived from the terms of the contract between the parties.

In other words, from a US perspective, a data transaction does not involve the transfer of property as such, and does not grant rights in property. Rather, it involves a right of access to information in raw, processed, or summary form. Even so, US tax concepts of "intangible property" as expressed in certain parts of the Code may be sufficiently broad to refer, in some circumstances, to data. This creates an inconsistency, where traditional notions of property law might not apply to a data transaction, but US tax principles might nonetheless suggest the arrangement could be treated as a property transaction in some instances (or, equally important, an underlying premise in the US tax framework is that property law concepts can be applied to the item being characterized – which simply is not the case with data).

This report discusses the current body of law that may be applied to determine character of income (or other US tax consequences) in various fact patterns. In many cases, the answer is not clear, though broadly speaking, the existing US tax framework seems to support the view that transactions in data should be treated as transactions involving the performance of services, giving rise to services income. This triggers a variety of consequences, including that the "source" of the income is determined by reference to the location where the services are performed, itself a particularly fact-intensive determination because data can be gathered and analyzed by computers, servers, and equipment that might be located anywhere in the world. Given the ever-increasing importance of "data" in today's global economy and value chains, clarification would be welcome.

---

[3]   The fundamental task of determining the proper character of income derived from a data transaction arises in numerous contexts in the Code, including but not limited to the following: (i) determining whether a payment to a non-US person is subject to gross-basis US withholding tax (and whether it is within the scope of, for example, the royalties article of an applicable treaty); (ii) categorizing the income in the context of the foreign tax credit "baskets"; (iii) determining the "source" of the income under the withholding or the foreign tax credit regimes; (iv) categorizing the income for purposes of applying the subpart F controlled foreign corporation ("CFC") rules; and (v) determining the most reliable method for transfer pricing a data transaction between related parties.

Branch reporters
Andrés Hessdörfer[1]
Andrea Laura Riccardi Sacchi[2]

Summary and conclusions

The purpose of this report is to analyse the incipient phenomenon of data-driven transactions, both from a domestic and an international perspective. This topic is both current and complex, provided that – as it happens in the Uruguayan case – the speed with which this type of businesses developed, taking a leading role in the economy, has not yet allowed the amendment of the legal framework (including the tax framework) to take fully into account the different modalities in which such transactions can be performed.

We will start by presenting the main "non-tax" domestic legislation with an impact on this topic. In particular, after framing the concepts of data and big data, we will focus on the current regulations on personal data protection, as well as on those of copyright, which comprise software protection.

Later we will aim to characterize the different types of data transactions involved, with the intend to resolve its tax treatment. In general terms, the three main categories of businesses that we identify are: (i) data transfer; (ii) data analysis services, and (iii) entitlement to use data and information for a time period.

The above will help to frame those transactions within the tax legislation in force – which does not have a specific solution for these businesses -, and then focus on the issue of source and nexus, which is very complex for any type of transaction in the digital economy, where geolocation of production factors is extremely difficult.

In the second part of the report, we will focus on international taxation and, in particular, on the application of tax treaty principles derived from the conventions entered by Uruguay. In this section we will emphasize the authority-to-tax distribution rules, with special reference to the permanent establishment case (and, in particular, the services permanent establishment).

The third part of the report will focus on transfer pricing legislation and the complexity in the application of its principles and rules to data-based transactions. An interesting aspect of this chapter is a recent judgment of the Administrative Claims Court, in which the tax authority relied on DEMPE functions to support its position in determining the place of value creation.

The fourth part of the report highlights the existing special tax regimes, such as incentives regarding corporate income taxation for software development activity and

[1] Doctor in Law and Tax Law Professor at the University of Montevideo's Law School. Master in Tax Law and Postgraduate in International Tax Law at the University of Montevideo. Partner at Olivera Abogados.
[2] PhD (Faculty of Law, University of Valencia, Spain) and tax advisor to the General Directorate of the Uruguayan Tax Administration Office.

The opinions contained in this report are the strict responsibility of the authors, not compromising in any way the opinion of the institutions to which they belong.

related services. It also refers to the so-called digital services tax, extended internationally but still without reception in our country, notwithstanding the regulations in force under the income tax law for some specific digital transactions that we will examine in detail.

The fifth part of the report is centred around indirect taxation. We will explain current solutions regarding Value Added Tax to determine the taxable event and point out a number of provisions – particularly in relation to services exports – that are of interest for the present report as they are related to digital services.

In the sixth part of the report, we will concentrate on the tax accounting aspects related to data-based transactions, with a special focus on intangible assets recognition and depreciation rules.

Finally, and to close the report, we will analyse some aspects of the cases proposed by the general reporter, in order to illustrate the different points developed throughout the report.

The above mentioned are aspects on a current and living topic, and even though the present report is a first general approach to it, we can conclude that the legal framework (including the tax one) still needs to adapt its rules to these new data-intensive businesses, in order to be able to offer specific and adapted responses to this challenging scenario, in which doubts prevail over certainties.

Annex

CAHIERS DE DROIT FISCAL INTERNATIONAL

The Cahiers are an invaluable source of information of lasting scientific value for any specialist interested in international or comparative fiscal law. The complete list of the Cahiers published since 1939 follows below.

Vol. 1.   1939:   *The Hague (Netherlands)*
                  Taxation with regard to the earnings of limited companies with international interests

Vol. 2.   1939:   Would the incorporation of fiscal law in a separate system independent of other branches of the law, tend to facilitate international agreement?

Vol. 3.   1947:   *The Hague (Netherlands)*
                  Tax treaties since the outbreak of the war

Vol. 4.   1947:   Trans- and postwar tax legislation

Vol. 5.   1947:   Double taxation conventions concluded by the United States since 1939

Vol. 6.   1947:   Trans- and postwar tax legislation (France and Belgium)
                  V. 1/6 (one combined volume)

Vol. 7.   1948:   Summary record of the 1947 Congress

Vol. 8.   1948:   Summary record of the 1947 Congress

Vol. 9.   1948:   *Rome (Italy)*
                  Computation of taxable profits (part 1)

Vol. 10. 1948:   Computation of taxable profits (part 2)

Vol. 11. 1948:   Effects and benefits of tax conventions
                  V. 7/11 (one combined volume)

Vol. 12. 1948:   Summary record of the 1948 Congress (has never been published)

Vol. 13. 1948:   Summary record of the 1948 Congress (has never been published)

Vol. 14.	1950:	*Monaco* The effect of fluctuations in the value of currencies upon taxable income, from the national and international viewpoint
Vol. 15.	1950:	Tax obstacles to European economic integration and proposals for removing them V. 14/15 (one combined volume)
Vol. 16.	1951:	Summary record of the 1951 Congress (has never been published)
Vol. 17.	1951:	*Zürich (Switzerland)* The fiscal domicile of the physical persons as regards direct taxes
Vol. 18.	1951:	Juridical interpretation of treaties concerning double taxation and necessity or advisability of establishing an international fiscal jurisdiction
Vol. 19.	1951:	Experiences in the field of extraordinary property taxes
Vol. 20.	1952:	Summary record of the 1951 Congress; Belgian report about 'Fiscal domicile of physical persons as regards direct taxes'; Italian report about 'Fiscal burden and production costs of industrial enterprises'
Vol. 21.	1952:	*Brussels (Belgium)* Comparison of tax provisions for reserves and depreciation allowances. The incidence of fiscal and parafiscal charges on the costs of production
Vol. 22.	1952:	Tax concessions to be made by a country with a view to attracting capital and enterprise from foreign countries – including special problems of sea- and airtransport enterprises; Multilateral conventions between the countries of Western Europe in order to avoid multiple, extra-territorial and discriminatory taxes
Vol. 23.	1953:	Summary record of the 1952 Congress
Vol. 24.	1953:	*Paris (France)* The reform of taxation on turnover, transactions and sales in the various countries of Western Europe, with a view to their unification. The different conceptions, whether already accepted or possible, for defining the fiscal value of tangible goods (the subjects should deal at the same time with the valuation of immovables, of goodwill, stock and cash and of non-quoted securities). Fiscal measures capable of facilitating international capital transfers within the European framework or world economy or of a more limited continental economy
Vol. 25.	1953:	Summary record of the 1953 Congress

Vol. 26. With Annex	1954:	*Cologne (Germany)* Tax measures to facilitate international movements of capital. Tax measures likely to encourage private savings both in movable and immovable property. International companies in national and international tax law; the influence of the existing relations between undertakings established in different countries on the determination of the taxable profits in each of these countries. Double taxation resulting from the taxing of company profits as well as from the taxing of the same profits as far as they have been distributed to shareholders viewed from the standpoint of comparative law as well as from that of tax policy
Vol. 26.		Annex
Vol. 27.	1954:	Summary record of the 1954 Congress
Vol. 28.	1955:	*Amsterdam (Netherlands)* The common assessment of income tax for members of one household. International double taxation in the field of turnover tax
Vol. 29. With Annex	1955:	Double tax burden on earned and distributed profits of limited companies
Vol. 29.		Annex
Vol. 30.	1955:	Summary record of the 1955 Congress
Vol. 31.	1956:	*Rome (Italy)* The international double taxation in the field of turnover taxes from the legal and economic points of view
Vol. 32.	1956:	The influence of the legal form, the nature and the size of enterprises on their tax regime and vice versa (from the national and international point of view)
Vol. 33.	1956:	The juridical guarantees of the taxpayer vis-à-vis the fisc. Survey of the Mitchell B. Carroll Prize Studies 1955
Vol. 34.	1956:	Summary record of the 1956 Congress
Vol. 34a.	1957:	*Vienna (Austria)* The juridical guarantees of the taxpayer vis-à-vis the fisc. The position of permanent establishments in national and international fiscal law; the concept of permanent establishments and allocation of capital and profits among the various permanent establishments of the same enterprise. Taxation of intellectual and industrial property (study theme)
Vol. 35.	1957:	The number 35 has not been used

Vol. 36.	1958:	*Knokke (Belgium)* Taxation of revenue from patents, trademarks, and designs, particularly from the international point of view
Vol. 37.	1958:	The onus and methods of proof (income tax law). The balance sheet and account in commercial and fiscal matters
Vol. 38.	1958:	The number 38 has not been used
Vol. 39.	1959:	*Madrid (Spain)* The verification of tax liability; its legal, psychological and economic aspects Tax measures designed to facilitate international capital movements
Vol. 40.	1959:	Unilateral measures for the avoidance of double taxation
Vol. 41.	1959:	Summary record of the 1959 Congress
Vol. 42.	1960:	*Basle (Switzerland)* The treatment of capital gains for tax purposes; The interpretation of the double taxation conventions; The treatment of debts and interests thereon in international taxation
Vol. 43.	1961:	*Jerusalem (Israel)* General reports on the two subjects of the 1961 Congress, viz.: Unilateral measures for the avoidance of double taxation, especially as regards fiscal aspects of the relationship between capital-exporting countries and countries in process of development, and: The taxation of interconnected companies
Vol. 44.	1961:	Unilateral measures for the avoidance of double taxation, especially as regards fiscal aspects of the relationship between capital-exporting countries and countries in process of development (national reports)
Vol. 45.	1961:	The taxation of interconnected companies (national reports)
Vol. 46.	1961:	Summary record of the 1961 Congress
Vol. 47a.	1962:	*Athens (Greece)* The fiscal regime applying on the importation and exportation of goods
Vol. 47b.	1962:	Fiscal problems arising in connection with investment trusts of international character
Vol. 48a.	1963:	*Paris (France)* The comparative tax treatment of process of merger and capital reconstruction of enterprises
Vol. 48b.	1963:	Fiscal measures in capital-exporting countries for the purpose of encouraging investments in countries in the process of development

Vol. 49a.	1964:	*Hamburg (Germany)* International problems of depreciation and valuation including revaluation for purposes of profits taxation
Vol. 49b.	1964:	The delimitation between the country of residence and other countries of the power to tax corporations and/or their shareholders
Vol. 49c.	1964:	Summary record of the 1964 Congress
Vol. 50a.	1965:	*London (United Kingdom)* The interpretation of tax laws with special reference to form and substance
Vol. 50b.	1965:	Advance rulings by the tax authorities at the request of a taxpayer
Vol. 51a.	1966:	*Lisbon (Portugal)* The problems that pose on the fiscal plan of the movements of integration between countries as well as for grouped nations or non-grouped nations as for the multinational groupings (national reports)
Vol. 51b/c.	1966:	Idem (general report) The fiscal treatment of the gratuitous distributions and its repercussions from the international viewpoint (national reports)
Vol. 51d	1966:	Idem (general report)
Vol. 52.	1967:	*Stockholm (Sweden)* Changes in the tax system as a part of stabilization policy - their technical and legal implications The development in different countries of the concept of a permanent establishment, notably from the point of view of the harmonization in future double taxation agreements
Vol. 52a.	1967:	Summary record of the 1967 Congress
Vol. 53I.	1968:	*Montevideo (Uruguay)* The reports between the structures of the fiscal systems and the economic development in the countries in process of development
Vol. 53II.	1968:	The territorial competence of the fiscal authorities in the field of succession and property taxes
Vol. 54a.	1969:	*Rotterdam (Netherlands)* The recognition of services and license of incorporeal rights between parent companies and their foreign subsidiaries. Avoidance of double taxation in case of non-recognition by tax administrations

Vol. 54b.	1969:	The possibilities and disadvantages of extending national tax reduction measures, if any, to foreign scientific, educational or charitable institutions
Vol. 54c.	1969:	*Addresses* Allocution d'ouverture par Prof. Dr. K.V. Antal, Président du Groupement néerlandais de l'IFA. Opening address by Dr. Mitchell B. Carroll, President of IFA. Address given by Dr. F.H.M. Grapperhaus, State Secretary of Finance at the opening session of the 23rd IFA Congress. Development in world shipping and the Dutch mercantile marine by J.J. Oyevaar, President of the Board of Directors of V.N.S. Tax treaties between developed and developing countries by Prof. Dr. Jan H. Christiaanse
Vol. 55a.	1970:	*Brussels (Belgium)* The multiple burden on dividends and shares by taxation on income and capital of both corporations and shareholders; possibilities of modification
Vol. 55b.	1970:	The national and especially international tax problems arising from the merger of enterprises
Vol. 56a.	1971:	*Washington (USA)* The fiscal treatment of international investment trusts and mutual funds, having regard to the major regulatory and foreign exchange features in the various countries
Vol. 56b.	1971:	Criteria for the allocation of items of income and expense between related corporations in different states, whether or not parties to tax conventions
Vol. 57a.	1972:	*Madrid (Spain)* The income, fortune and estate tax treatment of household units
Vol. 57b.	1972:	Tax consequences of changes in foreign exchange rates
Vol. 58a.	1973:	*Lausanne (Switzerland)* The taxation of enterprises with permanent establishments abroad
Vol. 58b.	1973:	Partnerships and joint enterprises in international tax law
Vol. 59a.	1974:	*Mexico-City (Mexico)* Tax consequences of domestic and foreign interests' establishing corporations as vehicles for joint ventures
Vol. 59b.	1974:	Tax problems resulting from the temporary activity abroad of employees of enterprises with international operations
Vol. 60a.	1975:	*London (United Kingdom)* Tax treatment of the importation and exportation of technology, know-how, patents, other intangibles and technical assistance

Vol. 69b.	1984:	Social security contributions as a fiscal burden on enterprises engaged in international activities
Vol. 70a.	1985:	*London (United Kingdom)* The assessment and collection of tax from non-residents
Vol. 70b.	1985:	International double taxation of inheritances and gifts
Vol. 71a.	1986:	*New York (USA)* Transfer of assets into and out of a taxing jurisdiction
Vol. 71b.	1986:	Currency fluctuations and international double taxation
Vol. 72a.	1987:	*Brussels (Belgium)* The fiscal residence of companies
Vol. 72b.	1987:	Tax problems of the liquidation of corporations
Vol. 73a.	1988:	*Amsterdam (Netherlands)* Recognition of foreign enterprises as taxable entities
Vol. 73b.	1988:	Tax treatment of computer software
Vol. 74a.	1989:	*Rio de Janeiro (Brazil)* The disregard of a legal entity for tax purposes
Vol. 74b.	1989:	Administrative and compliance costs of taxation
Vol. 75a.	1990:	*Stockholm (Sweden)* Taxation of cross-border leasing
Vol. 75b.	1990:	International mutual assistance through exchange of information
Vol. 76a.	1991:	*Barcelona (Spain)* The determination of the tax base for real property
Vol. 76b.	1991:	Protection of confidential information in tax matters
Vol. 77a.	1992:	*Cancún (Mexico)* Transfer pricing in the absence of comparable market prices
Vol. 77b.	1992:	Tax consequences of international acquisitions and business combinations
Vol. 78a.	1993:	*Florence (Italy)* Interpretation of double taxation conventions
Vol. 78b.	1993:	Non-discrimination rules in international taxation
Vol. 79a.	1994:	*Toronto (Canada)* Deductibility of interest and other financing charges in computing income
Vol. 79b.	1994:	National and international tax consequences of demergers
Vol. 80a.	1995:	*Cannes (France)* International income tax problems of partnerships

Vol. 91a.	2006:	*Amsterdam (Netherlands)* The tax consequences of restructuring of indebtedness (debt work-outs)
Vol. 91b.	2006:	The attribution of profits to permanent establishments
Vol. 92a.	2007:	*Kyoto (Japan)* Transfer pricing and intangibles
Vol. 92b.	2007:	Conflicts in the attribution of income to a person
Vol. 93a.	2008:	*Brussels (Belgium)* Non-discrimination at the crossroads of international taxation
Vol. 93b.	2008:	New tendencies in tax treatment of cross-border interest of corporations
Vol. 94a.	2009:	*Vancouver (Canada)* Is there a permanent establishment?
Vol. 94b.	2009:	Foreign exchange issues in international taxation
Vol. 95a.	2010:	*Rome (Italy)* Tax treaties and tax avoidance: application of anti-avoidance provisions
Vol. 95b.	2010:	Death as a taxable event and its international ramifications
Vol. 96a.	2011:	*Paris (France)* Cross-border business restructuring
Vol. 96b.	2011:	Key practical issues to eliminate double taxation of business income
Vol. 97a.	2012:	*Boston (USA)* Enterprise services
Vol. 97b.	2012:	The debt-equity conundrum
Vol. 98a.	2013:	*Copenhagen (Denmark)* The taxation of foreign passive income for groups of companies
Vol. 98b.	2013:	Exchange of information and cross-border cooperation between tax authorities
Vol. 99a.	2014:	*Mumbai (India)* Cross-border outsourcing - issues, strategies and solutions
Vol. 99b.	2014:	Qualification of taxable entities and treaty protection
Vol. 100a.	2015:	*Basel (Switzerland)* Tax incentives on Research & Development (R&D)
Vol. 100b.	2015:	The practical protection of taxpayers' fundamental rights
Vol. 101a.	2016:	*Madrid (Spain)* Dispute resolution procedures in international tax matters